IT'S ONLY A BADGE

PHIL RIBERA

This book is a memoir—a collection of stories that took place many years ago. As such, the events described herein are subject to the frailties and imperfections of human memory and the differing interpretations of others who were there. My best efforts were made to adhere to factual accuracy; however many of the characters in this book are composites. Individual names and identifying characteristics have been changed, as have those of businesses and organizations. Any similarities to actual persons or organizations are strictly coincidental.

ISBN 978-0-578-05112-3

Published by Phil Ribera
Cover design by Terry VanderHeiden

Visit Phil Ribera on the World Wide Web at: www.philribera.com
Learn more about this book online at: www.itsonlyabadge.com

For Gale—
You've stayed with me through thick and thin
. . . and thinner

Acknowledgements

To those who have given their support and encouragement during my transition from cop to artist, I am forever grateful. Thank you to Gil and Tyler Ribera for our Wednesday morning breakfast Meetings; Terry VanderHeiden for technical help and photography work; Buck Spillner, the cover model; Mary VanderHeiden for her editing expertise; my friends, Seth Harwood, Tammy Durston, and Wendy Baker, for their valuable feedback; and to all the police department employees who helped to keep me safe and made my 31 years with them so rich with memories. Most importantly, I want to thank my two daughters, Cari and Megan, and my wife, Gale, without whom I wouldn't have had a wonderful home to come back to at the end of each shift.

IT'S ONLY A BADGE

Prologue

I'm not a big guy. It seemed like most of the young men the police department had hired were much beefier than my 145 pound, 5-foot-9 frame. I considered wearing elevator shoes to my interview, but eventually dismissed the idea as weird. Somehow, I needed to find a way to appear larger than I was.

It was early September, and the date of my oral interview at City Hall happened to fall on the hottest day of the year. I was sweating like a goat and I hadn't even gotten dressed yet. First I slid the long sleeve sweatshirt over my head, and then another, and then a third. I pulled on the sweatpants, then another, and then a third pair. My dad's suit barely fit over them. I knotted the necktie as best I could, and then stepped back from the mirror to view the entire ensemble. I looked like an idiot–an obese idiot.

At that point it was too late to change my outfit, and my buddy, Terry, had already arrived to give me a ride. We'd been friends since junior high school and had built an entire relationship on practical jokes and pranks carried out upon one another. I knew I should have been more guarded, but I was too nervous about the interview and too damn hot to worry about it right then. "Just drive!" I snapped, as I wedged myself into his passenger seat.

The panel members must have felt sorry for me. I was perspiring all over their table and they kept asking if I wanted some water. At one point I felt like I might get sick or pass out. I had an overwhelming feeling that my *enormous man* idea was an enormous mistake. Then, just when I was certain my interview couldn't get any worse, it did.

"Don't hire him—he's a hothead," an amplified voice boomed from outside. My stomach turned as I remembered that Terry's van was equipped with a microphone and external loudspeaker. "Don't hire him—he's a hothead!" The words repeated over and over, making me dizzier each time.

The interviewers rushed to the window and watched the mustard colored van as it circled the parking lot below.

"Do you know that person?" one of them asked. All I could do was give a sorrowful shake of my head.

Like I said, they must have felt sorry for me. A few months later I received a letter telling me I passed the process and was being hired as a police officer.

I had stumbled onto a path upon which I would travel for the next 31 years. Though I didn't know it then, I was embarking on a uniquely personal journey—one that would allow me to experience people at their neediest, their angriest, their most hurt, and their most fragile. People whose lives would interestingly and unpredictably become part of mine, shaping the lens through which I would forever see the world.

Some of the scenes are funny, some are provoking, and some are simply too sad for anyone to ever have to experience. These were nights working mostly alone in my patrol car, with only the dispatcher's voice and the grimy smell of the street to keep me company. Nights that would furnish me with a million laughs, a million tears, and a million insights into human nature.

Chapter 1

The bulletproof vest I'm wearing feels like a straight jacket. My wool uniform itches, but not nearly as much as this turtleneck that someone told me I'll need. I'm weighted down at the hips by a wide leather belt that squeaks every time I move, a radio I don't dare touch, a ring full of keys, a gun, handcuffs, extra bullets, a whistle, and all this other stuff I've been issued. *God help me if I have to chase after anybody tonight.*

9:59 p.m.

I walk into lineup feeling as conspicuous as a kid on the first day of high school. Rows of tables and chairs fill the room—about two dozen seats in all. A raised dais stands at the front between the United States flag and the California flag. I set my brand new leather field case on the floor next to an empty chair. Before I can sit down the old cop next to me says the spot is taken. He grabs the handle of my case and gives it a bowling ball style slide all the way across the room. I retrieve it and put it down in another empty spot.

"This one is taken too," says someone else as my case is sent off in another direction. I end up on a tiny stool in the back of the room taking notes on a clipboard balanced on my knees.

My training officer later tells me to get used to it. "They just want to see how you handle it. What you're all about."

After lineup he takes me to the back lot to check out our car. Apparently there's a whole process to it. The night is damp and the air is cold, but I'm still boiling under this uniform. We stow our cases in the trunk and I get into the passenger seat. Somebody really heavy must have been sitting in it, because I sink down so low that I can barely see over the dashboard. We drive past the other cops on our way out the gate and I feel like a little kid on an outing with his dad.

"Don't worry," says my training officer. "You won't be doing any driving tonight."

It's a little bit of a relief. With everything so new and cumbersome, I'm not sure how well I'd handle the car. He could have ended it there, but he doesn't.

"You won't be touching anything, thinking anything, or doing anything either," he says. "And for God's sake, that gun better not leave your holster . . . unless I get shot. Then I don't give a damn what you do."

Let's see how much more of a dumbshit I can be made to feel like tonight.

The smells of the street at night in a patrol car are different for some reason. It's a crude greasy odor, on top of which is a mixture of cigarettes, car exhaust, wool, fresh leather, and my training officer's pungent cologne.

A carload of teenagers pulls up and they stare into the cruiser. Realizing I'm not much older than them, I try to sit taller. It hits me that I'm in a police car—not as a bystander but as a real cop. People will actually expect me to know what I'm doing. What if I have to pull out my gun? I'm already overly aware of it on my side—as if it might go off on its own at any second. I'm really hoping that I'll feel more comfortable after I get through the academy.

My training officer stops at the city facilities yard to gas up the car. Several of the cops who were in lineup are there, laughing and joking while they wait for an empty pump. It's easy banter that no one seems to take seriously. I try to look beneath all the jokes and the nicknames, and wonder if there is a passionate loyalty to one another that their lives depend on.

I ask my training officer what I can do to help, but he tells me to stay in the car.

11:03 p.m.

We leave the pumps and he drives me around, pointing out the boundaries of our beat. It's a brisk February evening and the streetlights shimmer on the wet pavement. Thankfully it's not raining, because I don't think I could move if I had to wear a raincoat on top of everything else.

Our first call comes and I nearly jump out of my skin. It crackles over the radio as a possible burglary in progress. "Respond to the Ford dealership on Mission," says the dispatcher.

"I used to work there," I say, intentionally omitting my former title.

"Do you think they'll give you your old job back?" My training officer flashes a crooked grin.

He shuts off his lights and coasts to a silent stop next to the dealership. He gets out and eases the door closed without a sound. I take my first step and feel the tug of my seatbelt. It catches and my flashlight goes clattering into the gutter. My training officer snarls.

I wipe it against my pants and flip the switch to make sure it still works. It illuminates both of us and I quickly shut it off. He stops and just looks at me.

"Sorry," I whisper.

We find a side door open, but nobody inside. It turns out the burglary isn't in progress. On the contrary, whoever did it is long gone. Someone had broken into the building through a skylight and drilled their way into the huge safe in the sales manager's office. The dealership's security company called it in when the thieves set off the silent alarm on their way out. All this is explained to me by my training officer while we're waiting for a company rep to show up.

As we pass time in the brightly lit showroom, my training officer checks out the new cars. My gaze settles on the covered area just outside the showroom doors and I find myself replaying a scene that took place at that very spot, less than two years ago.

I was on my hands and knees picking cigarette butts off fake outdoor turf. My palm came down on a piece of chewed gum, still wet with saliva. I eyed the two men standing a few feet away.

Pricks! One was the sales manager, Al Bianchi, and the other was one of the salesmen. They were talking about women, money, cars, whatever, and holding their cigarettes between their thumb and forefingers like they thought they were a couple of wiseguys. It seemed like they always left more of a mess than was necessary, and then got a kick out of watching me clean it up.

A siren distracted me from my janitorial duties and an unmarked sedan with flashing red dash lights whizzed past. The police car jumped the curb and pulled around stopped traffic on the wrong side of the boulevard.

"Bunko Squad," Bianchi proclaimed with arrogant satisfaction. The salesman nodded vigorously.

Knowing nothing about police, or what a *Bunko Squad* was, I assumed that Bianchi was right. However, for my money the guy was usually just full of shit. Either way, whatever emergency we were witnessing was clearly impressive. The three of us were like spectators at a sporting event, and for the first time I felt like an equal.

I rose up on my knees to watch the cop car slow as it approached a red light and then accelerate through it. Glancing back at the two men, I half expected some acknowledgement of our newly formed male bond. Instead, Bianchi took a long drag on his cigarette and flicked it onto the ground next to me. So close that a few of the glowing embers bounced off my arm. I glared at him with as much malice and challenge as a skinny 19 year-old could put into a silent look. Underwhelmed, they both sauntered back into the showroom laughing.

I knew in five minutes they wouldn't even remember it, but I was left seething on all fours like a dog. From then on I did a piss poor job of cleaning Bianchi's office, and when everyone left at night I used his private bathroom to shower. I even helped myself to sodas from the small refrigerator under his desk. Of course, at the time I truly believed that all my anger was really at Bianchi; never considering I was pissed off at being a janitor with mediocre grades and a Volkswagen in dire need of a muffler.

Two weeks later I was fired.

"Al Bianchi," a booming voice announces from behind me. He walks in with one hand extended toward my training officer in his typical salesman style, and the other holding the short end of a cigarette. Bianchi looks just the same as he did when I worked for him.

A crime scene tech pulls up and comes in carrying a camera. My training officer excuses himself from Bianchi and shows the tech around the crime scene, pointing out what he wants photographed and which pieces of evidence he wants collected. Meanwhile, I'm trying to look like a grizzled old salt in front of Bianchi. He eyes me curiously, and I eye him back. *Why do I feel like I've got a price tag hanging off my uniform?*

"Looks like they came in through the skylight," I say pointing overhead, as if Bianchi wouldn't know where the skylight was located. "Probably set off the alarm on their way out."

I thought it sounded good, but I can feel my training officer's scrutinizing gaze. He hustles over and snatches the conversation back. I don't dare say anything else to Bianchi, but I see him watching me when he doesn't think I notice. I probably look familiar to him, though I doubt he remembers where he's seen me before. My fantasy is that he does remember, and returns to work the next day to hold a meeting with all the employees who treated me like shit. In the meeting he tells them that the kid who used to clean up our mess is now a cop.

In any case, the irony of returning on my first call to the very spot where I initially thought of becoming a cop is not lost on me. I wonder if it's a sign of some sort, or just the way the universe works.

12:31 a.m.

My head is on a swivel. Everywhere I look there's something happening, but I'm not sure whether any of it is important. Thuggish men on motorcycles, people on dark street corners, someone in a long coat outside a liquor store—all of it's going on at the same time. I watch a woman barely stop for a red light, then look over at us and back her car up behind the crosswalks. All the while our radio discharges an endless repartee in a language foreign to me. My training officer sees and hears and understands all of it, amazingly processing it with ease. Crippled by my ignorance, I let out an unintentional sigh.

My training officer glances at me with an intuitive smirk. "You'll figure it out."

I would like him to expound on the crumb of encouragement, but he doesn't. A flurry of radio traffic catches his ear and he instantly turns up the volume. His foot hits the accelerator and I'm thrust against my headrest.

"Get ready for action," he says. "You got your hat and bat?"

I'm not exactly sure what he's talking about, but I presume it's police jargon for helmet and long nightstick. "Yes," I respond weakly.

"Good. The party on Urbano Court is turning into a riot and the beat cop is calling for all available units."

Besides not knowing where Urbano Court is, I hadn't been aware of a problem party on the beat next to ours. I grip the dashboard as we snake our way between cars at terrifying speeds. I'm listening intently to the radio and I hear car after car arriving at a staging area. Any headway I've made to steady my breathing during the ride is wiped away when we turn the corner. A beer bottle whistles out of the sky and crashes against the side of our patrol car. A line of cops in riot gear has formed up along the street at the mouth of the court, each of them wearing a helmet with a plastic face shield and holding a 36 inch riot baton. Many of them are slapping their sticks against their palms, eager to put them to use.

I spring from the car, impatient to prove my worth. The trunk pops open and I snatch my long stick and slide it into the ring on my belt. It nearly reaches the ground, so I decide to simply hold it in my hands. I find my helmet, but somewhere during the wild ride the plastic face shield came unsnapped. I feel around for it, but can't find it in the dark trunk. I throw on the helmet, hoping a lucky bottle doesn't find its way to my face.

A few quick steps and I'm right behind my training officer. He shoulders his way into line with the dozen or so other cops, and I do the same.

He says, "Stay right on my ass, no matter what happens."

I gulp and nod my head. A sergeant starts at one end of the line, checking everyone's equipment and giving out orders. I realize this is the real thing. I'm about to go into battle. My heart feels like it's going to rocket out of my chest, yet I'm trying hard to appear cool on the outside.

I suddenly feel myself being shoved forward. "Hey, check out the kid," a voice hollers out from behind me. I wheel around, and now I'm facing the row of cops. One of the senior officers, the one who pushed me, lets out a side-splitting laugh. "He's got his helmet on backwards!"

A surge of heat instantly rushes to my face and I'm pretty sure I'm turning red. I reach up and feel the snaps for the face shield facing the back. *Son-of-a-bitch!* A cackle works its way down the line as I flip the helmet around the right way. I consider trying to explain how it was dark and there was no face shield, but it would only make me look worse.

I put my best effort into a laugh and then I get back into line. There's a fleeting hope that I'll perform well when we move to control the insurrection, but that too is quickly dashed. The partygoers see we mean business, and promptly start leaving. Our presence is reduced to traffic direction until the bulk of the crowd is gone. Two or three of them are picked off for public drunkenness, but I'm involved in none of it. I slink back into the car next to my training officer. Mercifully, he chooses not to comment on my performance.

1:19 a.m.

We park in front of a donut shop and my training officer just looks at me. I'm wondering if it's some kind of test. I mean, the whole cops eating donuts thing seems too obvious. I stare back at him, determined not to take the bait.

"Well? Aren't you going to buy me a donut and a cup of coffee?"

"Sure," I say, realizing there was no trick. I go in and buy us two coffees and a couple of donuts. I've never really been a coffee drinker, but the whole experience somehow makes me feel more like a real cop.

I wolf my jelly-filled donut and wash it down quickly. I look up to find my training officer staring at me. He's only taken one bite of his.

"Look kid," he says. "You're gonna vapor lock if you keep this up. We got all night ahead of us. Just relax and find your pace."

I'm not sure what he means by that, other than I shouldn't eat so fast. My mom used to tell me the same thing, though somehow sitting at the dinner table as a kid wasn't usually as nerve-racking as where I'm sitting now. I'm so ready for something to happen that I'm almost shaking. The black coffee didn't help.

1:40 a.m.

We're back out to our beat. The dispatcher blurts out a long broadcast and I'm able to pick out the words *vehicle pursuit*. I lean closer to the radio and hear something about the Highway Patrol. My training officer tells me they're chasing a stolen car through the city. I'm trying to decipher the specifics, but I'm not sure what's happening. From the speed of our car though, I'm assuming we're going to join in.

"Damn it." My training officer suddenly slows the car. "Suspect bailed out. Now he's on foot."

Still sounds exciting to me, but apparently my training officer has little interest in helping with the foot search. We find the area where the car was abandoned—a parking lot behind a warehouse that backs up to a huge, weed covered field. I see the CHP cop walking around an empty white Toyota. It doesn't look like he's interested in the foot search either. My training officer tells him that we'll check around the area for the guy who ran. We barely pull away when our car comes to an abrupt stop.

"Look to your right," my training officer says, shining his spotlight into the field. "There he is."

I see the glint of a white tee shirt bobbing over dark mounds that look like waves in the ocean. My door is open and I'm out of the car before he says anything else. I'm running in a flat out sprint. What appeared close when I started out now seems miles away. The ground raises and falls beneath me, causing me to stumble in the darkness. With each stride, I'm more aware of all my layered clothing and the overabundance of equipment I'm carrying. Then, about half way across the field, the donut starts to make its move. My insides feel like a can of Coke that someone has sadistically shaken, yet I keep running. I see the guy ahead of me, stumbling and running, then stumbling some more. I think I'm gaining on him. Another few seconds and I'll have my hands on him. My first arrest.

I come over a crest and he's right there, inching his way up a small incline to a street. He looks like he's ready to collapse, but so am I. I make one final lunge and fall short by a few inches, ending up in the dirt. I look up and see that my training officer has driven around the field to head us off. He's standing next to the car, waiting quietly. I see his cup of coffee on the hood. The guy I was chasing is on all fours gasping at his feet, too tired to resist any further. My training officer orders the guy onto his belly and then calmly takes him into custody.

Having reached maximum velocity, the donut and coffee spew out of me like I'm possessed. I spend the next several minutes retching until there's no more to retch. I think I saw the Clark Bar I ate back in the fourth grade. By the time I'm done, the suspect is handcuffed and in the backseat of our car. I brush myself off and we drive the guy back over to the CHP unit. Besides feeling like hell, I'm embarrassed. I'm grateful only that the other cop has no idea about what I just did. But my good fortune lasts only a minute.

"Ever see anyone pass a jelly donut through his nose?" my training officer asks the cop.

He tells the story and they both have a jolly good laugh. *I'm really glad I've been able to entertain everyone so well tonight.*

We stop by the station and I clean up a bit.

2:39 a.m.

We're cruising the western part of our beat, beyond which is an industrial tract extending out to the bay. A small Mazda buzzes past us, and my training officer cranes his neck to watch it.

"Someone we're looking for?" I ask.

"What business is open out here?" he asks, without addressing my question.

"None that I know of."

"Then what the hell are two guys doing out here at this time of night?" I don't think he really wants an answer, although I can actually think of a couple of legitimate reasons why they might be out here.

I ask what he thinks they're up to.

He flips the car around. "That's what we're going to find out."

We locate the car tooling slowly around the fence line of an auto dismantler. The two guys see us and start driving even slower. They use their turning signals and come to complete stops at each intersection. There isn't another car on the road. Even to me they're trying too hard to look innocent.

My training officer hits the lights and they pull over—still out in the middle of nowhere. He walks up on the driver's side and I go to the other side where I can watch the passenger. Both of them have eyes like saucers. They face straight ahead while they're being questioned. I have my flashlight in hand, determined not to miss anything.

Over the top of the car, my training officer gives me a signal I don't understand. He pulls the driver's door open. "Step out of the car."

I'm not sure if I should go help him or stay where I am, keeping an eye on the passenger. There's a scuffle on the other side of the car and my training officer drops to the ground. I run around to help him, and I see he's on top of the driver who's struggling to get free. I fumble to put my flashlight away and I'm trying to find my handcuffs. Everything is so new and I'm grabbing all the wrong stuff. I can't find the slot for my flashlight, and the whole time they're fighting at my feet. *The hell with it!*

I drop to my knees and grab a handful of the driver's hair with my left hand, wrapping it in my fist. It whiplashes his head back so his face is only inches from mine. The metal flashlight is still in my right hand. I lift it high over my head as if I'm about to wallop him.

"Stop fighting or I'll split your head wide open!" I surprise myself with my own words, but more importantly it surprises the guy. He stops struggling and my training officer quickly puts him in handcuffs. Fortunately, the passenger stays put.

"Why did we arrest him?" I ask as my training officer as he stuffs the guy into the backseat of our car.

I follow him back to the Mazda's open driver's door. He points to an enormous hunting knife wedged in the space between the seat and the car door.

"He went for the knife as he got out," he says, still breathing heavily.

I feel like a chump. I hadn't grasped what was happening when it was happening, and I couldn't react quickly enough. All this damn equipment!

I feel even worse when we get to the jail. While our prisoner is being searched and fingerprinted, one of the other cops on the shift pulls my training officer aside.

"How did the kid do during the fight?" he asks, eyeing me up and down.

They both know I can hear their conversation, and I'm standing before them like a criminal waiting for a verdict.

My training officer glances in my direction. "Hesitated a little at first, but then jumped in."

Fair enough, I guess.

The other cop persists. "Jumped in how?"

"Let's just say he got the crook's attention."

He's being generous, but I'm not going to argue. I still need to find a way to prove myself tonight.

4:12 a.m.

Another alarm call. This one is at my old high school—another ironic coincidence. Fearing additional wisecracks, I elect not to tell him I went to school there. Even after getting the call, we continue driving along as if we're going out for a Sunday ride—no lights, no siren, and no hurry. I fidget in my seat and my training officer gives me the once over.

"What? You wanna go fast, kid?" he asks with a puff of a laugh.

I shrug, thinking that burglars already got away once tonight.

"Thing is . . ." He slows the car in an obvious attempt to prove a point. "Ninety percent or more of these alarms are false. You bust your ass getting there only to find out the wind set it off."

I nod in agreement, and he continues, "Notice how wet it is out on the road?" I nod again. "You go speeding to a call like this and stack it up, the sergeant's gonna come down hard on your ass."

The dispatcher comes over the air with an update. "Alarm company advises they have broken window activation and motion detected inside building F."

Now he puts his foot into it, and I feel like I've been shot out of a cannon. We take the turn toward the school and slide sideways out of control, nearly hitting the opposite curb. He corrects, fishtailing back into our lane.

"See what I mean?" He acts as if he did it intentionally as part of my training.

Another cop car is behind us, and then a third. I feel my pulse in my throat as all three cars suddenly go completely dark. We haven't slowed down at all, just flying along with all our lights out. I hope he knows what he's doing. It's hard for me to believe I'll be driving a patrol car like this some day.

One of the cops comes over the radio, "Where's building F?" Nobody answers.

"I used to go here," I finally tell my training officer. "Building F is in the back by the soccer field."

He looks at me for the first time like I might be worth a shit. "Good," he says. "You can show us."

A campus security officer pulls up behind the group. We all get out at the front of the school, and the security officer hands one of the cops a set of keys. I lead the parade through the maze of outside walkways to the back of the campus.

"There," I whisper, pointing proudly at the building. I step toward the doors and feel a fatherly hand grip the back of my collar.

"You wait out here," my training officer says. "And don't do anything."

Son of a bitch! The perfect chance to redeem myself and I'm stuck outside.

The three cops tiptoe their way in, followed closely by the security guy. I move around to the soccer field where I'm able to watch a long row of windows. I step carefully through the muddy turf until I'm about 50 yards out. It's pitch dark, and I can see the beams of the cops' flashlights working their way slowly up the hallway. Suddenly, there's some movement at a window about midway down. I think at first that it's one of the cops giving me the *all clear*. Then, two dark figures slither out and drop to the ground.

I'm paralyzed. Two burglars are running right toward me, unable to see me in the darkness. I can't move. My hands fumble for some piece of equipment—the radio, my gun, my whistle, a flashlight, my keys, it doesn't matter. It's useless. The gear I've been hauling around with me all night never sees action.

"Freeze!" I hear my own voice yell; mimicking every police show I've ever watched. Both guys immediately stop right there in their tracks and give up. *I'll be damned. It worked.* I'm almost more amazed than I am excited.

"Don't move!" one of the cops hollers from near the building. There's more yelling, and I see flashlights pumping up and down as the cops sprint toward us. Too stupid to put handcuffs on them, I stand there holding each burglar by the arm. Probably couldn't find my handcuffs anyway.

As the cops get closer, I see one of them isn't slowing down. *Does he think these guys are resisting?*

"It's okay," I call out. "They're under control."

He continues sprinting toward us as if he doesn't hear me. With his head down, and at a full sprint, he tackles all three of us. I'm knocked backward to the ground. I feel myself sliding on my back, and then the sensation of a drenching wave of mud washing over me. The wind has been knocked out of me, but I jump to my feet as quick as I can. I'm wondering if I did something wrong—some code or signal, something I was supposed to say. The two burglars are as confounded as I am. For a minute I feel more of a connection with them than I do my police partners.

As I wipe the mud from my eyes, I can see the other cops already giving the linebacker a bad time. He apologizes to me, claiming he couldn't see where we were.

5:52 a.m.

My uniform is trashed and I don't have another one yet. There's not much left of the night, so the sergeant tells my training officer to keep me inside the rest of the shift.

"We have reports to write anyway", my training officer says.

We? I can't drive, can't think, and I can't touch anything, but he's gonna have me write the reports?

Some of the guys come by to make cracks about my muddy uniform. One asks me if I want a donut. None of it bothers me. They all know that I did something halfway decent, and I guess this is all just part of the ritual.

8:00 a.m.

We're in the report writing room with the rest of the squad. My training officer finishes reading the last of my paperwork and tells me they look okay. I gather my equipment while he heads to the sergeant's office to turn them in. I look around for my field case, but it's not where I set it. Suddenly, it comes sliding over to me from the corner of the room. I look up and see the old veteran who gave me such a hard time in lineup at the start of the shift.

He grins widely. "See ya tonight, kid."

Chapter 2

5:00 p.m.

I've been assigned to the swing shift. This is my first lineup without a training officer sitting next to me. I can't believe I'm actually part of a squad now—*Five to Three, Bad Days*. We call it that because the hours are five at night until three in the morning with Tuesday, Wednesday, and Thursday off—hence the *bad days*. The other side gets weekends off, but I'm happy where I'm at. More action on the weekends!

One sergeant reads all the bulletins while the other one passes out reports and subpoenas. They tell us that one of them will be on the street working the northern half of the city and the other will work the South End. The watch commander stands by the door with his arms folded, saying nothing.

I watch the South End sergeant work his way between the tables and I'm thinking he's the one whose good side I'll need to stay on.

5:18 p.m.

The other sergeant stops lineup to answer the phone on the wall next to the patrol board. He looks around the room as he's talking. Not quite audible, but everyone knows it's dispatch calling to ask if someone can clear for a call before lineup is even over. He locks eyes with me and everyone else laughs.

By the time the sarge hangs up the phone, I've already stashed my clipboard and I'm carrying my case toward the door. He smiles as I pass him. "I didn't even have to say anything," he says to the rest of the group.

As I drive out of the back gate, I tell dispatch that I'm in service.

"3-Edward-46, we have a caller on the line asking for police at the family clinic across from St. Theresa's Hospital."

The E-Edward beat is about half residential and half industrial. The city's two hospitals are both in this beat, so some nights on Edward can be extremely busy. Apparently, this is going to be one of those nights. I acknowledge the call and the dispatcher adds, "Unknown problem."

I notice she didn't send a cover unit, so I'm assuming whatever the problem, it mustn't sound too bad over the phone. This would be my first lesson on making assumptions.

I find the building on the opposite side of the street from the large hospital complex. The clinic is smaller with only three stories. It's painted yellow, and the building has exterior walkways that make it look more like an apartment house. There are only three cars in the parking lot and most of the adjoining offices appear to be closed.

The clinic door is unlocked, so I carefully slide it open. I'm peering around the door frame from the relative safety of the hallway. Nobody is yelling, and there's no blood on the pale green carpet. That's a good thing. I see a doctor dressed in a white lab coat standing by the front desk, and there's a nurse standing next to him. They're talking with a lady in the waiting room. She's a pretty young woman wearing a pleasant yellow summer dress and holding a pink blanket.

"Hello." I take a step inside. "Did someone here call the police?"

Though neither says a word, the doctor and the nurse both have a look of unease. I glance to the woman with the blanket.

"Everything is alright," she says softly. "I don't know what their problem is. I brought my daughter to the doctor's office because she has a little cold."

As she's explaining this to me, I notice the nurse inching toward me.

"Is anyone else here?" I ask, half wondering if I'm at the right place.

The doctor shakes his head. "Nobody else is here."

The strange expression on each of their faces tells me that something is wrong. The doctor and nurse look as if someone is holding them hostage. I might otherwise wonder if the woman in the waiting room has a shotgun wrapped in that pink blanket, but I can actually see a little tuft of dark hair on her baby's head. The woman has a distant look though, one I can't really read.

By now the nurse has made it to within earshot of me. She leans close and whispers words that nothing in the police academy prepared me for. "The baby is dead."

I take an involuntary suck of air. I almost ask if she's serious. Not that I don't believe her, but only because I'm not accustomed to this level of sudden seriousness. I fight the urge to ask if she's sure the baby is dead. I suppose a doctor and nurse are pretty sure when someone is dead.

The nurse leans closer again, "The doctor is going to distract her so you can grab the baby."

Now I really want to ask if she's serious. I'm not feeling at all good about this plan. The last thing this poor woman needs is a bunch of strangers having a tug of war with her little girl.

The woman sees the nurse whispering to me and takes a defensive step back. "No!" she shouts; her eyes wide and unfocused. She tucks the blanket around the baby as if to keep her warm. "My daughter is just a little cold," her tone softens a bit.

"May I see your little girl?" I gently say to the woman.

It takes her a second to decide. She moves slowly toward me, glaring at the doctor and nurse the whole time. I can't say I have even the slightest idea of what I'm *supposed* to do, and I haven't really got any kind of a plan. In the absence of both things, I'm just sort of going with my instincts.

The woman peels back the blanket exposing a pale, little, angelic face. The baby's closed eyelids and lips have a bluish tint, but otherwise her outward appearance is unblemished. I'm struck by how peaceful she looks. Without warning or control, my eyes start to tear up. I'm not sure what to do, but it doesn't matter. The woman's eyes meet mine and hers also begin to tear.

"It's alright," I assure her. I extend my arms toward the woman, and slowly a look of resignation edges into her consciousness. She brings the baby to her face and inhales deeply, taking in a last memory. She kisses her daughter gently on the forehead and then carefully hands her to me. The distant look now gone from the mother's face, she collapses on the floor crying.

I walk to an examination room in the back while the doctor and nurse tend to the woman. I take time to gather myself, and then think back to one of my academy courses. I check the baby's body for any obvious signs of injury, abuse, or neglect. There are none. When the doctor returns, he confirms that it appears to be a case of Sudden Infant Death Syndrome.

They somehow track down the baby's father, and he arrives to comfort his wife. I wait in the back for the coroner to take custody of the baby. I know I should use the time to begin writing my report, but I'm unable to look away from the tiny body.

I can't imagine I'll ever get used to this.

6:59 p.m.

I'm driving through an area of my beat that I've never seen. My head is still back at the doctor's office. I'm mindlessly looking around at a rural neighborhood with dirt sidewalks and a hodgepodge of houses set on deep lots.

A rust colored Camaro jets through the stop sign about a half block ahead of me. He's probably doing about 45, and didn't even slow down. It's a residential area, so the speed limit is only 25 anyway. I'm already feeling drained, and I just started my shift. I wish I hadn't seen the Camaro. I catch up to the car and see a lone male driver inside. He slows down, and pulls into one of those long driveways that extends to the back side of the house. I know he sees me, but he keeps driving. He continues though an open gate and into a weed infested backyard. I tell dispatch that I'm stopping a car, and I give them the license number. What I don't tell them is that he's not stopping.

He finally stops the car and runs straight for the house. I manage to scramble out of my car and position myself between him and the back door. As I'm asking the guy for his driver's license, he's telling me, "Get the fuck out of my way, Pig."

They really do call police pigs? This is the first time anyone actually called me that. For some strange reason I feel kind of honored to be officially considered one.

I grab onto him as he tries to push past me. We both tumble through the door and into a kitchen. He's yelling and screaming, and his whole damn family just happens to be sitting right there in the kitchen. Bad luck for me. They are a Mexican family, as evidenced by the fresh handmade tortillas on the stove and the ample access to flour.

I'm grabbing the guy, and his family is grabbing me. Everyone is yelling and scratching, and I'm afraid one of them is going to get my gun out of the holster. I see my suspect disappear into a cloud of white powder, and I strategically back out the way I came in. The mother chases me out the door with a rolling pin.

As I get outside, I see that another young man has followed me out of the house. He arms himself with several rocks from the driveway and begins pelting my car with them. I figure he's the brother of the driver who's still hiding somewhere in the house. Finally, after backing my car out to the street, I get on my radio.

"Edward-46, can you send me a cover unit?"

I look down and see my badge dangling from my torn uniform shirt. I did manage to hang on to my gun, however. After a long ten minute wait, my cover unit arrives. It's Clyde Beasy—an older guy who works the overlap shift. He's a well respected cop who probably could have retired years ago.

"What the hell happened to you?" He says, glancing from me to the house and back.

I briefly explain what happened. He tells me that it sounded like a routine cover call, and then apologizes for not getting here sooner. Clyde then chastises me for failing to come on the radio sooner.

"This could have legitimately been an *11-99* call," he says, shaking his head in frustration.

I don't really have a response for Clyde. I know that *11-99* is an all units call for help, but I've never actually heard one go out. I sure don't want to call for help on my first day on solo patrol. Everyone would think I can't handle the job.

"The city limits are two blocks back," he says. "You're not even in the city anyway."

I tuck in my uniform shirt and glance at the house, hoping the people inside can't here me getting scolded by the old timer.

The last bit of advice Clyde gives me is that this is a well-known family of trouble makers, and the kid driving the Camaro is the worst of the bunch. His name is Johnnie Lopez.

I'm ready to rally the troops, kick down the door, and go take my prisoner back. I tell Clyde that I've got enough probable cause to arrest the brother and the mother, too.

Clyde rubs his chin pensively. "We could do that," he says, "...or, since we know who they are, we could send a report to the district attorney and get warrants for their arrests. We can come back and get them when the advantage is on our side."

As wounded as my pride is, I know Clyde's is a better call. I can only hope that I'll be able to even the score with Mr. Lopez sometime down the road. It doesn't feel right, just driving away. But that's exactly what we do.

7:38 p.m.

On my way out of the industrial area, I find myself behind a guy in a big Chrysler that looks like it should have a *wide load* sign hanging off of it. I probably wouldn't have noticed him, except that he's weaving from one side of the lane to the other and driving well below the speed limit. I'm watching the car, and I'm thinking that this guy looks drunk. Except, the one type of case that I never had during my training was a drunk driving arrest. So I'm a little apprehensive.

I decide to stop him, and pull him over right at a busy intersection. It's the tail end of rush hour, and I find myself with an audience of people in cars, restaurants, stores, and on foot. I walk up to the driver's side window and ask the guy if he would mind pulling off the road into the parking lot. *The last thing I need is to be fumbling through giving my first sobriety test out in the middle of Grand Central Station.*

He gets out of the car and I see he's an older man, maybe about 60 or so. Apparently he didn't hear me, because he leaves his car where he stopped. He seems cooperative though, and tries his best to follow what I'm saying. As he walks to the front of the car, I see he's a little wobbly. I get close enough to smell his breath, and I think I detect a slight odor of alcohol. *But how much is too much?* This time I ask for a cover unit.

While waiting for my cover, I ask the man if he's been drinking. He tells me he's had "a couple of Scotch and sodas". I've never had a Scotch and soda, and I have no idea whether *a couple* is enough to make someone drunk. Besides, I have no way of knowing if he really just had *a couple,* or if he's had ten of them.

My backup arrives and it's Clyde again—thank God. He doesn't say anything, just leans back against the front of his car watching me. I'm kind of hoping he'll jump in and take over, but no such luck. I administer the sobriety tests we were taught in the police academy; touching his nose with his eyes closed, and walking an imaginary line, heal to toe. He does okay, but when I ask him to hold one foot off the ground, he wobbles and has to touch a foot down for balance. *Ah-ha! I got a live one!*

I'm ready to arrest the guy and put him in the back of my car when Clyde steps off his bumper and approaches me.

"What do you think?" I ask him.

"What do *you* think?" He asks me back.

I tell Clyde that I think the guy has failed my sobriety test, and that I'm going to arrest him for drunk driving.

Clyde pauses and rubs his chin. "You know," he says as if he's picturing something off somewhere in the past. "I was like you once; all piss and vinegar. But I don't want to see you piss down your own pant leg."

If there's a message in there somewhere, I'm not getting it. "What do you mean?" I say. "You don't think he's drunk?"

Clyde goes on to tell me that I have to factor in the guy's age. "A young man can stand on one leg forever," he says. "But older guys have trouble maintaining their balance, even when they haven't had anything to drink."

Meanwhile the driver is just standing there, trying his best to hear what Clyde's telling me. It crosses my mind that the guy is actually a friend of Clyde's, and this is all a ruse to get the guy off. Then, I realize Clyde is just trying to help me.

"Watch this," Clyde says. He gets out in front of us, with people all around, and tries to do all the sobriety tests that I just gave the driver. When Clyde gets to the one leg balance, he wobbles like he's just had a couple of Scotch and sodas. I'm looking around, embarrassed as hell, wondering what people are thinking. It must look like I'm giving a sobriety test to another cop.

"Give the guy a break," Clyde says. "He's about half drunk and half old man." Clyde lumbers over to his car and lowers himself into the seat. "Save the handcuffs for the ones who are really a hazard on the road."

I give the driver back his license, and he drives off. I thank Clyde for the help, and he heads into the station. I wonder if I'm ever going to get this stuff.

8:10 p.m.
"3-Edward-46, take a domestic disturbance . . ."

They taught us in the police academy that *domestics* were the most dangerous calls. Right now I'm just glad to have something I've handled before. I hear them dispatch a cover unit, which is pretty much standard for this type of call. My backup is a guy named Ryan Kalani. He's a new guy too, so I know he won't be looking over my shoulder or second guessing me. He's a big guy who just transferred from another police department. I don't know him very well, and I haven't gone on any calls with him yet.

We pull up in front of the house at the same time. Kalani gets out of his car and immediately puts on his cap. He throws his nightstick into the ring on his belt and swaggers toward me like something out of an old movie.

"What's with the hat?" I ask.

He glances skywards, almost crossing his eyes, trying to see the cap on his own head. "What, the hat? Don't you ever wear yours?"

I don't want to admit that I haven't been working long enough. I haven't been to a promotional ceremony, haven't' been to a funeral, and haven't even had an inspection yet. In fact, my cap is sitting in my briefcase with the plastic liner still covering the inside of it.

"I came from an outfit across the bay," Kalani says before I can respond. "That place, you even think about getting out of your car without your hat on and your sergeant writes you up."

I tell him that it doesn't sound like a fun place to work, and he says, "Why do you think I left?"

Now I understand why he wears the hat, but it still doesn't explain the swagger.

A loud crash rattles the windows of the house, and a woman inside screams. We're on either side of the door and I give it a good rap.

"Police department!"

It's answered right away by an elderly lady in a flowered housedress. "Oh, thank God you're here! My sons are going to kill each other." Behind her are two adult men—probably in their 30's— beating the shit out of each other. One brother has the other in a headlock, and the other looks like he's trying to tear his brother's ear off. The mother shrieks at the sound of her coffee table overturning.

I feel my hand reaching for my duty belt—surely there's something amongst all this gear that will help me quell this melee. Kalani suddenly steps in front of me to address the old woman.

"Let's see what you got cooking over here on the stove." He drapes an arm over the woman's shoulder and the two of them walk right past her two sons, into the kitchen.

Is this guy for real? He acts like the fight is the last thing on his mind. I'm standing in the living room while these two pummel each other, and Kalani is in the kitchen with his head over a pot of beef stew.

The old lady is giggling and asking if he wants a taste. "I might as well," Kalani says loudly. "Since your two knucklehead sons would rather fight than eat this nice dinner you made for them."

Both men suddenly stop fighting, clearly not getting the reaction from the police they had expected. They watch Kalani in disbelief, and then they start laughing at him.

"You two!" Kalani says, finally coming out of the kitchen. "Go wash up for dinner. And when you're finished eating you can fix your mom's coffee table!" They both look at the table, overturned and askew against the wall.

Kalani gives the old lady a squeeze and tells her to call back if her sons get out of hand again. I look back as we're leaving to see the two men sitting down to dinner while their mother contentedly serves them.

"How did you do that?" I ask in amazement.

"Do what?" he says, swaggering toward his car. Then he stops and nods toward the house. "Did you see the size of those two guys? I didn't want to mix it up with them—especially the way I feel right now."

"What do you mean?"

"Why do think I'm walking like this?" He winces in pain. "My hemorrhoids are killing me!"

10:10 p.m.

I'm cleared for my dinner break. My wife, Gale, has packed some leftover spaghetti in a Tupperware container for me, and my mouth is watering for it. It'll have to be heated in a microwave and eaten without parmesan cheese and French bread, but I'm not complaining.

When I get to the station, Davis pulls in just ahead of me. Interesting guy. They call him *The Glove*. He walks into the building wearing a single glove on his left hand. I guess he doesn't want anything to interfere with the trigger finger on his gun hand.

Before I eat, I run out all the information I can find on my friend, Johnny Lopez. I want my report to leave no doubt in the district attorney's mind that this guy needs to go to prison. While I'm up in the front office, I notice that the desk officer and Tina Lynch, one of the night clerks, are enmeshed in a quiet conversation about two inches from one another. She's a tall lean woman with a pretty face and a round butt, which she has tightly packed into a pair of gray slacks. I only notice this because she's positioned herself over his desk with her butt in the air, so that nobody in the front office could possibly miss it.

The desk officer is called back to the jail for one thing or another, and Tina flutters away. He asks me to keep an eye on things at the front counter for a few minutes, until he returns. I gather up my paperwork and move over to the desk where he was sitting. No sooner does he leave when Tina buzzes over and assumes the pose in front of me.

"Can you believe him?" She says.

"Who?" I'm wondering if I somehow missed the first part of the conversation. "Him." She motions over her shoulder towards the desk officer as he disappears around the corner. "He's been flirting with me all night."

Although I wouldn't put it past the guy, what I saw was pretty clearly a two party game of grab-ass.

Whatever. I just shrug and go back to my report. Tina leans down so close that I feel her blond hair tickling my neck.

"And can you believe he's married, too!" She whispers as if it's a fact too incredible to say aloud.

Imagine that.

11:15 p.m.

As I clear the station, one of the guys working downtown gets a hold of me on the radio and wants to do a bar check. He's been on the force about a year longer than me, and I get the impression he's kind of a golden boy. We rendezvous in a municipal parking lot between an adult book store and a gay bar.

"We got a bunch of complaints of drugs here," he tells me, pointing to the bar. "Bathrooms and outside in the rear patio."

"Okay," I say. I haven't done much self-generated stuff up to this point, but it's the kind of thing that all the really good cops do. I have a momentary fantasy of walking into the middle of a drug deal and seizing a nice bag of cocaine or something. Not only would it impress the golden boy, but it would make my sergeant take notice.

As we're coming around to the front of the building, I remember a little trick I heard about in the police academy. Close one eye, so when you walk into a dimly lit environment you're at least partially accustomed to the dark. It is a technique I have been dying to try, so I shut my eye and continue toward the door.

We walk into the bar, packed solid with steaming bodies. The music is so loud that I can't hear my radio or my partner. It is my first foray into a gay bar, and it surprises me to find the open display of physical affection between men a little distracting. I'm hit with a heavy scent of body odor mixed with beer, and the humidity reminds me of a sauna. The music stops and a round of wolf whistles shoot out from the bar on my right. I'm unable to see anything to that side, since my right eye is closed. The overall effect of the situation has me wanting to do a quick U-turn and get the hell out.

My partner wades off into the mass of tank top-clad men, and my right eye springs back open to get a better view of things. I can't tell whether or not the technique has helped me see any better, but there's an unintended outcome. One of the men on the dance floor, a guy in chaps and a cowboy hat, thinks I'm winking at him. As I inch forward in an attempt to catch up to the other officer, I find myself engulfed in the middle of the dance floor. The music starts back up even louder than before, playing *He's So Shy*. I turn sideways to squeeze past someone, only to find myself boxed in directly in front of the cowboy. He starts swinging his hips to the beat, and then mimics each move I make. I know that to anyone observing, it looks like we're dancing.

By then my partner has checked the bathrooms and has made his way to the back patio. Apparently there were no drugs being used or sold, because he emerges from the hallway empty handed. His look of disgust as he passes me is noticed by the rest of the bar, and they all break out in hysterical laughter. I back my way out of the front door as if I might be attacked from behind. The last thing I see before leaving is my cowboy friend blowing me a kiss.

"What the hell!" my partner says, still walking ahead of me. "I look around for you, and you're out there dancing with some guy."

I try my best to explain the eye thing, being trapped, the music, but he's not really interested. He's shaking his head as he gets back in the car, and I have the distinct feeling that I haven't heard the end of it.

12:38 a.m.

I'm heading back to my beat when I monitor some radio traffic in the south end of the city. It sounds like there are problems at *Sneakers*, a large dance club catering to eighteen to twenty-one year olds. After midnight they kick out all the kids under twenty-one. As I understand it, that's usually when the problems start.

I head down that way, hoping to get in on some action. Whatever happens, I am determined to avoid the dance floor at all costs. I never make it in though, because as I pull up to the front of the place one of the officers flags me over. It's the same guy who I did the bar check with. He's on foot with another cop, trying to clear a crowd of about 100 out of the lot.

"Ticket that car," he says pointing to a small green hatchback. "They blew the stop coming out of the lot and wouldn't yield for us."

Not wanting to look any worse to the guy, I speed off to catch the car. It makes a turn, and I come up behind it on a side street. As I light it up, another cop pulls up behind me. He's an older guy, Don Richards, and he's working overtime on swing shift tonight.

I walk up to the car I stopped and see it's packed full of people. I ask for the driver's identification, and my flashlight illuminates six young girls all dressed for a night of clubbing. One of them calls out my name from the backseat. I stoop to peer into the heap of purses, colorful dresses and ruffled hair, and I catch a whiff of heavily perfumed air. It's a stark contrast to the bar I was just in. A tiny hand with pink painted nails snakes its way out of the backseat, and grabs my wrist. She repeats my name. She's a cute little girl that one of my friends used to date in high school. The driver hands me her license with a broad toothy smile that says: *I just got out of a ticket.*

In my pea brain, I'm thinking that giving her a break just because her friend knows me would be tantamount to accepting a bribe. I don't want to embarrass myself in front of the older cop, and I certainly don't want to go back empty handed to the cop who sent me after them in the first place. I clumsily shake the hand of the girl I know, and I write the driver a ticket. She quietly signs it. The young ladies drive away, waving goodbye with dumbfounded looks on their faces.

My backup hadn't even bothered getting out of his car. I thank him for covering me, but he doesn't say anything. Instead, he scratches his head and winces, as if he has something distasteful to tell me.

I stand there at his open window, "What?"

"You didn't *really* write those young ladies a ticket, did you?"

"Yeah, why?"

He shakes his head. "You know, you don't have to write up everyone. There are enough people out here who really need it."

Where have I heard that before? Oh yeah, Clyde. What's with these old guys? They want to give everybody a break.

Richards notices my skeptical expression and turns his car off. He gets out and stands there under the streetlamp, leaning back against the door. "Listen, Kid," he says. "There aren't many perks in this job. Most people are going to hate you, cuss you out, spit on you, or worse. So when you stop a carload of young, pretty girls, enjoy it. Talk to them, be nice to them, and give them a break. They're few and far between. The next guy you stop is probably going to want to kick the holy shit out of you anyway. That's the one you want to write up."

He drives off, and I'm left standing alone on the now empty street. The thumping music from the club and the crackling radio drift in and out of my consciousness as I think about what he said. *Somewhere in this job I have to find my own balance.*

2:08 a.m.

I'm driving through a strip mall; a block long row of shops, offices, a liquor store, and a Chinese restaurant. For the most part they are in a straight line, except for an insurance office that is set back about 50 feet from the parking lot. The whole place is deserted this time of night, and I'm just wasting time patrolling my beat until the shift is over. My window is open, even though it's colder now, and I find myself still reliving the earlier incident at the clinic.

I glance to my side as I pass the insurance office, and see someone sitting back in the dark on brick planter box. I stop my car and put myself off on the radio. As I'm walking toward the guy, I notice his head is down and he's got a white paper bag on the pavement between his feet. I throw a light on him and see his hands are empty. He glances into my beam with a disconnected look.

"How's it going?" I ask, as if it's perfectly normal to be sitting in the dark in front of a closed office in the middle of the night, and that I just happened by to find out how his night is going.

"Not too good," he says.

He reaches for the bag and I step back, training my light on his hand. The guy pulls out a fat donut covered in powdered sugar. I lean over the bag and see that it's full of donuts. He crams it into his mouth in one gargantuan bite, leaving a powder goatee from his nose to his chin. I watch as he pulls out another one and eats it the same way.

"You trying to get yourself sick?" I ask with a pathetic half laugh.

He looks up at me as serious as can be and says, "No, I'm trying to kill myself."

I'm struggling to figure out the riddle, but I'm not getting it.

"I'm diabetic," he says. "I'm not supposed to eat sweets—they can send me into a coma."

I gently slide the bag away with my foot and sit down beside him on the planter. We talk for the next twenty minutes or so, and he tells me the story. It's something about the girl he lives with falling out of love with him. He's sure of it, though his evidence against her is dubious at best. My gut feeling is that he's not really suicidal, but just trying to prove a point. If he really wanted to die, there are much more certain ways than eating yourself into a coma.

He agrees to throw the rest of the donuts away and return home to work things out. I give him a ride the few blocks to his house, and drop him off in front. There's a light on inside and I can see a woman's silhouette pacing behind the living room curtain. She opens the door and there's a tearful reunion. *They'll be fine.*

2:39 a.m.

I unpack my car and walk into the report writing room to join the rest of my squad. I set my case down and find an empty chair. I notice the room becoming quiet, and I turn around to see why. Nobody is facing me. They're all looking down at their work.

In low, off-key voices, they all start singing, *He's So Shy*.

3:00 a.m.

My sergeant peers over the top of his reading glasses as I drop my reports into the basket on his desk. He says nothing, but gives me a funny smile. They all have their sources of information on the squads, and he's no different. As I walk down the hall toward the locker room, I wonder what he knows about my night.

Chapter 3

5:00 p.m.

I walk into lineup holding the equivalent of a winning lottery ticket. It's the arrest warrant for Johnny Lopez, charging him with resisting arrest and battery upon a police officer—a felony offense. I've waited five weeks for the district attorney's office to file the case and for the judge to issue the warrant. Whatever the process, it's finally here, and tonight Mr. Lopez is going to be my special project!

5:30 p.m.

We break lineup, and I'm the first one into the back lot. As I check out my car, I'm thinking about exacting payback at the Lopez house. At least to the extent that I'll take their beloved Johnny to jail, and this time there will be nothing they can do about it. I'm all ready to request a couple of cover units to join me, when a double unit pulls through the back gate. The two cops inside both give me a sheepish look as they come to a stop in front of me.

"Hey, we got your dude," one says, motioning toward the handcuffed guy behind the metal screen. It's Johnny Lopez . . . and I'm pissed.

"The sergeant sent us out, doubled up, to serve warrants tonight," the other guy says, half apologetically and half in justification. "We didn't know until after we had him in custody that it was your case."

The copy of my police report on top of their clipboard exposes them as liars, and I let the two glory hogs know I'm not pleased. I decide right then, never to screw one of my fellow cops in order to make myself look good. It was my case. I was the victim, I prepared the report, and I've been waiting for the warrant. It was mine to serve, not theirs.

The two chumps hustle Lopez into the jail and I'm still standing in the back lot fuming. *Assholes!*

Some guy passes by me as if he owns the place. He's a black guy wearing plain clothes and sporting a stubby beard. The secured back lot isn't accessible to the public, and anyone authorized to be here should have an ID tag of some kind. Instead of confronting him outright, I give him a nod and introduce myself—just in case he's somebody important that I'm supposed to already know.

"Harold Gumbs," he says, offering a half-hearted hand shake. He jumps into the patrol car parked next to mine and starts it up.

"You with the maintenance garage?" I ask. He shakes his head and tells me he is a new cop. So new, in fact, that he's only in his second week of the police academy. He goes on to say that he's taking the car to show some friends. I'm assuming that his friends are here at the station, and maybe he's going to pull the car around to the front of the building or something.

"You might want to double check with the watch commander or the sergeants," I say. "Got to be really careful, especially when you're new."

He gives me some corny salute and drives off out of the gate.

6:05 p.m.

I'm dispatched to KB Toys on a theft report. It's one of about 100 stores in the mall on my beat. I maneuver my way through the shoppers and past See's Candies, to the front of the toy store. I'm heading toward the door when a man walking with his wife and two kids comes to an exaggerated stop right in front of me.

"I didn't do it!" he yells, throwing his hands up in the air. The dork gets a courtesy laugh from me, which is more than he gets from his family.

In a small storage room at the back of the store, I find the store manager seated next to a kid the size of a squirrel monkey. The kid is slumped in his chair, his chin resting on the chest of his Ninja Turtle shirt. The manager, a nicely dressed woman in her thirties, tells me that the kid stole some yo-yos from a display case and then left the store without paying for them. She chased the boy through JC Penney, finally catching up to him outside the mall and wrestling him into custody.

I have a difficult time picturing the kid running away, much less putting up a struggle. The manager says the five stolen yo-yos are valued at $47.79. I now have a difficult time picturing yo-yos being that expensive. I take down the manager's name, and give her a report number.

"You're prohibited from coming back in the store," she yells to the kid as we're leaving.

"What's 'prohibited'?" he asks me. I tell him he can't go back. I find out that his name is Jeffery Miller, he's only seven years old, and he has no juvenile record on file with the police department. I'm thinking about the advice the two older cops gave me about not having to write up everybody I come across. I decide to release Jeffery to his parents with nothing more than a verbal reprimand.

We drive to his house, a shabby flat-top on a busy street a couple of blocks from the mall. Nobody answers the door, so we walk in. I find the kid's mother in a back room watching TV. She looks up at us, not in shock, but more as if life had just presented *her* with another problem. She picks up the remote and turns the TV volume down to about half of what it was. Then, as I'm explaining what happened at the mall, she continues to steal glances at her show. She interrupts me a couple of times to blurt out that Jeffery is "grounded." She finishes it off with a harsh, "Just wait until your father hears about this one."

I leave, wondering if I'm missing a couple of red flags here. The first being that Jeffery stole not one yo-yo, but five. I can almost understand a kid snatching a toy he couldn't afford, but five? The second is the mother's comment, "Just wait until your father hears *about this one.*" Sort of makes me wonder if there were others.

7:07 p.m.

A small motorcycle is in front of me on a narrow residential street on the south end of my beat. I'm not thinking much, except that the driver's butt looks too big for the seat. In fact, his body looks way too big for the bike. He keeps looking back at me as he's riding, to the point that he's paying more attention to me than the road in front of him.

He's finally got me curious enough to pull him over. I find out that he is a big fourteen-year-old with no driver's license. His name is Jacob McDonough, and he lives a block away. He keeps asking me why I pulled him over, and if he had committed a traffic violation. I tell him that it doesn't matter because he's too young to be driving.

"Ah-ha!" He cries out as if he's won an important point. "Then I didn't do anything wrong. You had no *just cause* to stop me."

The area is semi-rural and much of it is still undeveloped. McDonough's neighborhood was recently annexed from the county—meaning it's now inside the city limits, but is not fully constructed with sidewalks and the like.

Again, I consider the advice of the older cops. If McDonough had been riding a mini-bike on a dirt trail it probably wouldn't have been illegal. His motorcycle isn't much bigger than a mini-bike, and the street isn't much more developed than a dirt road. I decide to escort him home with a warning not to ride his motorcycle on the street until he has a driver's license.

As I drive away, I'm feeling pretty good about this newfound generosity. Although, my sergeant might not see it the same way when I turn in crappy stats at the end of the month.

7:39 p.m.

I get a call to cover Felix on a domestic disturbance. We were in the academy together, and he's been riding the beat next to mine. Felix is a big ex-football player, with a pock-marked face and a ready smile. Not the smartest guy around, but he always seems to do something funny without intending to.

I pull up to the house and find Felix waiting for me in front. It's a one-bedroom cottage sandwiched between two larger houses in an older section of the city. We knock on the door and a man yells, "Come in!"

I follow Felix inside and notice that the place is trashed. Furniture is overturned and clothes have been dumped out of drawers and closets. It could have just happened, or it could just be the way these people live. I spot an overloaded cat box on the floor in the kitchen, which explains the urine stench.

A man of about 25 stands in the middle of the living room, panting like he's just gone a few rounds. He's a thin guy, wearing bell bottom Levis and no shirt, and his hairless chest is red with scratches.

"What's going on here?" Felix asks.

"I found out my wife is having an affair!" says the guy.

"That's not true and you know it," a woman hollers from behind a closed door.

For whatever reason, Felix rushes the door and throws it open. The woman screams that she's not decent, and Felix turns back, red faced. I can already feel the laughter starting to bubble up inside me. The husband glares at Felix, pissed off that Felix saw his wife half naked.

"Now you're showing it off to the cops!" he yells to her. The argument escalates from there. Initially from either side of the bedroom door, the two of them yelling back and forth, and then face-to-face. Somehow we all end up inside the tiny bedroom—Felix positioning himself between the man and the woman. I'm standing there mesmerized by the enormity of this woman. She's not tall, but must weigh 400 lbs. She literally takes up most of the bedroom. I look back at her fuming husband, only a fraction of her size.

I'm standing on the opposite side of the unmade bed, crammed against one wall, wondering how I got in this position. Felix tries to calm the situation by telling the husband there's no way his wife is having an affair.

"How would you know if she's cheating? the man asks.

Felix stammers, "Look at her...I mean, she's kind of..."

I jump in to help him. "It's just that your wife seems like such a nice person, it's hard to believe she would be unfaithful to you."

"Oh yeah?" The guy reaches into a bag on the floor. "Then what's this?" He holds out an enormous pair of women's panties, yellowed with wear. "Look here," he says, turning them inside out. "Those are semen stains!"

Felix's mouth drops.

The man thrusts the panties toward Felix, swinging them around like a cape at a bull fight. "See there?"

Felix's eyes widen with horror. "Get back," he says.

The man advances with the panties. "Send them to the crime lab!"

Felix steps back into a defensive position and pulls out his nightstick. I can see he's about to loose it. Then Felix screams, "Get those shit stained skivvies out of my face!"

The poor woman is mortified, and I'm laughing so hard I can't breathe. I work my way out from behind the bed, and usher the husband into the living room. He calms down after a bit, and in the end they both agree to go to counseling.

8:28 p.m.

Felix and I stand outside the tiny cottage reliving the domestic call, when a woman walks up to us carrying a large shoulder bag overflowing with papers. She has the look of homelessness or craziness, or both. She's dirty and her skin is baked from the sun, but she's somehow managed to find the resources to apply an abundance of mascara on her eyes. The woman stops in front of me and starts talking at warp speed. Her words are clear enough, but they don't all fit together to form a rational thought.

Something like this: "I've been followed for thirteen years now by members of a secret society; many of whom are arthroscopic tunes that only I can decipher. My attorney has instructed me to follow the oblong methods. Do you get that? Everybody is torn asunder, and all of them take liverwurst in the morning when they pray to the supposed statue of Jesus. But we have proof it's really the image of Orson Welles. My ex-husband is the one that started all of this, and it's all been well documented."

The woman pulls a few loose papers from her bag. "The FBI has copies but they haven't done a Goddamn thing! It's pretty clear they're involved too."

Felix asks her name and she says, "Nancy Molfetto." As Felix makes small talk with the woman, I run her name to see if she's been reported missing from a board and care facility. While I'm waiting for dispatch's response, I see that Felix has managed to agitate the woman by looking through her shoulder bag. *Like she's carrying a sawed off rifle or a pound of cocaine-- she's just a nut, for Christ sake!*

But now, Ms. Molfetto is pissed and is accusing Felix of "playing footsies with the Feds, and abusing puppies with wooden nickels."

She's not wanted, nor is she reported missing. I tell the woman that we have another call, and ask if there is anything that she would like us to do for her before we leave. She wants us to arrest her husband for assaulting her, and make sure he's "prosecuted to the fullest extent."

Felix asks Molfetto how her husband assaulted her. Suddenly, she turns to Felix and delivers him a backhanded slap in the middle of his forehead.

Felix is so stunned that he stands frozen, his crossed eyes gazing upward at the red handprint on his head. As if what she did finally sinks in, he does this little Three Stooges style shuffle step, and then grabs Molfetto by the arms.

"That's a felony!" he yells. "You just assaulted a police officer!"

And again, I'm laughing almost too hard to speak. "You asked her," I say.

Felix reluctantly agrees to let Molfetto go on her way, and not arrest her. As she shuffles off, Felix looks at me with that goofy crooked grin and says, "I guess I just got a Molfetto slap."

8:50 p.m.

Dispatch is trying to raise me on the radio, so I let them know I'm clear the DV call. They tell me to head to the St. Theresa's Hospital Emergency Room for a possible child abuse.

I contact the head ER nurse who ushers me to a quiet hallway outside the waiting room.

"His parents are in there," she says, looking back toward a Latino man and woman. "They wanted to stay in the exam room with their son, but the doctor and Social Services wanted to talk to the boy alone."

I ask for some basic information about him, and I'm told he's a seven-year-old by the name of Ruben. According to the nurse, he was brought in 25 minutes ago by his mother and father, for injuries to his genitals.

Not wanting to overwhelm the boy, I wait just outside the exam room while the staff questions him. A few minutes later the doctor comes out and tells me that it appears the boy has been tortured. I ask if the boy told him what happened, but he says that the boy has not admitted anything.

I follow the doctor back into the room and find Ruben sitting quietly on the exam table. He's a slightly built boy with huge brown eyes that stare at me from beneath straight, black, soup bowl cut hair. He's wearing a green and yellow sports jersey, green shorts, and green and yellow knee socks. There are no visible injuries anywhere else on his body, and he doesn't appear to be in any pain.

"The policeman needs to see your penis," the doctor says.

Now, I don't know if there are better ways of saying that, but I'm thinking there must be. At least explain to the kid why I'm here. Anything. Any context at all would be better than, *"The policeman needs to see your penis."*

Before I'm able to add my two cents, the doctor reaches over and lowers the kid's shorts. He swings a large crane-like exam lamp overhead to expose a pair of shriveled, dark purple testicles and a matching purple penis. Not swollen, not scratched or cut, just a purple color, so dark they appear nearly black. The rest of his body's pigment is what I would describe as light olive, the same as both parents.

I ask Ruben if he was kicked or injured somehow, and he shakes his head no. "Did anybody touch you there?" I ask, and he gives the same response.

When we step away, the doctor tells me that he knows of nothing medical that could cause the injuries. It is his opinion that someone took a hammer or blunt object and pounded the boy's genitals. *Hammer to the balls? Seems to me the kid might be in a little pain.*

I take a seat next to the parents in a relatively quiet area of the waiting room. They seem like very nice people who are genuinely concerned for their boy. They offer nothing to help me figure out what happened. I describe the doctor's hammer scenario to them, and they are visibly shaken. They claim they never so much as strike the boy. We go over the boy's activities during the past few days: school, soccer practice, dinner, homework. No injuries, no disciplinary issues, very little time away from the parents. It all seems pretty uneventful.

A check of police department and Child Protective Services records show no history with the family whatsoever. Another doctor is consulted by the first, and the Social Services counselor consults with her supervisor. They all reach the same conclusion: the boy has been abused and should be taken into protective custody.

The parents are devastated by the news. Though respectful and cooperative, they cry and beg me not to take Ruben. I call my sergeant and run the story down to him, including my gut feeling that the parents are not responsible for hurting the boy. I think I detect a muffled chuckle about my *gut feeling* comment, which I assume is because I'm too new to have one. In any case, the sergeant tells me that I have to do what the doctors and social workers say. Take the kid.

Ruben weeps softly all the way to the temporary foster home in the north end of the county. When I get a load of the place, I feel like weeping myself. The ghetto neighborhood alone probably put Ruben in more danger than if I had left him with his abuser. The interior of the house is painted a bold violet color, and the thick shag carpet is olive green. A TV is blaring in another room, there's a baby crying, and somebody is coughing like they've got tuberculosis.

The large grandmotherly black woman who runs the place sees that Ruben is upset and offers him a cookie and a glass of milk. I give her the boy's information and the police report number. I kneel down next to Ruben and tell him that everything will turn out okay. He looks at me through his tearful brown eyes and I can see that this whole thing is wrong.

I've always believed the phrase, *my hands are tied*, is nothing more than a cop out by someone too lazy or too weak to do the right thing. I drive away from the foster home feeling like a coward.

10:30 p.m.

I get back to the station and pitch it again to my sergeant. I wouldn't say he's annoyed, but he's getting there. No, is his answer. "Just leave it alone," he says. "Let the justice system sort it out when they go for a custody hearing in a couple of days."

I describe my astonishment at the condition of the foster home.

"Yeah," he says dismissively. "Most of them are shit holes. Hey, how about staying in so you can get your reports written?"

What sounds like a generous offer turns out to be a clever way to assign me as the desk officer for the rest of the shift. Yes, I can stay in and write my reports, but I'll be at the mercy of whatever comes my way at the front desk.

I get a sandwich from the vending machine in the lunchroom and eat it at the desk. It tastes like it's been preserved with formaldehyde, but I devour it just the same.

Tina, the front office clerk, spots me from across the office and heads my way. I pull out my reports and huddle over them hoping she gets the message. She doesn't. Tina parks her round bottom on my desk and wants to know if anything "cool" has happened on my shift tonight.

"Not really," I say. "Nothing too *cool*."

11: 05 p.m.

Tina's about to delve into another line of questioning when the jail alarm goes off. It's an extremely loud buzzer that signals someone needs immediate help. There are a series of red buttons throughout the jail and someone has obviously hit one. I glance up at the closed circuit jail monitor and see one of the community service officers flailing with her hands in the air, as if she's being pummeled by someone just out of the video frame.

I sprint down the hall and half a dozen officers already crowd the jail door ahead of me. We jostle one another like wildebeests on a riverbank. The truth is that everyone is clamoring for the chance to tune someone up.

We find the community service officer on her ass against the wall, holding her arm. The cell door is open and whoever did it to her has apparently retreated back into the cell. By the time I get my head in there, I see the five occupants of the holding cell have been thrown to the ground and are getting twisted and pulled like Gumby figures.

"No," says the community service officer in a weak voice. "They didn't do anything."

I turn to listen, since I'm the last one in line and can't get my hands on a prisoner anyway. "It's hot applesauce," she says, holding out her arm.

Turns out she had mistakenly put a sealed cup of applesauce into the microwave with a prisoner's meatloaf TV dinner. She opened the cell door to give the guy his meal and when she pulled back the seal on the applesauce, its hot contents exploded all over her arm. She must have fallen backwards against the alarm button. By the time I manage to convey what happened, those at the leading edge of the dogpile have already gotten in some licks.

The sergeant shows up and hears the screwball story. He isn't too pleased. Two of the prisoners want to make formal complaints. There's no way to clean this thing up, so the sergeant wants me to write a report covering the incident. He says whatever happens in the jail is the responsibility of the desk officer. *First I ever heard of that.*

I tell the sergeant that I'll be glad to write it, *exactly the way it happened.* That seems to concern him a bit, so he ends up going with plan B. The two guys who want to complain are let out of jail with a citation to appear in court at a later date. Technically it's a legal option, and given the circumstances, probably a good call. It saves

them from having to post bail, and quickly takes the wind out of
their desire to stick around and make a formal complaint. It's the
kind of thing I never knew happened, but I'm learning. Best part is
there will be no report.

12:29 a.m.

I take a break from writing and walk down the hall, past the jail,
into the back parking lot for some fresh air. Writing about the abuse
case has got me feeling wrung out, and I can use the break. It's a
beautiful night—crystal clear sky, lots of stars, and a light breeze
that is just enough to cool me down. These vests are like a half inch
of insulation under the uniform. Some guys take the vest off when
they're on the desk, but I can't bring myself to do it. My luck, some
nut case charges into the lobby with an Uzi while I'm sitting there
writing.

I'm thinking about Ruben and wondering if he'll ever get to
sleep tonight. I wish I knew what caused his injury. At least I'd
know whether or not I did the right thing.

The clank of the back security gate opening jars me out of it. I
look over and see a patrol car inching in, not balls to the wall like
usual. I remember once after a good rain when some cop came
hauling ass through the back lot at the end of his shift. He hit a
puddle right as the captain stepped off the curb. It looked like a
tsunami washing over him. Drenched his nice pinstripe suit. Every
single cop in the back parking lot was out of there within 10
seconds. Nobody wanted to catch the frags of that blast.

Something about the car coming through the gate doesn't seem
quite right. As I look closer I see it's missing a door. The drivers'
door is completely sheared off and is sitting catawampus on the
backseat. The patrol car rolls by me and there's the new guy, Harold
Gumbs, behind the wheel. He's looking straight ahead as if there's
nothing remarkable about the car. *Hello! The freaking door is gone!*

I'm trying to keep a straight face as he parks the car and then
approaches me. "What's up?" I say.

"Door's all fucked up," Gumbs says, shaking his head as if the
damn thing just fell off on its own.

He tells me that he wanted to prove to his buddies that he's really a cop now, so he drove the car to his old neighborhood in Richmond. When he opened the door to get out, another driver sheered it completely off. As Gumbs heads off to tell the sergeant what happened, all I can think is that the sergeant is going to want me to write the accident report.

I hurry to my desk, but I can't hear what's being said behind the closed door. Both the watch commander and the sergeant are in there talking to Gumbs and it doesn't look too good. My guess is he ain't going to make it through the academy.

Here comes Tina to chat it up some more. *Doesn't she have any work?*

"I'm leaving for the night," she says.

"Okay, thanks. Have a good night."

She hesitates, then turns back to me. "You know? You're the only officer who doesn't try to hit on me. You have a good marriage, and you're a good husband."

"Thanks," I say. "Yeah, I'm one of the lucky ones."

12:42 a.m.

Dispatch calls me at the desk. They want to transfer a non-emergency call to me. I answer, and hear a squeaky voice of an old lady. She's saying something about half and half milk, but I can barely hear her. I cover my other ear and ask if she can speak up.

"Is there anyone there who can pick up some half and half for me?"

"Ma'am, this is the police department."

"Yes, I know," she says kindly. "But I have nobody else I can call. I have an ulcer and it's the only thing that settles my stomach."

I ask her to hold while I check with the watch commander. He's done with Gumbs, and the sergeant is in another office reading reports. I explain the old lady's request to the watch commander, telling him that she wants me to go buy her some half and half. He keeps nodding at me, but doesn't give me an answer. Finally I have to ask him right out.

"So, what are we going to do?"

The lieutenant looks at me like I'm a mental case. "We're going to go to the store and buy her some half and half."

It wasn't the answer I expected, in fact up until then I thought he was going to throw me out of his office. Instead, he digs into his pocket and hands me a couple of bucks. Then, he gives me a set of keys and tells me to take his car.

I drive the watch commander's car down to the 7-11 store, buy a quart of half and half, then take it to the lady. She's a tiny thing with a sweet round little face and eye glasses secured around her neck with a neat little chain. She's very thankful, but not the least bit surprised that we, the police, actually did it for her.

I think about it as I'm driving back to the station. I guess it's really not such an unreasonable request. A kind thing to do. A public service. The type of thing cops probably used to do a lot more of in the old days.

2:00 a.m.

It's quiet on the street and a handful of the guys on my squad have come in to write. They're sitting in the report writing room and I'm at the front desk when the call comes over both the radio and the building's loudspeaker.

"3-David-79 needs expedited cover on La Paz across the street from the PD."

La Paz is a private street inside a townhouse complex kitty-corner from the police department. I had monitored his call but it didn't sound like anything that dangerous—some kind of noise disturbance in the hot tub.

I leave the desk and run directly out of the front doors. I hear the hooves of the cavalry behind me—probably all the guys who were in the station writing. We get to the complex, but rather than run the extra couple of hundred yards to the entry gate, we climb over the fence. What I see when I get there makes me wish I had never left the comfort of the station.

The guy who initially responded to the call, 3-D-79, the guy we call *The Glove*, is in the center of the complex near an outdoor jacuzzi. Apparently somebody who was trying to sleep called to complain about a man and a woman in the hot tub after hours.

When The Glove gets there, he sees that the couple is naked. They've been drinking, but they're not particularly uncooperative or unreasonable. They're just an amorous couple in a hot tub at two o'clock in the morning.

Granted, I wasn't there at the beginning, and I have no idea what might have caused this situation to digress. But The Glove called for expedited cover and for whatever reason, decided to arrest them for public drunkenness, or indecency, or some crazy thing.

I come to an abrupt stop. The Glove is trying to yank the woman out of the hot tub. She's half in and half out, and her ample white boobs flop against the wet pavement with each violent tug. She retreats a few inches back into the water, and then The Glove adjusts his grip and gives another yank. It looks like he's trying to land a ling cod. The boyfriend is sitting there the whole time, half lit, and not doing much of anything.

The other cops have slowed down considerably as well. The Glove is asking for some help, but nobody is stepping forward. Finally, The Glove gets the woman all the way out. There she lies, whimpering and cold, and on display like the catch of the day. This screwup might well take the spotlight off of old Gumbs.

It's dark and chaotic, and there are enough cops that I'm able to slip away without being noticed. I find myself sprinting back toward the fence, glad that I hadn't come on the radio to tell anyone I was going to the call. Three other cops are right behind me as we hoist ourselves over and race back across the intersection to the station. We all make a pact with one another in the hallway outside the report writing room: If anybody asks, we were never there.

Ten minutes later, I'm walking past the watch commander's office on my way back up to the front desk. The sergeant and lieutenant are in there having a cup of coffee, appearing calm and relaxed. That changes the minute the lieutenant looks up at the jail monitor. Both bosses watch in shocked annoyance as The Glove ushers a sobbing, naked woman into the jail. As all hell breaks loose, I pretend to burry my head in my paperwork as if I never noticed a thing.

2:57 a.m.

I take a last phone call at the desk before turning in my paper and calling it a night. It's the clerk, Tina Lynch. I glance at my watch.

"Didn't you get out of here a couple of hours ago?" I ask.

"Yeah," she says, slurring her words as if she's had a few drinks since she left. "Well, I was wondering . . . Did you want to come over when you get off work?"

I'm standing there, speechless and wondering if I heard her correctly. Wasn't I the happily married guy she was so impressed with? "No thanks," I say. "I think I'll go home to my wife."

3:00 a.m.

The child abuse investigation hits the sergeant's in-basket with a thud. Even with statements from the doctor and the social worker, I suspend it as *inconclusive*. The sergeant looks at me with a quizzical expression.

"You're convinced the boy wasn't abused," he says.

"Not by his parents."

He picks up the report and begins reading. "You knew Gumbs was taking the car to Richmond?"

"No." My answer is technically an honest one.

He still hasn't looked up from the report. "You one of the guys who responded to the cover call across the street?"

I pause, unable to tell an out and out lie.

"Never mind," he says. "Go home."

"Goodnight, Sarge."

3:22 a.m.

On my way home I drive down the street where Ruben's family lives. I'm not sure why. I guess I'm hoping for something to tell me whether I did the right thing or the wrong thing. It's almost three-thirty and the kitchen light is on. I slow down and see Ruben's mom and dad sitting under a lamp at the kitchen table. They're holding each others' hands, and I think they're crying. Or maybe it's just because I'm crying.

I know I'm right. They didn't do it.

Chapter 4

4:55 p.m.

The lieutenant stops me as I'm walking into the lineup room. He tells me that Child Protective Services called about an abuse case I had a couple of weeks ago—the young victim by the name of Ruben. He says there was no abuse after all, and the boy has been released back to his parents.

The sergeant gives me a nod, indicating he heard the news as well. I'm not used to talking with the lieutenant, so I keep the conversation short, forgoing any questions. Though I have many, and the sarge knows it. He watches me take my seat before filling me in on the rest of the story.

"It was a medical problem," he says. "They couldn't figure it out at St. Theresa's, so they brought the kid to Children's Hospital for more tests. Turns out he caught a soccer ball in the nuts during practice the day prior. Kid had a rare condition that hadn't previously been diagnosed—bruises really easily."

I thank him for the information, and take out my notepad as lineup begins. I feel like paying the family a visit, just to apologize or something, but I guess I'm probably the last person they ever want to see.

The lineup room is crowded. Not only is our squad on duty, but the opposite side is working tonight as well. Their normal training was cancelled for some reason, so we've got twice the number of cops on the swing shift. The sergeant announces that we don't have enough cars for everyone, so some of us will have to double up. As he goes around the room matching partners and making car assignments, I notice he skips over me. My guess is I'll work a regular beat in a solo car like always. The really sweet assignments usually go to *golden boys*, like those two dogs who stole my warrant.

I hear my name and I perk up. Sarge tells me I'm assigned to an unmarked car, doubled up with a guy named Tom Scheper. We both worked in the jail together before becoming police officers. He's a great guy, if you can stand him. Scheper is the loud, animated type. He's always late for work, and rambles into lineup half dressed. He's got a ruddy face and a nose that looks like it's been broken fifteen times. In his two years on as a cop he's already managed to break his ankle and blow out his knee. He's scarred up and beat up, but he thinks every woman has the hots for him. What's worse is he wants to date my sister. *Fat chance!*

When lineup is over, the sergeant pulls me and Scheper aside. He tells us about a case where a guy torched his girlfriend's house in an attempt to kill her. She survived, but the guy has been on the run for a few weeks since it happened. The sergeant hands us the suspect's mug photo and says, "I want this guy in custody by the end of your shift."

Those instructions seem pretty clear to me. Unconsciously I straighten up, feeling like a soldier who's been given secret orders. I always wondered if the sergeant viewed me as sort of a screw up, but now I've got the chance to show him otherwise. Not only has he put me in an unmarked car, but he's given me a sweetass assignment. I fight the urge to salute him, and instead tell him we'll do our best.

He smirks as if *our best* won't be worth anything unless we deliver. As we're walking out to set up our car, I can't help wondering if this assignment was just an oversight or perhaps even a test. Maybe it's meant for Scheper, and I was simply an odd number without a car. Whatever. I decide to make the most of the opportunity and prove myself, not just to the sergeant, but the lieutenant as well. We decide the wanted guy isn't likely to be out and around town until later in the evening. In the meantime, Scheper has other plans.

"Starsky and Hutch," he says to me as he loads his gear in the car. "That's who we're going to be tonight—a couple of undercover cops."

"Yeah, except we're wearing our full uniforms," I say. "Starsky and Hutch wore plain clothes."

Scheper doesn't answer with words, but gives me a devious grin instead. He reaches into his bag and pulls out a cowboy hat.

With a wiggle of his eyebrows he says, "And I have jeans and cowboy boots in my locker!"

Against my better judgment, I'm already picturing my closet at home, planning the sort of getup I might be able to come up with for myself. Scheper changes out of his uniform and into the cowboy costume. He looks the part, all the way down to the revolver hanging off his belt. We take a detour by my house on the way to the gas pumps. In my garage I find an afro wig from a high school play, a pair of tight slacks, and sunglasses. I change into my outfit, and Gale just rolls her eyes as we head back out the door.

Now somewhere in the back of my mind I know the sergeant wouldn't approve of our plan. If he had wanted us in plainclothes he would have said so. But it just doesn't make any sense to go out in an unmarked car, wearing a uniform. *It defeats the purpose, doesn't it?*

6:15 p.m.

We're tooling along past a big park and community center when Scheper tells me he needs to use the bathroom. I pull into the loop in front of the building and park in the shade to wait. It's still light out and the park is full of people.

POP! I hear a sound that is either a gunshot or a firecracker. I'm hoping for the latter. I start walking around the building toward the park, forgetting to bring my hand-held radio with me. In the uniform there's a holder on your belt so you can't forget it, and apparently what I'm now missing is the dispatcher broadcasting a "shots fired" call in the park.

As I make the corner of the building, I see a middle-aged man slumped against a tree. It looks almost as if he's sleeping, except for the odd position of his head, and the fact that there is a gaping hole in it. His hands are at his sides, and I see that one of them has a gun in it. I hear sirens close by and realize that it has already been called in. I look around and there's nobody even close to the victim. People in the park are watching from a distance, probably not knowing if someone shot the guy or if he shot himself. Then, I remember what I'm wearing, and realize they might think I shot him. I pull my wig off just as the first cop arrives. She runs over and immediately yells at me to back away and don't touch anything.

I tell her that I'm a cop, and I see the recognition overtake the panic in her eyes. "Sorry, I didn't recognize you," she says, eyeing the wig in my hand.

Scheper appears out of the bathroom, and makes his way toward us at a half jog. He's got his cowboy hat on, and he's hobbling over the blotchy grass in his boots. I'm hoping he can get through the shift without blowing out his other knee.

"What the hell did you do?" he says, staring down at the dead guy. "Why did you shoot him?"

After convincing Scheper it was a suicide, I write a supplement statement for the uniformed cop who's taking the report. Scheper tells her that we would stay and help but we're on a "special detail" per the sergeant. By now the fire department is there and two other cops have pulled up.

"Let's get out of here before someone sees us in these clothes," I say, hurrying toward our car.

Scheper slows to adjust his hat in the reflection of a window. "What's wrong with the way we look?"

7:02 p.m.

I had grabbed a bunch of arrest warrants before leaving the station, thinking it would be nice to have some stats to show at the end of the night. Since double cars aren't usually assigned to a specific beat, they aren't directly sent to handle many calls. Consequently, they're free to roam around and get into whatever mischief they want, or in some cases do nothing at all. That contributes to a perception the bosses have about guys riding double, unmarked or not, that all they do is screw off. These things always have an origin in the department—usually part fact and part fiction. The way I understand this one, a couple of guys were doubled up a few years back, and told to do some drug enforcement at a park in the south end of the city. They showed up at the end of their shift with nothing to show for the night—no arrests, no citations, no nothing. When the lieutenant asked them what they'd been doing all night, one of the losers answered, "We've just been honking around the South End."

"Check out this one." I show Scheper a warrant card for Armando Torres—a notorious troublemaker from a notorious troublemaking family. It's only a minor traffic case, but it's enough to arrest the guy.

We decide to walk right up to the front door in our cunning attire, and ask for Armando. *I knew these getups would come in handy.* We park around the corner and make our way on foot to the front of the house. This time I'm carrying my radio in my back pocket with the shirt tucked out over it. We both know Armando on sight, and as we're walking up the walkway we see him through a window.

"What do you want?" an old woman's voice calls to us through a screen door.

"Armando here?" we both say in awkward harmony.

Two other family members step into the living room to join the old lady. They must not get many visitors who look like us, because they don't seem even slightly fooled by our disguises.

"He's not here," says a man whom I'm guessing is his father. "You two can take your sorry asses on out of here."

Scheper and I exchange looks, trying to decide how long to continue the supposed charade. "We're police officers and we just spotted him in the house," Scheper says as we both bulldog our way through the screen door. No sooner do we cross that threshold and the fight is on. I don't know where all these people come from, but this is the second time it's happened to me. An entire extended family suddenly appears out of nowhere when it's time to fight the cops.

We're pushing and swinging our way through the living room, trying to get to wherever Armando is hiding. We're taking a few blows during the scuffle and I nearly lose my wig. We find our man hiding in a linen closet, and now we're cornered in a dead end hallway. Armando is fighting us, emboldened by his family. They're all taking turns with a swing or a kick at us, too. Even the old grandma is screaming and cursing at us. At one point she gets up from the couch and ends up getting bumped in the leg. She exaggerates a leg injury and flops herself back onto the couch, hollering the whole time. Scheper is trying to drag Armando toward the front door while I'm on the radio hollering for assistance. Almost immediately I hear sirens, and right away I'm second guessing whether I overstated our situation. Someone pushes Scheper, and Armando nearly breaks free. We surge forward and someone slams into curio, shattering glass everywhere. Someone in the house threatens to "call the cops," and I'm thinking it's a strange logic. *We are the cops, dumbshit. Did you think our partners were going to race over here to arrest us?*

Uniformed cops are arriving en masse; so many that we still can't get our prisoner out the door. With the family now outnumbered, the melee quickly dies down. Nobody is seriously hurt, but there will undoubtedly be some bruises and sore muscles in the morning. We drag Armando to jail, and end up taking his brother and father as well. They are both charged with interfering with a lawful arrest.

We get them booked as fast as possible so we can get back out on the street. We've got bigger fish to fry tonight.

Unbeknownst to us, Old Grandma Torres is on her way down to the police station to lodge a complaint against us for a variety of conduct violations. Had we known it, we might have tried to head it off by pitching our side of the story to the sergeant.

9:00 p.m.

We get back on the street, annoyed at the how much of the night is already gone. *So much undercover work to do, yet so little time.*

"What about doing an undercover prostitution sting?" I say.

Scheper gives a thumbs up, and we head downtown. I don't know much about prostitutes, or where they hang out, but I know we get complaints about discarded used condoms in the parking lot behind the adult book store. It seems like as good a place as any to do our sting operation.

We end up cruising through the municipal lot at a snail's pace. A man parks his car well away from the book store before maneuvering his way on foot through the lot, eventually slipping in the back door. A while later he emerges carrying a bag of who knows what. Scheper and I do a walk-through of the book store — me with my afro wig and him with his cowboy hat. No prostitutes here, but plenty of pornography. Behind a wall of dildos are a series of individual booths where a dollar will buy a few minutes worth of movies from the nightly playlist. We hear echoed grunts and moans, presumably from the films, but possibly from the viewers as well. A sign on the wall reads, *1 person per booth*, but there doesn't seem to be anybody enforcing the rule.

Back out in the parking lot, things are starting to pick up. I notice a car with the outlines of two figures, parked right in the middle of the lot. The engine is off and they don't appear to be coming or going — just sitting there in the car. Scheper and I discuss the possibilities. We decide that it's worth further investigation, so Scheper watches from behind a bush while I walk up to the open driver's window.

"How's it going?" I say, sticking my head almost all the way inside. I'm hoping to catch them by surprise, but I'm the one who gets the surprise. There's a man sitting casually in the driver's seat next to a woman, and he's got his hand up the woman's short skirt. He's vigorously working his hand between her legs.

"Hey," the guy says as if we were old friends, "why don't you come in here and find out how it's going." The woman smiles coyly, and they continue without missing a beat. My eyes must be registering the shock I'm feeling inside, but thankfully they're too into it to notice or care. Once I catch my breath, I'm thinking she's a prostitute and he's her pimp. *Bingo! We got us a real undercover case! I mean, what else could be going on?*

Recognizing that I haven't actually been solicited yet, I decide to take them up on their offer to join them in the car. As I walk around the back of the car to the passenger side, I take a little detour behind the bush were Scheper is hiding.

"I think it's a pimp and a whore," I tell him in a rapid whisper. "Keep your eyes on me and I'll give you a bust signal once I get the solicitation."

Before he can even ask me what the signal is, I'm climbing in beside the woman. She's an attractively shaped woman of about 30 years, with an innocent face and short blond hair. He is about the same age and a little overweight. As I settle in, he uses his hand as a wedge to prop her legs apart even further.

"C'mon," he says to me. "She wants you to feel her fur panties." She smiles at me and I'm so panicked I can barely breathe. There hasn't technically been a solicitation for prostitution, but they're inviting me to rub her "fur panties." Embarrassingly enough, it doesn't occur to me right away that there are no fur panties. It's when I see the woman's panties crimpled on the dashboard that I realize the fur panties he's been referring to is her pubic hair. Regardless, right now I have bigger things to worry about. Like, what the hell am I going to do?

The guy, probably getting a little impatient with me, grabs my wrist and pulls it down under her skirt. I stop short of the *fur*. "I don't want to startle you," I say. It is the only thing I could think of at that very second. "My hands are so cold from being outside." I then put my palm against the inside of her thigh—proof, I guess, that my hand was indeed cold.

I'm wondering when he's going to bring up money, or what sex acts she will or won't do. But still, nothing that even hints at solicitation. I'm beginning to wonder if I could have been wrong. Then he starts the car!

"Where are we going?" I ask, again trying to conceal the panic in my voice.

"Just a few blocks," he says. "It'll be fun. She likes two dicks inside her."

Two dicks! Did he just say two dicks? I never heard of a pimp that has sex with the girl right along with the customer!

By now we're driving out of the lot and I'm getting ready to jump out of the moving car. I hear a zipping sound followed by a friendly chuckle. He pulls his wang out and starts stroking it.

"Let's see what you've got," he says. "C'mon, I showed you mine."

I feel like I'm in the twilight zone. I have my hand on the door handle, ready to jump. No way is anybody going to see what I've got. I look back and see that Scheper is following us in the unmarked car. He's so close behind that I'm afraid he'll run me over if I jump. I decide to make my escape at the next stop light. Then, suddenly, he turns down a driveway running the length of an average looking, green, single-story house.

The couple slides out of the car and they head for the door. I don't see Scheper's car, but there's no way I'm going in the house with them. "Hold it right there," I say. I pull out my badge and show it to them. "I'm a police officer."

Scheper's car suddenly comes fishtailing into the driveway, his high beams lighting us up like an old black and white photograph. He bails out of the car with his gun in his hand, "Nobody move."

The woman is crying and the guy looks scared shitless. "Are we under arrest?" he asks. "Did we break the law?"

Unfortunately I don't have a good answer to either of those questions. I assume there is some law on the books about stroking yourself in a public place, but I have no idea what it is.

Scheper and I take down their identifying information, and I realize they are husband and wife. He's an insurance agent and she's a nurse. I'm wondering if I've ever run into her before on a call at the hospital. With any luck, she wouldn't recognize me with the wig on. I tell them I'm going to submit a report to the district attorney for a criminal complaint. In the meantime they are not under arrest. Watching the man console his wife as they slink into their house makes me feel kind of bad for them. They probably aren't bad people.

Scheper and I are probably as shaken as the couple. I fill him in about the parts he hadn't witnessed, as we drive back to the station. We discuss the possible crimes they committed, but still can't come

up with anything. Though neither of us is in favor of it, we decide
we have to ask the sergeant for his opinion about criminal charges.
The last thing we want to do is look stupid or make him regret
giving us the unmarked car for the night.

11:35 p.m.

We slip in the back door and go directly into the locker room.
We take off our undercover outfits and dress in our uniforms before
hunting down the sergeant. We find him in the lunch room,
drinking a cup of coffee with the lieutenant. They both look at us in
a way that immediately gives me a bad feeling.

Without a word, the sergeant and lieutenant get up and leave.
Something tells me we're supposed to follow them. Scheper shrugs,
and we head down the hall behind them like a couple of dumb
puppies.

"We wanted to run a case by you," I say to the sergeant.

"We'll talk about your case in the watch commander's office,"
he says flatly. *That's usually not a good thing.* They walk in ahead of
us. Once inside the office, we're told to close the door. *That's never a
good thing.*

The lieutenant picks up a notepad from his desk. Though I don't
know it at the time, they're his notes from the complaint filed
against us by the grandmother of Armando Torres. At this point, I
still don't even know a complaint has been made. I'm guessing he's
pissed because he thinks we've been *honking around the South End* all
night. Or perhaps he's pissed that we haven't got his arson guy in
custody yet.

The lieutenant slaps the notepad on his desk and glares at us.
I'm trying with all my might to decipher the upside down writing
on the pad, but I can't make out a word.

"I got a citizen's complaint against you two from a woman who
claims you terrorized her," he says sternly.

Scheper and I glance at each other. I can feel my mouth drop
open and I make a conscious effort to close it. "She . . . she, said we
terrorized her?" I ask, unable to fathom that the nurse, or her
husband for that matter, would complain. Especially to say we
"terrorized" them.

"She says you forced your way into her house without a warrant," he says, reading from his notes.

"That's not true, sir." I feel myself breathing hard as I try to explain. "We never actually went into the house. The entire contact took place in their car and outside the house on their driveway." The lieutenant looks at his notes again. It's obvious he doesn't believe me. I need to start from the beginning. "Lieutenant," I say with as earnest a look as I can muster. "I thought she was a prostitute. That's why I contacted them in the first place."

"The old lady?" he says in disgust. "She's a grandmother, for Christsake!"

"I don't know, sir. She didn't look that old to me." Scheper and I look at each other and shrug. I try to continue in a controlled voice, trying to focus, but I'm so nervous I'm all over the board. "Anyway, it was her who invited me into the house."

"Not what she says," the sergeant chimes in. "In fact, she claims at one point you were rough with her. Hurt her leg."

"No way," I blurt out a little louder than I mean to. "She wanted me to feel her fur panties but I wouldn't do it." The sergeant and the lieutenant exchange frowns.

"I barely put my hand on the inside of her thigh," I say, demonstrating by placing my hand on my own thigh. "I wanted to show her that my hands were cold."

"What's this about her panties?" The sergeant yells.

"Are you sick?" The lieutenant looks like his head is going to blow off.

They look at Scheper and then back at me, trying to figure out what in the hell we've just done.

"She wanted two dicks in her at once," Scheper says.

The lieutenant slams his notepad down and it slides across the desk. They're about to bring us up on charges when I see the name of the complainant on his notes. It's Old Lady Torres, not the nurse. We do our best to explain the misunderstanding, describing first the lawful arrest of Armando Torres after observing him flee into the back of the house. Then, explaining the convoluted case in the municipal parking lot behind the adult book store. Once they realize that we had both been talking about different cases, they don't seem so pissed off. Satisfied that Grandma Torres' complaint is unfounded, they're no longer interested in pursuing it with us.

Sarge tells us to get back on the street and catch the arson suspect. It seems like we dodged the bullet, and Scheper and I are grateful to leave the office and still have our jobs.

"One last question," the lieutenant says. "Something in the Torres complaint that still doesn't make sense."

"What's that?" I'm stopped in the doorway with Scheper right next to me.

"She describes the cops who arrested Armando as being a black man and a cowboy."

Scheper and I are paralyzed. For a few seconds we can't think of an answer that will work. At this point the truth will make us look almost as bad as we did when they thought I molested Grandma Torres.

"You know what?" The lieutenant says, reading the look on our faces. "Forget it. I don't think I even want to know."

Scheper releases a long thankful breath, and I do the same.

"Just find the sergeant's arson suspect and we'll call it even."

2:41 a.m.

We've been parked outside the victim's mother's house since leaving the watch commander's office. It's where the suspect's girlfriend has been staying since being burned out of her place. There has been no sign of our man all night. We leave to make a pass through his old neighborhood, hoping to spot him there, but no luck. It's the end of our shift and neither Scheper nor I want to go back and face our bosses empty handed.

We're thinking that we must have waited too long. There's a damp mist shrouding the neighborhood and nobody's left on the streets. "He's probably home in a nice warm bed," Scheper says. "Where we ought to be."

I agree. We start up the car and cut through a large parking lot between the Amtrak station, and the Rapid Transit line—Bay Area's equivalent of a subway. Two dark figures walk towards the lighted station entry. Scheper and I look at one another.

"Why not?" I say as he pulls into the nearly empty lot. We stop the unmarked car in front of the station, a good distance in front of the two guys. I pull out the suspect's mug photo and we set it on the dashboard where we can both see it. The two guys are both wearing hooded sweatshirts and the lights above cast shadows over most of their faces. One of them is a lot taller than our guy, but the other one matches the size of the suspect.

"What are the chances?" Scheper says.

As they continue toward us, we realize we're only going to have one shot at seeing his face. It'll be right as he passes in front of our headlights. If he looks away, we're screwed. Or if he looks towards us, and sees the uniforms, we're screwed. He'd probably take off down the tracks and be gone before we could even get our cold tired bodies out of the car.

"Here he comes," I say.

They pass right in front of us, and we both focus on the shorter of the two. They both keep their heads down, leaving all their facial features masked by the darkness. Then, just after they pass, the taller guy says something to his partner. They both turn back to check us out—probably thinking we're a couple of thugs looking to fight them or rip them off. Their challenging faces are exposed, if only for a second, but it's clear the shorter one is our man.

We spring out of the car and put the grab on him before he has a chance to run. The identification in his wallet confirms it's him. His friend is sent on his way, and we transport our suspect to the jail.

3:00 a.m.

I follow Scheper into the watch commander's office where the sergeant sits talking with the lieutenant. They both pause as we enter. I place a copy of the arson suspect's arrest booking sheet onto the desk, along with his mug photo. A little smile creeps across the sergeant's face, then disappears. The lieutenant leans back in the chair and folds his arms.

"Well, well," he says. "Glad to see you two weren't just honking around the South End all night."

Chapter 5

4:05 p.m.

The locker room is buzzing when I walk in. The story was all over the news, but I was asleep and missed it. I guess it happened last night after we got off. I take a seat on a bench and listen to one of the cops who was there. Poor guy looks like hell. He's been here since it happened, being interviewed by the detectives, the DA's office, and the upstairs brass.

"We had the store surrounded," he says. "There was nowhere for them to go. We caught one kid coming out the back door, but the other one was still hiding inside a storage room."

From what I can gather they're talking about an alarm call at a hardware store last night. I heard the original call go out over the radio just as I was leaving for home at the end of my shift. It must have been around 3:30.

"Who was it?" someone on my squad asks.

"Guy Woodruff. He's all fucked up over this. His attorney is in there with him now."

"How old was he?" Felix asks.

"The attorney?"

"No, the kid he shot."

"Fifteen or sixteen, I think. Maybe younger."

"Let him finish," someone shouts. "So the kid's hiding in the box."

The midnight cop continues, "Yeah, so we go in there and call the kid out. We know he's hiding in a cardboard box, because we can see it moving. I grab the top of the box and Woodruff grabs the other side. Woodruff still has his gun in his hand. I guess when he yanks the box he accidentally squeezes the trigger. Or the kid kind of comes out on his own, I don't know. It all kind of happens at the same time. Anyway, the kid kind of pops up and the bullet hits him right in the head."

"Did he die?" asks Felix.

"Shut up!" a chorus of voices yell. "Of course he died, you idiot."

Holy shit. I stand up and walk around to the other isle. I sit on the bench in front of my locker, feeling numb and a little weak. "Guy Woodruff," I say to myself. He's a young guy like me, started with the department a few months after I did. He's on the midnight shift. Our beats are next to one another. I go on calls with him all the time. I can't believe he accidentally shot someone. Not just someone, a kid.

5:00 p.m.

Lineup is more serious than usual. The lieutenant is there along with the sergeants. He gives us a sanitized version of the shooting, but most of us already know a lot more about it from the locker room.

It's our last night of the week and there's also a double shift. When lineup is over and the bosses leave, one of the more veteran guys suggests going out for a beer after work. We're all kind of down about Woodruff's shooting, yet everyone halfheartedly coughs up a few bucks as the hat passes by.

5:42 p.m.

There are so many cops on my normal beat that I've been reassigned to work downtown tonight. I drive around for a while, getting my bearings and trying to acquire a sense of what's happening on the street.

I come around a corner and a spotless, bronze colored Oldsmobile cruises past me with its trunk open. Not tied down or anything, just sticking up in the air and bouncing up and down with each dip in the road. I flip a U-turn and get behind it. The driver is sitting so low in the seat that it almost looks as if nobody's driving. I follow for a block or two before flipping on the overhead lights. A turn signal comes on, and the car pulls into the parking garage of an apartment building. I follow the car through the gate and into the garage beneath the building. I broadcast my location to dispatch and give them the license number of the car I'm stopping.

Under the building, the red and blue lights bounce off the walls and become nearly blinding. The Oldsmobile's brake lights immediately come on and the car screeches to a sudden stop. I walk up and find a white haired man with a very confused expression. I ask if he knows his trunk is open. He turns back and frowns at it like he's never seen one before.

I ask his name and he hands me a license. Morris Sanborne.

I'm trying to figure out exactly what I have here when dispatch calls me. They ask, "Do you have an elderly man in an Oldsmobile stopped?"

"Affirmative."

"We have the manager of Safeway on the line. She says a subject fitting that description just drove off and left all his groceries sitting in their parking lot."

I ask Mr. Sanborne if he just came from Safeway. He shakes his head no.

"Wait," he says with a hand in the air, "Safeway, you say?" He thinks about it for a moment and finally gives up. "I don't remember."

I have him park his car and then get in with me. We drive about five blocks back to the Safeway store where a young employee stands with a basket full of grocery bags. The kid identifies Sanborne as the customer who forgot them. We load them into the trunk of the patrol car and Sanborne gives him a few bucks.

We drive back to the apartment house and I help him carry the groceries in. He loads a few things into the refrigerator, then turns and stares at me. He suddenly looks confused again.

"Why are you here, officer?"

I remind him about leaving the groceries and driving home with his trunk open. He nods politely, but I'm thinking he already forgotten all of it. I find an address book on the counter and thumb through it.

"Is Rick Sanborne a relative?" I ask.

"Yes, he's my son."

I dial the number in the book and talk to the son. He confirms that his dad suffers from Alzheimer's, and this isn't the first time something like this has happened.

"I worry about my dad's driving," he says. "But the old guy is stubborn. He refuses to give up his license or his independence."

After the call I take a look around the apartment. It's tidy and seems to have everything one would need to live comfortably. Dozens of notes cover the refrigerator door; reminders to take certain medications, reminders to lock the door, reminders to unplug the iron, turn off the stove, etc.

I phone our Youth & Family Services Bureau and talk to one of the counselors. She specializes in elder abuse cases and I'm thinking she might be a resource. The best she can suggest is for me to write a report.

"I can forward it to Adult Protective Services," she says, "and they *might* check on Mr. Sanborne from time to time."

I'm thinking that I could probably check on him myself. I give the old guy my business card and circle my name and the department phone number. I tell him to write a note on it so he remembers to call me if he needs anything.

7:50 p.m.

I hear the sound of loud motorcycles somewhere in the area as I'm driving down a one way street into the business district. Engines race with deafening intensity, echoing off the buildings and making it difficult to pinpoint where they are. In my mirror I spot two motorcycles coming up behind me, weaving in and out of traffic and revving their unmuffled engines. They slow when the spot my car and the revving motors go quiet. I watch the drivers in my rearview mirror, hanging back and talking to each other. They're bearded guys with leather vests—the kind of stop my sergeant loves.

I act like I'm turning, and then cut through a block-long parking lot. When I come out on the other side I'm behind the two bikes. I give my location over the air and then hit the siren. They pull over right in front of a bar. Not the best place for a stop. Another cop, one of my buddies from the academy, shows up to cover me. I call him Timmy. He's one of those guys with a great instinct, and he always seems to be there when you need help.

The bikers start tough talking, encouraged by a couple of their cohorts who've come out of the bar. The friends stand there with their beer mugs in hand, taunting us through frothy beards. Timmy tells them it's a violation to remove alcohol from a bar, and they'll be cited if they don't go inside. Incapable of parting with their beers, they stumble back in.

I give the motorcycles the once over and then write each of the drivers a ticket for the mechanical violation—no muffler. They call me "chickenshit," and I don't disagree. On the other hand, I wouldn't have noticed had they not drawn attention to themselves. Besides, it's getting toward the end of the month and the sergeant jumps our asses if we don't have a certain number of tickets on our monthly stat sheet. They won't call it a quota though; it's a, "minimal expected standard of traffic enforcement." Whatever that is.

A radio check turns up a warrant on the thinner of the two guys I have stopped. It's for an unpaid speeding ticket. I tell him the bike will be towed at his expense unless he can have someone move it off the street. He gives the keys to his partner. I handcuff the guy with the warrant, search him, and put him in my car.

The guy is much less of a tough guy when I get him into the jail and away from his pals. He takes on a pouty attitude with the jailers, answering their questions with childlike defiance. He takes his keys and drops them onto the counter with a clunk, then tosses his wallet next to them. The wallet hits the keys and knocks them onto the floor.

"Just keep your hands on the booking counter," I tell him. Then, I reach into his pockets myself to help inventory his property. I take out some change and some mints and set them on the counter. I go into another pocket and pull out a hair comb and a sandwich baggie full of a grayish powder. The baggie is old and weathered, and some of the powder is spilling out. I plop it on the counter amidst a small cloud of dust.

"Hey!" the guy cries. "Be careful with that, it's my brother."

The jailer and I look at each other. We both bend down and examine the baggie and its contents. Clumps of gray dirt is all it looks like. Definitely not drugs.

"Your brother?" I ask.

"Yeah, he's dead."

No kidding! I straighten up and finish searching the guy.

"Must have been a tiny guy," I say.

"That's not all of him. After he was cremated, everyone in the family got some of his ashes. I carry mine with me wherever I go."

I tell him that he'll have to part with his brother for a while, but we'll keep everything in a secure locker and return it to him when he gets out.

The jailer writes *brother's ashes* on the property receipt.

"Can I scoop him up off the counter?"

I tell him, "Sure."

He unties the top of the baggie and uses the blade of his hand to brush the dust back inside. He knots the bag but some of his brother still trickles out.

"Guess it's time to get another baggie," he says.

I go behind the counter, find a white mailing envelope and give it to the guy. He picks it up and stares at the printed logo.

"Got anything that doesn't say police department on it? I don't want him to feel like he's in jail."

The jailer hands him a plain manila envelope and he seems happy with that.

8:55 p.m.

I'm really hungry for some reason, and don't think I can wait for my lunch break to eat. Before clearing the station, I go into the break room and pull my bag out of the refrigerator. Although I leave some food for later, I take the tuna sandwich with me to the car.

My plan is to find a good place to park, and eat while I'm writing. Dispatch assigns me a cover call as soon as I clear the gate and I get the feeling my plan will have to wait. The Adam beat unit has stopped a car in the hills above the university, and he's asking for backup. I switch my radio to the scanner setting and hear that the driver has a suspended license and an arrest warrant for failing to appear in court on a DUI charge.

I use one hand to steer the car and the other to eat my sandwich. Switching the radio gets a little tricky, but I manage by clamping the sandwich in my mouth. Strange looks from a family driving next to me are reminders that someone's always watching. Even when it's dark outside, the lights from my radio and monitors illuminate me.

I take my last bite as I pull up behind the other patrol car. The cop is a guy named Leland, but everyone calls him Lee. He's got the driver out of the car and is talking with him casually near the curb. We're stopped on a stretch of road where residential construction has given way to a regional greenbelt. The land on either side of the street is hilly and thick with brush. Across the street the hill goes up and next to us it drops away sharply into a canyon.

Apparently Lee hasn't told the guy he's going to jail yet, because they're both chatting it up like old friends. The driver's demeanor changes abruptly when he spots me pulling up. I can see it before I even get out of the car. He grows quiet, the smile fades from his face, and his posture becomes rigid. I hurry out but I'm not close enough to help when he makes his move. The driver head butts Lee in the center of the chest, knocking him back toward me. The guy then pivots around, and in one graceful move, he disappears down the side of the hill into the blackness.

Lee recovers his balance and puts out over the air that we're involved in a foot chase. I'm over the ledge first and I hear Lee right behind me. We've got our flashlights on, but the brush is so thick the light isn't much help. I can hear Lee grunting and cursing as each limb I push through thwacks back, hitting him in the face. We slow to a near stop and listen. There's rustling and panting somewhere to our left. Off we go again, slipping and sliding as the contour of the hill changes before we can react. Lee takes the first tumble and his flashlight goes bounding past me. I reach to grab it, slip on wet leaves, and end up toppling into a thicket of low shrubs. Lee slides on his butt right into me and we're both tangled in some kind of thorny vine.

"Son of a bitch," Lee yells, as he retrieves his light. "This is poison oak!"

We pick our way out and turn off our lights.

"Listen," I whisper. There's a faint noise close by, like a twig snapping.

I lean close to Lee in the dark. "He's just ahead of us."

"Can I ask you something?" Lee whispers.

"What?"

"You ate a tuna sandwich, didn't you?"

There's a crackle in the bushes in front of us, and then plodding feet and heavy breathing. We both take off again after him. There are a couple of sirens off in the night, and although more cops are coming, they're still several minutes out.

We stop again to listen. Without warning the guy charges out of the dark with his head down. He rams Lee from the side knocking him into me. I swing my flashlight and catch him on the shoulder. Three of us are fighting in the dark, in the bushes, on a steep hill. I can't tell who's hitting who. Somebody goes down and I only know it's not me. I aim my flashlight and see it's the guy. Something about his eyes strikes me as odd, but I'm not really in a position to delve into it right now.

He's on his butt, backed up against a bush. I'm groping for my pepper spray as the guy struggles back up on his feet. Lee is off to the side of me yelling something at the guy; "Give it up," or "Put your hands up," something like that.

I find my spray and raise the canister in front of me. Holding the light with my other hand, I see the guy squat down slightly and clench his fists. He lets out an animalistic growl and starts coming at my light. The scene reminds me of a wildlife show where they film nocturnal predators in the desert at night. Only this one is charging at the film crew.

I spray a single straight stream right at his face. It's a direct hit right into his left eye. He stops, shakes his head like a wet dog, and growls again. *My pepper spray isn't working!*

"He's got a glass eye," Lee shouts to me. "Try the other one."

By then Lee has joined me with his canister in hand. The guy charges at us again and we let him have it. Two streams of pepper right into his good eye. He yells, drops down cradling his face in both hands, and starts coughing and gagging. We handcuff him and drag him all the way back up the hill.

We've already advised dispatch that the guy's in custody, so none of the cops who've arrived venture down the hill. The three of us emerge from the brush out of breath, and find the other units all talking and milling around. We toss the guy into the back of Lee's car, leaving the windows up.

"Let him suck on the pepper spray for a while," says Lee. The other cops gather with us on the side of the road to talk about Woodruff. There's a lot of speculation about how it might have happened. One guy demonstrates how when one hand gripped the box, Woodruff's gun hand reflexively squeezed. Another thinks that when the kid jumped out of the box Woodruff jerked and inadvertently shot. Nobody knows anything for sure, and I think we're all trying to convince ourselves that it couldn't happen to us.

I follow Lee and his prisoner back to the station. After dropping the guy off in the jail, we head for the locker room where we both shower and don clean uniforms before heading back out.

11:18 p.m.

I'm glad I grabbed the sandwich earlier because it doesn't look like I'm going to get a lunch break. I'm asked to clear the station for an in-progress call—a prowler possibly trying to get into a woman's apartment.

I don't waste any time getting there. It's a four-story structure with balconies off of each apartment, providing sweeping views of the bay. The woman who called is on the top floor. I take the elevator up and don't see a soul along the way. I check the interior hallway before knocking on the woman's door.

She peers at me through the peephole, and then I hear several latches being unlocked. The woman is breathing hard, her face is red, and she looks as if she's about to collapse. I wonder if I'm too late and the guy got in and assaulted her.

I ask if she's alright, and she says she is. She's an attractive, athletic-looking woman in her late 20's or early 30's, wearing sweatpants and a t-shirt. She tells me she's lived here alone for several months, and nothing like this has ever happened to her. I'm invited inside so she can actually show me what took place. We walk over to the sliding doors that look from her living area onto the deck and the view beyond.

"He came up this way," she says, motioning toward her balcony. "I was right here in the living room."

I unlatch the door, walk out to the rail and look down. There's a parking garage on the ground level, so her unit is actually five stories high. It's a long way down. I get that shaky feeling, like I'm going to fall over, and I pull back. I tell her that it's an awfully long distance to climb from the ground up. Seems like someone in one of the lower units would have seen him pass their balconies. But she's adamant that a man crawled up and peeked in at her. She says he clung onto the wrought iron railing as he lifted himself, and she could clearly see his head, arms, and shoulders.

Her story seems improbable, and I still can't figure out why she looks so physically taxed.

"Why do you think someone would climb all the way up here to look in at you?"

She flings her hair nervously. "I was naked . . . He saw me naked."

Wasn't he the lucky boy. Climbs five stories up the side of a building on the off chance the top apartment is rented by a single woman who spends time naked in her living room.

I give the room a quick glance. It's a living area connected to a small kitchen. There's a breakfast table, a couch along one wall, and an entertainment center with a TV along the other. The bedroom and bathroom, I presume, are down the hall.

"Mind if I ask what you were doing when he looked in at you?"

The woman shifts her weight, exhales, and turns her head away. "I was exercising." She takes a long breath before turning back to face me. "I workout naked, okay?"

Well, at least that explains the flushed face and rapid breathing. I nod as if I completely understand. "And you do this every night?"

"Most nights," she says. "During the week, usually. When I get home from work."

I jot down her information and tell her I'll be right back. I take the elevator to the floor below, and locate the corresponding apartment number. I knock, and the door is answered by a young man of about 30. He's well built, athletic looking, with dark hair and eyes. He's shaking his head.

"Did my upstairs neighbor call you?"

I tell him she did. "Says somebody hoisted themselves up to her balcony and looked in at her."

"Yeah," he says repentantly. "It was me."

I'm a little dumbfounded. First of all, because I've been pretty doubtful that it even happened, and secondly, because the guy admitted it so quickly.

"You risked falling to your death just to get a glimpse of the girl upstairs?"

"I didn't even know it was a girl," he says. "I've only lived here a couple of weeks. I start work one o'clock in the morning, so I'm usually asleep when most people are coming home. I haven't gotten to know any of my neighbors yet."

"That probably isn't the best way to meet your neighbors."

The guy smiles. "I wasn't trying to meet her. I just wanted to know what in the hell was going on up there. Every night since I moved in I hear this thump, thump, thumping sound. It wakes me up every time—sounds like a damn herd of elephants. Finally I couldn't take it anymore. I had to know what the noise was."

"And?"

"All I did was stand on the rail of my balcony and pull myself up far enough to see in."

"And? What was the noise?"

An embarrassed grin sweeps across his face. "I guess she was exercising. From what I could tell she was doing some kind of jumping jacks."

The guy comes across as completely sincere. He seems like as nice a person as she does. In fact, I get the feeling they would make a perfect couple. They're both physically fit, nice looking people, both single and live alone. Perfect!

"You might want to go up and apologize to her sometime," I say. He says he will.

I return upstairs and tell the woman what happened. I tell her that he works nights, and I emphasize the curiosity motive. She still seems a little creeped out, but she decides not to make a complaint.

I drive away wondering if they'll ever get together.

12:10 a.m.

Dispatch asks my location and I give them the nearest intersection. Since I'm the closest unit they send me into the hills again, this time to cover Ernie Rivas, another guy I was in the academy with. Someone in a ritzy home overlooking the state university campus called to report hearing firecrackers.

I see Ernie's taillights ahead of me and follow him up a steep street to Grandview Avenue. The homes on the street are all set on one side facing a steep drop-off on the other, and offering expansive views of the bay. Ernie stops in the middle of the street and sits on the hood of his car. I pull up next to him and roll my window all the way down.

"Check this out," he says to me. "How would you like a view like this?"

I look around, and then up at the huge homes. "Maybe some day." I don't see any cars around, and I'm wondering if the firecrackers were set off in the dry canyon below us. "Do we know who called it in?"

Ernie shrugs. "Anonymous informant. These wealthy people probably don't want to get involved."

I park my car and step to the edge of the roadway. Ernie joins me and we stand quietly for a few minutes listening. There's nothing below us but darkness. Anybody could be hiding there. After a while we walk back to where we're parked. We talk about Woodruff's shooting for a minute or so before getting back into our cars.

I hear Ernie broadcast the disposition of his call. "We'll both be clear of Grandview and back in service. The fireworks appear to be unfounded."

1:00 a.m.

I'm driving toward the station to drop off a completed report when I hear Bosworth stop a car a few blocks away. He's kind of a strange guy who's fairly new to the squad. He would like to be called Boz, but ever since the squad found out his real name is Bosworth, we call him that.

His patrol car is stopped in the slow lane behind a black Ford Falcon. Bosworth is standing behind his open passenger door writing a ticket. As I walk up I see there's a young kid, about sixteen years old, sitting in the passenger seat of the patrol car. Bosworth nods to me.

"It's just a speeding ticket," he says. "I should be fine."

I lean over to check who's sitting in his car, and see it's a police explorer scout. They're high school age kids who volunteer one night a week to help out. Sometimes they wash the patrol cars, sometimes they file papers, whatever's needed. But they all want to be cops, and they love riding along and observing the officers.

The Ford's driver is sitting in his car waiting to sign his ticket. They seem okay, so I start back for my car. As soon as I do, I hear tires screeching. I turn in time to see the Ford take off through a cloud of grey smoke, and Bosworth jumping in his car to chase after him. Only he doesn't get in the drivers seat. Instead, he shoves the kid over to that side of the car.

"Go get 'em!" He yells at the bewildered explorer scout. Bosworth's now climbed into the passenger side, and has the microphone in his hand. He hollers into it, "We're in pursuit!"

I can't believe what I'm seeing. The patrol car's turning signal comes on and the kid's checking his mirror. I'm in my car now so I can't hear them, but it looks like Bosworth is working the radio and emergency lights while the explorer scout does the driving. I'm thinking that this cop has lost his mind.

They take off and I'm right behind them. In less than a quarter mile I see the flashing lights of two other cops behind me. The Ford has slowed down and it looks like its engine is sputtering. Since the guy is now only going about 10 miles an hour, the kid is able to stay up with him.

The parade of cars inches down the street behind the Ford and the pursuing police car, driven by a sixteen year old kid who may or may not even have a driver's license. I can feel myself starting to laugh at the whole fiasco. Now the Ford turns into a Denny's, where late night diners watch curiously from their booths. The whole line of patrol cars, sirens wailing, files through the lot behind the Ford. I'm about midway through the lot when it appears as if the Ford is on its last legs and about to stop. I jump out of my car and run toward it. The two cops behind me abandon their cars and do the same.

The Ford sputters and jerks forward, still barely rolling. Bosworth and his scout continue after it in their car. I'm in one of those positions where you wonder: do I go back to my car or continue on foot after them? I find myself running after the Ford, behind Bosworth and his scout. Felix is barreling along behind me, and I can hear him laughing. I'm not sure who's running behind him.

The Ford makes it through the lot and pulls back onto the street, circling around back toward the driveway again. Bosworth's patrol car is behind it, and the three of us are still running. We cut across the landscaped front of Denny's, huffing and puffing and laughing. People inside the restaurant are now on their feet, crowding the windows to watch the spectacle. Fortunately, the cars are still going slow enough for us to stay up. The Ford rounds the corner and turns back into the Denny's lot, again. I hear another siren behind me, and I just hope it's not one of the sergeants.

When the Ford gets to the patrol cars we've abandoned, there's nowhere for him to go. We've inadvertently blocked the driveway. Now that he's stuck, the driver shuts off the car and raises his hands in the air. I'm running up behind the procession, and I hear the newly arriving patrol car skidding into the lot behind me. It screeches to a stop next to me and out jumps one of the sergeants. He's a big guy—both tall and heavy. He's grabs his nightstick and starts running toward the Ford. He has a very serious look on his face, and not a happy one. I slow down to give him a wide berth and he sprints ahead of me. I notice he's building up a pretty good head of steam. Bosworth is still in his car, not certain if the suspect is going to drive off again. Bosworth waits for a second before deciding to jump out and get him, but his timing couldn't be worse.

Bosworth throws open his door right as the big sergeant chugs past his car. The door flings right in his path, and before the sergeant can even slow himself, he runs into it with full force. There's a thunderous crash as the sergeant wallops the door. It distends forward with his hefty mass behind it, nearly tearing it off its hinges. When the door reaches its tensile limit, it rebounds back with a vengeance, throwing the 300+ pound sergeant flat on his back. There's a deafening thud and we're all trying to figure out if we should take off before he gets up, or go help him.

I streak past the downed sergeant to the Ford, and handcuff the driver. I figure Felix and the other cop can help the sergeant, and Bosworth can deal with his own mess. I pretend to encounter difficulty getting my cuffs locked, so I have ample time to stop laughing before I turn around. By the time I do, Bosworth and the explorer have switched seats, and the other two are helping the sergeant to his feet. He's so disoriented by his impact with the door that he doesn't even know who opened it.

2:00 a.m.

When I get back to the station, I'm summoned to the watch commander's office. I know they're going to ask me what happened during the pursuit. I don't have time to think of how best to phrase it. The lieutenant eyes me as I walk into his office.

"Want to go home?" he says. "We got more than enough cops here tonight, so I'm letting your squad leave an hour early."

I thank him, and thank him again. I stop before someone comes by and calls me an ass kisser. I quickly finish my reports, turn them in, and unload my car. I'm eager to see what these after work get togethers are all about. Until now I've been too new to be invited. I wait for a couple of the other guys to finish up before we head over for a beer.

2:30 a.m.

A bunch of the veteran guys are clustered under an overhang in the courthouse parking lot. One of them, a guy named Jack Dixon, brought his cabover camper and backed it up near the group. There's a small portable barbecue and a couple of coolers next to it.

Me and the other younger guys saunter over with our hands in our pockets, a little self-conscious but excited about being there. After a beer we're all equals. Mostly we're talking about Woodruff's shooting, and how it could have happened to any of us. Just what we didn't want to hear. The subject changes to history-making cases. We're eating hotdogs and drinking, and we're hearing all the stories from the guys who've been there. There's more drinking, more talking, and more laughing. I also notice a little more bravado. The stories get raunchier and louder, but it's nice to be part of it.

The younger guys whisper among ourselves, asking how long these things usually last. It'll be light in a while, and we're not sure how much we can drink and still be under the alcohol limit. Three of us decide to walk back over to the department and give ourselves breathalyzer tests. As we're jogging through the lot, I trip on a concrete parking strip and slide headfirst on the pavement. The other two guys are laughing so hard they can't even walk. Although I maintain that the strip couldn't be seen in the dark, my buddies insist that I already failed the sobriety test.

Nevertheless, we go inside and check each others' alcohol level. Barely below the legal limit, we decide it's just about time to go. We start back to get our jackets before leaving.

By the time we get back, the party has degraded into a rowdy shouting match. Dixon, the guy who brought the camper, is trying to load his barbecue into the back—hot coals and all. He's pissed off at someone, and he gets madder when someone else tries to stop him. There's some yelling and then some shoving. The thing is just short of a brawl, and the fact that everyone here is armed is a little disquieting to me.

Finally a couple of older guys wrestle the barbecue from Dixon and throw him on the ground. They forcibly remove his keys from his pocket. Someone else goes into the back of the camper and comes out with a folding lawn chair, a garden hose, and a roll of duct tape. Several them lift the Dixon onto his lawn chair and lash him to it with the hose. We younger guys just stand watching in astonishment.

Once they've secured him to the chair, they duct tape him like a mummy. They finish with a wide strip over his mouth, and then load him into the back of the camper. The guy with the keys goes around front and gets in.

Somebody asks where they're taking Dixon. He says they're going to leave him like that on the front lawn of his house. One of the guys is following in another car, so they can drop the camper off with Dixon. They all take off, and the party clears out as quickly as it started. The younger guys are in disbelief.

With raw abrasions on both hands, and the knee of my pants torn, I get into my car and drive home. I wash up and crawl into bed just before the sun comes up.

Chapter 6

2:20 p.m.

A terrible rash on the inside of Gale's arm is itching her like crazy. She can't figure out how she could have gotten poison oak.

"That's strange," I tell her. "Me and Lee actually chased a guy through poison oak last week.

She tilts her head and looks at me without saying anything.

"What? We showered and changed uniforms afterward."

"Would that be the uniform you had me bring to the cleaners?" She holds her arm out as if carrying an imaginary bundle of clothes. It's a vivid demonstration that only adds to my feeling of stupidity.

To assuage my guilt, I remind her of a guy on the department they call The Village Idiot, or V.I. for short. He earned the name when he forgot to take a tear gas canister out of his BDU cargo pants after training. He brought the pants home to wash and then tossed them into the dryer. The canister heated up and detonated just as his wife opened the dryer door. The poor woman was engulfed in a cloud of tear gas. What made it worse was that he went back to work and told his squad all about it. One of the guys called him The Village Idiot and it stuck.

"So, see?" I tell Gale, "It could have been worse."

She's less than amused by my story. She rolls her eyes and heads off to look for some calamine lotion. I know she'd be laughing if it didn't itch so badly. Gale's a good sport and the perfect cop's wife.

My Sunday at home is cut short. I'm called to work early because the overlap shift is below minimum staffing. Too many people called in sick, or the sergeant let too many people off. Whatever the case, I'm the one who pays the price. It doesn't mean I'll be getting off any earlier, just that I'll be working longer. It's another little perk that comes with my low seniority.

The watch commander is sitting at his desk watching a football game on the monitor that's supposed to be tuned to the jail. He tells me I'll be riding the C-Charles beat.

2:30 p.m.

First call out of the shoot is one that's been holding since early this morning. A burglary report at a small kiosk in the middle of the mall. The place sells knives of all sorts, and apparently a bunch of them were missing when they opened up at 10 a.m.

I meet up with the "manager," but for the life of me I can't figure out who he manages. The place is the size of a broom closet, and only one of us can fit inside at a time. The guy shows me the types of knives that were stolen—over a dozen surprisingly expensive Swiss knives.

Everything is intact, and we can't figure out how someone might have gotten inside the kiosk without a key. I have him roll down the security cover to show me how the metal flanges near the bottom are secured with padlock. With the exception of a tiny space along the floor, it's a pretty tight fit. I step back to get a better look.

"Too small for anyone to climb under," the manager says. However, I'm not so sure. I glance across the mall at the KB Toy Store and recall the size of my little friend, Jeffery Miller. The one I was kind enough to give a break to. I find out that the interior of the mall actually opens a few hours before the stores do in order to allow senior citizens a place to walk in the mornings. It would be a perfect opportunity for a kid like Miller to slip in and out unnoticed.

I give the manager my card and tell him I will be following up on a couple of things. In the meantime, I ask that he get me a list of all his employees.

"That'll be easy," he says. "There are only two."

3:28 p.m.

I'm leaving the mall, about to take a spin by Jeffery Miller's house, when I get another call. "Charles-46," she says with a certain amount of pleasure only a dispatcher enjoys.

I let out a sigh. "Go ahead."

She tells me to start toward the tracks off of Industrial Boulevard.

I know the area. It used to be nothing but fields and manufacturing plants before the new housing tract was built. Now, it's an odd mix of nice homes that back up to old warehouses. I'm about to ask her what's on the tracks when she tells me. At this point I realize why it took her a second to say it.

"Report of a person down," she says. "Possibly struck by a train."

I drive there with my lights and siren on, but I'm not sure why. I mean, what's the hurry? There's little chance anybody hit by a train would live to tell about it. In any case, I'm almost there and people who call the police about something that serious would probably be disappointed if I pulled up like I was stopping for coffee. Besides, it's my first train accident, and to be honest I'm a little keyed up.

When I get there I see the massive freight train stopped on the tracks. It stretches on for a good half mile from where the accident happened. It's not immediately clear who called, and then a man who's clearly shaken introduces himself as the conductor. He says he radioed in after the train hit the man.

I ask him what the man was doing prior to the train hitting him.

"Nothing," he says. "The guy just walked onto the tracks and stood there looking up at me. I sounded the horn several times, but he just stood there." He points to a spot up ahead about 100 yards. I have him sit down and take deep breaths while I go look for the point of impact.

As it turns out, the point of impact isn't difficult to find. And when I do, I realize it's me who probably should have taken some deep breaths. I'm carrying my clipboard and stumbling over the rocky berm along the train tracks when I come upon a chunk of something about the size of a football. It looks like an uncooked roast with about ten inches of bone sticking out of it. There's a shoe covered in blood, and a grey corduroy pant leg wedged under one of the cars. The blood is a deep red that looks almost black. Most of it has already sunk into the rocks, but a small stream has found its way out the side of the small incline next to the tracks. I'm feeling kind of numb. As I take another few steps, I see a couple of fist-size pieces of white skull with skin and hair still stuck to them. One piece has part of a nose and possibly an eye, I'm not sure. There's more blood, flesh, and clothing scattered along beneath the train.

"Oh my God," I hear a woman's voice in the distance behind me. I turn to see a middle-aged couple making their way along the tracks. "Was somebody hit by a train?" She asks.

I take a few steps in their direction, holding my hands out in front of me. Hoping to spare them the nightmarish scene I had just encountered, I say, "I don't think you want to see this."

"Do you know who was hit?" The man asks, trying to look around me.

"No, sir. There's no way to tell just yet."

"Oh my God," The woman says again, covering her mouth.

"I think it's my father," the man says calmly.

"Why do you think it's your father?" I ask.

He looks past me, his eyes suddenly growing wide. He points to a spot on the ground several feet beyond where we're standing. "Because that's his arm."

I turn around to see a complete arm, amputated at the shoulder. It's clothed in a blue and red plaid shirt sleeve, rolled up to the lower forearm. There's a shiny metallic watch strapped to the wrist, with a perfect undamaged hand facing palm up.

"That's the watch we bought him last Christmas," the man says, "and that's the shirt he was wearing today."

As I help them back the way they came, the man tells me his father has been depressed due to his deteriorating health. When we round the end of the train, we're met by the Southern Pacific Railroad police. I didn't even know the railroads had their own police, but they're telling me it's their jurisdiction. They're also telling me it's their investigation. *No argument here.* I pass on the information provided by the couple, and hand over the conductor's identification papers. I ask if there's anything I can do to assist, but he says they have everything covered.

"We investigate a lot of these," he says, out of earshot from the grieving couple. "I can knock out one of these reports in two hours, start to finish." I thank him and start back to my car.

"Hey," the railroad cop calls out to me. "What's the last thing that went through his mind?"

I imagine the victim watching the train coming right at him and shrug.

"His foot!" he laughs. With that, he turns with his clipboard and walks over to the couple.

4:46 p.m.

As soon as I clear the train accident I drive toward Jeffery Miller's house. It's nothing more than a hunch, so I don't want to come off as if the kid's a suspect. I'm thinking about what I should say to his mother, perhaps playing it like I'm just stopping by to see how Jeffery's doing. On the other hand, if they don't cooperate, I could say a witness saw Jeffery at the mall around the time of the theft. I make up my mind to tell the mother the truth and simply ask if the kid was at the mall this morning. Before I even get there I spot Jeffery walking down the street. He's about a block away heading toward his house.

I stop my car next to him and roll down my passenger window. "Hey Jeffery," I say with a genuine smile. "How've you been?"

His eyes register alarm, and I'm wondering if it's because I'm a cop or because he's got something more to be alarmed about. He unconsciously takes a step back from the car.

"I was just driving through the neighborhood," I say. "Saw you walking and thought I'd stop and say hi." He still hasn't said anything, and I'm focused on his body language. His left hand drops to his side, and it almost looks for a second as if he's going to run. I zero in on his hand and see it's covering a bulge in his pants pocket. I step out of the car.

"So, Jeffery," I stoop down to one knee so my eyes are in line with his. "You wouldn't happen to have some Swiss knives in your pocket, would you?"

His expression changes to one of resignation. He nods, digs his hand into his pants, and sets four brand new knives on the hood of my car. I check his pockets for myself and find nine dollars in single dollar bills. I'm guessing he's been out selling the others.

I take him back to his house where I find Mom on the couch with a death grip on the channel changer. I tell her what's transpired, and her reaction is similar to the last time. I ask if I can take a look in Jeffery's room, and she says, "Fine."

There's nothing noteworthy in his room, with the exception of a Polaroid photo I find of Jeffery sitting on a brand new bicycle. I take it with me, and I can see the expression on Jeffery's face change again.

We walk past Mom, through the kitchen, and into the single car garage. I find four bicycles there—the one in the photograph and three others. All are fairly expensive and in decent shape. In a toolbox near the bikes I recover all but one of the remaining knives.

I ask Jeffery if he has any brothers or sisters and he tells me no. When I ask about the bikes he starts with a story about how he found each of them, but finally admits that he stole all of them.

Because of his age, Jeffery is released, again, to his mother—this time with a notice to appear in the juvenile court. I load the bikes in my trunk and backseat for the short ride back to the police station. I log them into evidence and return the knives to the kiosk manager. According to Jeffery, the outstanding knife had been sold to an unknown teenager at the mall for $9.

6:44 p.m.

What a pain! Logging the bikes into evidence and researching the serial numbers took over two hours, and I haven't even started writing the report yet. My squad held lineup without me, and now they're all out on the street. Not that I expected them to call me in, but missing all the information bulletins and starting my shift without my squad is just a little unsettling. It feels something like leaving on a trip and forgetting to bring your wallet. Then there's all the internal gossip I missed out on.

Dispatch is calling me for another accident. *Aren't there any Traffic Units working tonight?* Fortunately, this one doesn't involve a train. In fact, it's a single vehicle into a light pole.

"Unknown injuries," she says, "respond code-3." That means use your lights and siren to get there right away. The accident is on a main six-lane street near a shopping center. It's twilight, but the weekend traffic this time of day isn't too bad.

On the opposite side of the street, I see what looks like a new sedan has run off the roadway and is up on its side. I jump the center median, making a U-turn and blocking traffic in the curb lane. As I pull behind the car, I see streamers and tin cans tied to its bumper. Several other motorists have stopped and are tentatively advancing on the scene. Most of them look like they can't decide whether to try to right the car, wait for instructions, or run in case the gas tank blows up. Although I have the same thoughts, I realize they all expect me to do something.

The car is on its passenger side, half way across the sidewalk. There's a path of crushed landscaping, and a dented light pole at the end of it. I pull my front bumper close to the sideways roof of the car, until I am flush against it. I climb onto my hood where I'm high enough to see down into the car. There's a jumble of arms, legs, and formalwear that has the distinct look of a wedding party.

"Are you two okay?" I ask.

"Yeah," the man grunts, righting himself and pulling the young lady up to a standing position next to him. It's unmistakably a wedding dress she's wearing.

I ask if they are able to climb up on the seat, and he boosts her up to me. With some help, they are able to lift themselves out of the shattered driver's side window. As soon as the woman's feet hit solid ground she starts yelling.

"That son-of-a-bitch tried to kill us!" She's pointing wildly, and it's apparent she's drunk. I'm looking around, wondering if she's referring to another motorist who ran them off the road.

"Who?" I say, looking as befuddled as the growing crowd.

"Him!" She slaps a slack hand against the groom's rumpled cummerbund. He drops his head down to his chest, looking both drunk and guilty.

I hear a few chuckles from the onlookers, and I feel an uncontrollable smile stretch across my face. "Tell me what happened."

She looks at the man for several seconds with seething eyes. "He got jealous!" She notices her dress is torn and curses before continuing. "He said I didn't give him enough attention at the reception. So, he starts yelling at me while we're driving to our honeymoon. He tells me that he wants to die. That's when he turned the car into the pole."

Now people in the crowd are laughing aloud.

Hey, I don't care if *you* want to die," she shrieks to the groom. "Just don't try to take me with you!"

I look at her husband and he's still staring at his feet. A traffic unit pulls up and a round cop called Chuckles ambles over to survey the wreck. "You two just get married?"

She nods, straightening her dress roughly.

"Congrats!" Chuckles says with a smirk. "Years of happiness to ya!"

I pull Chuckles aside and tell him that the guy may have tried to kill her in a murder-suicide attempt.

He nods. "Figured as much. Thought of doing the same thing to my wife a time or two."

I take a written statement from the bride, and then a short one from another driver who saw the car suddenly veer toward the light pole. Chuckles says he'll take the crash and the arrests. He takes the husband for DUI and the wife for public drunkenness. After handcuffing them and loading them into his car, Chuckles motions me over.

"Did you hear what's going on in dispatch?"

I tell him that I had to hit the street early and missed lineup.

He rubs his hands together. "You know that goofy guy in dispatch, with the gimpy leg?"

"Marty?" I say. I've talked to the guy once or twice. He's a fairly young guy, but he walks with a pronounced limp, has large crooked teeth, and talks with an abundance of spit in his mouth. My take on him is that he always wanted to be a cop but couldn't because of a physical disability. He's so awkward that I always wondered why we ever hired him.

"What about the guy?" I ask.

"Well, you know he's always carrying the baloney pony for that hot clerk, Tina."

I picture Tina—strange in her own way, but out of Marty's league just the same.

"She came in today and filed a harassment complaint against him," Chuckles says. "Says he calls her all night and comes by, banging on her door, at all hours."

"What did they do, send him home on admin leave?"

Chuckles shakes his head. "They were going to, but his mom died and he's off on funeral leave."

That's strange. I remember he took time off for his mother's funeral about two months ago. In fact, that was one of the times I spoke to the guy. I stopped by the communication center to give him my condolences after hearing his mother had passed. *Bizarre dude.*

8:10 p.m.

"Uh . . . Charles-46?"

The dispatcher's questioning tone gives me no hint as to what's coming.

"Go ahead," I answer cautiously.

"It's another dead body," she says, barely concealing her amusement. She tells me that the caller returned home to find his roommate dead. The dispatcher refers to it as a "Coroner's case," which usually means that there's no indication of foul play.

I park my car at the mouth of a narrow driveway leading alongside a triplex. I get out and walk toward the one in the rear. Two shirtless, beer-bellied men are barbecuing outside the front unit. As I approach, one steps back and raises his hands in mock surprise.

"I didn't do it," he says, nudging his buddy.

"It's only beer, I promise," the other slob says, holding up the can for me to see.

I try my best to smile politely, and pass without responding. I get to the back unit and find the guy whom I presumed made the call. He's sitting on the front steps shaking his head and rubbing his eyes.

I put my hand on his shoulder. "You okay?"

He nods. "I took him in because he didn't have anyplace to go. He's been staying here about two weeks." The man tells me the dead guy's name is Darryl Immakeetah, but he doesn't know how to spell it. I know Immakeetah. He's a local drunk who's been arrested dozens of times. Harmless enough, but when he starts drinking he doesn't stop until he's barely breathing.

The entire triplex is a rundown place owned by the State. I guess they plan to bulldoze the whole property someday, and continue building the highway. For the time being, they're nothing but cheap accommodations that remind me of a clubhouse my cousin and I built one summer in a redwood tree. As soon as I enter, I'm walloped by a conglomeration of contradictory odors.

"How long has Mr. Immakeetah been dead?"

The resident paws at the few remaining hairs on his head. "He seemed fine when I left this morning at eight."

We move through the kitchen where I notice a crock pot stewing away on the table. We end up in a back bedroom that looks more like a converted laundry room. There's a twin mattress on a faded laminate floor. The deceased is on the mattress, facing the far wall, on his knees with his butt up in the air. Apparently he died in that position. He's wearing white underpants, the back of which are caked with his final dump. He had also vomited and then must have died with his face mashed into it.

I suspect from the stench that Immakeetah was dead long before the resident left for work. The bodily excretions only intensify the smell of decay, all of which are infused with the broiling stew in the crock pot. The whole scene makes me gag.

I sit outside and work on my report until the coroner's people come to take the body. They give me a receipt for it, which I find a little weird.

10:10 p.m.

I clear the Immakeetah call and right away the dispatcher gets a hold of me. "You're clear to take your lunch," she says. I'm sure she's saying it with a grin, knowing damn well that I'm about to heave.

"I'll wait a little bit, if that's all right."

"Then, can you take a call out of your beat?" she snaps back.

I bite down on my lower lip. "Sure."

She sends me to a burglary that has just occurred. "The resident caught the suspect breaking into his house, and he's holding him under citizen's arrest," she says.

I stop in front of the address—a pleasant single home in a decent neighborhood. On the front lawn stands a burly man with pipe fitter arms, holding a skinny teenager by his long hair. I barely step out of my car and the man says, "Caught him breaking into my house." He flings the kid toward me. "Now do your job and take him to jail!"

I already have the feeling I'm not going to like this victim. Just to be obstinate, I reach back inside my car for something. Nothing really, I just don't like the way the guy is talking to me. I take my time and then reemerge from the car at half speed. "I'm sorry," I say to the guy. "You were saying something about a break in?"

The victim rolls his eyes and lets out a short huff. "Look," he says, "I already told you, this guy broke into my house and I caught him red handed. Now he goes bye-bye."

The supposed suspect/arrestee is just standing there with his hands in his pockets. I probably should at least put him in handcuffs, but I already feel there's something about this case that stinks. I ask a few questions of the victim, and he reluctantly explains that the kid had climbed through a window on the side of the house.

"Which window?" I ask.

"Why the hell does that matter?" he sputters. "It's the window right over there," he points over his shoulder.

I walk to the window and peer over the sill. It appears to be a young girl's room. *Hmm. Isn't that interesting?*

"Who's room was he breaking into?" I ask.

Another roll of the eyes. "My daughter's, okay?"

Hmm. That's even more interesting.

The daughter suddenly appears at the open bedroom window. She's crying. "Are you all right Donald?"

The suspect answers, "Yeah, I'm okay."

I look at the homeowner but he doesn't look back. After a few seconds he puffs out his barrel chest. "I don't care if my daughter invited him in. I catch someone, anyone, crawling through a window in my house, I'm going to have him arrested." He grabs the kid by the arm and shoves him toward me. "Now, book 'em Danno!"

I have the kid go stand by my car while I take down the homeowner's information. I tell him that I'm going to prepare a miscellaneous investigation report, but that no crime has been committed. I suggest he encourage his daughter not to invite her guests through the window.

The guy tells me that he pays my salary, and then threatens to file a complaint against me for refusing to do my job.

I drop the kid off at his house.

10:59 p.m.

I decide to give my lunch a try. I get to the station and wash up before hitting the lunchroom. I have a bag of chips and a leftover Sloppy Joe that Gale packed for me. I peel the foil off of it and find a paper plate to set it on. It looks a little like what I saw on the train tracks and a little like the Immakeetah stew, yet I'm really trying my best to push the images out of my mind. I open the microwave and there's a black glove in it. I stand there for a few seconds trying to make sense of it.

"That's mine," someone says. In walks the cop we call The Glove, only he's not wearing the glove.

I look back inside the microwave. "What the hell?"

"Oh, some blood got on my glove," he says. "I rinsed it off and everything, and I'm just drying it in the microwave."

I'm about to hurl. As I push past him, heading toward the bathroom, I see that two other people have overheard the conversation. From the looks on their faces they've lost their appetites as well. I forgo my Sloppy Joe and work on my reports instead. By the time I'm ready to go back on the street, someone has put yellow crime scene tape all around the microwave oven.

12:35 a.m.

I stop into the dispatch center to pick up some paperwork. As I'm standing there, an emergency call comes in from a guy who found his elderly mother not breathing. I'm listening as one of the dispatchers tries to walk the guy through CPR. She directs him to make sure she's laying on a flat surface. The man tells the dispatcher that his mother is propped up in her bed.

"Remove the pillows from under her head and make sure she's lying flat," the dispatcher says. There's a pause on the other end of the line. "Did you do it?" she asks.

"Yes," he says hesitatingly. "But, her head is still up."

"What do you mean, 'up'?"

"Well," he pauses again. "I took the pillows out from under her, but her head and back are still elevated. There's nothing underneath holding her up."

She explains to the poor guy that it sounds like rigor mortis, and that there's probably no use trying to revive her. The dispatcher covers the mouthpiece and turns toward me. "Would you mind? It's on your beat."

I pull up to number three for the night. When I get inside, I can see why the son thought his mother had died more recently than she had. The woman is wrapped in an electric blanket which had been left on the highest setting. Even though she's been dead for quite a while, she's still warm and clammy to the touch. It was not a totally unexpected death though, as the woman had been very ill for some time.

Her treating physician signs off on the cause of death and approves her release via telephone. Since there will be no coroner involvement, I don't have to wait with the family. I leave just as the private funeral home people arrive.

1:54 a.m.

I'm backed up to an elementary school's multipurpose building, writing my reports. They're nearly complete when dispatch calls my identifier. I'm told to cover a midnight unit a few blocks away from where I am. The dispatcher says a woman called screaming hysterically that her cat is on fire.

Dispatch broadcasts an update, just as I'm arriving at the scene. "The caller is a police employee. A front office clerk by the name of Tina Lynch."

I work my way through the maze of apartments to a center courtyard area. I find Tina's apartment, and the door is wide open. I call out her name but there's no answer. A few things go through my mind, like maybe she set it up to get me there. I mean, the cat on fire thing sounds a little unlikely.

But my ego is held in check as a small orange cat races past me with a smoldering tail, singed and charred from about midway down to the tip. Seconds later Tina rounds the corner, running spastically and sobbing. "Come back, Pumpkin. Come back, Pumpkin."

A couple of other officers arrive, including the guy whose call it is. Tina catches up with her cat and returns with it cradled in her arms.

"Her tail smells like lighter fluid!" she cries. "I know that twisted gimp, Marty, did it."

The cops all look at each other. I'm struck with the image of Marty hobbling after the cat, trying to squirt lighter fluid on her and light a match at the same time. It doesn't seem likely, but then again who knows? His mother did die twice.

I drive around the area without finding anybody, and then return to the station.

3:00 a.m.

I hand the sergeant my paper. He catches me staring at the receipt for Immakeetah clipped to the report on top.

"You had three death cases today," he says, not like a question. "You keep this up we're going to have to change your identifier to Coroner-46." He takes off his reading glasses to study me. "You know, I was a homicide detective for several years. Went to a lot of autopsies."

I'm not sure if he's headed somewhere or just reminiscing. But it's really the first time Sarge has taken the time to talk with me one-on-one. "I've never seen one, yet," I say.

He studies me again. "Tell you what." He swings his chair to face me. "You get up early and go watch the autopsies in the morning, and I'll give you the night off."

"You serious?"

He nods. "I think it'd be good for you to see. A good learning experience."

I'm exhausted. I've been at it over twelve hours and I'm looking forward to a decent night sleep. The idea of going home for an hour or two, only to get up, get dressed, and drive to the Coroner's Office for an autopsy, doesn't sound that great to me. However, I like the chance to learn something different, and I really appreciate that the sergeant has given me the opportunity.

7:00 a.m.

I wake up after an uncomfortable three hours in my own personal car. I'm in full uniform, and trying to figure out if that brutal pain in my hip is from the seatbelt clasp or my handgun. I open the window to let out some of the stale air, and remember I'm parked next to the loading dock. They said it would be alright when I called last night. They also told me the pathologist starts early.

I ring the buzzer at the employee entrance and an attractive young Asian woman answers. I suppose I expected a tall pasty man with a ghoulish head and huge hands. The woman seems to have been expecting me, and brings me into a small coffee room. She introduces me to the pathologist—another woman. She's a small white woman with wire rimmed glasses and her short hair bunched into a compact knot on the back of her head. She's probably in her late 50's. I notice her nametag says, Dr. O'Brian.

The doctor pours from a pot of coffee into a brightly colored mug emblazoned with, *World's Greatest Grandma*. With mug in hand, she motions toward a set of swinging double doors. "Shall we?"

As I follow her, I'm wondering if her grandkids had any idea where that mug would end up. And then I think about when I was called to work early the previous day. I had no idea where I was going to end up. There's a swoosh of air as she shoulders the doors open, and I'm struck, once again, with a menagerie of muddled odors. I recognize the putrid scent of decaying flesh, and it's merged with a chemical smell that I presume to be formaldehyde. There's another aroma that takes me a minute to figure out. It's sweeter than the formaldehyde but just as nasty. As Dr. O'Brian crosses in front of me I realize it's her perfume. I take a deep breath through only my mouth, and steel myself for what I know I'm about to see.

I tilt my head up and there they are; bodies of all colors, shapes, and sizes, laid out on stainless steel tables—five of them in all. They're all nude and their heads are propped up on U-shaped blocks.

I recognize Darryl Immakeetah, the drunk from last night. I don't see the old man from the train tracks, but there's an oddly shaped zippered bag on the back table, and I'm assuming it's him. Or, as much of him as they were able to collect.

"We'll save him for last," the doctor says, motioning with her mug. She pulls down an overhead microphone and adjusts the lamp. "Here we go."

With her mug never out of arms reach, she begins what I can only guess is her daily ritual. She filets Immakeetah like a sturgeon—from just below his Adam's apple to just above his genitals. Between gulps of coffee and clinical descriptions spoken into the dangling mic, the pathologist describes for me each step. I watch as she deftly slices and dices him until each of his major organs is removed, weighed, and sectioned for microscopic analysis. She's keeping her eye on me the entire time, probably wondering if I'm going to puke or pass out. I don't do either, but I certainly feel like it. At one point I have to step out of the room to remove my jacket. I'm not sure what made me wear it into the building in the first place. I guess I thought it would be like a giant refrigerator or something. I take some time to settle down before heading back in.

There's an assistant in there now. He's apparently preparing one of the bodies, an older man, for some type of more detailed examination. I watch from across the room as he makes an incision around the top of the cadaver's head and then peels the back half of his scalp down to the nape of his neck. When he starts pulling on the front half, the corpse comes up off the blocks. The dead man's face contorts involuntarily, as the assistant struggles to pull the front flap forward. With each violent tug, the corpse frowns, grimaces, and scowls, giving the twisted impression that he can actually feel what's being done to him.

I'm really struggling to stay detached. I'd like to be able to experience this in the same way a homicide detective would. However, the blood, the hollowed out torsos, and the mix of odors is starting to make me nauseated.

Dr. O'Brian thrusts a scarred and pock-marked hunk of Immakeetah carcass at me. "Look at his liver."

It looks nothing like the liver my mom used to make me eat, but I have no idea why she's showing it to me.

"This is what got him," she says confidently. "It's supposed to be smooth and a deep red color. Not all gray and swollen. This guy pickled himself with alcohol."

I tell her that he had been arrested dozens of times for public drunkenness and she nods approvingly. I'm still feeling a little queasy, and the liver in my face didn't help. We move over to the next table and I'm wondering how much more I can take. It's an infant.

This baby wasn't one of my cases, and I'm not sure how many of these Sarge wanted me to "experience". I guess I could watch this one instead of the train wreck, and we could call it even. Although, I don't know which of the two would be worse. I'm fighting memories of the little girl at the medical clinic several months earlier.

"This little boy," The doctor explains, as she cuts into his tiny body, "was in a highchair at a daycare." She tilts his head back to expose a slight red crease sideways across his neck. "He slipped down in the seat and the waist belt strangled him. Somebody took their eyes off him for only a few minutes and . . ."

It hits me in the chest, and I find myself taking deep quivering breaths to control the emotion. I keep telling myself to stay detached. Nothing more than a medical procedure, I remind myself. It's science.

She carves or saws into the back of his head, I'm not sure which. I'm unable to watch. When I turn back, I see the doctor retreat a few steps, as if to get another perspective of a painting. "What beautiful big eyes this baby has," she says delicately.

I brace myself for another strong wave of emotion. I turn away, take a few quick breaths, and then turn back. "Yeah," I say weakly.

Dr. O'Brian leans down as if she's going to cradle the baby, and gently slips her hand into the cavity at the back of the baby's skull. She props the body up admiringly. "Doesn't he have just the most beautiful eyes?"

It feels like she's crossing the line between science and humanness. The doctor, apparently, is able to move easily back and forth between those two worlds. But I can't. There's no way for me to stay detached, and at the same time talk about the baby's beautiful eyes. It's too real, and too damn sad for me to handle.

I apologize to Dr. O'Brian, and excuse myself from the remaining post mortem examinations. I rush outside where the air is cool and the smell of car exhaust is strangely restorative. I sit on the loading dock steps gathering myself before heading home.

9:20 a.m.

I pull into my driveway exactly nineteen hours after starting my shift. I wonder if I'm still smelling the autopsy odors, or if it's all in my mind. I walk through the house and into the garage where I remove and bag my uniform for dry cleaning.

Chapter 7

5:00 p.m.
As soon as I walk into lineup, I know what kind of night I'm going to have. The Edward Unit has called in sick and the sergeant is moving Bosworth over to cover the beat next to mine. Not that Bosworth is a bad guy, though he is weird as shit. It's just that things never go right when he's around. And with him working the beat right next door, I'm afraid we're going to see a lot of each other.

5:40 p.m.
First call out of the chute: "George-46, report of a vandalism. Possible shots fired from a pellet gun." The address is an apartment building on a street where apartment buildings line both sides for blocks and blocks.

Now, I like to take my time getting a feel for what's going on when I first hit the street. Tonight though, I barely even get out here and I get a nothing call that has probably been holding for two hours anyway. Guess I can't blame Bosworth for that.

I put myself off at the complex, wondering if the dispatcher could have misunderstood the type of weapon used—a shotgun instead of a pellet gun. I imagine myself walking, fat, dumb and happy into some apartment where I get my head blown off. *Now that would definitely ruin my night!*

With that in mind, I'm careful to stand off to the side as I knock. The door is opened by a pleasant looking black woman with a vaguely familiar face. She explains that a kid who lives in the apartment behind her shot a bb or a pellet though her bedroom window. As she shows me the tiny spider-webbed hole in the corner of the pane, I realize who she is.

"Brenda Johnson," I say. "I think we went to high school together."

She looks shocked. She doesn't remember me, and can't believe that I remember her. *How could I forget her? She scared me to death. She was one of the most militant girls in the school-- always looking like she was ready to kick someone's ass.*

"Of course I remember you." I take down the information for a report and tell her it's nice to see her again. I can't believe she's so nice. Maybe I had her all wrong in school.

Brenda tells me that she doesn't want anything done to the kid. She just wants me to talk to him so that he doesn't end up hurting someone. My face must have given away my astonishment.

"I have a kid of my own about his age," Brenda says with a half smile. She pauses for a second as if she's deciding whether or not to tell me any more of her story. She boils the rest of it down to a few words that make perfect sense. "I'm not the same person I was in high school."

The apartment complex behind Brenda's is bigger and not as nice. It's just about dark, yet everywhere I look kids are running around in shorts or diapers. It's hot and the wool uniform makes me feel like a greasy piece of linguisa. I figure out which unit the pellet was shot from, and knock on the screen door. A red-faced boy of about nine or ten stands there paralyzed. He's a chubby little guy, who I can picture firing away over the back fence like a mercenary. Probably never imagined he'd get caught. *Boy, how many times growing up did I feel like he looks.*

"How are you doing?" I ask. "Mom or Dad home?"

He takes a giant gulp and slowly looks over his shoulder toward the stairway leading upstairs.

"Who is it!" screams a raspy voice that I can only imagine is Mom. "Toby!" she shrieks again. "Who's at the door?"

Put down your cigarette and your cocktail and come see for yourself! I give the poor kid a smile. *No wonder he's run amok!*

The woman comes flying out of an upstairs bedroom like she's ready to take someone's head off. Younger than her voice, and with kind of a short round stature, she's still yelling wildly as she descends the steps. She stops suddenly when she sees me.

"Oh," she says in a newly crafted coquettish tone, "I didn't hear the door." The woman straightens her loosely tied robe. "Toby, honey, go on upstairs."

I tell her about the broken window, and that it appears to have been a pellet fired from the direction of her yard. She acknowledges that her son owns a bb gun, and that he, in all likelihood, is responsible for the damage. Although she seems more intent on disclosing her status as a single mother, and the fact that little Toby has no male role model.

She makes her way over to a large L-shaped couch that dwarfs the tiny apartment. As she reclines into it, her robe somehow gets hiked up high enough to expose her beefy white thighs. "Would you like to sit down?" She waves a hand in the direction of the kitchen. "I can make you a cool drink."

The cool drink would be great, but I couldn't handle what would come after that. "No, thank you. I really have to get back out on the street," I say in my best Joe Friday voice. *Just the facts, ma'am.*

I can hear the dispatcher trying to raise me on the radio.

"Forty-six, go ahead," I answer.

She wants to know how much longer I'm going to be off. There's a priority call on my beat, and she's already started another unit toward the address.

I take down the rest of the information for my report, and ask the woman to secure the bb gun until Toby is older and more responsible. *Good luck finding that male role model.*

6:27 p.m.

I jog through the complex out to my car. The kids take a quick break from hosing each other off to watch me, and then go back to their fun.

I back my car out, careful not to run over one of them. "3-George-46, rolling. Go again with the details."

"Code blue on Muir Street. 3-Boy-32 just went on-scene," she says.

It's a person who's not breathing, and Bosworth is there before the fire department—that's not good. Muir isn't far from Gading, and I get there in less than two minutes. It's all the way dark now, and I see Bosworth's car with its lights flashing, stopped in front of the house. I jump out to the sight of Bosworth dragging an elderly woman out of the house, with an elderly man closely following. The woman appears to be unconscious and unresponsive. Why he's dragging her onto the front lawn, one can only guess.

"She's not breathing," Bosworth says with dread in his voice. The eyes of the man standing off to the side show the terror identifying him as her husband.

"The fire department will be here in a second, sir." I'm trying to sound confident and comforting, yet I'm petrified. "In order to help her, we'll have to start CPR." I'm not really sure why I tell him all of that, other than to prepare him for what he's about to witness. On the other hand, I'm preparing myself as well.

"I'll do the chest compressions," Bosworth stammers, "and you can . . ."

He didn't have to finish. I know the role he just assigned to me. I put my flashlight down on the grass, illuminating the woman's grey face as I get down on all fours next to her. I use my fingers to clear her mouth. A set of dentures flies out and gets tangled in the woman's nightgown. I tilt her head back and cover her mouth with mine. As I start to exhale, I am vaguely aware of Bosworth's movements beside me. *Something's wrong—he's too low. The damn fool is pushing on her abdomen instead of her chest.*

A peculiar gurgle begins to radiate up from the woman's throat, and suddenly my mouth is filled with her vomit. I disengage and spit it onto the grass. Her husband's tear-filled eyes stare down at me with a mixture of hope and grief, and I force myself to keep on. She exhales a bubbling belch that echoes into my own mouth, but this time no vomit.

After what seems like an hour but is probably only a couple of minutes, the firefighters arrive with a little bag-like contraption that does the job for them. As their captain takes down information from the husband, it becomes painfully clear why he was so terror stuck. His wife had been terminally ill and had died peacefully in her bed more than an hour ago. Instead of calling the Neptune Society, he inadvertently dialed 9-1-1. Somebody miscommunicated something over the phone, and our hero, Bosworth, was sent. Without taking even a second to get some basic facts, he drags the corpse out of her bed and onto the front lawn to attempt resuscitation.

I have a few things I want to tell Bosworth, but I'm too busy gagging. I get back to my car and drive straight to the station, where I rinse my mouth and brush my teeth a dozen times.

6:59 p.m.

The night has taken hold. I clear the station still feeling a little grossed out. Strangely, I find myself wondering where the deceased woman's dentures ended up. Would her husband find them as he's mowing the lawn weeks from now?

I still haven't had a chance to sufficiently cruise my beat, so I hit the main roadway marking its southern boundary. The cockroach-like pedestrian activity reminds me that it's Friday night. A motorcycle pulls out of Kentucky Fried Chicken and heads east with no lights on. I get right on his tail before lighting him up— close enough to discourage him from even thinking about running.

He pulls over, removes his helmet, and stands with a look that says: *What the fuck do you want?* He's black and about my age.

"What did you pull me over for?" He asks flatly.

I tell him that he's driving at night without his lights.

He glances down at his dark headlamp, "Sheeeit!" I'm unable to tell if he's more pissed off at me or himself at this point. "I just left the . . . ah forget it." He seems resigned to his fate. I check his driver's license and run his name for warrants. "Psalms Johnson," I spell out over the radio. Dispatch tells me he's clear.

"Be careful, Psalms," I say, pronouncing the "P". I hand his license back without writing him a ticket.

"Thanks," he says with a look of skepticism. "And the "P" is silent!"

I try not to crack a smile as he gets on his bike and rides off.

7:13 p.m.

Another motorcycle buzzes past me. It's much smaller than the one I just stopped, and the driver is quite a bit larger. He's a chubby white kid with red hair. McDonough! *Now that's a ticket I'll write.*

I get behind him and hit my lights. He glances at me over his shoulder then leans forward, opening the throttle all the way. The tiny engine cries out under McDonough's girth. Top speed is all of 35 mph—not hard to keep up with. I tell dispatch I'm in pursuit, and then hit the siren. It nearly blasts him off the bike. He takes a wide, wobbly turn onto a side street, drawing me closer to his back wheel than I really need to be. At this slow speed, it's not all that dangerous, and I'm kind of enjoying the chase.

When he looks back again his eyes register panic, but he doesn't give up. I'm on the radio updating my location. Unable to get anymore power out of the bike, McDonough hunches down like a racer. It doesn't help. He takes an erratic turn, cutting across the roadway and up over the curb. He's trying to lose me in a grove of eucalyptus trees. He uses his feet for balance, ping-ponging off his left and then his right foot, as he bounces over the tree roots. Just when it looks like he's going to get away, he loses it completely on the loose dirt and leaves. As the bike slides out from under him, McDonough stumbles, but manages to stay on his feet. I'm out of the car now, gaining ground as he zigzags through the trees. His feeble attempt to evade me comes to an abrupt end as I grab the young desperado by the back of the shirt.

"Easy there, Big Boy," I say, turning him back toward his bike. "This time we're going to talk with the folks."

For the first time he realizes that it's me. He puffs out his red cheeks and looks as if he's either going to punch me or cry. He barely constrains himself, and marches defiantly ahead of me. I lock my car, and we walk his bike around the corner to the McDonough residence. I explain the series of violations their son has committed—not the least of which is that he's too young to even get a license. The kid wages an impassioned protest, claiming harassment and lack of "just cause." I write him a ticket, which he ultimately, yet reluctantly, signs. His parents are non committal, as if there son is old enough to make his own decisions about such things. To help them overcome their ambivalence, I tell them that the next time they will be cited for permitting an unlicensed minor to drive.

I see the frustration well up in the boy's eyes. "I'm a better motorcycle rider than most people who *have* a driver's license!"

I have to work to keep from laughing. *I like you, McDonough. You're not a bad kid.* "Just keep off the bike until you get your license," I say, giving him a friendly pat on the shoulder.

I drive off knowing that I've ruined the kid's day, but hoping I've saved him from something worse.

7:59 p.m.

I'm winding my way through one of the most troublesome sections of the entire city. It looks like the United Nations. There are people from everywhere, living shoulder to shoulder in sweltering apartments with paper thin walls. This 16 square-block area is the heart and sole of my beat. I drive slowly, with my windows open, taking in the heavy tang of Southern barbecue mixed with Indian curries. The air is filled with a fusion of mariachi, hip-hop, barking dogs, car horns, and an occasional gunshot.

I hear a downtown unit come on the radio asking for a license plate check. The car he's running comes back stolen.

A 3-second beep pierces the airwaves. The dispatcher follows it with, "3-Adam-10 with another unit to cover; 2-Boy-44 is behind a *roll'n stolen,* southbound Mission passing Grove."

I'm on the opposite end of the city, but I make a quick U-turn and head in that direction. The driver of the stolen car is not stopping, and it quickly turns into an all out chase through the congested downtown district. I'm listening to the radio as the chase gathers speed. The driver is blowing through red lights without even slowing. The pursuing cop sounds like he's losing ground as the chase takes a sudden turn and heads in my general direction. They're coming up on a sharp turn where the street intersects with a major thoroughfare.

A few seconds of an edgy silence passes before the cop comes back on the radio. His high pitched voice tells more than his words. "Suspect just crashed into a building!"

In my mind I picture the driver, unable to make the turn, catapulting across traffic into the Mexican restaurant on the corner. Several units are already on-scene, searching for the driver who has apparently fled over fences into the residential neighborhood behind the restaurant. They're trying to set up a 2-block perimeter in the hopes of containing him until a K-9 unit arrives. A sergeant is coordinating the response, directing officers to specific positions and organizing the search.

A few blocks from the scene I turn off into the neighborhood, listening for a recap of the suspect's description. I figure, if anyone is going to catch him it might as well be me. I'm driving up the street behind the restaurant, hoping to intersect with the suspect's path. I signal that I'm on scene to assist with the search. Immediately, the sergeant comes on the air and directs me to the La Casa Bonita crash site. *So much for catching the guy.* I make a quick circle around the search area hoping I'll spot the suspect before my sergeant spots me. No luck.

The crash isn't as bad as I had imagined. The car had indeed skidded though the intersection, up and over the raised center median, losing an axel in the process. It had continued rudderless into the restaurant parking lot, taking out a small planter box and a 6X6 entryway support beam. The unsupported roof is listing at an odd angle when I pull up. The car is another 45 or so feet further into the restaurant parking lot, having finally come to rest against an unfortunate BMW in the far corner.

Pam Halsey, a stoutly built crime scene technician, has arrived in her van and is already in the process of taking photos of the abandoned stolen car. The fire department pulls into the lot behind me and begins a perfunctory check of the building's gas and electrical lines—protocol for any vehicle collisions into a structure. The rest of the lot is littered with a half-dozen empty patrol cars— their drivers all well into the hunt, like greyhounds after a rabbit.

I listen with envy as my partners run here and there, shouting out the suspect's probable location. Dogs bark and radios echo in the darkness, yet I'm stuck at the crash site.

Pam squats to get a shot from a different angle and the flash nearly blinds me. She straightens abruptly, holding her camera chest high. Her eyes are wide and she's rock still. I barely pay any notice as I lean my head to better hear the action on my radio. Pam signals me with a terse wave of her free hand.

"Suspect's probably moving westbound through backyards," one cop gasps over the air. "Get a unit to the 7-11 store at the corner in case he comes out there," another one shouts. I look up at Pam and she's standing in the same position on the other side of the car. Her expression hasn't changed. She makes another cryptic gesture. *What! Can't she see I'm trying to catch this guy? I wish she'd just take her pictures and dust for prints.*

"Yeah?" I say with a forced nod.

She says nothing, but points down toward the car. I frown, wondering what in the hell she's pointing at.

"What?"

She mouths something which I can't understand. *Doesn't she know men can't read lips?* She points downward again. I use my flashlight to illuminate the interior of the empty car. I look back at her, unconsciously raising one eyebrow.

"What is it?" Suddenly a light goes on in my greyhound brain. Slowly, I move the flashlight downward. I keep squatting until I'm almost on all fours. In the deep shadows of the lot, wedged all the way under the stolen car, I make out a tennis shoe protruding from a torn denim pant leg. *I'll be damned!*

Reaching down with my free hand, I grab hold of the ankle and give it an authoritative tug. "C'mon out pal," I say. "Towards my light with your hands where I can see them."

He complies, worming his way toward me in the gravel. As he clears the side of the car, I fold his near arm at a 90 degree angle and handcuff his wrist. The other cuff is snapped to his second wrist as he fully emerges from beneath the car. Though I feel a charge of electricity, I know the credit goes to Pam, not me.

"CST Halsey located the suspect hiding under the car," I say over the radio. "He's in custody back at the scene."

"Confirm he's at the scene of the crash?" the dispatcher asks with a slight tone of annoyance.

"Affirmative," I say, unintentionally burning the pursuing officer who had missed him. Too bad, I think to myself. If this guy had been armed he could have killed both me and Pam.

I transport the suspect to the city jail as a favor to the primary unit. Other than dropping him off to be booked, my job here is done.

9:02 p.m.

I'm hungry now, even with the disgust of my earlier call on Muir. I picture the grieving husband, alone now for the first time in probably 50 years. He must feel completely lost. I wonder if they had any children.

There's a lull in the radio traffic, and I decide that now is as good a time as any. I pull away from the jail and turn north towards downtown instead of south to my beat. A quick stop at Wienerschnitzel, and I can whorf down a couple of doggies right here in the car. Then, I can use my *official* lunch break to get caught up on my reports.

Although it would be easier to hit the drive-through, I decide to park in front and walk in. There is a story in the department about a dumbass cop who once chose the drive-through. His patrol car was stuck in the middle of the Jack in the Box line, when he was sent to an armed robbery. Instead of making up something clever, he announced over the radio, "I'm in line for a Jumbo Jack. I got two cars ahead of me and two cars behind me, and I can't go nowhere!" That alone wasn't the cause of his demise, but a bunch of little screw-ups finally tipped the scale. He was fired before I was even hired. Still, a good rule of thumb is, the less attention you bring on yourself the better.

Though the two chili cheese dogs in the bag next to me are calling my name, my preference is always to eat on my beat, just in case I get a hot call. I skirt the center of downtown, trying to avoid running into something that will require me to take action this far from where I'm supposed to be. A flash of movement catches my eye, and I hit my brakes. I'm stopped just short of a cosmetology school building on my right. I swing my car's spotlight to the dark parking lot next to the building. What I'm seeing doesn't register at first. It's a rear view of three white butts squatting next to each other. *You gotta be kidding me!*

Three shocked faces turn briefly in my direction. They're girls! They quickly snap upright and hike their pants back up. As I swing my car into the lot, they are fully illuminated by my headlights. Three small puddles dribble across the pavement at their feet. I elect not to go off on my radio.

The girls huddle together in nervous laughter as I get out. I walk around to the front of my car, cross my arms and lean back against the bumper. "This ought to be good," I say with minimal emotion. They timidly step toward me and I see they are attractive girls about 18 or 19 years old. In bits and pieces, each of them contributes to complete the story. They are all cosmetology students there during the week. Their instructor, a Mr. Zachary Lim, had managed to anger each of the girls to the point of retaliation. But instead of confronting Lim directly, they decided to return after hours and urinate on the side of the building.

While technically a violation of city code, their transgression is more humorous than malicious. In my mind, they've been sufficiently embarrassed anyway. Besides, I've got two chili cheese dogs that are getting cold, and a sergeant that doesn't need to know I'm downtown.

"How about your three go home and I'll try my best to forget this ever happened?" They seemed okay with that.

9:17 p.m.

I'm still thinking about the Muir call as I'm waiting for the light to change. One benefit of working the street in a patrol car is that you can never get too far into your thoughts before the next thing happens.

That *next thing*, it turns out, is right in front of me. It starts with the telltale signs, signaling your subconscious that something isn't right. There's a sudden change of rhythm, or an abrupt variation in the street noise. It's my first clue that something is wrong. I'm scanning the five corners of the massive intersection. Horns start honking—my second clue. There it is, diagonally to my left across seven lanes of traffic, a small Toyota car has rear-ended a city bus. I'm out of position by three lanes, so with the radio mic in my hand, I'm looking over my left shoulder for a break in traffic.

"3-George-46, I'll be off on a two vehicle accident, southbound Mission at Jackson." I flick on my rear flashing amber lights.

"10-4, Mission and Jackson," she responds.

The signal has changed and cars are trying to get around me to go straight. I find a break and start to move into the left turn lanes, but Jimmy Do-Gooder stops directly next to me and rolls down his window. "There's a crash over there," he says pointing to the bus. *No kidding!*

I nod and say thanks, before squeezing past his bumper so I can get there. Now there's smoke billowing out of bus's backend. Drivers are slowing to watch, which doesn't make my approach any easier. Passengers are literally running off the bus in a panic, and I realize this is something more than a minor accident. The smoke is from the tires on the car behind the bus. They're spinning in place as the Toyota's engine races.

My overhead emergency lights are now on and I have cleared the last of the gawkers. As I pull up behind the car, now completely shrouded in smoke, I can barely make out a solo occupant behind the wheel. He's sitting upright and appears to be trying to push the bus. "46," I say, shortening my identifier. "I got something else here. Start a cover unit and roll fire." I don't wait for her response; I'm already getting out and grabbing my nightstick.

Two young men on the bus have kicked open an emergency exit, and are jumping out. I glance up to see the last of the bus passengers stepping off the front, followed by the driver. He is a frail looking man with grey hair and wide eyes. Though he tries to herd the passengers down the sidewalk, away from the bus, some want to get a better view.

I circle into the street in a wide arch and note that the spinning tires have now started a small fire under the car. The Toyota's driver looks into the flat rear wall of the bus without expression, his foot buried into the accelerator the whole time. I recognize him as Chuey Carvalho. He's from a local family, notorious for selling and using PCP. Although it answers the question of why someone would try to push a bus, it brings up a whole new dilemma. The drug not only causes bizarre behavior, but it kills pain. Superhuman strength, they call it. There is very little you can do to restrain someone who's on it. To make matters worse, the Carvalho boys are all very big.

He turns his head in my direction as I approach. The blank stare confirms in my mind that he's loaded. His eyes slowly register my presence. The door comes open and out comes Chuey, bigger than life. Has to be pushing 275. He turns and walks away with the drug's characteristic robot-like movements. If this guy wants to fight, it's not going to be good. I look back for my cover car, but no police cars yet. I follow Carvalho up onto the sidewalk and past the hoard of bus passengers, now flattening themselves against a computer store window.

Carvalho's walking at a brisk pace, but not a problem to keep up with. I quickly weigh my options. I could follow him until some help arrives. Then again, there is a restaurant up ahead, and a bar full of people next to it. Both could mean problems with customers if Carvalho were to go inside—families and innocents in one place, and hostile drunks in the other. Beyond those places the sidewalk gets darker. Then, there's always the possibility we could end up beefing in the middle of street traffic.

"Aren't you going to do something?" one of the bus passengers calls out to me, engendering a few chuckles.

The wisecrack helps me decide to make my move. I come up close behind Carvalho; my nightstick in my left hand and my right hand resting on my pistol grip. At the last second I switch the nightstick to my right hand and jab it into the small of his back, causing him to arch his head slightly backward. At the same time, I swing my left arm around his neck in a chokehold—officially called a *carotid restraint*. When it's done properly, it cuts off the blood supply to the recipient's brain and renders him unconscious within a few seconds. But those *few* seconds can be one hell of a bull ride.

My arm clamped firmly around Carvalho's neck, he begins to buck and kick. He tries to throw me off by spinning in a circle, like a dog trying to bite his tail, only it's me this dog wants to bite. We slam into the plate-glass store window, and I'm amazed it doesn't break. My adrenaline only causes the noose to cinch tighter, but in reality, I'm gripping on for dear life. In the back of my consciousness I hear someone yell, "That's brutality!" Probably the same jerk who wanted me to "do something".

Finally Carvalho succumbs to his own adrenaline and increased blood flow, none of which has made it past my chokehold into his pee-brain. He collapses at the curb, just short of propelling us both onto the highway. His eyes are rolled up in his head, and there's a putrid stench from the number he just dumped in his shorts. I snap the handcuffs on him while he's still flopping—a distinctive finale I've heard referred to as *The Funky Chicken*.

I turn around to see Bosworth, my cover unit, abandon his car in the middle of the street and hustle over to me. A fire engine pulls up and they start hosing off the Toyota. It looks like they got it before the fire spreads to the bus.

"I need to take a couple of statements here," I tell Bosworth. "Mind transporting him to the jail for me?"

Carvalho is coming to, and I hustle him into Bosworth's car before his pantload becomes noticeable. I give Bosworth a half-baked salute, "Thanks, my man! I owe ya!"

9:38 p.m.

I spend the next hour and 25 minutes at the station booking Carvalho, logging evidence, and getting started on my reports. It also counts as my hour lunch break, so I retrieve my dogs from the car. By now the chili is cold and the cheese is hard, but at least the department has purchased a new microwave oven.

11:03 p.m.

I timed it just right. The midnight shift is just hitting the street, so they'll start picking up the slack. Once they come on, the swing shift is used more for back-up than as the primary unit. In theory anyway. I hear a unit go off on a pedestrian under the overpass about two blocks from the police station. I'm just clearing the station, so I head over there to cover him.

I find them in a dark area alongside the train tracks. The cop is taking down the guy's name and checking him for wants. I've seen the guy before. He's kind of a fixture downtown; tall and lanky with frizzy hair and huge feet. He walks everywhere, taking large elongated strides with each step. A couple of us have dubbed him, *The Keep on Truckin Guy*, after a 1970's comic character. The guy never actually does anything wrong, as far as I can tell. He just walks around late at night, listening to his transistor radio and getting stopped by the cops. I can never understand why everybody stops him, other than he just looks like he isn't all there.

After several minutes he goes on his way and we go on ours.

11:22 p.m.
I need to find a quiet place to write.

12:44 a.m.
I've finished most of my reports, and I'm part way though the supplement on the stolen vehicle arrest. I'm on the west end of my beat, just outside my beat actually, but close enough. It's a quiet industrial tract that backs up to the bay wetlands. I'm down a dark driveway to the rear of a warehouse where I won't be bothered. I'm also in a position to see someone coming before they see me.

With the clipboard on my lap, I'm writing under the tiny overhead map light. I suddenly notice a faint glow in the middle of the mud flats, out toward the water. I shut off my light and let my eyes adjust to the dark. As the figure becomes clearer, I realize it's a car parked out there only a couple of hundred feet away. I pull the binoculars out of my case and focus in on it.

Oh shit! I realize I'm seeing something I wish I wasn't seeing. It's my sergeant, Don Clawson. He tilts his head back and takes a swig from a bottle. A Jack Daniels bottle. His outline is perfectly illuminated under his car's dome light. I pull the binoculars away and then look through them again, as if I'll see something different this time. The sergeant takes another pull, and I swiftly become aware of the situation I'm in. I've got to get the hell out of here before he sees me.

I can't back up or use my brakes, or he'll notice the lights for sure. Even putting the car into drive will momentarily activate the brake lights as I shift. I unscrew the dome light and remove the bulb. Then, without starting the car, I drop it into neutral and push my patrol car back down the driveway to the street. Once I'm around front and the building blocks his view, I drive like my ass hairs are on fire.

1:16 a.m.

"3-George-46," the radio crackles. I look at my watch and wait an intentionally long time before answering. *She ought to know that I've got paper to write and I'm at the end of my shift. Whatever call she has should be given to the beat unit working the midnight shift.*

"Go ahead," I say unenthusiastically. Then, in the moment before dispatch responds, I wonder if Clawson spotted me. Could he want a meet somewhere out here, so he can confront me about what I saw? What would I say? *Admit nothing—it wasn't me.* How could he prove it? *He couldn't.* Anyway, wouldn't he be in deep shit for drinking on duty? *No way, they would never take the side of an officer against a sergeant. I'm screwed.*

"Start for an injury accident on Industrial south of highway 92," the dispatcher says. "A traffic unit is enroute from the station and we're starting fire and ambulance."

Great—mangled bodies. Just what I want to see before going home to bed. I guess it's still better than Clawson.

It's cooled off quite a bit and the streets are nearly empty, at least out in the industrial section. I wonder who hit what. I'm thinking that at this time of the night it's got to be a drunk who's slammed into a pole or something.

I get there and find a long dark stretch of road with nobody around. It's dead quiet, and there's an eerie mist hanging overhead. I slow to a crawl, checking to the sides in case someone went off the roadway. Up ahead, I detect a dark mass of something. As I get closer, I see it's a Cadillac sedan, or what's left of it, completely enmeshed into the back of a big rig parked on the side of the road. There are no skid marks, and it looks like the Cadillac driver had been moving along at a pretty good speed. I train my high beams and spotlight on the wreck, only then getting a full picture of the damage. The area is littered with bits of broken glass and car parts. The force of the impact has sheered the car's top back to a crumpled metallic heap on its trunk, and crunched the chassis down to half its original size. *No way anyone can survive this.*

I come back on the radio, "Let the fire department know they'll probably need to bring extraction tools. Unknown how many occupants, but it looks like it's going to be a fatal."

I move closer, trying to figure out where in the heap the driver might be. I'm bracing myself for what is sure to be a gruesome sight. A chunk of glass falls from the wreckage and I instinctively jump back. Another piece falls, and then a fragment of metal that looks like it was a portion of the window frame. I'm standing in the dark silence of the empty road, watching the unbelievable. A hand emerges from the tomb-like mass of twisted metal. I lunge forward and reach in to grab it. Slowly and carefully, more of the body emerges. I don't believe this. It's a complete person!

A few minutes of maneuvering and he climbs all the way free. He's a Chinese man in his 50's, dazed but not badly hurt. I tell him that the ambulance is on its way, and I ask if there's anyone else in the car. He says he's alone, and that he was on his way to pick up his wife from work. He declines my advice to lie down. Other than a tiny cut on the side of his forehead he appears to be fine.

The fire department arrives and then the traffic unit. We all stand in the street, looking at the mashed car and then back at the driver in disbelief. He's got to be the luckiest man I've ever seen. I tell him he's my hero, and ask if he would mind me taking his picture. He gives a humble wave to the camera.

We take him to the hospital to be checked out, and tow what's left of his Cadillac. Another unit is directed to his wife's place of business, where she is told what happened and driven to the hospital.

2:38 a.m.

I pull into the police department's back lot and take my gear out of my car. There are three patrol cars in line waiting to get into the jail. I pass them by on my way to the back door. I spend the next 20 minutes finishing my reports. I drop them off in the sergeants' office where Sergeant Clawson sits reading them—his eyes at half mast. "Goodnight, Sarge," I say on my way out.

He gives me a nod and says, "Nice work tonight."

3:00 a.m.

I walk to the locker room to change before heading home. *I wonder what he meant by that.*

Chapter 8

5:00 p.m.

It's our last day of the workweek, and one of the guys is collecting a few bucks from everyone on the squad for some after work refreshments. We call it *choir practice.* I suppose it's a takeoff from one of the Wambaugh books. Though I'm not much of a beer drinker, it's all they ever buy—that and some chips. However, at three in the morning after a long tour of duty, the camaraderie, the storytelling, and the blowing off of a week's worth of steam is an indulgence I look forward to.

The sergeant calls me up to the front of the room just before the end of lineup. With only fleeting pomp and circumstance, he hands me a pin for my uniform and tells me that I've been selected for SWAT. I applied and tried out for the Special Weapons and Tactics unit as soon as I got off probation, but I didn't think they would take a cop with only two years experience. I'm really excited and I'd like to immediately call everyone I know, but I keep my enthusiasm in check.

"Let's give him the clap," somebody yells, and in unison the entire squad does a single clap. It's their way of allowing a person some acknowledgement without giving them too much. This place is packed to the rafters with egos, and nobody wants to give anyone else an edge. It took me a while to figure out the double meaning; still I'm thankful for being given *The Clap.*

5:49 p.m.

After a quick phone call to tell Gale, I hit the street. There's a call waiting on my beat of an indecent exposure report. I'm told to contact a woman at a business called Action Silk Screening, on Corporate Avenue.

I find the building in a manicured business park on the western section of the city. I glance around and see the lights are off in the Silk Screening business, and there's a lone car parked in front. A woman sitting by herself inside the car watches me as I pull in. I park my car ahead of hers, so she can see who's coming. I know this sort of thing is likely to make a woman a little jumpy. I take a few seconds to gather my clipboard and report forms before walking over to her. Although I know she's seen me, her driver's side window is up and she's now staring straight ahead.

"Excuse me," I say, tapping lightly on the window. "Did you call the police, ma'am?" She sits there for at least another full minute before slowly cracking her window about an inch. Not sure if she heard me, I try again. "Did you call the . . ."

"Yes, yes! I'm the one who called!" She's still facing straight ahead as she answers. Now I'm getting kind of amused. Instead of responding back, I just stand there at her window holding my clipboard. Neither of us says anything for what seems like several minutes. Finally she looks over at me, I think to check if I'm still standing there.

"Well?" I say, "Did you want to report a crime?"

The woman turns her face forward again and answers without looking at me, "I told the woman on the phone, he exposed his genitals at me."

I stoop as if I'm talking through a mail slot, twisting my head this way and that, exaggerating the difficulty I'm having conversing in this manner. I'm not sure what she's trying to prove. I wonder if she's in some kind of post traumatic shock, or maybe she's just angry at men. In either case, I'm careful to give her plenty of personal space. She reluctantly opens the door and comes out.

The woman says she was the last one to leave the office. After locking the front door and setting the alarm, she turned to see the man standing next to her car. She describes the suspect as a tall, thin, white man in his 20's.

"He looked at me, and I looked at him," she says. "And then he unbuckled his pants and aimed his erect penis at me."

Something about the woman's mannerisms and word choice seem strange to me. I write down the description and then broadcast it over the radio. I hear another unit come on to say he'll be checking the area for the suspect. It's a guy named Danny Cleary, whom I've known since we took a class together in college.

I reassure the woman that another officer is looking for the suspect.

Pulling out a statement form, I begin explaining that I'd like to get a written statement from her in case she's able to identify the man later.

"Yes, I know all about it," she says. "I've been through this before. About a year ago a man came in the office and masturbated in front of me for forty-five minutes."

Now I know there's something wrong with her. I'm struggling to keep a straight face. "Wow, forty-five minutes is a long time. Were you able to leave or call the police during that time?"

"No," she says, as if I should know better. "He was sitting right on my desk; there was nothing I could do."

I finish her statement, making sure to include that last tidbit. I want to be certain that the investigators get the full picture. I leave there wondering if she's got some kind of emotional disorder or just a woman with really bad luck.

6:52 p.m.

I'm driving around the area looking for the "flasher" when dispatch asks me if I'm clear yet. "Contact the ER Nurse at St. Theresa's," she says. I assume this has something to do with my last call until she clarifies. "They're reporting a patient with some type of domestic violence injury."

I arrive and walk through an uncharacteristically quiet waiting room. A woman sitting alone near the nurse's desk catches my eye. She's obviously been crying, and the sight of me walking through the room definitely doesn't have a calming effect on her. Her eyes widen and then she buries her face in her hands. *Probably not a good poker player.*

The desk nurse buzzes me in and I find the person in charge. "Whatcha got for me?" I ask.

She smiles and holds up a small glass jar with a finger in it. Well, the top digit of one. Maybe an inch worth, including the nail. I consider making a joke. Something like, this gives a new meaning to giving the finger, but I resist. Partly because it's too corny and partly because it would likely be viewed as a typical cop come-on.

"I assume it's from the husband of the woman in the waiting room?"

She smiles again. "Yep, they came in together."

I ask about the domestic violence angle and she tells me that it was something the doctor picked up on. He apparently noticed several scratches on the guy while he was treating him for the amputated finger.

"Are they going to sew it back on?" I ask, peering at the pale little nub floating around in the jar.

"Can't. The bone's been crushed." She wiggles her index finger to demonstrate. "It wasn't severed cleanly enough to reattach."

With clipboard in hand, I move past the curtain. The patient appears a little pale, but other than that, and the finger of course, he looks in pretty decent shape. He's a good looking guy, kind of a construction worker type, with white teeth that show nicely against his tan.

I ask him to tell me how it happened and he flashes a mouthful of them. "Just caught my finger in the screen door."

"Doctor says you're pretty scratched up."

More teeth. "Work," he says. Something about his smile tells me that he's not only lying, but he knows that I know he's lying. It also tells me that he's not about to cave in, and he knows that I know there's nothing I can do about it.

I talk briefly with the wife in the waiting room, but she's obviously been coached. She repeats that her husband got the scratches at work, and he accidentally slammed the screen door on his finger. The screen door scenario sounds plausible based on the crushing injury, but I doubt it happened accidentally. I look into the wife's brown eyes and I see a hot tempered woman who's probably as jealous as the day is long. She's every bit as attractive as her husband, and my guess is that they love hard and they fight hard.

I use the ER phone to call in and have a records check done for prior domestic calls. There are none on record. Nevertheless, I write a report for informational purposes. In the event he changes his mind or ends up dead down the road, we'll at least have something on file. Regardless of what I think happened, he's going to protect his wife. I'd probably do the same.

7:59 p.m.
I'm just getting back to my beat, driving around and getting a feel for the night, when I get another call. It's at a mobile home park located about a mile away.

"Check on the welfare," the dispatcher says. "Family members called from out-of-town, stating that they haven't heard from the subject in several days."

That kind of call is usually a toss up. Sometimes it's nothing, and the person simply went on vacation and forgot to tell the family, and other times it's a ripe body that's been marinating in a closed up environment for days. Since it's in a mobile home, I'm more leery. They attract seniors, and that tends to skew the odds in favor of the dead body.

I get there just as a fire engine pulls up. They made so much racket with their sirens and air horns that every last resident of the park is making their way down the narrow street to see what's going on. *Thanks for that.*

By the time I get out of my car, the firefighters have already taken a sledge hammer to the front door; opening it easily enough but leaving the thing in pieces. Two of them charge in as if the place is in flames. I'm wondering what in the hell they're doing here in the first place, when a younger firefighter left outside bounds over to me.

"It's a retired fire captain," he says, "That's why we're on this call."

It definitely explains it for me. They tend to be fiercely loyal to their own, probably like I would have been if it were a police captain.

He leans close so nobody else will hear, "Great guy, but one hell of a drunk. He's probably dead in there."

The other two emerge from the mobile home, examining the damaged door with pride as they pass it. "He's dead," one says.

"Yeah, judging by the smell he's been in there a while," says the other.

Great! I sure hope it isn't a homicide scene, because you guys just trampled over any evidence we might have had.

"I hear he was one of yours," I say solemnly. "Sorry for the loss." They all nod with matching reverence.

We take a few deep breaths before heading back inside. A gaggle of onlookers, all of whom would like to tell us something *important* about the guy, follows us onto the tiny porch. Now that we have no door to block them, the younger firemen is assigned to stand guard.

The other two firefighters direct me to a living room area at the far end of the house. Apparently there's a main door there, but we had entered through the kitchen door. The carpet is a royal blue shag that a blind man couldn't miss, and the place is decorated with antique dolls. We find their beloved captain on a white couch, the fabric of which reminds me of something sparkly my grandmother used to have.

The deteriorated condition of the guy is in stark contrast to the immaculate state of the rest of the home. It's pristine. He, on the other hand, is gray and rancid, and has several days of an unshaven beard. His mustard colored sweater looks like it's rotting on his body, and his unbuckled pants are down around his ankles. A huge bloated stomach is exposed, distended out so far that it conceals his genitals. On the couch next to him is an empty bottle of Kessler Whiskey, and a couple of others are on the floor beneath him. It looks and smells as if the man sat right there in that very spot, and drank and drank until he died.

There's a gurgling sound. We all suddenly stop talking and look over at the couch. In a slurred voice the *dead* fire captain says, "Somebody help me to the bathroom. I got to take a shit!"

I'm not sure how we missed it, but apparently he had been breathing, if only scarcely. He looked and smelled every bit as dead as every dead body I've seen, but somehow he had managed to come very close without going over the line. They immediately call for an ambulance. I'm embarrassed and so are the firemen. Other than a few uncomfortable looks between all of us, there's no outward discussion about the misread. I'm sure it's a story that won't be told for quite a while.

The firefighter who was left guarding the door is baffled by the ambulance request heard over his radio. I pass him on my way out and he asks me what's going on.

I shake my head, "You wouldn't believe me if I told you."

8:33 p.m.

It's dark when I clear the trailer park. My sergeant calls me on the radio and says he wants a meet. As I'm driving to the 7-11, I'm trying to figure out what I did. Could the indecent exposure lady have complained? Maybe the guy with the missing finger thought I came at him too hard. I'm leery when I pull up, and even more so when he offers to buy me a cup. Turns out it's not so bad. One of the cops, a guy by the name of Barry Pigeon, had to take the rest of the night off, and Sarge wants me to move over to his beat. Apparently something urgent came up at Pigeon's home. He works the 'B' beat downtown, which is a whole different animal than where I am. For the remainder of the night I'll be Boy-46.

8:40 p.m.

I know the beat, but I'm familiarizing myself with a couple of the new bars. They're known to be trouble spots, especially at closing time. One is a Mexican bar that hosts boxing matches and provides cheap beer to anybody who comes in the door, regardless of their age. The other place is a gay bar where they tend to cram more people inside than is humanly possible. There are a lot of drugs bought and sold in the patio out back, although the place tends to handle any problems without involving the police. I'm convinced that we only hear about a fraction of what really goes on there.

After driving past it, I turn down a side street, cutting through a residential area back toward the Mexican bar. Sometimes just being seen cruising by is enough of a deterrent. As I round a corner, I notice the silhouette of a head in a car parked in the darkest area of the street. The head disappears momentarily and then bobs up again. I'm far enough back that the person couldn't make out the police car, only the approaching headlights. I slow down and keep watching. Head disappears, head comes up again.

I slide in behind the car and light it up. With my high beams and spotlight activated at the same time, it has a blinding if not shocking effect. The tactic provides me the time I need to get out and get up to the window in time to actually see what the person is doing. My hope is that I'll catch a guy in the middle of hotwiring the car. Wrong.

In the starkness of the illuminated car a second head pops up. Unless the two car thieves are working very closely together, all I've got is a couple of lovers. As I get closer, I see they're two guys— probably from the bar around the corner. I slow my walk and give them time to straighten up whatever they need to straighten before making my way to the passenger window.

The driver is thirty-ish with a shaved head and a big handlebar mustache. The one on the passenger side is much younger. He's an olive-skinned kid with dark hair, and the muscled look of a high school swimmer. He's still buttoning up his pants as I'm standing at the window. I ask for both their identifications. The driver hands me his but the kid hesitates. Something about him is familiar, but I can't place it.

"Your ID?" I repeat, with a flashlight beam in his face and just a touch of intimidation.

Reluctantly, he hands it to me. He's looking over his shoulder out the back window as I'm reading his name, and then I know why. I also know why he's familiar to me. Jason Cleary.

"You're Danny's brother," I say. He nods and wipes his lips. I get on the radio right away, "No assistance needed." His license says he's just turned eighteen. The look in his eyes is clear enough. Whatever he's choosing to do is something he'd rather keep private. Instead of running the names on the radio I just hand back their identifications.

"Thanks," he murmurs.

"This is a residential area," I tell them. "Best not to park here at night otherwise someone is likely to call the police. And you never know who'll show up next time."

They take off in a hurry.

9:05 p.m.

There's a light rain starting to fall and the temperature has cooled considerably. It'll keep the pedestrian activity down, but probably increase the accidents. Especially at two o'clock in the morning when the drunks are all making a mad dash home.

I drive by an all-night fast food stand at the corner of a busy intersection. An old man is sitting under an overhang beneath an electric heater. I hear a whistle, and check my rearview mirror as I pass. A man in a white apron and chef's hat runs into the middle of the street waving his arms like he's just been robbed.

I put myself off on the radio and hit my flashing lights. A quick U-turn and I'm in front of the restaurant.

"Can you do something about him?" The guy motions toward the old man sitting in the corner.

"What's he doing?"

"Those tables are for patrons only." He points to the faded yellow print of a prehistoric sign. I look around and the old man is the only person in the whole joint. He's not even aware I'm there. His head is down and his shriveled hands cling to one another, almost as if he's praying. His pants are secured around his waist with a bungee cord and he's wearing a thin cotton shirt. Next to him on the bench seat is a trash bag, which I imagine holds everything he owns. I come on the radio and cancel my cover.

The cook ducks back inside behind the counter, probably assuming I'm going to remove his problem. I follow him to the counter where I stand waiting.

"You want something?"

"Sure," I say with a smile. "A couple of small coffees, please"

He hands them to me and I walk over to the table where the old man is sitting. He looks up and I slide one over to him.

"You take cream or sugar?" I ask, depositing a handful of condiments and stir sticks between us.

The old guy grins as he inundates his coffee with cream and sugar. We sit there for a while, not really saying much, just watching traffic pass.

"You going to take him outta here, or what?" says the cook.

I motion to the coffee cup cradled in the old man's hands, "Now he's a patron."

The cook dismisses me with a wipe of his hand and goes back to whatever he was doing. I ask the old guy if he has a place to stay and he shakes his head.

"I stay here and there, but it's tough when it rains." He's shivering, even under the heat lamp. I'm thinking the cook is going to kick him out sooner or later. Even if he doesn't do it himself, he'll keep calling until he gets a cop that'll do it for him.

I ask the guy, "Can I give you a ride somewhere?"

"How about jail," he says with a toothless grin. I think he's joking, but he's serious. He tells me that it's the safest place for him on a night like this. He's had a little bit to drink, but not much. Not enough to be drunk in public, but what the heck. There's no criminal charge, no court, and no fine. It's just a night in the drunk tank, and he's let out in the morning.

On the way to jail I coach him. "You've got to stagger a little when I bring you in. And slur your words some."

He's into it. He practices on me from the backseat. I walk him in, and one of the jailers fills out his paperwork and inventories his bag. I tell them it's a detention only for public drunkenness. The old guy stumbles and swears at me, making like he's really pissed off.

I'm laughing as I leave the jail. I get into the freezer where we keep the prisoner meals. He missed feeding time by about three hours, but I heat him up a Salisbury steak dinner anyway. I get a couple of extra blankets from the jailers and toss them into his cell as well. The old guy gives me a sly wink, and for the first time tonight I feel like I've accomplished something.

10:14 p.m.

I check with dispatch and they say I'm clear to stay in the station and take my lunch. I'm writing my reports and eating chicken and rice leftovers that Gale packed for me. Two other guys come in to eat, and they're both pissed.

"What's with Pigeon going home early?" one of them says, slamming his Tupperware container onto the table.

"This is the third time in three weeks!" the other one yells. "And it's always on our Friday!"

The term "our Friday" doesn't necessarily mean it's actually Friday. It's just what we all call our last work day. It could be any day of the week, but in this case it is actually on Friday. Anyway, I tell them I don't know anything about Pigeon's time off, except that Sarge asked me to take his beat for the rest of the night.

"Humph!" They're both muttering as they eat. "No wonder he didn't kick in any money for choir practice," one says.

The other one slaps a hand on the table. "That son-of-a-bitch knew he was taking half the night off all along!"

At first I'm not too bothered by it, but then the more I listen to them, I'm realizing it's kind of a sideways thing to do. Leave your squad short, halfway through the shift, three weeks in a row? What's that about? Pigeon seems like a nice enough guy, but he's always smiling and you can't help wondering if he just gotten one over on you. Something inside me questions his sincerity.

Emergency at home, I doubt it.

11:45 p.m.

I'm just about to stop a car for making an illegal U-turn when I get a call. "Cover the fire department on a structure fire . . ." Usually that means we're needed to direct traffic around their hoses, but occasionally an investigation is required. In most cases it's better to let the firefighters get there first, although this time the fire is only a block from where I happen to be.

I double check the address. I'm looking for flames and smoke but I don't see either. It's a nice home with a semi-circular driveway in front. As soon as I reach the porch I hear screaming and crying inside. Before I can even knock, the door is opened by a small Filipino woman. She's yelling into a portable phone and waving her arms for me to follow her. Now I smell smoke. She leads me to a back bedroom where the smoke is a little more visible, lingering like a haze in the air. A young boy, maybe eight or nine, is on the floor in his underpants, holding a wet towel over his feet and lower legs. He's crying hysterically and is obviously in a great deal of pain. Beneath the towel I see dark skin, separated like a dried riverbed, with oozing pink tissue between the cracks.

The blanket on his bed is charred. The woman hangs up the phone and tells me that her son's electric blanket had somehow caught on fire. She awoke to her son screaming, and was able to pull him from the bed and unplug the blanket before the flames ignited anything else. I advise dispatch and they relay the information to the fire department. I also request an ambulance. I can hear the firefighters coming down the hall, their radios echoing everything I just said. They take over medical aid for the boy's burns while I get more details from the mother.

Everything adds up to an electrical malfunction, and the firemen confirm that they found a short where the blanket had previously been damaged.

"I can't get in touch with my husband," the woman cries. "I've been calling his work, but they say he's not there. I need to let him know our son is hurt." She tells me her husband's name is Manuel DeGuzman.

I realize that is who she had been calling. Poor thing, she's frantic and obviously at a loss without him. I imagine how Gale would be if it were one of our daughters in the same situation.

The ambulance has arrived and they're tending to the boy. Mrs. DeGuzman continues dialing and redialing the phone. I offer a ride to the hospital and she accepts. She tells me that her husband is a night security guard at a bottling plant only a short distance away. We take a detour there on the way to the hospital.

We get to the plant, and I get out and walk up to the security office housed in a small trailer in the lot. A middle-aged black man sits eating a sandwich and watching a panel of video monitors. I tap, and he opens the door as if he expected me.

I explain that we're trying to locate Mr. DeGuzman.

He shakes his head in disgust. "I didn't know what to tell his wife when she called," he says. "DeGuzman doesn't even work on Friday nights."

"Are you sure?" I ask, hoping there has been some sort of mix up.

He nods apologetically, "Yeah, I'm sure."

I get back to the car where Mrs. DeGuzman waits anxiously for some good news. Whether she can see the answer in my eyes or not, I'm uncertain. Maybe in her heart she already knows. She says nothing all the way to the hospital. I walk her inside where she is reunited with her son. I tell her I hope everything works out okay, but I can't think of anything more helpful than that to say.

12:50 a.m.

As I'm clearing the hospital, I hear several units going to a burglary alarm at Macy's Department Store at the mall. I'm not that far away, and if it's a good one, they'll need a lot of cops to cover the doors.

There are no broken windows or pried doors. It's still sprinkling outside, and the wind has started to pick up. In most cases we would assume that the weather set off the alarm, and as long as the building is secure, we'd leave. But the K-9 unit shows up, and he wants to give his dog some work. He motions the mall security officer over and has her open the store.

Three of us walk in behind the handler and the dog. The only light is from the green exit signs at the far end of the store. The support posts, the racks of clothes, and all the counters provide a thousand dark places for someone to hide. On top of that, the oddly posed mannequins give the place a wax museum feel.

The dog sniffs around, and the handler gives us a look like we're just wasting our time. I kind of thought that from the beginning, but it's a break from the car and the rain. I'm checking out the men's shoes when I hear the dog growling. I turn around and the damn thing is staring at me with his teeth bared. He's on leash, thankfully, and the handler is standing over him laughing. *Real funny.*

We're just about ready to leave and the dog handler says, "Watch this." He takes off the leash, and gives the dog a command in German. Immediately the dog attacks a mannequin standing on a pedestal. The dog growls and barks as he chews the pant leg of the nicely dressed businessman. There's a tearing sound and the pant leg flies outward. A plaster foot falls to the floor. The handler is laughing and telling the dog he's a good boy.

As we leave the store I can't help but think of a few things: that could have been my foot, the K-9 handler is psychotic, and I wonder what the store manager will say when he arrives in the morning.

1:42 a.m.

The rain is starting to come down with some authority now, and I'm counting on no more calls until I get off. I'd like to ignore the Volkswagen Beetle in front of me with no rear lights, but I can't. The bars are about to close, and in this weather another driver won't even see the car until they're on top of it.

I turn on my overhead lights, and the Beetle pulls to the curb next to a boarded up liquor store. I wonder if the driver is a drunk, trying to make it home. I stretch the plastic liner over my hat before putting it on. It keeps the hat dry, but only serves to redirect the rainwater straight off the back and down my neck.

"Your tail lights are out," I say, cutting right to the chase. No time for chit-chat in this weather. As I follow my flashlight beam over the lip of the fogged window, I'm surprised by an unexpected sight. The driver is an attractive young woman. She smiles warmly, and then giggles as a new torrent of water sloshes off my hat and dribbles down my cheek. Her expression says she feels sorrier for me than for herself. I'm completely struck by the contrasting scene. It's a miserable night, on a dark corner in front of a graffiti-covered liquor store, and suddenly I'm the recipient of a soft smile from a doe-eyed girl in a warm car, the interior of which smells curiously like fresh baked cookies.

As she hands me her license and registration, she actually thanks me for stopping her. Although she may just be working the sweet angle, it doesn't seem like it. She appears to be just a kind, and very attractive, young girl. Then again, the sweet angle wouldn't work if guys knew when it was being deployed on them.

"You know, it could just be a fuse," I tell her. Having had a Volkswagen myself a few years back, I know right where the fuse box is. "If you want, I could switch the bad fuse for one you don't use much."

"Are you sure it's no trouble?"

Of course not! There is nothing more I feel like doing than squatting down on the wet pavement, folding myself under the dashboard, and trying to change out a fuse, while holding a flashlight in one hand and wiping rain out of my eyes with the other.

Just then, she maneuvers herself over the stick shift and emergency brake to the passenger seat. "You can sit inside the car if that would be easier."

I swallow. My first reaction is to say, "No thanks." But the words don't come out of my mouth when my mind tells them to. I squint up at the angry rain, and then back in at her gentle expression. Somewhere inside I hear the advice of the old-timer, Don Richards, the night he told me to enjoy a pretty girl because the next guy I stop will probably want to kick my ass. So, going against every safety tactic I've ever learned, I find myself climbing into the driver's seat next to her.

It takes me a good five minutes to exchange the taillight fuse with one for the heater. She says she'd rather do without the heater the rest of the ride home, than without the windshield wipers or the radio. I snap the cover back on and straighten up into the glare of blinding light. It's the spotlight from another cop car pulled up next to us. *Damn it! He must have come to check on me and found my patrol car empty.*

I roll down the Volkswagen's heavily fogged window, and to my chagrin I'm face-to-face with one of the midnight shift sergeants. He's got the look that I'm becoming more and more familiar with. The right words don't come to me, and I find myself doing more pointing and stuttering than talking. The girl doesn't make it any better, waving cheerfully to Sarge from the seat next to me—like he's just another helpful officer who has nothing more pressing to do.

"Everything *copasetic* in there?" he smirks, dragging out the word just long enough to make me feel like a stooge.

"Yes, sir. Just putting the fuse . . ." I'm halfway through my explanation when the sergeant holds up his hand. It's clear that he prefers the visual story over the factual one. I can only shake my head as he drives away laughing.

The girl is puzzled by the exchange, but thanks me once again. I step out into a downpour, check to make sure the lights work, and wave goodbye.

2:28 a.m.

I look up from my quiet parking spot where I'm writing reports to see the rain has dwindled to a light drizzle. Not a sound over the radio for several minutes. I check the squelch button to make sure it's working. Thirty-two minutes left on my shift, and I'm finally caught up on my paper.

I'm heading slowly toward the station. Like a football team ahead by a touchdown, I'd like to run the clock down without turning the ball over to the other side. The radio is still silent and I'm about a block from my turn. After that it's a straight, quarter-mile shot to the police department.

Something catches my eye near a closed market on the corner. There's some movement over my right shoulder, barely noticed in the outer reaches of my peripheral vision. It's only a flash, and then it's gone. I keep driving as if I didn't see it, but then I circle the block. With my headlights out, I creep along the side street approaching the market. The building is dark and the parking lot is empty. Now I'm wondering if I was seeing things.

I use my emergency brake to slow the car at the corner in order to keep the car as dark as possible. I make the turn at a crawl, and right in front of me are two guys in dark clothes. They have a side door pried open and boxes of merchandise stacked outside. They see me at the same moment I see them. I hit them with my spotlight and immediately they start to run. The silence of the radio is shattered by my less-than-composed transmission. With the radio mic in one hand, I'm driving after one guy while trying to keep the second guy in sight. The whole time, there's a thought in the back of my mind that I know this guy.

He cuts through the lot and I jump out of my car. He's got about a 10-foot lead and we're running stride for stride. I'm hoping he slips on the pavement but it doesn't happen. He's headed for the darkest corner of the parking lot, where a wooden fence separates the lot from a residential backyard. In a fraction of a second, my mind plays out three different possible scenarios: he turns with a weapon in his hand; he turns to fight; or he tries to beat me over the fence. I stay focused on his hands, and although they appear empty, it's awfully dark. He could still have something tucked in the front of his pants. As we approach the fence, he's running so fast that I'm banking on the fact that he's going to try to jump it. Even if he stops and tries to pull out a weapon, I'll probably have better odds ramming him at full speed, into the fence.

He leaps for the fence with a thud, getting both elbows hooked over the top it. He tries frantically to swing his legs up, but I reach him first. I ram him from behind with my shoulder, and then grab hold of his belt and collar. By now the leverage advantage is mine and he looses his grip on the fence. We tumble to the asphalt, and he's fighting like a dog to get free. *How right Don Richards was!*

I smack the guy a couple of good ones in the back of the head with the flat of my forearm, and it stuns him a bit. Between the blows and the approaching sirens, he doesn't put much more into it and I'm able to handcuff him.

The first car slides into the lot illuminating us like two boxers in a prizefight. I flip the guy over, and I'm awash in the warm satisfaction that only payback can provide. It's my old pal, Johnnie

Lopez. He had gotten the better of me during our first encounter in his family's kitchen, and his warrant arrest had been stolen out from under me by two of my unscrupulous comrades. But in yet another cathartic irony, I get the last laugh of sweet revenge. *I only wish I had smacked him a little bit harder.*

There's some chatter on the radio, and it sounds like they've stopped my other suspect a couple of blocks away. They give me the name over the radio and all I can do is laugh. It's Lopez's brother, the one who had pelted me with rocks. *Got to love this job.*

Another midnight shifter pulls up. "Want me to take it?" he asks, referring to the lengthy report that lies ahead of me. "You're almost outta here, and I got all night to write it."

"No thanks," I say. "I won't mind writing this one."

He looks at his watch and shrugs. I have him transport Lopez to the jail for me while I go identify his brother as my second suspect. That done, I head into the station for a long night of writing.

6:10 a.m.

My sergeants are long gone. I find one of the midnight sergeants in his office with a cup of coffee and the morning paper. It's the same one who had found me inside the Volkswagen. I hand him my report, and let him know it's an *In Custody*. He peruses it and then gives me a nod.

"Everything looks *copasetic*," he says with a grin.

Chapter 9

4:00 p.m.
The worst part about working this swing shift is leaving the house. Once I get to work and change into my uniform, my mind is set for the street. However, driving out of the neighborhood, especially on a nice day, is a demoralizing gauntlet of backyard barbecues, street baseball games, and kids riding bikes over fresh-mowed lawns. I envy the guys who are off on weekends and can stay home at night with their families.

5:33 p.m.
I hit the street after lineup and there are no calls holding for me on my beat. Hopefully a sign it's going to be a good night. A couple of blocks off the main drag is an exclusive little residential neighborhood set on the crest of a hill. It's a nice reminder that the city isn't all stripped cars and government subsidized apartments. I drive past mansions, circular driveways and well landscaped yards. One of my favorites is a regal looking home with white columns and a rounded portico in front. It's where the former mayor lives, a large impressive man who can lay claim to dozens of valuable real estate holdings throughout the city. I've known him since my early teens when his daughter and I went to school together.

Down the street a bit the roadway veers to the left, and just as abruptly the houses turn to shit. A block later and I'm on the outskirts of downtown, where shopping carts are the new mobile homes and graffiti is an excepted form of communication.

5:42 p.m.

I barely have a chance to check my beat when three loud beeping tones come over the radio. It's the attention-getter that means a heavy duty call is about to follow. It's my call-sign followed by several other units as backup.

"Hysterical female caller states her ex-husband is trying to kill their baby!" The dispatcher's anguish transcends her words. She gives me the address on a nasty street in the heart of a nasty neighborhood. It's one of those government subsidized apartment houses.

I arrive before anyone else, and move quietly between buildings to find the right one. "Ground floor unit on the south side of the complex," I whisper over the radio. The frantic screams inside confirm I have the right place. A door behind me flies open with a loud smack and I turn with my hand on my gun. The next door neighbors, an Asian couple with two little girls, emerge from the doorway and run for the carport. A tattooed guy on the second floor walkway leans over the railing. With his hands stretched wide, he silently indicates the man inside the apartment below is big. I mouth the words, thank you.

I'm at the screen door and the neighbor upstairs is right. I'm staring at the broad brown back of a guy who's got to be well over six feet tall. The woman, whom I'm presuming is the "hysterical caller," is still hysterical. She beats on the man using both fists, but it has no effect. He bats her across the room with a bear-like swipe, and literally rips the baby out of a highchair. He wheels around to face the woman, and for the first time sees me, now frozen just inside the door. He's holding a long curved butcher knife tightly against the baby's neck. The baby, a chubby brown kid wearing only a diaper, appears to be about ten months old. He's already terrified from all the screaming, and now having been torn from the highchair straps, is wailing at an earsplitting pitch. So hard, in fact, that he only breaks long enough to take a gulp of air before starting again.

My own daughter is the same age as the baby, and I'm momentarily gripped by the insane notion of how someone could kill their own child. *It simply can't be true.* I'm startled into action when he suddenly clamps one hand into a chokehold grip around the baby's neck, and at the same time uses the other hand to press the tip of the knife against the baby's tiny heaving chest.

"Stay back or I kill him!" The man is shouting in an accent I'm assuming is Samoan, or maybe one of the other South Pacific Islands where everybody is his size.

"Take it easy," I say in as soothing a voice as I can muster. "I don't want to see anybody get hurt, especially *your own son*." I make a conscious effort to remind him of that little fact, in case with all his rage against the Ex he forgot this is his son. The Ex, on the other hand, is beside herself—screaming, crying, and begging him to put the baby down. The more she yells, the more agitated the man seems to get.

"Please," I look at her right in the eyes. "Please help me by stepping outside for a minute." I know other officers will be here any second, and there's no way they will let her back in once she's out. My hope is that he'll rethink his plan once his audience leaves and some of the hysteria is gone. Unfortunately, she's not having it. She remains between us, waving her arms witlessly and bellowing as if the boy is already dead.

"What's your son's name?" I ask the father. He ignores the question and repeats his threat to kill him. It generates a new round of howling from the mother.

I ask again and this time the woman answers. "Malaki," she says with a snivel, "after his father."

I hear other cops near the door behind me, but it sounds like they're not coming in. Shadows through the kitchen curtain tell me they're putting a tight perimeter around the apartment, and most likely evacuating any of the immediate neighbors who have yet to leave on their own. I feel my hand still on my gun and realize that it is now out of the holster and pressed against my thigh, on the side facing away from the older Malaki. *What am I going to do, shoot him?*

He notices some movement outside the window and renews his threat to kill the boy. This time, he raises the knife high in the air directly over the center of the baby's chest. "I'm going to do it!"

I can't watch this, I think to myself as my grip tightens on my gun. Continuing my efforts to calm him, I repeatedly refer to the child as, "your son, Malaki." At the same time I'm trying to prepare myself for the real possibility that I'm going to see him plunge the knife into the baby. I'm also weighing the use of deadly force option. The way he's holding the baby gives me a narrow head target, only inches from the baby. I could kill the father and save the baby, or I could miss and kill the baby myself. Or, I could hit the father, and he could still drop on top of the baby, knife first. I'm just an *okay* shot at the gun range anyway, and I really, *really*, don't want to shoot anybody.

He retreats into a back bedroom and I follow him to the doorway. It provides me with my first chance to get the wife behind me. One of the cops, a guy named Bryan, also uses the opportunity to our benefit. He quickly steps in, grabs the mother by the arm and yanks her outside.

Big Malaki raises the knife again and glances around with wild eyes, apparently realizing he's physically boxed himself into a tight spot. I'm afraid he might panic. "Listen!" I say in desperation. "I have a daughter the same age as Malaki."

"Just stay back!" He shows no reaction to my words.

"Think about when he was born," I continue. "Remember? Remember how happy you were to have him. Whatever went wrong here can be undone."

He grits his teeth and pushes the knife tip right up to the baby's chest, dead center. His breathing increases and I find myself talking faster.

"It can all be worked out. Your son loves you. You haven't done anything we can't fix . . ." I'm just rambling, trying to hit on something that works before he plunges that damn knife into the baby. I'm overwhelmed by the insanity of this. I can't understand it. I realize I've been standing at the doorway talking with him for 30 minutes. Sweat is dripping down my chest under my vest, and my legs are like rubber. There's nothing more I can think of to say.

We lock eyes and I try to see all the way into him. I still don't see it. There's no way he can do this. Without thinking, I slide my handgun back into its holster.

"You're can't stab your own son to death." It was only a thought in my mind at that second, and it somehow came out of my mouth. It wasn't a challenge or a taunt. It wasn't a threat. It was just the quiet realization that this simply can't happen. He just kind of stares off with a glazed look.

"Good job, kid." I feel a hot whisper on my neck. I turn slightly to see Sergeant Dave McCreedy, his huge, sweaty, white face taking up my whole field of view. "See if you can get him round the near side of the bed, and then we'll rush him."

I hadn't even been aware that McCreedy and a few others were stacked in a line against the wall behind me. "Rush him?" I ask. "He's still holding the knife."

McCreedy nods and a bead of sweat rolls off the tip of his nose. "I know. When we do it, you grab the baby and me and Bryan will grab the knife."

It's like somebody injected me with adrenalin. My mouth is instantly dry and my legs begin shaking. A lot of things can go wrong with this plan, but McCreedy has been a sergeant a lot longer than I've been a cop. I hope he knows what he's doing.

Another five minutes go by. Malaki is still on the other side of the bed holding the baby in one hand and the knife in the other. I don't know how I can get him to come toward me, other than to simply ask him, which is totally absurd. My mind races to think of something to say, then suddenly McCreedy's big hand grips my shoulder.

"On three," he whispers. "One...two...three!"

Malaki still hasn't moved from the far side of the bed. Our sudden movement is accompanied by a thundering stampede-like noise. I'm the first one through the doorway, and I see Malaki's eyes grow large at the sight and sound of our advance. He raises the knife, the baby screams, and we yell, all at the same time. McCreedy launches himself over the top of me, toward the knife. Malaki takes a step back but there's nowhere to go. The full weight of McCreedy hits Malaki like a truck. I'm stretched over the bed with my hands around the baby as if I were intercepting a pass. There's a huge crash and the sound of glass breaking. Malaki tumbles to the floor with McCreedy and Bryan on top of him, the girth of all three men wedged into a three-foot space between the bed and the wall. Meanwhile, the baby and I make a soft landing on the bed, though you wouldn't know it from the way the baby is wailing. I check him for injuries and he appears fine.

Several other cops rush in to help but there's no more room. McCreedy yells out, "Suspect in custody!" They carefully untangle themselves, and it's apparent nobody was hurt by the knife. Malaki, in handcuffs, is walked outside and stuffed into one of the patrol cars clustered there. I emerge with the baby, and am amazed at the resources this incident has attracted. There's a fire engine, an ambulance, two family counselors, a crime scene tech, a couple of detectives, a newspaper reporter, and over a dozen other cops. Not to mention the entire neighborhood.

The wife runs up to me crying, and I hand her the baby. It's the first time I get a good look at her. I realize she's Kitty Armstrong, a girl I went to junior high school with. She was the subject of a crush my entire seventh grade year, although she didn't know it then and doesn't recognize me now. Hardly the time to bring it up, I decide not to mention any of it.

I stick around to take statements and diagram the scene while Bryan transports Malaki to the jail for me. By the time I'm finished, the crowd has disappeared from the front of the apartment. I stow my clipboard, start the car, and pull out of the complex. Emotion suddenly wells up inside me, and I'm caught off guard by it. I'm neither happy nor sad, just relieved. Best I can figure, it's a pressure release of some kind. Undoubtedly from the intense emotions I've stifled for the past two hours. Anyway, it feels good to get it out. Luckily, everyone is gone and I'm alone in my patrol car.

7:50 p.m.

I get back to the station to take Malaki's statement. The jail is under construction and it's a mess getting in. Plastic and plywood covers one whole wall, and the prisoners are all confined to their cells. I have to walk around to the side of the building and call on an intercom in order to get inside. It would have been easier just to tear through the plastic.

Malaki is walked from his cell into the small holding area across from the booking counter. The rage now gone from him, Malaki sits on the bench next to me like a balloon with no air. His eyes never meet mine and I wonder if he even knows I'm the same cop who was at the apartment. Whatever the case, Malaki doesn't want to say anything, which is fine with me. The DA prefers that we at least provide the opportunity to someone we arrest.

I hit the bathroom, and I'm back on the street.

8: 20 p.m.

Dispatch calls me just as I clear the back gate. "Start for a possible coroner's case on Montgomery Street." *You gotta be kidding!*

I pull up to the front of a one-story house with a station wagon parked cockeyed in the driveway. The front door is wide open, and I hear a woman yelling inside. It's not a grief stricken yell, but more of an angry yell. As I come up the walk, I'm able to make out what she's saying.

"I told you to keep an eye on Grandpa while I was gone!"

"We did keep an eye on him," a boy's voice cries out.

"Hello?" I tap on the doorframe. "Police department." I'm squinting to see into the dark living room. A woman stands just inside, arguing with two boys in their early teens—their volume competing with an action movie blaring on the TV.

"Turn that down!" the woman barks at one of the boys, then motions to me. "Come in, officer."

As soon as I step inside, I see an old man lying comfortably on the couch. I notice he's not moving. He's got on a tan button up sweater and slacks, and is turned away from me.

"I told my sons to watch their grandfather," she says. "He's had a drinking problem in the past, and the doctor recently warned us he would die if he takes a drink."

"We did watch him," says one of the sons. "He didn't have anything to drink. It isn't our fault. He probably just died because he's old."

"Yeah," says the other one. "Why do you want to put the blame on us?" The boy points out two pillows on the floor between the couch and the TV. "We've been sitting right there the whole time you were gone."

About this time I step over and check the old man for signs of life. He's not only cool to the touch, but the underside of his face has already begun to turn purple. My guess is he's been dead a couple of hours. I'm debating whether or not to call the fire department and ambulance, just to play it safe. I take hold of an arm and lift it away from his body. It feels like the early stages of rigor mortis. As I lay his arm back down I hear a thud at my feet.

"Goddamn you! I knew it!" The woman grabs one of the boys by the back of the shirt, directing him toward the old man. "What the hell is that?"

I step back and see a Whiskey bottle had fallen to the floor. It had been tucked secretively under Grandpa's sweater. It's empty now, but had no doubt been enjoyed by the old guy while the boys were engrossed in their show.

"No television for a month!" The woman marches over and shuts it off with a slap of the hand. "I hope you're both happy now, Grandpa's dead."

With heads hung low, the boys shuffle off to their room. I stick around long enough to call the grandfather's doctor and find out that he will sign the death certificate. I explain to the woman that the coroner doesn't have to respond, and the family can deal directly with the mortuary. It also means that the old guy's medical condition was pretty bad already.

I tell her that in all likelihood the boys bare only a small amount of responsibility in the matter, if any. If she's catching the inference that she was also partly responsible, she doesn't show it. It isn't really my place anyway, but something inside me feels an affinity for the two boys. *Poor little shits.*

9:43 p.m.

I pull into the parking lot of a Quick Stop market where a gang shooting happened only a few nights ago. A plywood sheet covers a window shattered by gunfire while new graffiti spray painted on the side of the building threatens more violence. Yet, the store is open and neighborhood residents are lined up for their beer and pork rinds. I drive slowly through the lot, making sure I'm seen and hopefully preventing anything from happening on my watch.

Lights fade around the corner, and I find myself in the shadow of a rundown apartment house. A group of young men huddled on the sidewalk see me and slither off in all directions. I'm thinking gang retaliation.

One of them lurches awkwardly toward the corner, his baggy clothes making him look smaller than he probably is. I can't tell if he's got a bad leg or he's got a shotgun tucked down his pants. For whatever reason, he's the one I focus on as the rest of the group disappears into the darkness.

I put myself off on the radio. "Hey," I say as I bank my car into the curb and jump out. "What's going on tonight?"

He mumbles something I can't make out and then turns away from me. I light him with the flashlight and close the distance between us at the same time. "Keep your hands where I can see them!"

I'm almost on him, but I can't see either of his hands. Still facing away, he's fumbling with something down his pants. I'm sure it's a gun. I grab one arm with my free hand and spin him around. In an instant I realize it's not a gun. A flexible hose-like appendage springs from his trousers. A clip flies off and a putrid liquid squirts all over my leg. He tries to grab the end of it, but it's roiling around like a pressure hose. Finally, he gains control and directs the stream away from me.

"Colostomy bag," he says with some irritation.

"I see that." Shaking what I can off my pants before it seeps into the fabric, I release my grip on him. I take the light out of his eyes. The kid's a gang member, or former gang member, who was shot last year in a drive-by. However small the consolation, at least I had been right about the gang thing.

I start to explain what I thought he was doing, and he nods a cutoff to my words. It's clear we're both embarrassed, and to say anymore would be useless. He stoops to look for the clip, and I help him with my light. He finds it and clamps the end of the hose.

10:00 p.m.

I hit the station for a quick pants change and hand wash. I telephone dispatch and ask if I'm clear to take my lunch.

"We have a call holding on your beat and the midnight shift is still in lineup," she says. It's a missing child, so I decide to take the call first. The house is only a short distance from the police department, on the other side of the freeway near the mall.

I pull up and notice baseball team banners taped up on every window. It's familiar to me, and I think I might have taken a call here once before. When I get to the open door I remember them. It's the home of a mentally retarded man and woman who are raising a normal son. The living room is sparse; three folding chairs in front of a small television. Beyond that is an open kitchen with a table set for dinner. They're both standing in the kitchen hugging each other and crying. They see me and both run over to tell me their son is missing.

The husband holds up a finger to the wife, "One person at a time, Martha!" With her quietly holding his hand, he tells me that Ronnie is seven years old and has been gone since this afternoon. Apparently he missed dinner, but instead of calling the police, they've been out looking for him themselves. I broadcast Ronnie's description over the radio for the benefit of assisting units.

Almost immediately, the unit based at the mall comes on the radio. "He's been walking around the mall since closing. I have him here in the security office—Ronnie Hanson."

As the officer transports the kid home, I explain to the parents that he's been walking around the mall and he's okay. They cry again when they see him getting out of the car.

"Ronnie! Don't you ever do that again," they both take turns chastising and hugging him. It's clear that the boy just got carried away looking around the stores, and probably lost track of the time. Once the stores all cleared out at nine, the kid drew the attention of the security staff.

I take a quick look around to make sure they're capable of caring for him. There's adequate food in the refrigerator, clothes are stacked neatly on a small table in his room, and three toothbrushes, all color coded, hang from a mounted holder in the bathroom. It's not the cleanest house I've ever been in, but it's a long way from neglectful. Sadly though, they haven't got much in the way of furnishings.

I give them my card in case they ever need anything. I circle the 9-1-1 number on the back, and tell them to call right away the next time Ronnie is missing. As I leave, all three of them are sitting down at the table. It's a cold meal of meatloaf and string beans, but they're happy to be eating it as a family.

12:20 a.m.

I clear the station after my lunch and a little report writing. I'm just about finished the Malaki arrest, but still need to work on the dead grandpa report. I hope it's quiet. Just as I'm backing into a protected spot in front of my old school, I'm called to cover Thurmond Morris, the midnighter who's also on my beat. He's stopped a prowler near the back of a shoe store downtown.

When I get there, I see another car with two cops in it has also stopped by. All three cops now form a semicircle around the suspect. They wave me over, so I get out of my car. The words of a recycled old joke run through my mind: *How many cops does it take to arrest a prowler?* Of course the original joke, as I remember it, had something to do with Polish or Italians and nothing about arresting a prowler.

As I approach the group, I see a figure in a crouching position between the officers. *What the hell?*

"You're gonna have to remove it, sir."

"I'm trying," says the prowler. I'm able to view him more clearly now, and I see he's wearing pink lace lingerie that's right out of Victoria's Secret. A teddy or camisole, with garter straps holding up matching stockings. His thick torso and beefy legs couldn't contradict the outfit more. With the mild amusement quickly passing, I'm now wondering what they're trying to get him to remove. The squatting position is clue enough for me.

"I'm outta here," I say as I head back to my car. I pull forward to leave and my headlights illuminate the distasteful conclusion. The "prowler" is escorted to the police car in handcuffs—the string of the pink thong panties wedged into his hairy asscrack. With one hand on his prisoner, Morris's other (gloved) hand carries a gargantuan rubber dildo. *Nasty!*

12:45 a.m.

I'd like to get back to my writing spot before any other distractions happen. I take a side street back toward the school, and see something that I know is going to be a *distraction*. A large blue Chevy Impala with no lights is driving slowly down an alleyway behind a bar. On one end of the continuum, it might be nothing more than a forgetful driver, in which case I probably won't even write them a ticket. More likely though, it's a drunk trying to sneak home. Then, at the far end of the scale, it could be someone casing to do a robbery at the bar, just as they close with the day's receipts.

I circle around and put myself off on the radio just as I pull up behind the Impala. It stops immediately, leaving me in an uncomfortable position down an alley and out of view from the street. The situation worsens when I get to the driver's window. I see there are four Latino guys in the car, all wearing gang attire. While the driver gets his license out for me, I step back and peer into the backseat. The one in the back, closest to me, appears to be asleep. I spot an unopened bottle of beer on the floorboard between his feet.

In a momentary lapse of judgment, I reach into the backseat to grab the beer. My thought is that I'd like to secure my evidence before he gets a chance to discard it. However, in the second it takes me to reach my hand in, the previously sleeping passenger grabs my wrist with both hands. I pull back, but I'm off balance and his grip is too tight. My watchband snaps and the watch falls into the car. By now, the driver has jumped out and is behind me. He throws a chokehold around my neck and wrenches it tight. I finally get my hand free and push backwards into the driver, hoping to free his arm from my neck before I pass out. The rear passenger springs out of the car, and charges at me with the bottle in his hand. He raises it high and slams it down with a crashing blow, right across the top of my head.

Meanwhile, the other guys are out of the car trying to get their licks in. The guy behind me manages to rake my face with his fingernails while I've got my right elbow locked tight against my holster. Fortunately, none of them have made a move for my gun. I'm still conscious though, and trying to wage a decent fight. My intensity is aided by the likelihood that if I loose my gun, it's all over for me. I manage to break free of the chokehold and knee one of them. I also flip the switch on my radio, sending out an emergency signal that I'm in trouble.

I take a couple of shots in the ribs, neither of which do much damage, thanks to my bulletproof vest. The guy on my back, the one who loves to scratch, gets me another good one from the top of my forehead down to my chin. As I continue fighting them, I feel blood dripping down my nose. Whether it's from the bottle over the head or the scratches, I can't tell. I hear sirens, and I'm hoping my partners can find me back here behind the bar.

It takes what feels like a few hours, but is probably only a minute. The red and blue flashing lights, the tires squealing, the radios blaring, and the spotlight in my eyes never seemed so good. When the dust settles, my academy roommate, Timmy, has one guy on the ground and is tuning him up pretty good. I get the driver in handcuffs, and the other two are taken down by two sergeants who showed up. One of the sergeants, a heavyset woman, uses her weight to squash the guy into submission.

I'm banged up pretty good, and with the scratches and knot on the top of my head, I look much worse than I really am.

It takes me the next two hours to write that report, and another hour to finish the Malaki paper. The sergeant lets me put the dead guy on hold until tomorrow. "He ain't going anywhere tonight," he says.

By the time I'm done, most of my squad is gone. Timmy sticks around to help me with statements and logging evidence. He's a good man.

4:30 a.m.

I get home and see I have about 10 minutes before Gale's alarm goes off. I clean up in the kitchen, and take off my clothes there so she doesn't hear me. I tiptoe around to the far side of the bed and crawl in as quietly as I can. I face away from her, so there's no way she can see my injuries.

With a sudden click of the clock radio, a soft tune begins to play. Gale quickly shuts it off, and I can hear her slide out of the bed. I'm waiting for her to close the bedroom door on her way out, but the room is silent. Her tiny footsteps sound like they're headed in the wrong direction, and I casually tuck my head beneath the blanket. I resist the temptation to open my eyes to see where she is, but I have the feeling she's very close. Slowly, I edge one eye open and peek out of the blanket. I'm looking directly into her eyes, only inches away.

"I knew it!" she shouts. "I knew something happened to you, I could tell by the way you got into bed."

I tell her I'm fine, and not to make a fuss. She never listens when I do that valiant macho thing, and in reality, I'm glad she doesn't. Instead, she takes the first aid supplies out of the medicine cabinet and gently fixes me all up. The more I pretend I don't need it, the better it actually feels.

Although I assure her it won't happen again, I know there will likely be many more nights when I'll come home bruised and battered.

Chapter 10

7:30 a.m.

Even through tiny slits, my eyes burn as if someone squeezed lemon juice into them. I only got two and a half hours sleep last night, and I've got to get up for court this morning. At least I don't have to work tonight.

Gale looks at me strangely as I stumble into the kitchen.

"Subpoena," I say in my croaky morning voice.

She's feeding breakfast to the girls, and I kiss them both before heading for the shower. Gale calls out to remind me that our new living room couch is being delivered today. It will be our first new one. The old couch was given to us by my in-laws when they replaced theirs. It's still in great shape, but the dark blue velvety material never went with the tans and browns in the room.

I stand in front of the bathroom mirror cinching my tie. We have the option of wearing a uniform with long sleeve shirt and tie, or a business suit when appearing in court. Since I don't keep my uniforms at home, I'm going to court in a suit. Even after showering I still look wrinkled and squinty, like a guy who only had a couple of hours sleep. The scratches on my face have had a few weeks to heal, and the last of the scabs have all but disappeared.

8:30 a.m.

I check in with the district attorney's clerk and she buzzes me inside. I give her the name of the DA handling the case, a guy by the name of Bill Canaday. I tell her that I called the subpoena hotline last night, and the case is still on for this morning. I had hoped it was postponed.

She checks her list of cases. "Hmmm. Don't have anything on it. You can have a seat in the waiting room and I'll let Bill know you're here."

It's a concealed weapon case I handled in the parking lot of Toys-R-Us two days before Christmas. As I read through a copy of the report I brought with me, it's all coming back. It was a crazy shift—one of my first after getting out on my own. The rain was pouring down and the parking lot was a flooded ant hole of activity—total chaos. A dispute over a parking place ended when one guy shoved a revolver in the other guy's face. He got his parking spot.

I was met by a store security guard and a victim who seemed more interested in getting into the store to finish his shopping. The car was still in the stall, but the suspected gunman was nowhere in sight. Both the guard and the victim said he was inside the store. *Great—an armed man inside a toy store at Christmastime.*

My sergeant and another cop showed up just as the suspect wandered out carrying a bag full of merchandise. We searched him, and when we didn't find a gun, we took his keys and searched his car. We found a loaded blue steel .38 revolver in the trunk. The guy went to jail and I wrote the report. Doesn't seem like a tough case to win.

10:09 a.m.

A sharp noise jolts me awake and I realize I've nodded off. The police report is in disarray on my lap, and I quickly check the corners of my mouth for drool. I touch bases with the clerk again to see if there has been any word from Canaday. She tells me that there hasn't been a status update, and that Canaday is now upstairs in court on another matter. I pick up a frayed, year-old magazine about fishing, and thumb through it for a minute or two before falling asleep again.

12:15 p.m.

After nearly sliding off the chair, I walk to the cafe for a cup of coffee. When I get back, the clerk tells me that she still hasn't heard from the DA.

"He should be at lunch by now," she says. "You might try the breakroom upstairs."

I find the breakroom full of scattered newspapers and guys in gray suits. They're all boasting and one-upping each other in that uniquely male way. One loudmouth in particular is sitting with his back to me. He's lamenting about an upcoming vacation to Disneyland with his family—says he doesn't think he can stand being at a place that doesn't allow any liquor. *What a family man.*

It gets quiet when I walk in, and I'm suddenly back in third grade delivering a message to Mrs. Billings in the Teacher's Lounge.

"Excuse me; I'm looking for Mr. Canaday?"

A couple of them nod toward the guy with his back to me. He picks up the paper without turning around. Finally, after an uncomfortably long time he says, "That'll be me. What can I do you for?"

"I'm here on the Jonathan Yancy case. Any idea when it's going to go?" I'm standing there with my dry eyes and my police report waiting for an answer, but he's going to do another one of his long pauses first.

Finally he yawns and stretches his arms. "Oh yeah, the Yancy case. It's been continued. I knew it yesterday, but didn't have time to call. Had a cocktail party to go to."

The last line got everyone in the room laughing pretty good. He never turns around to look at me, but just goes back to his newspaper. I stand there for a second looking at the back of his head, imagining a lot of things I'd like to do to him. A couple of one-liners go through my mind, but none that would make me look any better than him. So, I just turn and leave, hoping that someday he gets his.

1:00 p.m.

I bypass the police building and head straight for my car in the back lot. Though I'd rather not get tied up inside on my day off, one of the sergeants has other ideas. He yells my name from across the lot, and I walk back to meet him.

"Didn't know you'd be here today," he says. "Investigations lieutenant wants to talk to you."

I hold up my subpoena and start to tell the sergeant why I'm here, but he cuts me off. "Might be able to catch him upstairs before he goes to lunch."

The lieutenant's office door is closed and he's in there talking with a couple of the homicide detectives. I wait against the file cabinet in the hallway, wondering what in the world the lieutenant of investigations could want with me. Hopefully he's happy with some investigation I've done, and wants to compliment me on it. *Yeah, I wish.*

The lieutenant sees me through the window and motions me inside. The detectives keep their seats as I come in and stand to the side of them. Whatever he's got to say to me, these two guys apparently have something to do with it.

"Didn't think you were here today," he says. "Left a message with your wife at home." The detectives raise their eyebrows—an apparent reference that I'm now busted by my wife for being somewhere I shouldn't be. *Whatever.* I start to pull out my subpoena, but decide it's not worth the effort.

"Anyway," he says. "Do you remember a call up on Grandview about a year ago?"

I'm caught a little off guard. I've probably been on Grandview a dozen times. "Any specific kind of call?"

The lieutenant looks to the detectives. One of them flips open a notepad. "It was in October of last year. The eleventh, at ten after midnight. You were covering Rivas up there."

"Fireworks," I say, recalling the detail. "I think it was an anonymous informant." *Why would they be interested in this? Obviously it's something more than fireworks.*

"Do you remember anything else about the call? A vehicle? Any witnesses?" The detective is poised to write on his pad.

I take a minute to recall the scene. "No vehicles or witnesses. I got up there right behind Ernie; we looked around for a few minutes and then cleared."

They each exchange glances as I stand there.

"Something happen?" I rest myself against the lieutenant's bookcase, trying to use my body language to insist on my inclusion into their game.

"We've been working with Stanislaus County investigators," the lieutenant says. "They recovered a body a while back, a murder victim, and they believe it's our case."

The detective who hasn't said anything yet finally chimes in. "They've actually made arrests in the case, a couple of bikers who they believe kidnapped the victim, shot him, and dumped the body in their county."

I work fast to connect the dots. "You think the call on Grandview had something to do with it?"

"One of the guys they arrested is talking," the lieutenant says. "He claims they dragged the victim down the hill off Grandview and shot him. He told Stanislaus investigators that a couple of uniformed cops showed up and were out of their cars right above them. Apparently these guys had made up their minds to ambush you and Rivas, but I guess you cleared before they did it."

I'm at a loss for a response of any substance, and I find myself just shaking my head. "Wow," I finally say. "Guess we were pretty lucky."

They tell me they've already questioned Ernie about the call and he remembers it the same as me. It doesn't sound like anyone is upset with the way we handled it, just amazed that such a simple call ended up being much worse. I'm lost in the images of how much worse it would have been if Ernie or I had looked around even a little longer.

1:55 p.m.

I'm home in time to slide the old couch into the garage before the new one is delivered. My daughters make good use of the temporary space by running in circles around the empty living room. When the new couch arrives, they both fight to be the first to sit on it, and of course the older daughter waits patiently while the younger one sits there like king of the hill.

Gale suggests we donate the old couch to the Goodwill, but I have a better idea. I call the police department and get the number for Jimmy and Martha Hanson, the parents of the boy who went missing a few weeks back. I get in touch with Jimmy, and although it takes a few minutes to explain who I am and why I'm calling, he eventually grasps it.

6:15 p.m.

We load the old couch into the back of my truck. All four of us cram inside the cab and drive to the Hanson house. On the way, Gale reminds me that a lieutenant had called the house while I was at court. I tell her that I already spoke with him while I was there. She seems to sense something in my voice, but lets it go . . . for now. Probably because the kids are listening.

I don't remember the Hanson's address, but I recognize the house from the baseball pennants taped to the windows.

We get to the door and I see their living room is still decorated with three folding chairs and television set atop a TV tray. Jimmy is waiting at the door and Martha is clearing the dishes from the dinner table. Little Ronnie is racing around like it's Christmas morning.

Jimmy helps me carry the couch in while Gale compliments Martha on everything from her hair to her son. My girls are standing there watching Ronnie in amazement. Without a brother, they don't often experience that kind of energy.

In the light of the room, the couch actually looks brand new. Jimmy and Martha embrace each other as if they're about to cry. Jimmy keeps asking me, "How many dollars does it cost?"

I assure him that he can just consider it a gift from the police department. It seems like that's a little easier to understand than from my home to his.

Little Ronnie takes a running leap onto the couch and begins yelling, "We're rich! We're rich!"

His parents immediately admonish him. My girls are nuzzled against each other giggling—tickled by the whole scene. Gale thinks they are the cutest family she's ever seen, and I have to pull her away before we end up having them all over for a barbecue.

It's a happy ending to a day that didn't start out so well. We head home and I can't wait to get into bed early. I'm exhausted.

Gale asks me if there is more to the call from the lieutenant earlier in the day. I give her a slightly sanitized and shortened version of the story—partly not to worry her, and partly because I can barely keep my eyes open. She rests her hand on my chest without saying anything more.

11:43 p.m.

I'm sitting up in bed with the phone in my hand and I don't know why. I'm trying to shake myself out of one of those deep, deep sleeps that you wake up from and don't even know what day it is.

"Hello?" a strangely familiar voice squawks into my ear. "I'm calling from the police department. Are you there?"

"Yes," I finally say. "I'm here."

"We've got a situation . . ."

I'm finally awake enough to understand her. Although I can't picture a face, I know the voice belongs to one of the dispatchers. What I can't understand is why she's calling me.

"We're calling in all SWAT team members," she continues. "The commander wants to know how long it'll take you to get here."

It's like she injected me with a strong stimulant. "Tell him I'll be there in fifteen minutes. No, make it ten."

One of the things I've been told about SWAT callouts is that you're never called out when things are going well. Not even when they're going bad. They only call you when a situation has deteriorated to the point that it can only be described as total pandemonium. The other thing I've been told is that they always happen at night, and usually when it's extremely cold. Although it is nighttime, the weather is warm. It's the kind of night where a dog's bark echoes through blocks of open windows.

I race to the station where I join a few others who live close by. I change into our *special* uniforms—dark blue jumpsuit with darkened patches that make us more difficult to see. We're all asking one another about the call, having only secondhand bits and pieces up to this point. The station has pretty much emptied out, with the exception of dispatch, jail staff, and clerks. As a result, there's really nobody left to ask.

We grab a set of keys off the board and the four of us, along with all our gear, squeeze into a black and white. I end up in the backseat behind the security screen, which given my inclination toward claustrophobia, doesn't thrill me. To mitigate it, I keep my door cracked open. One guy is working the lights and siren while the driver handles the radio.

We're given the location and a few details from dispatch as we clear the back gate. A patrol sergeant has set up a command post on Berry Avenue, near a gated apartment complex where the incident is occurring. We're told that one officer has been shot, and the watch commander is pinned down behind his car in the parking lot of the complex.

The new information increases our speed by about double, making me rethink the wisdom of keeping my door open. The group nearly loses me as we slide around one particularly sharp corner. I find myself wondering if I'll even make it alive to the actual call. We turn onto Berry and the street is lit up like Rockefeller Plaza at Christmas. There are ambulances, fire trucks, and police cars stacked shoulder to shoulder—all with their lights going. A young officer attempting to control traffic, lifts the yellow crime scene tape and directs us to a large SWAT van illuminated with generator-powered search lights.

As we unload our gear from the car, I hear gunshots coming from the complex. A flurry of radio traffic follows. The intensity must be a little too much for another guy, Louis, who is also new to the team. He's standing right next to me fiddling with his rifle magazine when a loud crack nearly deafens me. A round goes whistling over my head and I instinctively drop to the ground. The other two guys run over thinking I've been shot, but I tell them I'm okay. There's some chatter on the radio about another gunshot coming from outside the perimeter, and we all stand there looking at the smoking rifle in Louis's hands. He sighs into his radio, "Accidental discharge at the command post."

A patrol sergeant steams over and nearly clocks Louis. It's clear that everybody's nerves are frayed, and nobody's going to look forgivingly upon a dumb mistake. I flatten my hair with my hand, and again wonder if I'm ever going to make it to the scene.

The sergeant begins to brief us, then stops suddenly when another car pulls up carrying the SWAT commander and one of the team sergeants. We're relegated to listening to the briefing over the shoulders of the command group. What we hear is kind of a good news - bad news thing. The cop who was shot took a shotgun pellet in the foot, and he'll be fine. On the flip side, this situation is far from under control. The watch commander is still pinned behind his car, which now looks like Swiss cheese, and there's a gunman still on foot inside the gates of the complex. He's carrying a shotgun and wearing a bandolier of ammunition crisscrossed over his chest. To give the situation just another element of challenge, he's shot one of his neighbors in the neck. The poor guy is calling dispatch from his apartment, pleading for someone to help him. He's in there bleeding to death, but nobody can get to him because the gunman is still mobile.

Since I'm one of the newest guys, I doubt I'll get any of the good assignments during this operation. However, I'm hoping that since I'm one of only a handful of team members here so far, perhaps my brief tenure will be overlooked.

One of the snipers needs a ladder. I'm tapped for the job, along with the cop who almost shot me. It's not exactly what I was hoping for but it's better than nothing. We're on one side of the driveway, and the sniper wants to get onto a building on the opposite side. He's waiting for the ladder and there's obviously some urgency. We could play it safe and carry the ladder all the way around the block, or we could simply hustle across the exposed driveway and hope for the best.

We decide to cross, but do so in the shadows of the building directly across the street. We'll be exposed a little longer but we'll be more difficult to see. We each grab an end of the ladder and trot to a safe spot behind a parked utility truck. I look down the street behind me and see a bunch of news media vans. The reporters are gathered behind the crime scene tape with their bright lights and cameras, vying for a long distance shot of some action. I look across the street to the dark parking lot where I know the watch commander is lying behind his disabled car. I also know that somewhere in the shadows is a nutcase bent on killing someone before this night is over. I just want to make certain it isn't me.

We count to three and then run across a long open paved expanse, carrying a 12-foot extension ladder. When we're about half way across, there's a flash of light from the parking lot followed by a loud cannon-like explosion. *He's shooting at us!* The window above me shatters and I'm showered with tiny shards of glass the remaining twenty yards of our sprint. Another rapid volley of transmissions and then the radio is quiet again. The short silence provides a momentary reflection. I realize that only thirty minutes ago I was asleep in the safety of my own bed. In as many minutes I have been shot at twice—once by a crazed gunman and once by one of my own guys.

Transfer of the ladder is accomplished, and I now have to decide whether to cross back again. This time the only urgency is my desire to get in on the real action. I'd hate to be stuck delivering ladders when I could have been part of an assault team. The cop that came with me decides to stay and backup the sniper. I dart back across the open area to the command post. This time there is no gunfire.

As I'm waiting there for another assignment, a new barrage of gunfire erupts. Everyone freezes in place. A veteran cop, a guy who goes by Caldwell, comes on the radio. He reports that he took a couple of shots at the suspect, and thinks he hit him. Caldwell had evidently made his way into someone's second-floor apartment, and spotted the armed man from a bathroom window. With only his handgun, Caldwell took the shots. He says that in the darkness of the parking lot he can't be sure if the suspect went down or not.

The watch commander, who has been uncharacteristically quiet until now, comes on the air and says he can see the suspect on the ground. A team is hastily organized to enter the parking lot to make sure the suspect is *neutralized*. One of the team sergeants calls me over and I'm sure I've been tapped to go in.

"The investigators need someone to assist them," he says. "They need license numbers and descriptions of all the cars in the parking lot."

I nod my acknowledgement, unable to find the words of thanks. So, as the assault team rolls out, single file, into the thick of the action, I head back to the car for my clipboard.

They find the suspect dead of a perfectly placed gunshot wound in the back of his head, and they quickly evacuate the injured neighbor. I begin the lackluster task of recording information from 79 parked cars.

In short order, the investigators determine that the suspect is a resident of the complex. They identify his apartment, and another entry team is assembled to search it. Once again, I am not part of it. Only this time I'm not as disappointed. Turns out, our suspect had planned all this well in advance. He had taken the 220 volt outlet supplying his clothes dryer, and connected it to the metal handle of his front door. His plan, apparently, was to construct a booby-trap for the police, whom he knew would search his apartment after he was either arrested or killed. Thankfully, the team entered through the glass sliding door in the back and none of them were injured by the contraption.

Lights are on in the apartment next door, and there's a new fear that the suspect's bullets might have pierced the wall, injuring yet another neighbor. Nobody answers the door, and a third team is organized. This mission is more of a welfare check though, and I'm still not part of it. They force the door and find it unoccupied. Surprisingly, it's a giant greenhouse full of budding marijuana plants. They determine that it has no connection to our shooting suspect or his activities. The narcotics unit is now called out to pick up that part of the investigation.

The excitement for me wore off about a dozen cars ago. I finish my assignment in time to see the taillights of the last SWAT vehicle disappear around the corner. Even the media trucks are wrapping up. I find the investigations supervisor and give him my list of license numbers and vehicle descriptions. He doesn't seem to know anything about it, but thanks me anyway. I catch a ride back to the station with one of the patrol cops.

4:15 a.m.

Sliding into the cold side of the bed, I begin slowly inching southward.

I finally stop against Gale and hear her mumble, "How did it go?"

"Fine," I say, warming myself against her. It takes only a minute and I'm in a deep sleep again.

Chapter 11

5:00 p.m.

We've all gotten our hair buzzed. It was kind of a dare after work last week and almost all of us did it. I was a little self-conscious until I came in here and saw the rest of the squad looking as goofy as I do. They're collecting money for choir practice tonight, so I dig deep and throw in a few bucks. I just hope I'm not left in the report writing room again. At least it's our Friday.

Everyone is eyeing Pigeon, the guy notorious for bugging out halfway through the shift on our last night. He's also the only one on the squad who didn't get his hair chopped off. The envelope stops in front of him and he passes it on without putting anything in. The guy next to him hands it back, "You forgot to kick in your share."

"Oh, I don't like beer," Pigeon says. "I'll pick up some sodas for myself and anyone else who wants them."

Nobody presses him, but a couple of guys look like they want to kick his ass. It's not because he doesn't drink, it's because they know he's planning to sneak out again and leave the rest of the squad to cover his beat. *I'm beginning to wonder if he's got something on the sergeant.*

5: 40 p.m.

Since I'm working downtown tonight, I figure I'll take a spin through Wienerschnitzel for something to hold me until my break.

After that, I'll cruise down the street with all the stately old mansions.

I bite into my first of two chili cheese dogs and they call my identifier. It's a burglary alarm at the former mayor's house—on the same street where I was already heading. I've been to Mayor Lowe's residence several times before I became a cop. His daughter hosted most of our high school parties, probably because she had the nicest house in the class. The parties were tasteful catered affairs, though, and everyone respected the family enough to behave themselves. In fact, her parents were always in the next room watching television while the parties were going on.

I park a few houses down and walk up, so I don't telegraph my arrival. There are no cars in the driveway and the front of the place looks okay. There's a detached garage to the side of the driveway and I can hear something inside. I turn down my radio and listen. It sounds as if someone is rummaging through things. As another cop pulls up, I quietly motion to her that there's someone inside. She radios for a K-9 unit and then takes a position at the opposite end of the garage.

It suddenly quiets down inside. I have the feeling that whoever is in there knows we're here. It stays silent for several minutes, almost as if the person thinks we'll just leave. We don't. The dog arrives and they take a position right outside the rollup door. When the handler nods to me, I call out to whoever is inside.

"This is the police department; whoever is in there come on out with your hands where we can see them."

There's a rush of sounds, boxes moving, something being dropped, and clinking of glass. Nobody comes out. I nod to the K-9 handler and he gives his rote warning. He says it so fast that I can barely understand him.

"This is the police department canine unit. You have ten seconds to give yourself up before I release the dog. The dog will find you and will bite you." He never even has a chance to count to one.

"Hey, whoa, don't do that. I live here," a distinctly African American voice calls out from the garage. I might not be able to recognize Frank Lowe's voice when I hear it, but I can recognize when a voice is not his. And this guy isn't him. First of all, Frank Lowe is a huge, Santa Clause looking white man. He's also getting up there in years, and he can't move around with even half of the gusto that I've heard from this guy.

We throw open the garage door. A skinny, scruffy, homeless-looking black man is stretched out comfortably on a chaise lounge. He's wearing sunglasses and he's wrapped in a flannel bathrobe that I can only assume belongs to Mr. Lowe. The best part is, he's sipping a cocktail from a martini glass as if he's watching the Kentucky Derby.

If there was any consideration given for good acting, I would have to let this burglar go. He tips up the dark glasses to see us as he takes another sip of his drink.

"You live here?" I ask over the K-9's incessant barking.

"Why yes, I do."

"You're Frank Lowe?"

"Why yes, I am."

"You're the former mayor of this city?"

He pauses for a moment, figuring he might as well play it all the way. "Why yes, I am." He gets off the lounge chair with his drink in one hand and the other extended toward me. "And I hope you vote for me when re-election time comes around."

He gives me his best politician handshake accompanied by a broad smile. I smile back and shake my head. His grin slowly melts and his shoulders drop. He shakes his head to mimic mine.

"No?" he asks submissively.

"Sorry, no." I could tell him I know the real homeowner, but I don't have to. He already figured it out.

He sets his drink down, turns around, and clasps his hands together behind his back. "Damn."

6:33 p.m.

I pull into the police lot with Mr. Antonio A. Coleman III in my backseat. With the exception of a little gin, nothing was missing from the Lowe's garage. There was no force used to get in, and it's a tossup whether the district attorney will even charge it as a burglary. I suspect they'll reduce it to a misdemeanor trespassing, and extend the probation Mr. Coleman is already on.

There's a garbled transmission over the radio, and I see a commotion in the police lot ahead of us. It looks like two cops are wrestling someone to the ground. I throw the car into park and jump out to help. The back door of the building flies open, and out of my periphery I see more cops coming. Some of them in uniform and some in plain clothes.

I get to the dogpile, and I'm stunned to find that it's another uniformed cop they're fighting with. *What the hell? Who am I supposed to help?*

Something about the cop on the bottom doesn't seem quite right. I look closer and see it's a woman with long black hair and no shoes. She's in uniform, but it doesn't fit her very well. She's also kicking, scratching, and biting at the two cops who're trying to control her. I reach into my belt and pull out a small section of rope we call a *hobble*. As they get the handcuffs on her, I loop the hobble around her feet. The free end has a snap-latch, which I fasten to the handcuffs. It basically hobbles the woman's hands and feet together behind her.

All the other cops who had come to help are standing there as dumbfounded as I am. The back door flies open again and another cop comes running out in a panic. His name is Gary, and he's wearing nothing but a bath towel. Now everybody is looking at him, dumbfounded.

The door flies open again, and this time it's one of the captains from upstairs. He takes a look at Gary in his towel, then at the uniformed woman bound up like rodeo steer.

"Somebody want to tell me what the fuck is going on?" He eyes the rest of the group as he waits for an answer.

"She stole my uniform," Gary says.

"She escaped from the jail," pipes someone else. And then, little by little, the story starts to fall into place. Apparently, this woman has been in custody since this morning on drugs and weapons charges. She's so thin that she was actually able to squeeze her body through the phone slot in the cell. I'm talking about a rectangle no bigger than 10 inches by 14 inches. Once outside her cell, she gnawed through the plastic tarp that the work crew put up over the newly constructed section of the jail. *I knew that tarp idea would backfire.*

She was able to get all the way out to the back lot, but then instead of simply climbing the cyclone fence to freedom, she decided to don a disguise. So she finds her way back inside the building, and slips down the hall into the men's locker room. Gary is so busy lathering himself with Irish Spring that he doesn't notice the woman lifting his uniform off the hook just outside the shower. She slides her wafer-thin body into the uniform pants and shirt, and then heads back out into the parking lot. Two cops on their lunch break happen to see her, and the fight is on. That's when I drove in with my burglary suspect. *Oh yeah, my suspect!*

I work my way through the horde of cops back to my car. It's idling just inside the gate, and Mr. Coleman III is comfortably watching the goings on from the backseat. He's managed to maneuver the handcuffs from behind his back to the front.

"Hope you don't mind," he says. "Cuffs were starting to hurt. What'd that lady cop do, anyway?"

7:28 p.m.

After booking Coleman, I reheat my hotdogs in the department lunchroom. Somehow they never seem to heat evenly. The dog is cold, the chili is warm, and the cheese is burning hot. Through trial and error, I've found that once I chew everything around together, it all goes down as at about the same temperature.

I'm sent to a theft report at La Casa Maria—an old two-story motel that houses an assortment of truckers, prostitutes, drug dealers, and innocent travelers, in its two dozen rooms.

"Contact the caller, Andre Bunton, in room fourteen."

I arrive to find Mr. Bunton standing on the exterior walkway in front of his room, waving his arms wildly and yelling something unintelligible. Others meandering around the motel grounds don't seem to take notice. More than likely they're relieved I'm not there to investigate them.

Clipboard in hand, I climb the stairs to the second floor. He's calmed down a bit, but I'm still having trouble understanding him.

"Are you Andre?" I ask.

He doesn't answer. Instead, he opens his mouth and points his finger all the way inside.

"You ate Andre?"

He frowns, shakes his head, and points more vigorously.

"Your tooth is named Andre?" I continue the game of charades.

He rolls his eyes in disgust. "Day tole ma toot!"

It takes a couple of tries before I figure it out. "They stole your tooth?"

He nods with renewed enthusiasm and points into his mouth again. I shine my flashlight and there's a good sized gap in one particular spot. *But who would want this guy's rancid tooth?*

Andre tells me that it was a gold tooth, and according to him it has significant value. His story is that he left the tooth on his nightstand when he took a nap. He woke up, and it wasn't until he bit into a peanut butter pretzel that he realized it was missing.

I notice Andre's bad breath carries with it the scent of stale booze. We look around his room for the tooth, but other than the pretzels, cigarette butts and some empty beer bottles, there's nothing of interest.

"Who were you partying with?" I ask. It's a hunch based on the fact there are cigarette butts in the room, but no cigarette packs and no cigarettes on his breath.

Andre repeats my question before answering—a sure sign that what fallows will be bullshit. He stammers and starts with a story about someone breaking into his room. I stop him before he goes too far down that road. I pick up my clipboard and tell him I'm done unless he wants to tell me what happened.

Now the true story comes out. Well, almost true. He says he met a girl named Angel, and she and her "old man" came to his room for a couple of beers. When they left, the tooth was gone. He's sure Angel's old man took it.

My translation is that Angel is a prostitute and the guy is her pimp. They could also be a couple of other oddballs who got their kicks by having a threesome with Andre. It's a scenario I became painfully familiar with during my first foray into undercover work. Just for kicks I ask their descriptions, but they don't match my nurse and insurance agent friends. Which one snatched the tooth is moot anyway, because there's little chance we're ever going to find them. Andre says he met them on the street and has no phone number. I'm not sure what he expected me to do for him, but I take a report just the same. "Dispatch, I need a report number for a stolen tooth."

8:45 p.m.
Dispatch asks me to clear for a cover call. I give Andre a card with my name and the report number. As I'm coming down the stairs, a fire engine from the downtown station pulls out and turns west with its lights and siren on. I'm going to assume they're heading to the call I'm about to get.

I radio dispatch that I'm clear.

"Cover the David Unit on a report of a man down; A Street and Montgomery."

I follow the fire engine to the intersection where the man down was reported. Nothing there but a train stopped on the tracks, and a small group of people who have gathered off to the side. Think dispatch might have mentioned the "man down" is *down* because he was hit by the train? The other cop pulls up along with the sergeant. Bracing for what I already know is going to be a horrible scene, I'm both pleasantly surprised and saddened at the same time. With the exception of one bloody abrasion on his forehead, the body that was struck by the train is intact. However, I'm saddened to recognize that the dead man on the gravel next to the tracks is my Keep on Truck'n buddy.

His eyes are open, he's got his headphones on, and in a bizarre irony he's ended up laying in his trademark elongated stride pose. Nothing but a single mark on his head. I stand over him for a while wondering how it happened. I never even knew his real name. We always just referred to him as the "Keep on Truck'n Guy."

9:50 p.m.

Dispatch tells me I'm clear to take my lunch break, so I start toward the station. I'm just about there when they call me again. "Divert to cover the Adam Unit, responding to a violent family fight on upper D Street."

I'm backing up Felix which is usually worth a laugh, but the call doesn't sound like a good one. I hear Felix already arriving on scene. I'm almost at the station, so I have a pretty good distance to cover. I tell Felix that I'm still a long way out, and then I step it up. He comes back on the radio almost right away, sounding like he's in the middle of a fight. He yells for "expedited cover." I really put my foot into it now, with the lights on and the siren wailing.

I've written down the address, but it's really hard to see the numbers when you're going as fast as I am. I look for Felix's car instead. I'm racing down the narrow street at a pretty good clip, when I pass his car. It's parked at the curb, between two trucks and with no lights on. I nearly missed it. I slam on the brakes and crank the wheel, which sends me into a locked skid. The sound is horrendous. I'm stomping on the brake peddle as hard as I can as I slide toward the curb. I'm powerless to do anything at this point, and all I can do is hope I don't smash into anything. My front tire slams into the curb with a nasty jolt, and I jump out of the car. I hear hissing from my tire as I pass it, running toward what I hope is the right house. It's an old cottage. The place is just one of several dozen on this street, built back in the 20's, on small lots with no fences to separate them.

A young man suddenly sprints from around the back of the house. He sees me and veers across the front lawn. Felix tears around the corner in hot pursuit. Behind Felix is an older lady, running at a slower speed but making up for it with her mouth. She's yelling and cursing in what sounds like a mix of Spanish and English. I cut in front of her and join in the chase. Our quarry rounds another corner, heading for the back of the house. We sprint past the back door and around to the front again. As we pass the front of the house, we are joined by another young man—probably the brother. He's behind me but in front of the mother. Although I'm focused on keeping up with Felix, I don't really like the idea of this guy behind me. He could have a weapon of some type, and at the very least he'll be all over my back when we finally catch his brother.

I'm on my second lap around the house and I'm beginning to think it's funny. Then I come up with the bright idea to turn and go in the opposite direction. When I stop and turn around, the brother changes direction too, and heads for the front door. The mother rounds the corner toward me, and I see that she's wearing some kind of shower cap over a bunch of hair curlers. She also tries to change course, but slips and falls on the lawn. She's wallowing like a sea lion on a wet rock as I run past her.

I make the corner, now headed in the opposite direction, but I don't see Felix or the guy he's chasing. They should have been here by now. I continue back around the house and find Felix and the guy in a slugfest on the front porch. Another brother emerges from the front door, along with the one who had been chasing me. They throw a couple of blows that land on Felix's back. I'm almost at the porch, and as they see me they try to retreat back into the house. I manage to grab one of their shirts and there's a short tug-of-war at the doorway. I wrestle him out onto the porch, and now Felix and I each have a prisoner we're trying to take into custody. I end up on top of my guy with my knee buried in his back. Just then, brother number three reaches out from inside the house, and tries to grab me by the hair. With my new crew cut he comes up empty.

About this time the cavalry arrives. Felix and I get our two guys handcuffed and stuffed into a car. A couple of other cops storm into the house and come back out dragging the other brother behind them. Bosworth is the last of the cops to arrive. He bolts from his car just as Mom finally gets to her feet. Frustrated he didn't get in on the action, Bosworth dumps the old lady back on the ground and handcuffs her.

The sergeant shows up and we try to look like everything is under control—all being handled with the utmost professionalism. He takes a look at Bosworth straddling the old lady, then at the bent rim and flat tire on my car. Clearly, he isn't happy. I listen in as Felix's gives the sergeant his account of the incident. It sounds like it started as a fight between two of the brothers. When Felix arrived they turned on him. Sarge wants the old lady "dusted off", a practice used exclusively to prevent complaints from someone wrongly detained. Bosworth takes the handcuffs off her, and then spends the next 20 minutes basically kissing her ass.

Someone else has transported my guy to the jail for me. So while I wait for a tow truck, I get to watch Bosworth grovel. They replace the tire for me and I head for the station.

11:30 p.m.

I offer my suspect an opportunity to give a statement, but he wants nothing to do with me. Just as well. I work on my reports while eating the meatloaf sandwich Gale made for me. There's a note at the bottom of the lunch bag telling me to *be careful.* The radio sounds like things are slowing down around the city, and the midnight shift has finally hit the air.

12:33 a.m.

I get back out on the street with only two and a half hours left in my workweek. I could find a drunk driver easily enough, and that would take me right up to the end of my shift. I cut down a long thoroughfare that skirts the edge of downtown. A lot of people leaving the bars take this back way to avoid the main, well lighted streets where the cops patrol.

Ahead of me, a white station wagon pulls off a side street. It's heading the same direction as me and traveling very slowly. I'm sensing that I have my drunk driver.

I hit the lights and go off on the radio. The car pulls over under a canopy of trees that block the streetlights. With my flashlight turned off, I make my way around the back of my car and up to the passenger window of the station wagon. That way, I'm behind the lights and the driver won't know where I am until I tap on the window.

The driver is the only one in the car. He's a Mexican man, about 40 years old or so. I shine my flashlight through the window and he gazes into the beam, probably unable to see me behind it. His face is brown and weathered, and his hands are stained from years of hard work. He leans over and rolls down the window. It only goes half way, and he tries to explain that the handle is broken. His English isn't great but I get the picture. He gets out of the car and steadies himself with a hand on the door. It's pretty clear he's had too much to drink. His name is Ignacio Barajas, but he tells me that he's called *Nacho*. He digs through his wallet to find his license, thumbing through pictures of children in the process—a lot of them.

"Those all yours?" I ask.

There's a spark in his tired eyes. "Yes, I have nine children."

I ask him where he's coming from and he says he stopped for a drink after getting off work as a school custodian. He then tells me it's his only day off from his second job, a nighttime janitor in a convalescent hospital. I'm wondering what the difference between a custodian and janitor is, but I don't ask. I run a check, and find that he has no arrest record and a clean driving record.

I probe a little more and Nacho tells me that his wife is disabled. The car he's driving is their only car, and it gets his kids to school, his wife to her medical appointments, and Mr. Barajas to and from his two jobs. I know what will happen if I arrest him. The car will be impounded, he'll probably lose his license, lose his insurance, lose his job or jobs, and who knows what else.

"Mr. Barajas, do you have any idea what will happen if you are arrested for drunk driving?"

"Yes," he says quietly—his leathery hands clasped.

"Do you realize it would be even worse if you were to have an accident and hurt someone?"

He nods and makes the sign of the cross on his forehead.

I pull his car to a better spot off the road. I move my briefcase to the backseat and hold the passenger side door open for Barajas. I radio dispatch that I'm doing a transport run, and I drive the old guy home.

When he gets out he wants to thank me. He grips my hand in his and his eyes well up with tears. I think he's going to hug me, which would be all right, but he doesn't. I think he's too respectful of the uniform.

1:50 a.m.

I'm backed into a dark spot in the parking lot of a funeral home. The building sits adjacent to a large cemetery about 200 yards off the main highway. There are hardly any cars out and the radio is quiet. I'm working on my supplement report, describing my involvement in Felix's earlier fiasco on D Street. I'm nearly finished when sirens suddenly slice through the stillness of the night. I wait for a call over the radio, but none comes. A fire engine and then an ambulance make the turn off the highway, and they scream past where I'm parked. Still no call, and I assume it's a medical situation not involving a crime. I go back to my report.

A while later I hear a siren start up again. The ambulance passes me heading in the opposite direction, back toward the hospital. I've finished the report, and just start to proofread it when I hear a horrific noise. There's a piercing skid and the sound of a massive collision—metal on metal impact and shattering glass. The siren stops abruptly and there's total silence. I bolt upright and feel my heart thumping in my chest. I'm already putting it out over the radio and I've started my car. My paperwork flies onto the floor as I fishtail out of the parking lot.

The ambulance is lying on its side in the middle of the intersection and a large sedan is crumpled against a light pole on the near corner. The ambulance is completely dark and smoke is billowing from the engine compartment. One of the medics, a young woman, is helping an elderly woman from the cab of the upended ambulance. Another medic crawls out the back door pulling a fireman by the sleeve of his coat. The fireman's face is covered with blood, and large chunks of glass are imbedded in the torn flesh.

I help them out, and we lay the fireman on the sidewalk just as the engine pulls up. I ask the medic what I can do to help and she looks anxiously at the smoking ambulance.

"If we don't get the oxygen shut off, that whole thing is going to blow sky high!"

I'm thinking it's more appropriate for the firefighters to do, but they're tied up helping their comrade. The other medic is over at the sedan, checking what appears to be two women inside. I glance at the ambulance realizing that the longer I take, the more dangerous it becomes.

Between the darkness and the smoke I can't see much, even with my flashlight. I'm on my hands and knees crawling around the back of this ambulance, and I'm thinking it's about to blow up. I hear hissing from the oxygen tank, and use the sound to guide me toward it. I'm crawling over broken glass and assorted pieces of equipment that I'm not familiar with. I suddenly find myself on top of something odd and squishy. I reach down and feel skin. My heart jumps again and I keep going, finally feeling my way to the oxygen shutoff. I back my way through the smoke as fast as I can.

"There's someone in there?" I ask breathlessly.

The medic motions me away from the old woman. "It's her husband," she says. "We were transporting him to St. Theresa's before we were hit."

"Shouldn't we . . ." I motion toward the ambulance.

"We've already got three more ambulances on the way. The fireman goes first, then the two in that car." She points to the sedan. "The wife should get checked out too," she says motioning to the elderly lady. "But as far as the patient in the back, we had already lost him. We were just doing a PR transport."

More cops have arrived, and a motorcycle cop is assigned to take the accident report. I step back and watch the medics treat the two women in the sedan. In all likelihood, the accident was their fault for failing to yield to an emergency vehicle. I'm assuming they're both drunk as well. Yet, they are treated just as well as any other patient.

I have to wonder about the concept of a *PR transport* though. I assume it's nothing but a show for the surviving spouse; something to give them hope until they are ultimately told the truth. Their loved one has died.

3:00 a.m.

I drop my reports into the basket on the sergeant's desk. He glances up at me and nods.

"Night, Sarge."

I change in the locker room and head out the side door toward the courthouse parking lot. Most of the squad is there, gathered around a garbage drum that someone started a fire in, like a bunch of homeless people. There are chips, pork rinds, and beef jerky. And there's beer—lots of beer.

"Where's Pigeon?" someone asks. "Wasn't he supposed to bring his soft drinks?"

"Where the hell was he all night?" a guy named Bradford grumbles. He works the beat next to Pigeon, and out of all of us he has to pick up most of the slack.

Pigeon had left early again, taking half the night off on the sergeant's approval. The same guys from a couple of weeks ago are working themselves into a lynch mob.

There is more talk, more beer, some cursing, condemning comments, more beer, and finally a resolve to follow Pigeon on our next Friday night to see what he's up to.

"Hey, you gonna eat all those chips? Pass them over here," someone says, effectively ending the clan rally.

5:30 a.m.

I walk in and Gale's already up, stretching on the living room floor to an exercise tape. It's her few minutes of solitude before the girls wake up. I've stopped for donuts on the way home, and I'm holding one out like a gift, in case she didn't notice the big pink box.

She smiles, "Maybe later." I realize my timing sucks. She's working out and I'm trying to give her a donut. A dead giveaway I've been drinking.

"You smell like a campfire," she says between sit-ups. "Better throw those clothes in the wash."

I kiss the top of her head and leave the donuts on the kitchen table. I toss my clothes in the laundry basket and head off to bed.

Chapter 12

5:00 p.m.

There's an awkward feel to the lineup room. I look around and see the room is full. Training was cancelled for the guys working opposite us and they're all reassigned to the street duty tonight. I hear the tail end of a crude joke, and look back to see who's about to get us all in trouble with Internal Affairs. Chuckles, a traffic officer, sits behind me with his motorcycle boots on the desk and his mouth full of chewing tobacco. Traffic officers are supposed to attend lineup, though we rarely see them on our shift. They're an untamed bunch, and their sergeant is usually gone by 5 p.m. That gives the unit plenty of unsupervised time to run amuck. And they do.

The last time we had a sobriety checkpoint operation, they actually lost one of their guys. The checkpoint was a big deal, with lots of cops from all over helping out. The newspaper was there taking photos and working up a big story on all the drunk drivers we bagged. Suddenly one of the traffic cops went missing. They kept calling his numbers over the radio, but he never answered. Eventually, they had to close the checkpoint and reassign everybody to look for him. A search party finally found his car parked behind a strip club about a mile away. The cops who located him stayed pretty quiet about it, but rumor had it they found him at the end of the bar buggered up to one of the dancers with his face between her tits. He somehow managed to avoid getting in any real trouble though. Apparently, he had a few connections in high places helping him out.

Anyway, back to lineup. A new ball-busting sergeant just took over traffic, and I'm sure that's why we've been graced with Chuckles and his scuffed boots. He'll toe the line for a week or two, and then he and the rest of the traffic unit will be back to their shenanigans.

Somebody is collecting money again, which means it must be our Friday. Bradford's eyes meet mine and I know immediately what he's thinking: Pigeon's going to take another powder for one of his infamous *family emergencies*. Since there's a double shift on tonight we'll be able to get off early, and this time we're going to see what Pigeon's up to. Bradford nods at me and I nod back. Done!

The sergeant comes into the room and everyone quiets down. Chuckles refrains from his comedy routine, but keeps his feet on the table, just to be a jerk. The sergeant is unusually quiet. I would think we did something wrong, but we haven't had enough time to piss him off yet.

"I just got my ass chewed by the Captain!" he says to a silent room. Chuckles slips his boots off the desk. "And you guys are going to pay for it."

We all look at each other, wondering what the hell happened.

"There won't be anymore choir practices on our Fridays!" he says. "Did you imbeciles light a fire in a garbage can last week?"

Now nobody looks up. We're all staring at our clipboards, as if there is suddenly a very urgent bulletin we need to read. One knucklehead decides to mount a defense.

"We put out the fire with beer before we left," he says, "and piss." There's a murmur in the room that falls short of laughter.

"Well, thanks to you guys there's a garbage man with second degree burns to both hands. The fire may have been out, but that damn barrel was still red hot! We'll be lucky if we aren't sued."

Pigeon sits there beaming. *Suckass.*

"And what about Jack Dixon?" Sarge says. "His wife came out one morning a few weeks ago and found him taped to a goddamn stool on her front porch."

"Actually, Sarge, it was a lawn chair."

The sarge glares at the cop who said it. "Whatever! No more choir practice in the courthouse lot!"

It's a short lineup and we all head out to the back lot. The other shift shakes their heads as they walk to their cars, like we ruined it for everyone else. *As if they would never have done such a thing. Screw them.* The biggest concern now seems to be where we can go after work for a decent choir practice—not that it really matters to me and Bradford. If everything goes as planned we'll be on a surveillance of Pigeon.

5:29 p.m.

Some of the guys are doubling up due to a shortage of cars, but I'm solo tonight. The first call is to cover on a family fight at an apartment complex two blocks from the department. There are a couple of good things about double shifts. More cops are out here to spread the workload, and it's easier to get lost in the crowd. On a night like tonight when the sergeant is already pissed off, that's exactly what I plan to do.

I get to the apartment before the primary unit. He radios that he's held up in traffic. I walk through the interior hallway, and from the noises inside each of the apartments, it's difficult to tell which one we were called about. I find the right unit and listen at the door. It's quiet inside, so I knock.

"Police department."

"Come in, the door's unlocked." The man's voice is raspy and slurred.

I'd rather not, but then again I don't want to stand out here in the hallway all night. I step off to the side as I push the door open. No gunshots—that's always a good thing. I move out at an angle and see a white middle-aged couple sitting at a Formica table in a tiny kitchen. There are two things on the kitchen table, a nearly empty bottle of bourbon and a small serrated steak knife. However, both people seem calm, so I step inside.

"How's everything going tonight? I say, casually picking up the knife and placing it on top of the refrigerator.

The woman doesn't answer, just smiles. It's a peculiar smile that reminds me of a clown for some reason. I look to him for a response and he shrugs.

"Alright, I guess." He lets out a long wheezy breath, filling the room with the bouquet of his fermented stomach contents. I unconsciously groan.

"What's-a-matter? Having a bad day? the guy mumbles in drunken irritation. "Oh fawwk," he says to his wife. "You might as well just go ahead and show him!"

I look at her and she's still sitting there with her crooked grin.

"I did it," he says, slapping his thick, numb hands down on the table. "I cut her."

"Let me see," I say to her.

She starts to open her mouth and it just keeps opening. One side is sliced horizontally from the corner where the top and bottom lips meet. It's cut clean through to the middle of her cheek—about two good inches. Strangely, there is very little blood, and the whole disgusting wound is nearly camouflaged by her loose facial skin.

"Is that true?" I ask her. "Did he cut you with a knife?"

When she answers, it's apparent that she's every bit as drunk as him. Probably why it doesn't seem to hurt her much.

"We were arguing," she says. "He got mad at me for talking back. That's when he stuck the knife in my mouth. He said I was giving him 'too much lip', so he tried to cut my lips off."

The guy is nodding along with her as she's telling the story. He reaches for the bottle and I get to it first. "I think that's enough for tonight," I say.

He frowns like a kid who's been told he can't have any more cookies. The other cop comes in behind me.

"What do we got?" he asks in a chipper voice.

I look at the couple at the table. "Which one of you wants to tell him?"

I'm watching the cop's face as the woman starts to explain. From his disgusted expression, I can only assume her facial flap is fluttering like clothes on a clothesline. I've already seen the show, so I focus elsewhere.

The cop wants me to transport the husband to jail for him, while he accompanies the woman to St. Theresa's. I'd rather do it the other way around, but it's his case, his arrest, and his call. He's just trying to avoid the sergeant, same as me.

At the station, I read the guy his rights and take a written statement from him. He admits it without any sign of remorse, as if she got what she deserved. It's simple drunken logic. I leave the statement in the cop's mailbox and head back out to the street, having successfully steered clear of the sarge.

6:42 p.m.

Two quick beeps sound on the radio, followed by my call sign. Although three beeps is a high priority call, we really have nothing that spells out what constitutes two beeps. I can only imagine it's something that falls between sort of serious and really serious.

"Major injury accident, southbound Mission Boulevard near Fairway Park," dispatch says.

It's a long straight stretch of roadway at the southern end of the city. People tend to pick up a lot of speed out there, and my fear is that it's going to be a messy one. I hate car accidents anyway, because more often than not they involve innocent people who are the victim of someone else's stupidity.

I get to the scene before the fire department or ambulance. A couple of cars are pulled off to the side, and a motorcycle is lying in the middle of the roadway. Two people are standing next to their cars staring at what's left of the motorcycle. The front of the bike is smashed in, and it looks like the gas tank is charred and smoldering.

I ask if either of them were involved, and they say no. I ask if either of them saw the accident, and they say no. I ask if either of them know what happened to the driver of the motorcycle, and they say no.

There's a good size hunk of white fleshy meat on the ground next to the bike. I take a closer look to determine if it's part of the mystery driver, but there's no blood and it smells curiously like fish. My car is behind the bike blocking the roadway, which gives me ample room to move. I walk across all the lanes looking for smudges or grooves on the road that might be left by a tumbling body. There are none. I'm now looking off to the sides, over a fence, and up in a backyard tree. Could the driver have flown through the air and landed at some improbable spot? I'd hate to miss something like that.

I look further south on the roadway and something catches my eye. Near the front of a Jack in the Box restaurant, somebody's standing in the street waving their arms. The person is a good quarter mile up the road, definitely too far for the driver to have sailed, even if he had been driving at the speed of sound.

A traffic unit pulls up behind my car. Chuckles slowly gets off his motorcycle and props it up on its stand. "Whatda we got?" he says, spitting a brown blob of tobacco onto the pavement.

"Not sure," I say. "But whoever was driving this bike is missing. I'm going to drive down a ways and see if anybody at the Jack in the Box knows anything.

I drive to where the person was trying to flag me, and I see a couple of teenage kids in Jack in the Box uniforms milling around a cream colored station wagon. The car is parked at the side of the road with its right turn signal on. It's kind of a family wagon, with a roof rack and wood paneling along the sides. The back window of the wagon is shattered and there's a body dangling out of it. The upper part of the body has gone through the glass, leaving the rest hanging out the back. The feet actually touch the road.

The guy who had been waving his arms is standing off to the side, pale and stunned. Before I even get to the guy imbedded in the window, I hear gurgling and moaning. I get on the radio, and advise dispatch to have ambulance and fire respond past the accident site about a quarter mile south.

I've decided not to move the victim unless he stops breathing. On closer look, I see the side of his head is crushed in. I look at his feet and notice the tips of his shoes have been shaved off where they drug along the road. It amazes me that he hadn't fallen off during the ride from the crash site.

Once the fire truck arrives, I pull the station wagon's driver away from the restaurant kids and ask him what happened. It's clear to me he's one of those guys who hasn't had anything more serious take place in his life than a broken shoelace.

"Well, I just installed a new car stereo and speakers in my car." He's obviously started the story farther back than necessary, but I've got no place to go right now, so I just listen.

"I took it out for a drive so I could test out the sound," he continues. "As I reached over to turn on the stereo, there was a huge explosion, and a fireball came from the backseat. Look, it singed my neck hairs." He turns to show me a crinkled patch of nubs along his collar.

"I thought I had screwed up the wiring on the speakers and they had blown up, so I turned the stereo off right away." He stops to swallow as he's recalling the event. I give him a light pat on the shoulder and urge him to go on. "Well, I kept driving, and then I heard this really weird sound, like groaning. I thought it was coming out of the speakers, until I looked in the mirror and saw a guy jammed through my back window."

"Then what did you do?"

"I put on my turn signal and pulled over next to the Jack in the box." He motions toward the kids still milling around. "I went in and told them there's a dead guy in my car, and asked them to call 9-1-1."

"So they called for you?" I ask.

"No, actually they all ran out of the restaurant to see. I was the only one left in there, so I climbed over the counter and dialed it myself."

The ambulance arrives, and after taking down the man's information, I drive back to meet Chuckles at the crash site. He's taking measurements and recording them in his report. He shows me a paper bag and receipt he found beneath the motorcycle, indicating the driver had recently purchased four pounds of Ling Cod. It solves the mystery of the white gunk on the road.

As I go over the driver's statement with Chuckles, the new traffic sergeant drives up. Chuckles watches in dismay as the sergeant runs over the road flares he's just laid out to block traffic. A couple of them go out as the car rolls right up to us and stops abruptly.

"Fatal?" the sergeant asks nonchalantly through his open window. He flings the door open and comes out of the car, chest first, like a general surveying a battle scene. There's a squishy sound, and we all look down at his feet. He's standing squarely in the fish.

"What the hell?" he says. "What *is* this stuff?"

Chuckles shakes his head ruefully. "I'm afraid it's the victim's brains, sir."

As I'm driving away, I see the sergeant gagging while he feverishly chafes his boot against the pavement. *Way to score points with the new sarge, Chuckles.*

8:20 p.m.

As soon as the sun went down it started to get really cold. I pull over and grab my jacket from the trunk. Just as I'm getting back into the car, I get another call—a house fire. Although the fire department is already rolling, I'm only two blocks away. They could need me for anything from an arson investigation to guarding their precious hoses. It's usually the latter.

I look in that direction and see a golden haze illuminating the night sky. Now I know why they sent me. I beat the fire department by a minute or so, judging from the sirens. The back portion of the house is burning pretty good by now, crackling and popping like the Fourth of July. Bright red embers rocket high overhead through a gaping hole in the roof. I make my way through the crowd of gawking neighbors, looking for someone who might have an answer to the only question I have.

"Is anybody inside?" I say to a young man who's holding his wife and two children in a bear hug.

"No," he says with a panicked look. "Thank God we all got out."

"But what about the Pepper and Biju?" asks the little girl, her eyes as big and innocent as a doll. Without waiting for the answer, she buries her face into her mom's leg and begins to sob. Her brother's face slowly distorts, and he does the same on the other leg.

"Our two dogs," the father says. His expression is one of heartbroken resignation. The grip he's got his family say's, *I'm not letting go for anything—even the family pets.* I understand that.

I take a look down the block, but the firefighters haven't made it yet. Any second, I'm sure. With each one that passes, I watch as more and more of the house goes up in the raging blaze. I look back at the faces of the two kids, and start for the front door. It's an open mouth, growling and sputtering angrily, appearing almost unreal. It reminds me of a Halloween replica of hell, put up to scare the neighborhood kids. I hold my arm across my forehead, shielding my face from the intense heat. It does nothing. The furnace-like blast drives me back a few steps, and I immediately second guess myself.

Dropping to my knees, I start through the door again. I don't notice it being much cooler this low, but it's definitely less smoky. I can see an open kitchen, on the other side of the living room, across a tortoiseshell shag carpet. Beyond that, it looks like a step-down family room where the fire seems to be concentrated. The flames have already overtaken it, and the smoke makes it nearly impossible to see. I hear a faint sound of barking dogs and I crawl as close as I can, straining to see into the room. What's left of a small electric space heater lies on its side off to the right. It goes through my mind that it probably started the fire.

A heavy support beam crashes down, and I know there's no way I can go into the family room. As I'm backing out, I notice a dark hallway running off the opposite side of the living room. I use my flashlight to find my way through the smoke. I can stand now, but the light casts an eerie, slow-motion pallor, as if I'm moving through a dream. I get to a cluster of bedrooms in the back, where I find Pepper and Biju. They're huddled in the corner, barking and making small circles around one another. They're wagging their tails, but still reluctant to come to me. Without the luxury of time to bond, I tuck my flashlight back into my belt, leaving it on, and then grab each of the dogs under an arm. With barely enough light to see where I'm going, I run as fast as a guy can in a hot house, wearing a thick jacket and carrying two dogs. I weave my way back through the living room and out the front door.

Firefighters have already deployed their lines and are just starting to charge the hoses when I emerge.

"Anybody else inside?" one of them asks.

"Nope. It's all clear."

I move past the parade of trucks, hoses, and flashing lights, and find the family exactly as I had left them. The dogs start wiggling and squirming when they see the little boy and girl, and I have to drop to one knee so I don't loose my grip. There is a tearful, yet joyful, reunion as the kids nuzzle into the dogs. They respond back with wet noses and tongues. I realize it's been two minutes since we got out, and those two dogs probably don't remember any of it.

The parents thank me and I know it's sincere. Although, in light of what they've lost and the terror they've endured tonight, I'm uncomfortable with their praise. I know they'll all be haunted by this for a long time. Still, it's as happy an ending as I could hope for.

9:50 p.m.

I open my windows to get the smoky smell out, but it's useless. It must be imbedded in the fabric of my clothes. I've cooled considerably from the inferno of that house and I'm back to freezing. It seems to have dropped another ten degrees in the last hour. I leave the window open and turn the heater to high.

"Forty-six," the dispatcher says in a tone that's both apologetic and urgent. "Start for a . . ." There's a long pause, which always concerns me. It's never a good thing being sent to a call that dispatch doesn't even have a name for.

"Suspicious circumstance," she finally says using a catch all that only generates more questions. "We're not sure what we've got." There's a voice in the background, probably that of the call taker, relaying whatever she's being told on the phone. "We're sending the fire department as well. We've also got reports now of smoke coming from the same address."

I let out a sigh and click my acknowledgement without actually saying anything on the radio. It's a way to communicate displeasure without violating any radio policies. Sure, it's a little childish, but given the right set of circumstances, the simple act can be quite satisfying. First of all, I just came from a fire and I'm not really up for another one, especially if it involves, well, fire. And second; good luck getting the fire department to the call anytime soon. The firehouses in this part of the city are all pretty much empty because of the call I just came from. They'll probably have to dispatch a truck from the hills, which will take forever. The rational me knows it's not the dispatcher's fault. However, sitting here alone in my car, who else do I have to take it out on? Luckily the dispatchers know that. Likewise, I know that they're the ones who save me whenever I get into real trouble.

I hear her sending another police unit as a cover, confirming in my mind that there's something about this call they're not telling me. I guess I'll find out what it is soon enough.

The call is in an industrial area on the west end of the city. I arrive at a warehouse that shares a common driveway with an identical building configured in a mirror layout. The owner of that business, a muffler shop, meets me between the two buildings.

He points to the big rollup door where light can be seen through about a one-inch crack at the bottom. A wispy thread of smoke snakes out from the opening.

"I know they're in there," he says. "I banged on the door when I saw the smoke, but they won't answer."

My cover car pulls up and I see that it's Bosworth. My luck with him is never good. As we're walking toward the building, I tell Bosworth what the guy told me. I hold my hand up to the metal door, feeling for heat. It's as cold as the night. We listen for voices, but there aren't any. The low sound of a car engine idling somewhere inside the warehouse is the only noise we hear.

We nod to each other from opposite sides, grip the bottom of the rollup door, and lift hard. It rattles loudly as it retracts into its housing, and immediately a wave of grey smoke curls outward and upward. From a protected position off to the side, I peer into the bay. It's smaller than it appears from the outside, crammed with boxes and machinery and engine parts. An older model black Ford Galaxy sits in the middle of the acrid cloud, idling quietly.

"It's not smoke, it's exhaust." Bosworth, always quick to notice the obvious, then gets on his radio and cancels the fire department.

Meanwhile, I'm stepping through grease and over car parts to get a look inside the car. I don't have a really good feeling. I'm holding my breath because of the exhaust. I get right up to the car, and what I see stuns me for a second. Three grown men are seated upright in the backseat. I can only see their outlines, but they're positioned shoulder to shoulder as if enjoying a Sunday ride on a sunny country road.

I call out to Bosworth, who has gone back to talk to the guy outside. I've inhaled a bunch of exhaust now, and I'm coughing and hacking. I try the driver's door, but it's locked. They're all locked. The windows are down about an inch, but the space is too narrow to reach through. I pick up a socket wrench from the floor and bash out the glass with it. I unlock the door, open it, and turn off the engine. The men in the backseat don't move. I illuminate the ghostly trio with my flashlight. Two are around my age, mid-twenties, and the guy in the middle looks like he's pushing sixty. Their faces are gray and flaccid and their eyes are closed, as if they're asleep. No real sign of trauma, except that the one on the near side looks like he's vomited onto the front of his shirt.

"Oh, shit!" I hear Bosworth murmur over my shoulder. "I'll get the fire department started, again."

Ya think?

Bosworth and I carry the men out of the car and into the fresh air outside, one at a time. We lay them out, side-by-side, just like in news photos I've seen after a big disaster in India or Bangladesh. Only we don't have sheets to cover them, in fact, we don't know for sure yet whether they're alive or dead. We kneel down next to them and check for a pulse or breathing or any movement. There's none. Technically, we're supposed to begin CPR unless there are *positive signs of death*. That would be something like rigor mortis or their head is missing. Unfortunately for us, cold to the touch, no pulse and no respirations doesn't count. I find myself feeling that somehow Bosworth's bad luck is to blame for this. We've been through the same thing before.

Unexpectedly, yet happily, a fire engine pulls up right behind us. They've apparently gotten a handle on the house fire, and this engine company was cleared to help us. I suspect that dispatch ignored Bosworth when he cancelled them.

The paramedics work at half-speed to resuscitate the men, but it's pretty clear they've been dead for quite a while. The guy who works in the building across the way confirms he heard the car running inside the building for at least an hour before he decided to call. *Interesting.*

I mull it around in my head; is their any possible explanation, other than group suicide? I go back inside and look into the empty car. Doors locked, windows cracked open, engine running, and they're all in the backseat. I don't see any other probable scenario.

Something about the caller's responses gives me the feeling he knows more than he's saying. I walk back over to his shop. His place is littered with auto parts, too. They had to know each other fairly well.

"You don't seem all that surprised by this." I look him in the eye, not in an intimidating way, but obviously expecting a response.

He pauses for a few seconds. "No, not really."

I ask him what the relationship was between the three men, and he tells me the older guy is the father of the other two. I'm imagining me, my brother, and my own dad. It doesn't compute. Too weird for words.

"That's kind of strange, don't you think?" I'm looking at him and then over at the three dead men.

"They were kind of strange," he says, following my gaze. "I don't really know what demons they had inside, but they always talked about suicide.

"Did they discuss it with each other?"

"They'd talk about it with anybody. In fact, Pauley, the youngest one, tried to kill himself a few weeks ago."

"How do you know that?"

"I was there," he says. "So was the old man and his brother. Pauley just said, 'Hey, I'm gonna kill myself,' and then he ate some rat poison right in front of us."

"What did his father and brother do?"

"Nothing. They just said, 'Okay, do it. We'll do it too.'"

"Then what happened?"

"He got sick and the ambulance came. They pumped his stomach at the hospital and that was it. I guess they all decided to really do it this time." He turns and walks back inside his muffler shop.

A gust of icy air works its way up my back, and I'm not sure if it's the wind or this call. Either way, I'm left feeling cold and empty.

The fire department has decided to have the bodies transported to St. Theresa's, and two ambulances are sent. I'm not sure what my role is at this point, other than to write the suicide report. As much as I hate doing it, I call for a meet with the sergeant.

10:55 p.m.

I drive under the overhang of the closed and dark gas station, and Sarge pulls in from the opposite side. We inch up to one another, drivers' side window to window. I run the case down to him and he listens without a response. He takes a sip from a covered Styrofoam cup, and then carefully sets it on his dashboard.

"So, there's three corpses sitting down there at St. Theresa's?"

I nod. "On the way there now. The second ambulance arrived just as I was clearing the scene."

It seems he isn't any more certain about what to do that I am. After some deliberation, he tells me that I have to "guard the bodies" until the coroner's office picks them up. I say okay and start up my car, although I'm skeptical that there's any value in guarding bodies at a hospital. I suppose if it were a homicide case . . . which this doesn't seem to be. Well, if they had left the dead guys at the scene, I'd be standing guard out in the freezing wind. At least I'll be warm inside the ER.

"One more thing," he says as I start to pull away. "You can get out of here at midnight."

I give him a puzzled look, wondering if he's sending me home because I screwed something up. Am I in trouble for the bonfire last week?

"Bradford," he says. "He asked me if you two could get off early."

"Oh, yeah. Thanks, Sarge."

I almost forgot about our planned surveillance operation on Pigeon tonight. Bradford had actually borrowed his brother-in-law's car so Pigeon won't recognize he's being followed.

11:02 p.m.

St. Theresa's is hopping. All the beds in the emergency room are full, and a couple of CHP cops are towering over a drunk driver who looks like he's done a hard face plant in gravel. They nod to me and I nod back. The ER supervisor brings me about halfway through the room to a doorway next to the nurse's station.

"We had to put your boys in here," she says. I detect a note of pissed off-ness in her voice, so I tell her it was not my decision to transport them. Hospitals lose enough people on their own, I doubt they appreciate having cadavers delivered to them. I get that. Still, I'd rather be *guarding* them in here than outside.

I step into the room and it's a narrow storage closet. There's a sink and some janitorial supplies . . . and three dead men. The two brothers have been crammed onto a single gurney and their dad's has been wedged, head first, up against a hanging mop. The mop strings cover his head, giving the impression he's wearing a wig.

So much for the integrity of any evidence.

I check my watch and wonder if Bradford will wait for me if I'm here past midnight. I clip a blank report form onto my clipboard. Then, balancing it on the sink, I start hammering out the report. I'm using what little room there is on the old man's gurney as kind of a butt rest, intentionally not sitting all the way back against him. At first I keep looking at the bodies, I guess making sure they're dead. But after a while I stop looking.

11:43 p.m.

I'm startled by a sharp blast of an alarm. I've been writing straight through since I got here. I open the door into the emergency room and it's total chaos. The CHP guys are gone, but the beds are still full of patients. Nurses are running in every direction.

"What's going on?" I ask one of them.

"It's a fire!" she shrieks. "Come with me, we need you upstairs."

I hesitate momentarily, looking back toward the broom closet. I guess a hospital fire trumps guarding corpses. I follow her up the stairway to a critical care unit on the top floor.

"We need to evacuate these patients," she says. Some of the employees have already begun unhooking monitors and tubes full of bodily fluids. The hallway is backed up with rolling beds lined up for the elevator. It looks like the bridge approach at rush hour. These poor patients are too old, or too confused, or too sick to say anything.

"It's nearly freezing outside," I tell her.

"Hospital policy. We'll try to keep them as warm as possible." She checks her watch. "Hopefully they won't have to be out there long."

I grab the other end of the bed and work my way into the line of hallway traffic. I get on my radio and try calling for help from other units, but my radio isn't transmitting from inside the building. I'm looking for a phone and finally spot one on a desk. I call dispatch and tell them what's happening. They tell me that the fire department is on scene downstairs, and they're sending additional units to help with the evacuation.

The place is a madhouse. I don't see any fire or smell any smoke, but the alarm keeps sounding in alternating blasts. We get off the elevator downstairs, and the firefighters are already turning people around and sending them back up. I see a small group of beds out in the parking lot, each with a tiny head tucked beneath a pile of blankets.

"This is nuts," I say to one of the firefighters.

He shakes his head in aggravation. "You know what this was all about? A patient on the third floor tried to sneak a smoke and caught his pillow on fire. It was out before we even got the call."

He shakes his head again and skulks off. I glance down at the old woman in the bed I'm pushing. Her face is partly covered by a sweater someone had tossed over her. A weak pair of blues eyes stares back at me from underneath. I tell her everything is okay. I'm relieved of the bed by one of the nurses, so I make my way back toward the ER.

I find two bewildered coroner techs standing at the nurse's station. One guy raises an eyebrow and I say, "Don't even ask."

I show them where the bodies have been stored and they both look at me like: *You can't be serious.* They write me three receipts, one for each body, and that's that.

I walk out of the emergency room into the frigid night as the last displaced patient is wheeled past me. I check my watch—it's four minutes to midnight.

12:01 a.m.

I'm moving as fast as I can. I unstrap my briefcase, grab my reports and clipboard, turn off the radio, and check the backseat for anything dumped during the night. As I thread my way through the back parking lot, I hear, "Psssst!"

Slunk down in a brown Datsun hatchback is Bradford. He's wearing a maroon sweatshirt with the hood up and sunglasses.

"Hurry up!" he says. "The Pigeon's about to fly!"

I dump my reports with the sergeant, and head to the locker room where I change into my street clothes. I rummage around the tops of the lockers looking for something dark to wear over my white tee shirt. I find a black windbreaker, but it has "POLICE" printed across the back. I turn it inside out and slip it on.

"Did he see you?" Bradford asks as I'm getting into the Datsun.

"No, but I see his car on the other side of the lot. And I brought these." I hold out my hand showing him compact binoculars I've taken from my briefcase. Bradford peeks over the top of his sunglasses and smiles his approval. Satisfied that Pigeon will have to pass by us on his way out, we slink back down and wait.

12:13 a.m.

Pigeon waltzes out of the back of the building and heads for his car. The lightness of his step confirms he's up to something. If we're wrong, we just burned three hours of comp time for nothing.

Bradford lets out a childlike giggle as Pigeon drives by us without a care in the world. "We're going to find out what that little ass-kisser's been doing every Friday night."

"While we're getting hammered on *his* beat!" I add.

We wait a few seconds and then head out the back gate behind him. He hits the freeway heading north, and we follow at an even speed three or four cars back. We pass the city limits and we're approaching the turn off to his house. We consider the possibility he's going straight home, and really does have some family issues. When he passes his off ramp we give each other a high five.

Pigeon pulls off the freeway in Oakland, and then into a Safeway parking lot. We hover a few rows away until we find a parking stall with a decent view. Pigeon doesn't get out of his car. He's just sitting there in the dark. I wonder if he knows he's being followed, and he's watching to see who it is. Then, the light comes on inside his car and I grab the binoculars. Somebody gets into the passenger seat and quickly closes the door. All I see is a momentary flash of long blond hair.

Neither of us saw where she came from, but she was definitely moving quickly.

"I knew it was a chick," Bradford says with a clap of his hands. "We got that boy by the balls now!"

Pigeon and his *friend* drive slowly out of the lot, heading back toward the freeway. We maintain a safe distance, but keep him in sight. They take a turnoff heading west, toward the bay. They pass a few restaurants and a nightclub, and keep traveling west. We follow them over a small bridge into Alameda, an area neither me nor Bradford are familiar with. It's getting darker, and traffic has become almost non-existent after the bridge. We're forced to drop way back for fear he'll get hinked up.

He turns down a small driveway out of our view. We wait a few minutes before driving past. I glimpse his car, parked at the far end of a small paved lot next to a small row of wooden docks. The lot is dark, but there's a lamp dangling from a wire at the top of the boat ramp. It throws just enough of its pale light to distinguish the car from the murky bay behind it.

We maneuver our way to a raised area about 200 yards away. It's some kind of utility access road surrounded by low bushes, and it gives us a fairly camouflaged view of Pigeon's car. After about ten minutes, Bradford starts getting antsy. He wants to do some kind of low crawl up to the car and take a peek inside. It's freezing out there and the wind is blowing a fine mist onto everything.

We decide that I'll stay and watch with the binoculars while Bradford makes his move to the car. Then, Bradford throws open the car door before I can warn him about the interior light. It goes on, brightly illuminating me holding binoculars up to my eyes.

"Shit!" Bradford shuts the door with a clank. *Remind me never to do a serious surveillance with him.*

I watch as he works his way down the small incline, and then out of my line of sight. There is no change in Pigeon's car, so I'm assuming he's too busy doing whatever he's doing to have noticed the light. Bradford's dark figure suddenly comes into view, inching along the jetty behind Pigeon's car. He's got to be freezing out there.

He slides around to the far side of the car and he's out of my view again. I'm half expecting him to get caught or pound on Pigeon's car, but there's no sound and no movement. Several minutes pass before I see Bradford slide back towards the base of the access road. I quickly unscrew the overhead light bulb. Bradford appears at the door and jumps in, looking up at the empty socket as an afterthought.

"Well?" I say.

Bradford's too busy laughing to answer. Finally he chokes out, "They're doing it!"

"You're bullshitting me."

"No, I'm serious." Bradford rubs his hands together. "I listened at the side for a long time, but I couldn't hear shit. Then I poked my head up to the window."

"And you saw them screwing."

"Yeah. Well, not exactly. I saw Pigeon's fat ass up in the air and his pants down around his ankles."

"Could you see her?"

He shakes his head. "Poor thing was buried under that toad."

We sit there for a minute thinking about what to do next. Suddenly Bradford gets an eager look in his eyes.

"We'll call it in!"

Bradford leaves the lights off as we head back down the hill and out onto the main road. We pull up to a phone booth against the wall of a nightclub. A few seconds later, Bradford jumps in and we fishtail back onto the street. We return to our little observation point and he backs the car as far into the bushes as possible without losing our view. He tells me that he called 9-1-1 and told them there was a woman screaming. He described the location and Pigeon's car.

Within a couple of minutes three cop cars come whizzing down the road, blacked out. They descend on Pigeon's car, and then all at once they turn their spotlights on him.

There's movement in the car, and through the binoculars I can see Pigeon's shirtless back up against the window. It looks like he's trying frantically to get his pants back on.

"He looks like Sasquatch, trapped in a car!" Bradford and I are laughing so hard we're nearly pissing our pants.

The cops turn abruptly and head for their cars. They're clearly suppressing their own laughter as they start up and quickly drive off. We figure Pigeon managed to find his wallet and show them his badge. In some ways that's even more humiliating.

We wait a long time after Pigeon drives off before we leave.

3:00 a.m.

Bradford and I get back to the police station just as the rest of our squad gets off duty. They've moved choir practice to a park about two blocks away. Some of them are wondering where Bradford and I disappeared to for the past couple of hours, but we avoid the subject.

Bradford's eyes meet mine as he passes me a beer and we both start laughing. The others suspect something, but we don't give it up. It's all we can do to keep from telling them the whole story. It will get out sooner or later, it always does. Until then, we're keeping the whole thing quiet.

Chapter 13

5:00 p.m.

For the past couple of weeks, ever since our clever surveillance, Pigeon has been acting like everyone is out to get him. He must have told someone on the squad what happened during his midnight rendezvous because rumors are all over the building. The stories are even better than what actually took place. In any case, Pigeon hasn't figured out who did him, so he suspects everyone.

It turns out that a couple of the guys now feel badly for Pigeon. He's engendered sympathy by claiming that his wife somehow found out about his infidelity. I wouldn't have believed it except for an unfortunate coincidence that neither Bradford nor I could have predicted. Pigeon's wife knows someone on the police department where it happened. The cops who responded out there that night must have run Pigeon's license plate or recognized his name. From that point it was only a matter of time before it got back to her. Oh well, at least he's been working his whole shift on Friday nights.

.

5:30 p.m.

I finish checking out my car, and I hit the bathroom one last time before heading out. My portable radio is squawking my call sign while I'm standing at the urinal. I ignore it for the moment, but they're still calling. I finish what I'm doing, and then intentionally key the mic as I flush the toilet.

"Forty-six, go ahead." I say it with the rush of swirling water in the background. There's a pause before she answers and I'm content that I made my point.

"Take a family disturbance," she says. The address is on a narrow, block-long street right across from one of the hospitals on my beat. They don't send a cover unit because one of the parties has already left the scene.

I park near the house—a pleasant, single-story job with a few muddy pairs of kids shoes sitting on the covered porch. A birdfeeder hangs off to the side and there's a little wooden sign above the door that says, *The Shelton Family*. I knock and the door is answered by a white woman, early thirties, no makeup, wearing a pair of sweatpants and a man's flannel shirt. Her black hair is stringy and matted, and she's holding her hand against the side of her head.

I introduce myself and ask if she's the one who called police.

"Uh-huh. My husband assaulted me and then left." She's clearly in some pain. Her head is still tilted into her hand as she makes her way over to a couch. She plops herself on top of a rumpled blanket and pillow.

"Sorry for the mess," she says. "I've been sleeping on the couch." She goes on to tell me that she and her husband haven't been getting along, and this was the first time he was actually physical with her.

I don't see any blood where she's holding her head, but I ask if she would like me to call an ambulance anyway. She says she'd rather walk to the emergency room across the street. I wonder if it would be better to drive her in my car, but depending on where we find parking, she could end up walking the same distance. So, she locks up the house and we walk.

"Can you tell me what happened today?" I ask as we cross the street.

"My husband sent the kids to a friend's house this afternoon, and I thought that meant we were going to discuss a separation. I've been telling him for a couple of weeks that it's over between us. But when he got back from dropping off the kids, he just stayed in the bedroom."

We get to the emergency room and the doors spring open.

"After a while I dozed off on the couch. All of a sudden I hear this crack and the side of my head is killing me."

"What was it?"

"I don't know," she says. "I screamed and grabbed my head. It hurt so bad it made me dizzy. When I finally turned over, there was my husband standing over me, just staring."

"I yelled at him, 'What the fuck did you just do?'"

"And what did he say?"

"Nothing. He just walked out of the house and drove away.

"Did he have anything in his hands?"

She thinks for a minute. "He was holding something behind his back, but I couldn't see it. It felt like he hit me with a hammer or something."

The woman registers with the emergency room nurse. The nurse takes a cursory look at her head. "Thank you Ms. Shelton," the nurse says. "You may have a seat in the waiting room until your name is called." I find us a couple of seats away from other people where I can continue the interview in relative privacy.

"Do you mind if I take a look?" I ask.

The woman leans down and slides her hand away, holding a clump of hair off the wound. I use my flashlight to get a better look. A bruised area about the size of a quarter rises up under the hair near where she parted it. Even under the light there is only a small amount of blood. I notice a small blackish lump in the center of the raised area, and lean in closer with the light.

I straighten up for a second and blink to clear my eyes. *It can't be.* I lean in again, and sure enough.

"I think you've got a bullet in your head," I say. "Could your husband have shot you?"

She looks at me for a second with a shocked expression. "That son-of-a-bitch!" Her words are loud enough to earn a disapproving frown from the registration nurse. I walk back over to the nurse, and she looks up at me with a blank expression.

I motion toward my victim. "I believe this woman was shot in the head."

"Nonsense," the nurse says. "She's got a minor contusion. Do you think I'd make her sit in the waiting room if she had been shot?"

"I don't know, but I can see the base of a small caliber bullet sticking out of the skin." I'm trying hard not to embarrass the nurse, but she's decided to dig her heals in. On the other hand, I know what I'm seeing.

She glares at me. "Bring her back up here."

I walk over and escort my victim back to the counter. She leans forward, holding her hair back as she did before. I aim my flashlight into the wound as the nurse brings her face within inches. After a second or two the nurse abruptly straightens up. She glances right into my eyes for a fraction of a second, and then spins on her heel and storms away. I hear her yelling something down the hallway, ending with the word *stat*.

A doctor and another nurse hustle over and immediately help the patient to a gurney. At the same time, I hear my identifier being called over my portable radio. They're asking me to switch to another channel so I can speak directly to the desk officer. He apparently has an urgent question for me. I change frequencies and the desk officer comes on.

"Do you have a victim by the name of Christina Shelton?"

I check my notes. "Affirmative."

"Her husband's here at the station," he says. "Lawrence Shelton. He's saying he wants to turn himself in for trying to murder his wife."

"I'm here at the hospital with her, and she's got a gunshot wound to the head. You'll want to search him right away, if you haven't already." There's only silence after that. I suppose I'd have heard some emergency radio traffic if the guy had opened fire in the front office. More likely the desk officer didn't waste any time.

I finish up at the hospital, and then drive to the station to take a statement from Lawrence Shelton. I contact the desk officer first. He's a little pale. He tells me that the suspect had the gun in his pocket the whole time he was confessing, apparently never thinking to mention *how* he had tried to kill his wife. After talking to me on the radio, the desk cop immediately put the guy on the floor at gunpoint and relieved him of his pistol.

The gun has already been placed into evidence and the officer is writing a supplement to my report. *Good man!* All I need to do is take a quick statement from the suspect.

6:58 p.m.

We're sitting at a desk crammed into a tiny room in the jail. It was used as a holding cell at one time. There are no bars like in the old westerns, and no windows. Like all the other cells, this one is fully enclosed, reinforced cinderblock, painted high gloss yellow. It's claustrophobic inside, it feels like a refrigerator, and the acoustics are terrible. There's a doorbell on the wall to alert the jailers when I'm finished. Then they come and let me out.

I read Mr. Shelton his rights. He waives them and he tells me his story. It matches exactly with the wife's, except it's from his perspective. He tells me that he had decided kill his wife when she was asleep, so he wouldn't have to face her. He dumped the kids off with a family friend and waited in the bedroom until she had dozed off. Then, he tiptoed out, held the gun a few inches from his wife's head, and fired. Shelton was sure he had killed her.

"Suddenly, she started screaming at me," he says. "It was like she was possessed or something. I thought the fool at the store must have sold me blanks. I didn't know what to do, so I hid the gun under the back of my shirt and left. I drove around for a while, and then decided to go to the police department and give myself up."

I write down all of what he tells me. When we finish, I ring the buzzer and walk him back to the booking counter so they can take his prints.

"So where is she now?" he says meekly. I wondered if he was ever going to ask.

I tell him that he had, in fact, shot his wife in the head, but that the bullet hadn't completely penetrated her skull. He seems neither relieved nor disappointed, just perplexed. I leave him with the jailers at the booking counter.

I hear yelling as I pass one of the cells. It's the largest one, designed for up to 12 people in six metal bunks bolted to the wall. Everything inside the cells is either concrete or metal, except for the mattresses, blankets, and toilet paper. Even the toilet itself is a stainless steel, one-piece, combination toilet/sink. It sits against the wall just inside the door—out in the open for everyone to see, hear, and smell.

I keep walking, ignoring whoever is hollering, but then I stop in my tracks when I hear a loud crash. It's definitely not a sound I'm used to hearing inside the jail.

I go to the cell door and look through the tiny rectangle of etched safety glass. In the center of the cell is a man wearing one shoe. He's a small Latin looking guy, not much bigger than a racehorse jockey. The guy is holding his other shoe in front of him with both hands. He looks up at the ceiling and throws his shoe toward it. Another crash as it hits a metal box that houses the fluorescent lights. I squat to get an upwards view of the light box, which is a good 15 feet off the ground. The prisoner picks up his shoe and gives it another good lob, this time directly striking the plastic covering. The whole four-foot-long piece falls to the ground with a thunderous crash, echoing all the way through the jail.

I call for the jailers to bring the keys, and they come running. There are three other prisoners in the cell, all of whom are sitting on their bunks watching with indifference. By the time the jailers get to the door, the Latin guy is standing on the sheet of plastic, pulling it toward him. It bows to nearly a right angle and then snaps in an irregular shard. I know where he's going with this, so I swing around and hit the red knob mounted on the wall behind me. Immediately a loud buzzer goes off throughout the building.

The jailers slide the heavy door open in time for me to see what this guy had in mind all along. He's slicing the sharp piece of plastic hard across his forearms in a sawing motion, cutting as deeply as he can.

"Son of a bitch, this life!" he yells over and over as he continues slicing. "Son of a bitch, this life!"

I edge my way inside the cell, followed by two sturdy jailers—a male and a female. I snatch the wool blanket off the nearest bunk, and motion for the guy on the next bunk to toss me his. He does. I hold one blanket and the two jailers hold the other. I count to three and we rush the guy. He swings the plastic shard in our direction but its impact is muffled by the blankets. We take him down to the floor and roll him onto his stomach.

An ample pack of cops has arrived in response to the jail alarm, and all of them are more than ready to join in the fracas. They're disappointed to find that the situation is under control. Most of them make a hasty exit when they see all the blood anyway. Nothing fun about exposing one's self to any number of disgusting viruses this guy might be carrying. The jail is a virulent petri dish on a good day.

Turns out the guy didn't cut through anything major. He'll have to get cleaned up at St. Theresa's, and then taken up to the county psych ward for an evaluation. The watch commander assigns another cop to handle the transport, and has the desk officer deal with the paperwork.

Out of curiosity, I check to see what the guy was in jail for. Nothing more than a drunk driving arrest. He would have been cited out in a few hours. I wash up, clear the jail, and head back up to my beat.

8:22 p.m.
I get a call to cover another cop in a downtown parking lot. The dispatcher tells me he's off on a suspicious vehicle. The cop is a big guy by the name of Helmsley. He's a quick witted guy who fills up a room. People around the department seem to either really like him, or really hate him. I get the feeling that Helmsley would gladly spend his day off helping me move if I asked him. He would also spend a day off helping me move a body. I don't think it would really matter to him.

He nods to me as I pull up behind his patrol car. He's at the passenger window of a sedan, parked in a dark corner of the lot. The windows are fogged and I can't see who or what is inside, so I move over to the opposite side of the car. There's a kid seated in the driver's seat; a pale and pimpled kid with tousled reddish hair. If he's old enough to drive, he's just barely.

I hear Helmsley telling the passenger to get out. The response is a soft, affected voice that sounds like a Doris Day impersonation. She's confounded as to why she's being asked to get out of the car, but she does it anyway.

She's a big woman—nearly as tall as Helmsley, but not quite. Her muscular legs are covered in fishnet stockings and her dress barely covers her ass. Even from across the car I can see the phony wig, the pronounced Adam's apple, and the abundance of puttied face makeup—all sweaty and smeared.

Helmsley asks, "Are you packing a banana under that dress or are you just glad to see me?"

In a falsetto voice, the man tries his best to sound insulted at the suggestion he's anything but a woman. Helmsley turns him around against the car and searches him anyway.

"What are you doing to that poor kid?" Helmsley asks, turning the guy back to face him.

"Nothing, honest. We were just sitting here talking. I swear it."

Helmsley walks the guy back to his car. "Sit here." He locks him in the backseat without handcuffing him.

I get the kid out of the car and he's obviously shocked and confused. He's also dumber than a lug nut. Helmsley comes over and starts to question the kid. It turns out he's actually 17, and has a valid driver's license. He's stands limply with his mouth open, and is slow to answer Helmsley's questions. The kid still thinks he was with a woman. He also denies that they were doing anything in the car.

"Unbutton your pants," Helmsley says.

With his lower lip still dangling stupidly, the kid reluctantly complies. He unfastens his belt, unsnaps the pants, and unzips his fly.

"Now drop your boxers," Helmsley says.

The kid does it. Helmsley raises his flashlight and shines it on the kid's genitals. Flesh colored face makeup is smudged in a semicircle over his thighs and abdomen, and there are blotches of darker eyeliner on his belly. In the center is his now-wilted penis, smothered in bright red lipstick.

"You didn't just get head, Kid, you got the whole face." Helmsley walks back to his car and rousts the cross-dresser out of the backseat. He turns him, not too nicely, and handcuffs him. The guy protests as Helmsley tosses him back into the car.

A sergeant pulls up and wants to know what's going on. Helmsley tells him that the underage kid was getting a blow job from a man dressed like a woman. The sergeant was a vice cop for years, and likes those kinds of cases. Helmsley makes the kid drop his drawers again for the sarge.

The sergeant laughs at the evidence. "Looks like Tammy Fay Baker just went down on him."

Helmsley takes the suspect to jail. I have the kid lock up his car, and I take him down to the station where we call his folks. He's seated at a table in the front office near the desk officer while I take down his statement. He's technically a victim, so that's the way the statement reads. By this time, Helmsely's done booking the suspect and he joins us in the front office. The parents arrive looking like average working people. A genuine confused expression tells me they aren't ready for what they're about to hear. They look just as dense as their kid. I can almost imagine their expressions when they hear the news—same open mouth and hanging lip. I leave Helmsley to explain it to them.

9:49 p.m.

I call upstairs to the communications center and ask if I can take my lunch. The dispatcher is about to grant my request when a priority call comes in on my beat.

"Can you take an attempt suicide first?" she asks.

I tell her I will, and I head back out. It's starting to rain now, and there's not much traffic on the street. Dispatch tells me a family member of the victim called from out of state to report it. Says the victim, Randy, had phoned them from his motel room, claiming to have taken an overdose of pills.

The motel room is on the second floor of a large chain complex right off the freeway. I stop by the manager's office first to get a passkey. I also get Randy's last name and birthdate from the room registration—the clerk had made a copy of his driver's license. As I'm walking to the room, I request dispatch to run a check on the guy—31 year-old Randolph Luisotti.

The fire department had also been sent. I get up the stairs in time to see one of them, dressed in a helmet and heavy coat with his name stenciled across the back, hefting a huge axe over his head. I call out to him just before he swings it into the door. I hold the key up to show him, and he slowly lowers the axe. *Sorry to ruin your fun.*

I knock hard on the door. "Police department; open the door."

A withering male voice answers from inside, "Can't . . . get . . . up."

I slip the key in and open the door. An obese man lies nearly naked on the bed. Lit only by a small light on the stand, it's difficult to tell where his mammoth body ends and the shadows begin. I step past the end of the bed to glance in the bathroom. There's nobody else there. Two firemen follow me inside with their gear.

"Are you Randy Luisotti?" I ask.

He cracks one eye and gives me a half-hearted nod.

"What did you do tonight, Mr. Luisotti?"

He licks his lips slowly, as if crawling parched and thirsty through the desert. "Took . . . pills. Want . . . to . . . die."

I'm suddenly struck with a sweet smell that reminds me of Christmas. As I lean closer to the blob in his white underpants, I'm surprised to find that the smell is coming from him. I unconsciously glance at the sink looking for mouthwash, but don't see any. I'm wondering why a guy, supposedly on his death bed, would rinse with Scope before killing himself. Something about this guy seems way overplayed.

"What kind of pills?" I ask, as one of the firemen slips a blood pressure cuff on his arm.

Luisotti's eyes roll back and his head wavers unsteadily. He looks like he's about to lose consciousness, or more likely, he wants it to look as if he's losing consciousness. I ask him again, louder and more authoritative.

His head bobs back and his eyes spring open momentarily, then close again. A lazy hand flops across his bulging white stomach, pointing toward a dresser. "Top . . . drawer."

The fireman nearest the dresser opens the drawer and pulls out an empty Sucrets tin.

I inch closer to Luisotti's face. "Blow into my hand."

He lets out a feeble breath that smells like a mint julep.

"Did you take anything besides these sore throat lozenges?" I ask loudly into his ear. "Come on, stay with us! Stay with us!"

The firemen pick up on my act and they start in. One of them calls out that he's going back to the truck to get the defibrillator. The other one tells me that Luisotti may have to be catheterized.

Luisotti miraculously starts to come around. I have him put his clothes on, and amazingly enough he manages to do it. He's then able to walk down the stairs all on his own, although with an occasional Hollywood wobble. He starts toward the ambulance and I stop him. I slip a pair of handcuffs on him and sit him in my patrol car.

He looks at me incredulously. "You're taking me to the hospital in handcuffs?"

I tell him that we are only stopping briefly at the hospital so they can medically clear him. In the midst of his deathbed act, dispatch had radioed me back on the warrants check. I tell Mr. Luisotti the bad news: He's wanted on a felony bank fraud warrant for $20,000.

They do more than I expect at St. Theresa's. They give Luisotti ipecac to make him vomit. The ER doctor tells me that the lozenges contained a weak sedative that is absorbed through mucous membranes. He doesn't believe Luisotti ingested enough to hurt himself, but he's going through the motions as a precaution. They flush him like a radiator, and by the time they finish I think Luisotti wished he'd taken something stronger than Sucrets.

11:30 p.m.

I finish up with the jail paperwork and leave Luisotti to be printed and booked. I finally get time to eat, but use most of my break to write reports.

There's a wastepaper basket in the center of the lunchroom with water dripping into it. A brown ring is stained into the ceiling panel above it. This is just one of about a dozen buckets put up around the building when the weather gets bad. I've heard that it isn't actually the roof that leaks, it's the pipes between the floors. They shunt rainwater from the roof to the ground level, and have become rusted and cracked. In any case, it's now raining hard, and I'm wishing I didn't have to go back out there.

12:30 a.m.

As I head back onto the street, I hear radio traffic downtown about a rape that has just occurred. Several units are responding, so I start in that direction. From what I can gather, a woman working as a janitor in one of the businesses was attacked when she stepped outside to empty the trash. I'm familiar with those office buildings from other calls I've had there. They back up to a creek that runs through the downtown area and eventually out to the bay. Several bridges crisscross the creek, providing shelter for numerous homeless camps.

I drive to an area on the opposite side of the creek, where I park with my headlights off. A block-long row of exceptionally nice apartment buildings overlook the creek. Even though it's a secured complex, there are spaces between the buildings and even a footbridge where someone could cross. As the other units contact and interview the victim, I watch for anything moving. I'm waiting for an update on the suspect, but it takes a long time to get the description from the victim. I only imagine that the poor woman is hysterical and in shock. I wonder if she's been injured as well. Finally, they come out over the air with a description. He's described by the victim as a tall white male, in his late twenties, with short brown hair and a beard.

I'm sitting in the car hoping a guy fitting that description wanders up from the creek. I feel myself wishing I could be the one to catch him, if only to be able to reassure the victim that the guy who raped her is in prison.

I'm thinking back to a call I went on at one of those offices about a year ago. Two young women were cleaning the building after hours and some homeless guy kept pounding on the back door. They were petrified. It could have been one of those girls who were raped tonight. It could have been that same homeless guy who did it.

I remember another call I went to not more than two months ago, right here at these apartments. Another young woman had seen someone peering into her window one night. She didn't report it to the police right then, but called a few days later when she found that someone had gone into her car. It had been parked in the garage below the building, but she couldn't remember whether or not she had locked it. Something had dried all over the steering wheel and gearshift, leaving a tacky opaque film. The woman surmised that the same man who had been peering into her apartment had somehow found her car and masturbated in it. I remember being skeptical at the time, about whether the two incidents were connected. Now I'm second guessing myself. The whole thing angers me.

Groups of cops are coming on the radio, checking the homeless camps all along the creek. They're obviously thinking the same thing. I start to visualize the description, and wonder if perhaps the suspect isn't homeless. Lots of men have beards, and the fact the suspect had short hair might indicate the kind of grooming that a homeless man might not have the resources for. I begin to wonder if it is more than coincidence that these other cases occurred in the same area. Perhaps the guy who's responsible actually lives in the apartments. Crossing the creek on a rainy night like this would surely leave muddy shoeprints wherever he steps.

I give dispatch the address of the apartment building. It's the one at the end, nearest the creek, and the same building the woman victimized by the Peeping Tom lived in. I hold my raincoat over the back of my neck, against the pounding rain. It doesn't matter. By the time I get to the partially covered landing, I'm soaked. A gust of wind pulls at my pant legs, twisting them flat against my leg.

I try the buzzer labeled *Manager,* but there's no response. I shield my face and squint through the plate glass security door. The apartment nearest this end of the hallway has the number 110 on the door. I find that buzzer and press it. A woman's voice asks who it is, and I tell her it's the police department.

Nothing happens. She says nothing more, and the door remains locked. I wait a few minutes, whipped by the cold all the while, and then try the same buzzer again. There's no response. A moment later the door to unit 110 opens and a young woman steps into the hall. She's wearing a coat cinched loosely over what looks like pajamas.

"I'm sorry for waking you," I show her the badge clipped onto my black raincoat. "But we're investigating a . . ."

"Do you have any idea what time it is?" she rips into me. "No! No! I'm not letting you inside here."

I try to tell her that a woman was raped not far from the building and I'm looking for witnesses or evidence that might help locate the person who did it. She doesn't seem the least bit interested.

"How do I even know you're a cop?" She glares at me through the window. "I ought to call the police right now and report you."

I don't know why, exactly, but I'm deflated by the encounter. I had felt as if I was working, not just for the rape victim, but for all women who could be attacked by this guy. Especially those who live in close proximity to where this pervert may be stalking his victims. Of all the things I've tried to brace myself for, this one catches me unprepared. She ends the conversation by telling me to "go away and don't come back."

From what little of the building I saw through the window, there wasn't any mud on the hallway carpet. I convince myself that it was a long shot at best anyway. Demoralized, I amble through the freezing rain back to my car. I sit there for a minute trying to shake the feelings. Embarrassment, stupidity, just hurt by that kind of treatment by someone I didn't expect it from.

I tell dispatch I'm clear, and I drive off.

1:49 a.m.

I'm stopping by the department to drop my paper with the sergeant. He doesn't want to come out in the rain to pick it up, and he's told us he doesn't like getting a pile dumped on him at the end of the shift.

As I'm getting back into my car, a broadcast goes out to all units. An unmarked Oakland unit is in a high speed pursuit of a burglary suspect and they're coming toward us. They're on a wide, six-lane street, divided down the center by a raised median. The street runs north/south and they're coming from the north. I race about a half mile to the intersection they'll be coming through.

I monitor their locations over the radio and listen intently to the updates as they are broadcasted. The CHP has joined in the chase, and they're approaching at 90+ miles per hour. I see two cars stopped at the intersection waiting for the light. I turn on my rotating lights and jump out of the car with my hands held up to stop them from moving into his path. The two drivers are puzzled as they look up and down the vacant street, but neither moves.

A second later there's a muffled siren and roaring engines. A white van rockets out of the darkness, flying past us with its headlights off. A brown Chevy with a red light in the front window flashes past, followed by two marked CHP units running full lights and siren. The two guys in their cars just sit there stunned, still not moving.

I jump back in my car, ready to join in, but my sergeant has other ideas. He comes on the radio telling all our cops to stay out of the pursuit. "Just monitor it," he says, "and escort them through the city." *Sounds more like parade duty.* I give the *all clear* wave to the two stopped drivers and they cautiously continue on their way.

When the officer riding the beat on the southernmost end of the town advises that they've left the city limits, I start slowly back towards the department. The rain has eased quite a bit and now it's just freezing cold. I don't pass a single car during the half mile back.

"Forty-six?" The dispatcher calls my numbers. I tell her to go ahead.

"The pursuit has turned around and they're heading back your way." I hear the background squawk of the other agencies as she's relaying their information to me. "The suspect has rammed one of the CHP units and the other unit has spun off the road."

"Confirm only the unmarked Oakland unit is still in it?" I spin the car around and head back toward the intersection. In my rearview mirror I see a couple of other cars have cleared the station and are headed my way as well.

"Affirmative," she says. "Only the single unit. Per the sergeant, none of our units are to join in the pursuit."

That couldn't be right, I'm thinking to myself. She's got to be repeating what he said when they passed through the first time. The fact that the suspect already disabled two CHP cars, and the Oakland cop is chasing him alone, opens the door for a whole new set of rules. Surely the sergeant doesn't have all the information. I'm about to ask for clarification when I see the single red light from the unmarked car quickly approaching.

I look around and there are no other cars in the intersection. As the unmarked unit gets closer, I realize he's not chasing anyone. The van didn't pass me and isn't anywhere in sight. I'm wondering who the Oakland cop chasing? What did I miss?

With the suddenness of a gunshot, the van passes in front of me—its engine roaring like a jet. The van's lights are still off, and now it's on the wrong side of the divided road. The unmarked cop blows past me on the right side of the road, paralleling the suspect, maybe just a step behind.

I fall in behind him, forgetting for the time being how much trouble I'm going to get in for ignoring the sergeant's orders. I bury my foot into the accelerator in an attempt to catch up to their speed. I radio that the unmarked unit was alone and I've joined in the pursuit. I'm waiting to hear my decision countermanded by the sergeant, but there's only silence. The speedometer needle is in an area labeled with red, and it flashes through my mind what can happen to a body when it crashes at nearly100 miles per hour. The road is wet, and I know I can't afford to drive even a little bit over my head. Before I started with the department, one of our cops died in a crash during a pursuit. As I remind myself of that, I ease up on the gas just a bit.

We're approaching a good sized intersection and I instinctively start to brake. The unmarked car does the same, but the van sails right through the red light without even slowing. Driving on the wrong side of the street with no lights on, and at his speed, it amazes me that he hasn't killed someone by now. I find myself wishing it was over, not so much because of my own fear, but the thought of seeing an innocent driver killed by this guy terrifies me. The farther we drive the angrier I feel inside.

We go under a freeway overpass and the echo from our sirens momentarily deafens me. I see the headlights of an approaching car, and it looks as if the van is headed straight for it. I grip the wheel and cringe, not wanting to watch. The van fishtails, and somehow passes the car without hitting it. In my mirror I see the car stopped in the middle of the street, the driver probably scared beyond belief, and wondering what just happened.

We're approaching another big intersection. There are dozens of flashing lights ahead. It looks like the city we just entered has set up a roadblock. I see they're all the yellow and orange signs, and realize it's a construction zone. Part of the roadway is blocked and coned off for traffic. There are large, orange, plastic barricades diverting the lane around the work. I'm thinking, with any luck the driver of the van will lose control and crash into them. He doesn't.

He turns left at the intersection, skidding in a wide arc but avoiding the blockaded construction site. The van's back end keeps sliding and it looks like he's going into a spin. The rear end smacks an overpass support causing sparks and pieces of fender to fly, but he manages to control the van and continue west toward the bay. I know the area. Turning off the main roadway may have been a tactical mistake for him. The street narrows into a residential area, and eventually dead-ends about two miles further down. I can feel it—this thing is coming to an end.

I make the turn, a little shaky but without crashing. I see the Oakland car start to lose it, but regain control. He's lost a step or two and I'm now the lead car. There was only one set of emergency lights in my rearview mirror last time I checked, but he was quite a way behind. Probably someone from my own department.

I broadcast our change of direction. We're moving quickly toward another big intersection, but thankfully we have the green light. We roll through at sickening speeds, first the van, then me, then the unmarked car. Our emergency lights whirl around overhead, reflecting in the mist that hangs like a shroud in the night air.

It's darker up ahead where there are fewer streetlights. My heart pounds as I prepare for how this thing will unfold. I remind myself that this guy is desperate and may be armed. He's run at least one police car off the road during his rampage, and his flight has involved several different jurisdictions. If he was going to give up, he would have done it before now.

We're getting close. I know there isn't much road left ahead of us. The Oakland car is right on my tail, and I'm right on the van's. I ease off just a bit as the road narrows, leaving some reaction room in case he turns. One final opportunity lies ahead where we cross a four way stop. If he misses it, the road ahead funnels down to nothing—a wooden barrier with a cyclone fence behind it.

He slows slightly as if he's thinking about it, so I take a risk and press my bumper right up to his. At these speeds I know what I'm doing is insane, but it works. He can't slow or swing out to make a turn because I'm leaving him no room. So he abandons the idea, and accelerates westbound into the dark abyss. It's obvious to me now that he doesn't know the area. Missing that last turn effectively ends his chance to keep the vehicle pursuit going. He's either got to fight or run.

Now I lay back a bit so I don't crash into him, and so the unmarked car doesn't crash into me. The van's brake lights come on as the driver sees the outline of a fence through the mist. I can imagine he's looking around frantically for a way out. The brake lights go off and he picks up speed again, as if he might try to ram through the barricade. He suddenly slams on the brakes, probably hoping we lose control in our attempts to avoid him. We don't. The unmarked car behind me has given me room and I have given the van room. The van goes into a four wheel skid, headed straight for the fence. We're on gravel now, and for a second it doesn't look like he's going to be able to stop in time. I'm braking rapidly too, but not in a full skid.

The van comes to a stop with only a few feet to spare. There's a whirlwind of dust and rocks, and the only light is from our cars. I've already broadcast our location, unhooked my seatbelt, thrown the car in park, and opened my car door. Within a second, I find myself out of the car with my handgun out of the holster. The van's backup lights come on and the wheels start spinning in the opposite direction. It only moves a few feet before I hear the jarring sound of metal on metal and glass breaking. He's smashed it into the front of my car.

I'm at the driver's door now. He's inside, blinded by the headlights behind him, and he's thrashing like a feral cat. A thicket of curly black hair and a mustache, maybe. He's dark and wiry and moving. I'm pointing my gun and I'm screaming at him to shut off the engine. His eyes are wild. He turns away and reaches across the seat. It's dark. I can't tell if he's arming himself. I hear the engine rev as he twists. My arm rears back and comes forward with an earsplitting crack. The window shatters with the weight of my handgun, and I hear myself yelling. Threatening. Challenging. The barrel of my gun is pressed into the side of his temple, hard, like it might drill right into his skull. I'm yelling for him to get out of the van, put his hands up, shut off the engine. I'd settle for any one of them. But he still won't give up. He dives across the passenger seat and flings the door open. Out he jumps, and into the arms of the Oakland cop. By the time I get around to them, the suspect is on his face in the gravel and his arms cuffed behind him. Another cop has arrived, but the action is over.

"Are you okay?" I ask the Oakland cop.

He smiles widely. "Some chase, huh?" Then he looks down at my hand. "We better get you some help."

I hadn't noticed the knuckles and fingers on my right hand are bleeding. I wipe them off and hold my hand in front of the headlight. A couple of deep gashes, no doubt from my *gun through the window* performance. I wrap them in gauze from a first aid kit in my trunk. The damage to my car is minimal. The bumper is out of whack and the license plate frame is broken, but it'll drive fine.

About a dozen cops are there now; some from my department, CHP, San Leandro, and a couple from Oakland. My sergeant pulls up, and I'm hoping he doesn't dress me down in front of all my counterparts. He asks me if I'm alright, and I tell him yes. He checks out the scene without saying much, then conferences with a boss from one of the other cities. The suspect is carted away to Oakland, and a tow truck is called to haul the van. It's full of stolen property, and they're talking about where and when to inventory it all.

My sergeant gets back into his car. From the window he only says, "See you back at the station." He doesn't look mad, but he doesn't look happy either. I can't tell.

3:02 a.m.

I get back, unload my car, and pack everything into the locker room. Blood has soaked through the gauze, so I get some more supplies from a first aid kit in the building and rewrap my fingers. I'm using band-aids instead. They won't last long, but they won't draw as much attention as gauze.

I've prolonged the inevitable long enough. I look for the sergeant, but he's not in his office. I find him in with the lieutenant, running down the chase to him. They're looking at a memo of some type that the sergeant has apparently written. I walk in and they both ask me if I'm okay. I tell them I'm fine, but they both eye the band-aids on my hand. They ask me a couple of questions about the pursuit, but nothing too inquisitive—not like they would if I were in trouble.

The sergeant asks me to take a look at his memo, saying he wants to make sure it's accurate. I scan through it, looking for any mention of my insubordination. I get to the part when the van first passed through the city, and see that he mentions his orders over the radio not to become involved in the chase. I take a gulp and keep reading. The sergeant goes on to write that the situation had changed by the time the suspect entered the city the second time. There is mention that Oakland's unmarked car was the sole police vehicle pursuing the suspect, and that I had advised I was joining him. The sergeant wrote that he heard my radio transmission, and that he *"acquiesced"* to my decision to cover the unmarked car. I suppose I know what the word means, but I have never actually heard anyone use it before.

I hand the memo back to him. "Looks good to me."

He gives me a nod and hands it over to the lieutenant. I'm not sure what just happened, but I think I was taken care of.

I turn to leave, and stop at the door. "Thanks, Sarge."

He gives me another nod. "Good job," he says. "You did the right thing."

I'm sitting on the bench, taking off my boots and feeling kind of numb. I slide my pants off and run my hand along the crease before hanging them neatly in my locker. There's talking and laughter on the next row over, as the rest of my squad starts to file in. I'm sitting in my underwear in front of my open locker, thinking.

What had just taken place was a defining moment for me. It was the first time I hadn't been treated as just another snot-nosed rookie working the night shift. The sergeant took care of me, he sided with me. He stuck up for me and for the decision I made. Some cops get hung out to dry and some get taken care of. The difference seems to be whether they're viewed as a screw up or someone who's got their shit together. He and the lieutenant must see me as someone in the second group.

3:32 a.m.

I'm sitting in the emergency room waiting for the doctor to look at my hand. The injury is technically a Workers' Compensation situation since it happened on duty, but I'm getting it taken care of on my own. I'd rather not go to the city doctors and have them fill out a pile of paperwork that goes back to the department. It may not be the smartest thing to do, but I would hate to get a reputation as a wimp. Besides, I don't want to give the sergeant second thoughts about going to bat for me.

They stitch up two fingers, clean out a couple of smaller cuts and I'm done.

5:10 a.m.

As I pull into my driveway, the dog next door starts to bark. Gale pulls the curtain aside to see who it is, and then goes back to her exercise video. I come in and wish I had the energy to join her. She finishes and asks me if I want anything to eat.

She turns on the wall heater on her way to the kitchen, and I snuggle into the recliner right next to it. Gale brings me a couple of warm slices of pumpkin bread and a cup of decaf tea. She notices the bandages on my fingers and gives me a chastising look.

"How bad?"

"Not bad," I say. "A couple of stitches."

She shakes her head without asking me anything more. I'm sure any guess she has is close enough to the truth.

After eating my breakfast, dinner, or whatever it is, I fall asleep in the chair. When the girls wake up an hour or so later, Gale eases me out of the chair and into bed. I hear the door close and Gale whispering to the girls, "Be as quiet as you can so Daddy can sleep."

Chapter 14

4:20 p.m.

Eyeing the other cops in this classroom, I realize I'm probably the youngest one here. These guys are all big names, detectives and narcs from all around the county. Bettis and Glover, the two DA inspectors teaching the course, are icons in the field of investigations. I've heard their names since they were undercover superstars in Oakland. They've probably wondered all day who this young patrol cop is. Two months ago when I signed up for the search warrant writing class, it seemed like a good idea. Now, I'm having my doubts.

I check the clock and slip out just in time to grab my certificate and beat the afternoon commute down the freeway.

5:01 p.m.

I rush into the lineup room a second after the sergeants begin. The lieutenant eyes me as I pass him, and I have a fleeting urge to tell him how I spent my own time and money on the class. Instead, I hold my watch to my ear as if I think it might have stopped. *Lame!* The lieutenant only rolls his eyes.

Among stolen vehicles, wanted suspects, and other bulletins, they pass around the photo of a missing juvenile. Gloria Ferris, a fifteen year old runaway who lives on my beat and has been missing for nearly a week.

"This kid's always running away," Lee says, as he slides the flier to the next cop. I glance at the photo when it gets to me. She's a pretty blond girl with contemptuous green eyes traced with thick black eyeliner.

I glance up to see the lieutenant standing over me. "Stop by my office before you hit the street."

The sergeant finishes lineup and everyone starts to file out. A couple of the guys tell me it's been nice working with me. Although I know I haven't done anything to piss off the LT, there's always that one percent of uncertainty. I load my case into my car and then walk into the watch commander's office.

"I have an important assignment for you," he says, handing me a printout.

I look at it, thinking it might have something to do with the runaway girl, but it's an airline itinerary.

"The Police Chief is returning from a conference tonight at 8:30 p.m. sharp. He'll be arriving at the Oakland airport, gate twelve. I don't give a shit what else you do tonight, just make sure you're there on time to give him a ride home when he gets in."

"No problem, LT. I'll let dispatch know."

I stick the itinerary on the front of my clipboard and turn to leave.

"Go change into a long sleeve uniform shirt and put on a tie," he says. "And I mean it, don't be late."

I let dispatch know what my instructions are, and then quickly change into the more formal attire. More than likely they'll just give me cover calls until I pick up the Chief. Little stuff that won't keep me tied up.

6:10 p.m.

The first call comes just as I'm pulling out of the lot. "Cover on a suspicious person loitering in the parking lot of the Value Inn Motel." The dispatcher describes the suspect as a scruffy looking, white male with a beard and wearing a green jacket.

It's a short drive from the station, so I arrive before the unit I'm covering. I pull off the main street and see the guy getting out of a van. He's scruffy alright, and wearing a green army jacket. I've already committed into my turn into the lot as it dawns on me that the suspect is Moose, one of our undercover narcotics cops. He looks in my direction and quickly looks away. I have to fight the instinct to wave. I can see from his serious expression that his isn't a pleasure trip to the Value Inn, and he's most likely in the middle of some drug deal. I can't back up, so I pass through the parking lot as quickly as I can and then get the hell out of there. I advise dispatch that it's one of our UC units, and tell them to cancel the other cop. I'm going to feel like a real jackass if their case was blown because of me.

6:39 p.m.

I'm called back to the Value Inn to cover the narcs on a search warrant. They meet me at a carwash down the street before they hit the place. I apologize all over myself for screwing up their surveillance, but they tell me not to worry about it.

"The people we've been watching never saw you drive through," Moose says, "and besides, we should have let dispatch know we were running an operation down here."

They show me photos of the couple they're after. Apparently the man and woman are heroin dealers, believed to be armed and paranoid. One of the undercover cops has made a series of drug buys from them over the past two weeks, and wrote a search warrant for their motel room. Moose had been watching the place from the parking lot when I was sent there the first time.

"You cover the back," their sergeant tells me. "We'll go in through the front."

I ask if they want me to get the passkey from the manager.

"We brought our own key." Moose lifts up a huge, solid steel battering ram.

They want me to park my patrol car at the carwash and jump in the van with them. There are no windows and no seats in the back section of the van, and the interior is encased in a thick, red shag carpet. I find myself on my knees, sweating profusely, and wondering how pieces of hay have gotten all over my uniform. It's a short bumpy ride down the boulevard to the motel with six of us crammed into the back.

A guy named Stu Banyon is driving. He hits the lot sliding sideways and the van bounces hard over a speed bump. The sergeant curses Banyon as the case notes and all their paperwork fly onto the floor. I throw open the van door and sprint around to a narrow alley behind the row of rooms. I count the windows until I find the right room. I'm behind what appears to be a bathroom. Its translucent window only allows me to see shapes and movement on the other side. I hear the sound of water running and realize I'm watching someone showering. I can make out flesh tones, and recognize the motions of a figure washing their hair, but can't distinguish much else.

The sound of yelling suddenly billows through the complex, followed by the jarring crash of their *key*. Whoever was in the shower is no longer there. I step back out of the line of fire, just in case someone inside starts shooting. I'm hoping the window pops open and one of the suspects tries to jump out, but nothing happens. They quickly come over the radio advising they've got both people in custody. I come around to the front and find a gargantuan hole in the door where the knob should be. They want me to transport their prisoners to the jail, so I have to hoof it all the way down the block to get my car. Meanwhile, the male half is allowed to towel the shampoo off himself and put on some clothes.

I keep checking my watch to make sure I don't loose track of time. The drug suspects are booked into the jail, and I make sure they don't get any phone calls until the narcs say they can. I drive back out to the Value Inn with the arrest paperwork on their suspects.

Stu Banyon and the sergeant are in the lot next to the van when I pull in. I roll down my window, but quickly roll it back up when I hear the sergeant tearing into Banyon's ass. I drive past them, stopping instead in front of the motel room. Moose and the others are inside, so I leave the paperwork with them.

"Banyon still out there with the sarge?" Moose asks.

I tell him they're in the lot, talking.

Moose shakes his head. "That dumbshit, Banyon, took the narc van home last weekend and used it to move a bunch of goats."

"That explains the hay all over my pants."

Moose tells me that Banyon's father owns a farm out in the valley. Nobody copped out to how the hay got in the van, but the sergeant was able to put two and two together. Anyway, it looks like Banyon will be in the doghouse for a while.

7: 44 p.m.

I radio dispatch and let them know I'm clearing the motel and heading to pick up the Chief. Forty-five minutes will give me more than enough time. I cruise down the freeway and get to the airport a few minutes before eight o'clock. I park directly in front of the terminal and make my way to his arrival gate. I'm 30 minutes early.

The terminal is crowded with people, many giving me a second glance as they pass by. I'm standing at the foot of the jetway with my back to a pillar, probably looking more like a security guard than a cop. The waiting area fills up with passengers taking the next outbound flight. I smile politely and answer a few questions while I wait.

A couple of college age guys amble across the waiting area, laughing loudly and leaning against each other for support. They're drinking from large plastic cups, but it isn't long before I suspect that they contain more than soda. The two men look at me, then whisper something between them and let out another round of laughter. One of them salutes me as they stumble by. Evidently, they're waiting for the next flight, because they park themselves near where I'm standing. I check my watch: 8:15 p.m.

As time passes, the two men become louder and more obnoxious. Their language has garnered some raised eyebrows from the other passengers, many of them glaring expectantly at me. Under normal circumstances I would have at least asked for their ID, and run warrant checks by now. But with the Chief's plane about to land, I'm trying to avoid getting involved. I check my watch: 8:25 p.m.

One of the men belches loudly and the other stumbles backward in laughter, knocking over another passenger's suitcase. The one who belched seems to be the drunker of the two. He belches again, and a woman glares at him.

"What's your problem?" he slurs, raising the straw clumsily to his mouth. The man takes a long, slurping draw from his drink cup.

The woman is still staring at him, but has yet to say anything. Then, in one quick movement, the drunk tosses his drink cup in the air. The lid pops off and ice flies out all over the waiting area and some of the passengers. I feel a hundred eyes on me now, and I'm on the guy before the last ice cube hits the ground.

"Put your hands behind your back, you're under arrest." I put him into an arm bar and press him against the wall. The other guy steps forward like he's going to come to his buddy's aid. "Step back," I tell him, "or you're going to jail with your pal." He mumbles a weak response, but does what I tell him. With the worst offender of the two in handcuffs, I check my watch: 8:28 p.m.

I glance frantically around the area for a cop or some kind of security officer, but there's nobody. Out of the corner of my eye I see the Chief's plane pulling up to the gate. I grab my arrestee by the arm and thrust him through the throng of travelers. I'm at a half trot that's just short of a jog, heading back through the terminal. I still haven't found someone to take this guy off my hands. I finally come across a sign pointing to the security office. I bang on the door and two Oakland cops come out. I explain briefly what has taken place, and they take the guy for me. They replace my handcuffs with theirs, and I give them my card before leaving. I check my watch: 8:35 p.m.

Hoping the Chief's plane was late to disembark, I'm at an all out run through the terminal. People think I'm chasing someone, and everyone is stopping to watch the emergency. Little do they know that the emergency is me about to lose my job. I slide on the marble floors as I take the turn into the waiting area. It's now empty, except for the Chief of Police who's standing regally in his blue pinstripe suit, holding his coat and briefcase and looking at his watch. *Son-of-a-bitch!*

"Sorry, Chief," I gasp, grabbing his briefcase from his hand. "Here, let me take that for you."

He relinquishes it. "I thought my flight might have been early."

"No, sir. I ran into a little problem while I was waiting." I'd rather not get into it with him. Arresting a drunk at an airport in another city would probably be considered a bonehead move. The whole thing is an embarrassment that he doesn't need to know about. The fact that I was late picking him up is all that matters.

We hustle through the terminal, past the security office on our way. One of the cops sees us and waves me over. "Your guy had a warrant for his arrest, too." He hands me a copy of the booking sheet. "We're waiting for a transport unit to take him to the Oakland jail."

I thank him and turn back to the Chief. "What's that all about?" he asks.

My teeth clench. "That was the problem I was talking about. I, uh, had to make an arrest just as your plane landed."

"You arrested somebody? Here at the airport?"

"Yes, sir." I swallow. "A drunk was causing some problems."

I'm waiting for a rebuke, but instead a firm palm swats me on the shoulder. "Good work, Son. Good work."

I'm pleasantly surprised by the Chief's reaction. Thankfully, the subject of my being late never comes up between him and the lieutenant.

9:00 p.m.

Dispatch asks me if I want to eat early since I'm already at the station. Though I'm hungry, I take a pass, figuring I've already spent enough time off my beat tonight. I'm rolling through a small shopping center at the south end of the city, watching a party break up at an East Indian event hall. I can smell the food from all the way out here, and consider doing a walk-through in the hopes they'll offer me some. Instead, I keep driving.

I pass a convenience store, and see a young girl loitering out front. She's approaching people as they enter the store, and I infer she's either panhandling for money or asking them to buy booze for her. I turn my car and pull up beside her.

"How are you tonight?"

She flashes a pair of angry green eyes I've seen before. I hear her grunt, and then she says, "Don't worry, I'm leaving."

"Hold on," I say, getting out of my car. "What's your name?"

"I said I'll leave." She turns away. "Don't you guys have anything better to do?" I'm trying to remember the name of the runaway, Gloria something. I glance at my clipboard on the front seat, but I never wrote it down. I ask her name again.

"Donna," she says. Her hand swipes back a strand of hair. "Donna Miller."

"How old are you, Donna?"

She rolls her eyes. "Eighteen."

"Do you have any identification?" I glance at the purse clutched under her arm.

The girl juts out her chin and stares at me defiantly. I'm looking back at her with a friendly smile. "Donna?" I say, raising an eyebrow. "You sure it isn't Gloria?"

She closes her eyes, and then opens them with a new, cooler expression. "Go ahead and take me back, I'll just leave again."

I move my things off the passenger seat into the back, and tell Gloria to take a seat. While she waits, I let dispatch know where I am and what I'm doing. I also ask if any of the youth and family counselors are working tonight. There's one.

I step into the convenience store and buy two of my favorite drinks. I returned to find Gloria with arms crossed, staring out the side window. I set the cup on the dash in front of her and start drinking mine. It takes a few minutes, but she eventually opens the lid and peers into.

"My own concoction. Half coffee and half chocolate."

She wrinkles her nose, and then slowly begins sipping it. I ask her what could be so bad about home that she keeps running away. I have a pretty good idea of what some kids might face at home, but definitely not what I would call a thorough knowledge. Each situation is different, and I'm hoping she'll open up about hers.

Gloria shakes her head in disgust. "Doesn't matter. I'm not going back."

I ask if she's willing to talk to one of our counselors, but she doesn't answer the question directly. "If you take me to a foster home, I'll run away as soon as you leave."

We drive back to the police department where I pull the flier out of the lineup box. After confirming that Gloria Ferris is the girl I have, I ask dispatch to update the missing person system entry. Vaughn Tinsley, the on-duty crisis counselor, is waiting for us when we arrive. He's a tall, soft-spoken man with round glasses and a grey beard. He's dressed in a cotton flannel shirt and tan corduroy pants, and he's seated in his small office when we come in. She keeps the hard shell for a while, responding with either short or sarcastic answers.

Vaughn takes the lead, and I offer my input when occasionally asked. We establish that when she's not on the run, she lives at home with her biological mother, father, and two sisters. One sister just turned eighteen and the other is a year younger than Gloria. It isn't until Vaughn keys on the younger sister that we start to see through Gloria's solid veneer. Gloria's fourteen year old sister is her soft spot.

Through teary eyes she tells us, "I don't want the same thing to happen to my little sister. It quickly becomes clear that this girl's home life is a living hell.

"My father. He touches me."

I feel my stomach drop. My head buzzes while we listen for the next hour as she describes dozens of incidents of sexual abuse that started when she entered puberty. After struggling in silence for over two years Gloria began running away, the entire time vexed with worry and unrelenting guilt about her younger sister.

"Does Dad touch your little sister?" Vaughn asks.

"I don't know." Gloria's eyeliner is reduced to muddy streaks extending to her chin. She wipes her nose with the sleeve of her sweater. "By now he might."

"What about your older sister?" I ask.

Gloria shrugs. "I don't think so. She just had a baby." Vaughn and I exchange a foreboding glance.

"That's nice," I say casually. "Does the father come around much?"

She shakes her head. "We don't know who the father is."

I'm betting the baby looks a lot like Grandpa. I excuse myself from the room to do a file check on the family. In reality, I'm finding myself barely able to suppress my emotions, and I need to take a break. I wander around the cold back lot, letting the wind dry my eyes.

After a few minutes I come back inside. Unfortunately, neither the police nor Child Protective Services have any record of the Ferris family. I find my sergeant in the front office and run the case down to him. He tells me to take the girl to a foster home and write up what I have for the child abuse detectives.

"I still have plenty of time left to see this thing through tonight," I say.

He checks his watch. "What do you want to do?"

"I'd like to interview the other two sisters, at least. Depending on what I find out, I might take them into protective custody as well."

The sergeant drums his fingers on the counter, thinking. "How about this? Why don't you call the parents, and have them come down here on the pretext of picking up their runaway daughter. We'll delay them with some bullshit story while you drive out to the house and interview the two sisters."

I like that plan better. That way the father isn't there to influence anybody. I coordinate the whole plan with the desk officer. Meanwhile, Vaughn explains to Gloria that we're going to make sure her sisters are safe. Reluctantly, Gloria agrees to go with him to a temporary foster home. I make the phone call to the house, telling Gloria's mother only that I picked up her runaway daughter and she's being held at the police department. I add that I'll need both parents to sign for her. As stupid as it sounded, Mrs. Ferris doesn't seem concerned. She tells me that she and her husband will be right down to get her.

Lisa Baranova is a female cop on the midnight shift, and I ask dispatch to have her meet me at the house. I tell her about the case and ask her to stand by with the older daughter while I question the younger one.

I knock on the door and it's answered by a freckled girl with strawberry blond hair. She tells me that she's Gloria's little sister, Jane Ferris. They think we're there regarding the runaway investigation only. I eventually manipulate Jane into the kitchen area, away from the other sister and the baby. Slowly, I ease the conversation in the direction of ensuring their welfare.

Jane doesn't show the hard exterior that Gloria did, but it still takes her a while to disclose any abuse. Eventually she does. Jane tells me that it started on her thirteenth birthday, when her father told her he had to *examine* her. Apparently these exams happened more than once, and were conducted with their mother's full knowledge. I take a written statement from her, just as I did with Gloria.

I find the older sister, Joe Ellen, sitting with Baranova in the living room. Next to them is a small white bassinet. I ask Joe Ellen if she would mind speaking with me in the other room, but she wants to stay close to her baby. Baranova takes Jane into the other room, leaving me and Joe Ellen and her baby.

I work the conversation around to the statements made by both of her sisters against their father. Joe Ellen regards me with a blank, unresponsive stare. She appears neither surprised nor emotionally connected to it. There's no defending or condemning of her father, just the blank stare.

I ask, "Do you think what your sisters said about your father is true?"

"I don't know."

"Were you ever aware of anything like that going on?"

"No."

"Did anything like that ever happen to you?"

"No."

I pause, realizing this girl isn't going to admit anything. She keeps looking over at the bassinet, and it finally dawns on me that she's fearful of losing her baby. That's the only thing she cares about right now. I ask a few questions about the baby and she answers them happily. But when I ask who the baby's father is, she clams up.

I get up and walk over to the bassinet. "Mind if I take a look?"

She shakes her head.

I peer in at the tiny infant, awake sucking on its fingers. The baby has an odd look. Its head is large, the eyes are off kilter, and it is obviously suffering some impairment. Whether it's the result of inbreeding or just coincidence, I might never know.

I try not to register revulsion on my face. "Is it a boy or girl?"

"He's a boy," she says. Joe Ellen is an adult, and has not admitted to being the victim of anything. All I can do at this point is give her my card and ask her to get in touch with me if she has anything she'd like to add. I plan to send copies of the report to the sex crimes investigator and child protective services, but for now I leave Joe Ellen and her baby at the house.

Jane comes with us back to the station. I slip in through the back door in order to avoid a face-to-face with her folks. I bring her down the hallway to Vaughn's office. He's returned from dropping Gloria at the foster home and will now talk with Jane.

I ask the desk officer to keep an eye on Mr. Ferris while I move his wife to an interview room. She's wearing a button up smock that's something between a bathrobe and a housecoat. Since there has been at least one allegation that Mrs. Ferris knew what was going on, I follow the rules and recite the Miranda rights to her. She waives them and agrees to be interviewed. We start slowly, with me asking basic questions about where she lives, how long she's been married, and how many children she has.

"By the way," I interject with a cheesy grin, "congratulations on your new grandson."

"Thank you." Mrs. Ferris smiles back politely, but I can't tell what's behind it.

The conversation eases into my discussion with Gloria, and the statements she made against her father. I don't feed Mrs. Ferris any specifics, just that Gloria told me she was molested by her father.

Mrs. Ferris protests immediately. "Gloria is a troublemaker. Always stirring things up." I make a mental note of the fact that she didn't deny it.

I tell Mrs. Ferris that daughter Jane made essentially the same allegations, and her face goes pale. She had no idea I had even spoken to anyone other than Gloria. "Now, can you tell me why both of your daughters would say the same thing about your husband?"

"Mr. Ferris is a good and decent man." Again, she doesn't deny any of it. I also find it really weird that she refers to her husband as *Mr. Ferris*.

She sits mute, staring at the desk. I'm not sure whether it's the slight drawl in her voice or misuse of basic words, but Mrs. Ferris doesn't come across as very intelligent. I get the impression she's completely dominated by Mr. Ferris, and wouldn't know wrong from right if it jumped up and bit her in the ass. Maybe there's a better way I could go about this. I'm being too nice to her. She's used to following orders.

I slap my palm on the table and Mrs. Ferris jumps. I glower at her. "I want you to tell me about these examinations your husband does on your daughters!"

"It's nothing." She pauses, straightening her coat. "When they get to be of a certain age, he just checks them."

"Checks them how?"

She motions to the table. "Like a doctor. He gives them an examination to make sure they're still in tact, you know."

I feel my insides wrench. "No, I don't know. Explain it to me."

Mrs. Ferris goes on to describe this rite of passage, or coming of age, or whatever it is. Starting at puberty, her husband has taken each of the daughters and conducted these exams. Usually done with her knowledge, Mrs. Ferris is apparently under the impression it's all normal. When I tell her that Gloria's examinations had progressed into clearly sexual acts, she turns away. Somewhere behind that dumb expression she knows it. I get as much from her as I can onto a written statement, which she signs.

I seat Mrs. Ferris in the lobby and take Mr. Ferris to an interview room before they have a chance to talk. I read him his rights as well.

Lyle Ferris is wearing work boots and grey overalls. He's got about the same intellect as the Mrs., but definitely a more arrogant manner. One look into his heartless eyes and I know he did everything they say he did. It takes a while to crack this nut, but I manage it by challenging his authority. When the conversation gets around to the family I say, "Must be hard to raise three daughters these days. They're always sneaking out to meet up with different boyfriends—a new flavor every month." I let out a goofy laugh.

Ferris looks at me like I'm crazy. "Mine are good, God-fearing girls. They don't sneak around with nobody!"

I get Ferris to obligate himself to a few more comments like that before springing it on him. "So, tell me about the examinations." I say it as if it's no big deal.

He hesitates long enough to wonder how many of his family I've talked to, and what his wife told me. He downplays it at first, but then admits to exercising what he considers his, "fatherly right."

I have to really work at suppressing my anger. "Tell me exactly what your fatherly right is."

Ferris describes examining his daughters to make sure they are still virgins, and then goes a step further. "When they're of age, I use my finger to bust through. You know, make sure they're not a virgin no more."

I don't know if I'm going to heave or reach across the table and slam his head into it. Instead, I nod calmly and write what he says. I ask about other sexual acts, but he denies it.

"Nothing like that," he says. "Everything is on the up and up. Very sterile, like in a hospital."

I still can't zero in on the older girl. For some reason, which I have a pretty good guess why, he avoids any mention of her or the baby. By the end of the interview I have enough to bring several felony charges against Lyle Ferris, and a couple against Mrs. Ferris. The two younger daughters, both juveniles, have been taken into protective custody. Vaughn Tinsley successfully placed them together in the same foster care home.

I meet briefly with my sergeants to go over the case. They both concur that it would be best to let the Mr. and Mrs. Ferris leave tonight, without being arrested. Their rationale is that the juvenile and sex crimes investigators may want to complete additional follow-up before bringing the case to the DA. If I were to make the arrests tonight, the clock starts ticking and there are time constraints. They'll get arrest warrants later, I'm told. Though fairly common practice in these kinds of cases, it irks me not to be able to put them behind bars tonight.

12:14 a.m.

I spend the rest of my shift writing the sex abuse report so the investigators will have it when they get here in the morning. It's a long and complex report, but I want to make sure I get it right. I finally finish it up and carry it to the sergeant. I'm standing there while he reads it, and suddenly I remember I still have an outside assist to write for the arrest at the airport.

I sit down in the report writing room and pound out a quick drunk report. A couple of guys from my shift come in and start giving me a hard time.

"We need to buy you a three legged stool," Kalani says. It's a worn out joke that has to do with milking a farm animal. It's a metaphor for me *milking* my investigation, thus keeping off the street all night.

Van Kirk leans over to see what I'm working on. "A drunk? You spent all night in here writing a drunk report?"

I know they listened to what I was doing on the radio, and they're both probably thankful that it wasn't them who got the sexual abuse case. I'm too tired to mount any kind of defense. Instead, I just laugh along with them.

3:15 a.m.

I'm driving home, alone with my thoughts and the soft music from my radio. Wind whistles sideways over my car, and across the all but deserted street. I can't shake the image of that little baby looking up at me through his screwy eyes.

From the outside, that family looks like any other. The daughters are pretty, attend school, talk with friends, and go home. You'd never know what was happening behind those doors.

So much of what I see doesn't add up to anything recognizable. It's beyond my frame of reference. It makes me wonder about everyone. Most of all it just makes me sad.

Chapter 15

4:15 p.m.

Before I do anything else, I have to hoist two big trash bags out of my backseat and carry them into the building. I made the mistake of mentioning to Gale that the department was collecting used clothes and toys for a Christmas giveaway. She used the occasion to clean out the girls' closet.

As I set the first bag into the bin, I see she also took the opportunity to relieve me of a couple of my favorite jackets. She's always telling me that I have more than enough, and I tell her that a guy can never have too many jackets.

The second bag, stuffed mostly with toys, fills up the donation bin. I hope these things actually go to a needy family with kids. You always wonder where they really end up.

5:00 p.m.

The sergeant is late for lineup. That's a first. We all sit around looking at each other wondering what's up. Thurmond Morris, a day shift guy, comes in and cautiously closes the door behind him.

"Lieutenant and sergeants are having a big powwow in the watch commander's office," he tells the squad, all 250 pounds of him standing there smiling like a simp.

"And?" Lee shakes his head.

Morris grins. "Lieutenant's been pork'n Front Office Tina."

"Tina Lynch?" says Lee. "Who hasn't been pork'n her?"

The shift's only woman looks like she doesn't think it's funny. I wonder if she's offended by the crude talk or if she's also had some of Tina.

Morris shifts his stance like a guy who's got to take a leak. "Well, apparently she's going cookoo. Ever since the gimp dispatcher torched her pussy cat." He gives the squad another goofy smile. "Tina's been calling the LT's house, and apparently that's got his wife all stirred up."

A couple of the guys look more worried than they should be. "So what's the powwow about?" I ask Morris.

"They're trying to figure out how to shut the bitch up. They're talking, maybe, a psych hold or something like that."

The door opens quickly and the sergeants walk in. Morris makes like he was in there for something else. "Thanks for taking care of that warrant for me," he says. He turns and walks out, his uniform pants bunched into a painful looking wedgie.

5:30 p.m.

A few of us stand by our cars in the back parking lot discussing the latest Tina Lynch saga. I'm concerned that she lives on my beat, and I tell them I plan to stay busy tonight. The last thing I need is to be called to her apartment again. Especially if the lieutenant wants me to commit her to the psych ward in order to save his marriage.

I toss my field case onto the passenger seat and bungee it to the headrest. "How does Morris know this shit anyway?"

Kalani laughs. "Who knows? But that stooge can't keep his big mouth shut!"

"No shit," Van Kirk says. "That's why they call him Morris Code. Fastest way to pass information around here: telephone or tell Morris."

5:55 p.m.

"They're calling you," Kalani says to me.

I realize we've been in the lot talking for nearly thirty minutes. I answer the dispatcher's call and let her know I'm clearing the station now.

"Cover on a shots fired call," she says. "The informant says someone inside his house is shooting."

"Was anybody hit?" I jump into my car and take off.

"Unknown."

The unit I'm covering is Bosworth. Even though it's his call on his beat, I still get there before him. The address is in a relatively nice neighborhood on the west side of the city. It's a two story house, white with blue shutters. Could have been the Brady Bunch house. I park next door and listen, but don't hear any gunfire. There's a man in his 60's standing on the porch with the front door open behind him. He's wiping his eyes with a handkerchief.

I call out to him, "Is everything alright?"

He nods. "Yes, everything is alright."

I walk up carefully, watching him, the windows, and the doorway behind him. "You called about a shooting?"

"Upstairs," he says. "My son's killed himself."

The man looks like he's about to pass out. I steady him and help him sit down on the steps. I get his name and his son's name before heading upstairs. He tells me that his son, "Jake" has fought drug addiction and mental health issues for years.

At the top of the stairs, I slowly push the bedroom door open. Jake is on his back, lying on a wide, low bed. It looks like a king mattress with no box spring, propped on a sheet of plywood a few inches off the ground. There's a shotgun on his chest with the barrel resting below his face. Jake's tattooed arms are draped over the gun with one hand on the barrel and one on the trigger housing. As I inch closer, I see his chin and lower jaw are gone, and the top of his head has been blown off. A blast pattern starts just above his pillow, and goes straight up the wall all the way to the ceiling. It's a mixture of blood, bone, and brain, in tiny bits that look like someone put a raw meatloaf in a blender and forgot to attach the lid.

An electric guitar is propped next to the bed and a bong sits on the floor next to it. Magazine photos of heavy metal bands are taped up on the walls, and a large confederate flag hangs over the window like a drape. I check a pharmaceutical bottle on the dresser.

It's a prescription of lithium issued to Jake Striker by a Kaiser doctor named S. W. Howell.

I hear a noise behind me. Bosworth has arrived and Mr. Striker has brought him upstairs to Jake's room. It would have been better if Bosworth had left him sitting outside, but whatever, it's his case.

Mr. Striker dabs his eyes again with the handkerchief and turns toward the window. "He had so many problems."

"What was your son's name?" Bosworth asks.

I hand him the prescription bottle. "His information's on here."

Bosworth stares at the label in disbelief. "Your son was Doctor S. W. Howell?"

I nearly choke. *What kind of imbecile is he?*

"No," says Mr. Striker. "Howell is my son's doctor."

7:25 p.m.

I get out of that place as quickly as I can. I feel really badly for the dad, almost more because he's now at the mercy of Bosworth. There's something just not right about that guy.

"George Forty-six," dispatch says.

I pick up the mic and respond. They're sending me to a family fight without any cover. It means the aggressor is no longer there. The call is on a tiny street tucked up against the railroad tracks in an older neighborhood in the middle of the city.

The flat top roofs are a dead giveaway that the homes were built in the 1940's after the war. They must have slapped these babies together by the hundreds, maybe even the thousands, and this blue collar town ate them up as quickly as they could put them together. The people who could, have long since moved out. Some rented their places out to those who couldn't afford to buy—mostly ethnic minorities, and mostly below any recognizable standard of living. A small number of residents chose to dig in and stay. Their homes are easy to identify, with their neatly mowed lawns, decent paint, and fake waterfalls that you can buy at Home Depot. Just fill with water and plug it in.

This place is a blah, mustard yellow with white trim. Could go either way—rented or owned. I park on the other side of the street and walk across. I have to step around a black stain on the asphalt where someone's car leaked all its motor oil. Nothing is parked there at the moment, but a Honda Accord is parked in the driveway. The car's rear window is missing and a piece of cardboard is duct taped in its place.

Unconsciously, I switch my clipboard out of my gun hand. A woman stands behind the screen door watching me with an uncommitted expression. She's Latino, perhaps in her late forties, with a worn out look that makes her seem older. Her physical appearance reminds me a little bit of an avocado—small upper body, wide stomach and hips, and thin, toothpick-like legs.

In a moderate accent, the woman tells me that her husband is the culprit and has already left. I take down their names; he is Manuel Espinoza, and she is Lupe Espinoza. Lupe tells me that her husband got drunk and threw an ashtray at their daughter, Leticia. Leticia is in the living room icing an injury on her head.

"Hi." I step into the house. "Are you alright, or do you want to go to the hospital?"

She shakes her head. "I'm okay."

I check the damage. She's got a good sized welt with a two inch, purplish, horizontal line across the center of it. It looks like it really hurts. I pick up an ashtray from the floor and hold it in front of her. The width matches closely with the length of the bruising.

Leticia identifies it as the ashtray her father threw at her, and I slip it into an evidence envelope. She tells me her dad was recently laid off, and has been drinking more than usual. He spent much of the afternoon in the garage with a 12-pack of beer, and when it was depleted he came back inside the house for more.

"He saw me on the couch watching TV, and started in on me."

"Started in on you, how?" I pull out a statement form.

"You know, trying to pick a fight, and telling me I'm a lazy bitch." Leticia's eyes start to moisten. I stop asking questions, and give her time to collect her thoughts.

"Anyway, he threw the ashtray at me," she says.

Lupe is standing beside me nodding at everything the daughter says. "I divorced him already once," she says. "But then he went to AA and we got married again."

Leticia rolls her eyes. "You should have stayed divorced!" She turns to me, "I tell her that all the time."

Leticia looks about 18 or 19, and tells me she's studying to be a dental hygienist at the local community college. She's a slender girl, with almond shaped brown eyes and straight white teeth.

Her mother beams with pride. "My daughter, she's going to work for a dentist office."

They both agree that Manuel is a drunk and is prone to violent outbursts. Leticia says this is the first time he's been violent with her, and I believe it. Lupe says he's never been violent with her. That, I don't buy. Her tired eyes tell me the whole story without a word. She's spent a lifetime covering up for things she's too ashamed to admit.

The house is immaculate. In the corner of the living room is a statue of the Virgin Mary with a rosary draped over it. There are photographs propped up around the statue, old cracked black and white photos of family who must have passed away. It's a sad little shrine, but sweet and meaningful. There's a kind of simple perfection about it.

I take written statements from the two women. They sit next to one another like close friends. They hold hands, as if it's the two of them against the world. Manuel must have made their lives miserable.

When I'm finished with the paperwork, I ask them to tell me exactly what they want to happen. They both want him gone, for good. I tell them I will do everything I can if they're prepared to follow though. I tell them they have to be sure. They are.

We talk for a long time, and we go over what they should do when Manuel returns. I tell them to call 9-1-1 immediately, and to get the locks changed in the meantime. I prepare a bulletin for lineup, describing Manuel and his car, and advising that he's wanted for a felony assault. It also includes a request for other units to extra patrol the house during my off hours. In the interim, we make plans to meet with the district attorney's office the following day to get a temporary restraining order against Manuel.

9:02 p.m.

Dispatch is asking me when I'll be clear, and I realize I've spent over an hour and a half with the Espinozas. I hope the extra time has been well spent, and that they actually show up tomorrow.

I'm sent to a suspicious person wandering around a residential neighborhood, talking to himself. I'm actually covering another cop on a beat that adjoins mine. We get there together and speak with the man who called it in. He gives us the person's description—a white male in his late 20's wearing dark clothes.

We cruise around the neighborhood and locate the suspect a few blocks away. He's talking and gesturing as if speaking to someone else, but there's nobody there. We stop our cars just ahead of the guy. He looks over to the imaginary companion and says, "Oh boy, here we go again. Let me do the talking this time."

The cop I'm covering is my buddy, Ryan Kalani, and I'm thinking I could really have some fun with this call. I could start conversing with the invisible person as well, but I resist the temptation.

The guy appears to be just under six feet, with a tight sinuous body. Guys like that can be a handful if they want to fight. He's got a card identifying him as Peter Valentini, with an address of a board and care home a few blocks away. He seems nervous, eyes darting everywhere, and his voice modulation is all over the board. It's almost as if he's talking to us and then talking to someone across the street. Of course, there's nobody there. He doesn't strike me as being aggressive or violent, though. At least not now.

He knows who he is and where he is, but he believes that someone is speaking to him through a transistor in his mouth. We ask what the voice is saying to him and he starts getting agitated.

"Passages from the Bible," he says with frustration. "And I think you know that!"

We do our best to keep him calm while we have dispatch phone the group home he belongs to. Rather than risk upsetting Valentini by transporting him in the patrol car, we decide to wait for the group home counselor to pick him up.

A small Filipino woman arrives a few minutes later and takes Mr. Valentini back. She's by herself, so Kalani follows them back to the house, just in case.

I hear him go back in service, so I guess it all went okay.

9:25 p.m.

I'm driving back toward my beat, and turn down a street that cuts through a retail section of downtown. It's windy, cold, and most of the places are closed by this time of night, except a couple of restaurants and a handful of bars. A bus stop shelter on the corner catches my eye. It's one of those three-sided structures with plexiglas walls. There's a figure lying inside it, dark and curled in a ball.

I put myself off on a security check as I pull up to the open front. The person inside looks up at me with blurry eyes as I join him under the shelter. It provides a small amount of protection from the wind, but does nothing to lessen the cold. I notice that the wide bench must have been replaced recently. In its place is a row of spring loaded rubber seats that are barely a few inches wide, with no back or arm rests. Somehow, this poor guy has managed to fold down three of the seats and balance himself across them on a makeshift bed.

I illuminate my uniform and badge with the flashlight so he doesn't think he's about to get rolled. I ask if he's alright.

"I'm fine, officer," he says in a gravely voice. "I'll move along if you want me to."

"No, that's okay." I glance up the street. Except for a cluster of leaves clattering in a whirlwind beneath the streetlight, there's nothing moving. Even if the busses are still running, I doubt any of them would stop.

"Are you trying to get somewhere?" I ask, thinking I could give him a ride to a warmer spot.

"Nowhere to go," he says.

"What's your name?"

"Clem McMillen," he says with a shiver.

He catches me looking curiously at his thin cotton button up shirt. "Somebody stole my coat and hat." He forces a laugh. "Hey, what's a guy gonna do?"

I recognize Clem as a local drunk. I check to see if he's wanted for missing a court appearance, but he's clear. I tell him to be careful and I get back into the warm car.

I watch him curl back into a ball as I'm driving away, and I feel bad for the guy. Then, I get an idea. One that I think will make him feel better, and I know will make me feel better.

I drive to the station and go into the lunchroom. Two cops from my squad are eating lunch, Van Kirk and a woman named Baranova. They stop and watch me rifle through the donation bin, then shrug and go back to eating. I find the bag containing my clothes and pull out my old jacket. A favorite of mine since high school, it's a collegiate looking thing with a wool body and leather sleeves. The only thing missing is a school name and a varsity letter. It has a thick lining, elastic in the cuffs to block the wind, and will keep old Clem toasty on a night like this.

I get back in the car and drive downtown. My friend is still sprawled across the seats, now with a wad of newspaper for a pillow. I step out of the car and walk toward him.

He groans as he lifts his head, "Not again."

I realize he doesn't recognize me—his eyes only see a uniform and badge. I tell him I'm the same cop who just talked to him a few minutes ago. I must not have made much of an impression, because he just sits there expressionless.

"Anyway," I say, "I got this warm jacket here, and thought you might be able to use it."

"No, thank you." He starts to lay his head back down.

I stand in the dark for a few seconds, holding the jacket like a salesman at Macy's. Doesn't he at least want to try it on?

"You sure?" I ask. "It'll keep you warm."

He shakes his head. "Nothing to give you for it."

"No, no. I'm not trying to sell it. I'm giving it to you. You can keep it."

Clem sits up and two of the seats spring back with a thud. He reaches out for it, slowly, eyeing me the whole time. "Free for nothing?"

He slips an arm in and I work it over his shoulders, then I help him with the other sleeve. Now I really do look like a salesman. I scan the street to make sure one of my cohorts isn't driving by. Not that it's a bad thing I'm doing, it's not. It's just something that's not usually done. Since we're supposed to be impervious to feelings and emotions, it would be a little difficult to explain.

I step back to check him out. His craggy old face and wizened body looks out of place in the jacket, but he seems to like it. He smiles approvingly at his new ensemble, and then reaches out to shake my hand. Clem grips me with both of his and smiles. Doesn't say anything, just keeps smiling.

I tell him goodnight, and I get back into my warm car. I don't feel so guilty this time.

9:58 p.m.

I see a set of headlights in my rearview mirror, and wait for him to pass before pulling into the lane. I watch the old guy stretch back across the folding seats in his snappy new jacket. The car slows as it passes, and the sole driver makes eye contact with me. He has a scared, guilty look that's already enticed me to find a *legal* reason to stop him. No sooner does he pass me than he takes off. Maybe he read my look as well as I read his.

I note his license number and put it out of the radio. "I'll be trying to catch up to that vehicle," I say. It's the terminology we use to let everybody know that he's moving pretty good and to get ready for an all out pursuit. He blows through the empty intersection against the light, and makes a right turn onto the main boulevard. I give his new direction over the air.

When I catch up, I turn on my lights and give him a blast of the siren. Something in his driving tells me he's drunk, and I'm just as ready for him to pull over as I am for him to speed up. He does the latter. I update my status over the air to *in pursuit*.

I see flashing lights in my rearview mirror and know that my backup isn't far. We don't go but a few more blocks, when the guy suddenly takes a left turn down a narrow side street. He slows abruptly and I see him reaching down under his seat. Now I'm thinking he might be going for a gun. The last time this happened I reacted without thinking and ended up with a handful of stitches. My fingers are just about healed now, and I'd rather not go through that a second time.

I pick up my microphone. "He's slowing now, and it looks like he's reaching for something under the seat." Dispatch repeats my radio traffic to make sure the cover unit hears it. Now that we've slowed it gives him time to catch up to us. I see his lights swing around the corner and now he's right behind me.

The suspect is still rolling, but his foot is on the brake and he's only doing about five miles per hour. I see him bending and reaching, and I'm preparing myself mentally for the guy to jump out of the car firing. Suddenly, he stops.

In the back of my consciousness, I'm aware of a dog barking and realize that my cover is a K-9 unit. I'm thinking of that as I get out and start running toward the stopped car. I wouldn't be the first cop to run across the trajectory of a police dog, only to come up missing a nice chunk of ass. So, when I hear the rustling of footsteps and growling behind me, I freeze. The dog passes me by and I fall in behind him. The handler, a guy named Zaragosa, is right behind me.

The driver is still hunched forward when we get to the door. I fling it open. The dog lunges inside and locks his jaws around the guy's left upper arm. He shakes and tears, ripping the guy sideways out of the car. As his upper body hits the ground there's a clattering sound, and a metallic object rattles across the pavement beneath the driver.

"Gun!" I yell, as Zaragosa wallops the guy with his police baton. I dive for the gun and Zaragosa and his dog drag the guy free of the car. The driver's foot leaves the brake peddle and the car starts going again, now with nobody in it. I grab the gun as Zaragosa stands over the dog, telling him what a great job he's doing. I'm trying to figure out if I need to stay and help him or go after the runaway car. Another police car comes barreling around the corner. It looks like the dog has the guy pretty well detained anyway, so I take off running down the street.

The car is rolling at a snail's pace, but it's got a head start on me. It's not going straight, either. I notice it's slowly veering to the right where a whole row of cars are parked. I'm in an all out sprint, wondering if it'll even be possible for me to jump sideways into the car while running at this pace. At least the car door is already open. I stuff the handgun into my jacket pocket as I'm running. When I catch up to the car, I grip the door with my left hand and grab the steering wheel with my right. I swing my legs in at the same time. At that exact second there's a grinding crunch, and I'm jammed forward as the car smashes into a parked truck. I look in the mirror and see that the second car that arrived was the sergeant. He's standing in the middle of the street with his hands on his hips.

I'm not really happy about the way this went down either, but at least nobody was shot. I hear the sergeant jamming Zaragosa. He seems to be mainly pissed off that he let the dog yank the guy out while the car was still in drive. Besides the pursuit and the firearm report, we now have a vehicle accident and a dog bite report to write. The sergeant divides the work between us. I write the crime reports, since it's my case, and Zaragosa writes the crash and the dog bite. Turns out the driver's drunk, so I get the DUI as well.

11:00 p.m.

The doctor finishes sewing up the suspect at St. Theresa's. At the jail, I get a urine sample from him and leave him there to be booked in. He's mad about the dog bite, so he isn't about to give me any kind of statement. I unload the handgun in the back lot, and then log it into evidence.

I'm cleared to take my lunch, but I've got a ton of writing to do. I grab my bag from the lunchroom refrigerator and head back out. I park my patrol car in front of the Espinoza house. There's no change there—Manuel's truck is still gone. I unwrap my sandwich, and under the dim glow of my overhead map light, I eat and write.

The curtain inside the house moves a few times and I see either Lupe or Leticia, I can't tell which, glancing out at me. I'm hoping it gives them some piece of mind to see me out here. Things are slow on the street and dispatch has left me alone. I stay through my lunch and well beyond.

12:40 a.m.

The radio calls my numbers. "Forty-six, security check at the Eucalyptus Woods Apartments. Manager states the tenant hasn't been seen for several days, and there's a bad odor coming from inside."

Swell. Glad I just finished my sandwich, apple, and cookies. I thank the dispatcher and head in the direction of the complex.

The manager is waiting for me out front. I recognize her from previous calls there, and I know she's got her act together. If she called, then there's a good reason. As I approach the woman, she holds out a copy of the rental agreement with all of the renter's personal information. The unit is rented to Sheila Washburn-Chalmers, a 61 year old white woman with no emergency contact listed. The manager also hands me a passkey.

"Sorry to lay this one on you, but I'm afraid we got a ripe one," she says. "Next door neighbor called me about the smell. Had to get themselves a hotel room for the night."

It's a two-story building, and the apartment in question is a lower unit at the end of the building. She tells me the unit above is vacant. I get her information and the name of the neighbor who reported it to her. I inch up to the porch sniffing the air like a hound, trying to gauge how bad it's going to be. I smell it by the time I reach the door. I knock a few times as a precaution, and then let myself in.

The place looks vacant, and for a second I'm wondering if we've zeroed in on the wrong unit. But then the odor hits me like an invisible punch. It's so strong that I almost expect to see a nasty green cloud. I immediately start breathing only out of my mouth, though still able to taste a rancid tang.

A weak glow comes from somewhere in the back of the apartment. I walk through the dark living room, over an olive colored scalloped carpet. There's barely any furniture. The kitchen alcove also appears empty, except for a small table and two chairs. Not so much as a salt or pepper shaker is visible. I turn down the hallway, which I know from prior calls at other units in this building, leads to a bedroom on the left and bathroom straight ahead. The bathroom door is open and it looks barren as well.

The single light is coming from the bedroom. As I start down the hall, I see the carpet transitions to hardwood flooring in the bedroom. I also see the top of someone's head. It's a woman, lying on the floor in a sleeping bag. The bag is blue canvas, zipped all the way up around everything but her head. The woman is turned on her side away from me and her knees are tucked up slightly, causing the bag to form an 'S' shape. I step in, and around to the side she's facing. Her eyes are completely sunken in, and the skin on her face is a mottled purplish black. Some of the skin has cracked and is oozing. The woman's mouth is open, exposing rotted teeth and a long black tongue hanging sideways down her cheek.

The smell is unbearable. It's a sick, sweet, rotting meat, that smells very human and very much like death. Once you know it you'll never forget it. Even with my nose plugged, I still smell it all around me.

A large plastic water cup sits on the floor next to her, along with a 1.75 liter vodka bottle. Nothing else. Both the cup and the bottle are empty.

I'm chased back outside by the stench. The manager is waiting on the grass, the sleeve of her sweater covering her nose and mouth. I let her know what I found inside. *As if she hasn't already figured it out.* She thanks me, and tells me she'll be in the office if I need her. I switch my radio to a utility channel, and then ask dispatch to notify the coroner and give me an ETA.

I check the entire house, looking for any possibility that Ms. Washburn-Chalmers could have been murdered. There's nothing—all the doors and windows had been locked from the inside. There is no sign of a struggle, and nothing appears disturbed. Not that there is much here to disturb. Suicide is another possibility, but there is no note and no obvious means—except the vodka.

I open a narrow linen closet in the hallway, and step back to take in the scene. Empty vodka bottles stacked from floor to ceiling, probably a hundred of them. No food, no books, no furniture. Just her vodka.

I look at her for a little bit, wondering what she had accomplished in her life. Is a closet full of empty bottles her only legacy? *What could have gone so wrong?*

I go back to the car to get my clipboard and paperwork. I sit on the steps outside the apartment. It's quiet. A yellow bulb over the porch provides enough light for me to write. I sit with the open door behind me until the end of my shift. Dispatch finally gets a hold of me on the radio to tell me that the coroner's office hasn't called back yet. The sergeant has sent a midnight unit to relieve me. When she arrives, I give her the key and ask her to return it to the manager when the coroner is done.

3:00 a.m.

The sergeant is sipping a cup of coffee as he reads reports. I set my paperwork in his basket and he sets them down. I had hoped to get in and out unnoticed.

"Natural death at Eucalyptus Woods?"

"Yeah," I say. "Sure looks that way. I think she drank herself to death."

"Was she an 'O' or a 'Q'?" He peers at me over his reading glasses.

I cock my head sideways, frowning at my report and trying to figure out what the hell he means.

The sergeant takes a slow sip of his coffee. "You know, was her mouth like this?" He purses his lips in a round circle. "Or was her mouth like this?" He opens his mouth and flops his tongue out to the side.

I think back to the blotched skin, rotten teeth, and her dried up black tongue. Giving him a courtesy chuckle, I answer, "She was definitely a 'Q', Sarge."

As I make my exit, I glance into the watch commander's office across the hall. The chair is pushed in, the terminals are shut down and the light is off. The lieutenant must have taken off early. I wonder if he's home, or if he's paying a late-night visit to Tina. A couple of the guys had the same idea and are discussing it in the locker room when I come in. They quiet down for a second, but start up again when they see it's only me. Van Kirk is trying to organize a few of us to stakeout her apartment, and see if the LT's there. This is a lieutenant we're talking about, and I want nothing to do with it. Neither does anyone else. I get into my own car and pull out of the lot. In my mirror, I see Van Kirk head in the other direction. I wonder if he's going to drive by Tina's place.

3:32 a.m.

On my way home I take a detour downtown, past the bus stop where the old guy was sleeping earlier. He's not there now. I take a spin around the block, but don't see him anywhere. I hope old Clem found a better place to sleep.

Chapter 16

8:00 a.m.

My alarm goes off and I sit straight up in bed. What day is it? Where am I? And for that matter, who am I? The four hours of sleep I got wasn't enough. I can hear the girls in the other room playing dolls—it sounds like they've turned their closet into Barbie's motor home. It's a good sound, and one I could easily fall back asleep to if I didn't have something important to do.

I get up, shower, and dress in a sport coat and tie. Gale is surprised to see me up so early. I tell her I'm going in for court, and I give her an abbreviated version of the Lupe and Leticia Espinoza story. She fixes me some toast with jam, and a cup of tea. I kiss the girls and I'm out the door.

9:45 a.m.

To my delight, both Lupe and Leticia have shown up. Leticia takes her mother's arm as they sit in the small waiting room outside the district attorney's office. Lupe is wearing a yellow skirt and jacket with big white buttons. I'm sure it's what she wears to church, and it's a nice respectful image to project. One I'm hoping will compel the DA not only to charge the case as a felony, but also to push for a restraining order.

We do well on both counts. The case is charged as a felony, and the judge goes for the restraining order. It's nearly noon by the time we're done. I ask the Espinozas if they've heard from Manuel, and they say they haven't. I'm thinking he probably went somewhere last night where he continued drinking until he passed out. Whether in his truck or at a friend's house, either scenario is only temporary. I'd lay odds that he'll show up at the house today. I go over the drill again with the two women, making sure they know who to call and what to say.

By the time I get home, it's too late to go back to bed and too early to head into work. I spend some time playing with the girls while Gale goes out to do some shopping. Christmas is less than two weeks away, and she's been trying to get some time by herself.

4:45 p.m.

Sometimes I get to work and there's just a feeling in the air telling me that something's not right. I feel it when I walk in the building tonight. My eyes are burning because I'm so tired, and I'm not sure if it's that or there's really something going on. My suspicions are confirmed when I pass the cluster of bars and stripes in the watch commander's office. The clerical supervisor is also in there, which makes me think it has something to do with Tina, the amorous front office clerk.

I make a quick call home, just to touch bases before lineup. Gale tells me that my dad called for me after I left. Apparently he and my stepmom are having a Christmas party tonight, and he invited me to come. I call my dad and tell him I'm working tonight. I know he and his buddies get a kick out of seeing me in uniform, so I tell him I'll try to make it by.

I overhear some whispering about Tina during lineup, and only one of our two sergeants shows up to give tonight's briefing. Everything supports my inkling that something's going on. Should be an interesting night.

5:30 p.m.

I bust out of lineup and head straight down to the Espinoza house, hoping to find Manuel trying to weasel his way in. There are no cars in the driveway and all the lights are out. I drive slowly around the neighborhood, ready to find him parked off to the side watching the house. There's nothing.

5:39 p.m.

They send me to a call on the west end of my beat. The "distressed caller" is asking for the police, the dispatcher says. "Unknown problem."

I arrive at an upscale two story home at the end of a court. It's outfitted with a ton of Christmas lights, fake reindeer and a lighted sleigh on the lawn. I wonder what the caller is so *distressed* about.

I'm met by a young woman, maybe a year or two younger than me. She's a pretty girl, dressed warmly in a fur-lined parka.

"I can't get my car out," she says, her bottom lip in a pout.

I look around and see a silver Toyota parked between two other cars in front of her house.

"The neighbors are having a party," she says. "They parked their cars all over the place, and I have to take my finals tonight. How am I going to get to class?"

I take a closer look at her Toyota, and see the wheels cockeyed and the rear bumper is flush against the truck parked behind her. I think for a minute, and I suspect the dispatcher knew exactly what this girl wanted. They were just hesitant to give me the details of what they knew was a bullshit call. Then, I remember the old woman who needed half and half.

"Sure," I say. "Give me the keys and I'll try to pull'er out of that spot for you."

It takes about five minutes of inching backward and forward before I free her car. "Here you go," I say, as I get out of her car. "Now you have to do something for me."

The girl looks at me blankly, probably thinking I'm going to ask her out. "You have to get an 'A' on your final." I smile at her. "My reputation is on the line here."

She laughs and says she'll do her best.

6:00 p.m.

A call goes out to a cop on the adjoining beat, and I'm dispatched to cover him. He's a guy named Zabinski, a good guy, maybe even the smartest person on our squad, but he puts more effort into getting out of work than he does just doing his work. I'm always wondering if everything Zabinski does is just part of some intellectual social experiment he's conducting.

The call is an assault with a deadly weapon, a stabbing. I roll with my lights and siren, dodging around mentally impaired drivers who apparently all missed the question on the test about pulling to the right when an emergency vehicle is behind you.

Zabinski is already at the apartment complex and out of the car when I arrive. A guy is leaning against the stairway holding his stomach, and a group of woman are surrounding him. He appears to be East Indian, wearing a tall purple turban and sporting a long untamed beard. The women are all yelling, crying, and wagging their tongues in a high-pitched wail.

"This guy was stabbed by his brother-in-law," Zabinski says to me. He reaches over to hold up the guy's top, which looks like very comfortable pajamas. "Look, it's barely bleeding."

I see a narrow slit, maybe an inch long at the most, on the side of the Indian's belly. Like Zabinski said, it's barely bleeding. The victim acts as if it doesn't hurt, and he's talking to the women in his native language. Despite the unique cultural differences, I recognize it as ordinary male machismo. He's downplaying the whole thing.

I'm not as certain that it's a big nothing as Zabinski seems to be. I once went to an accident call where a guy had crashed his motorcycle. The guy was unconscious when I got there, and the ambulance people thought he was just drunk. Turns out he was, but he ended up dying later that night from a traumatic brain injury. My lesson was that injuries aren't always what they seem.

I tell Zabinski that we might want to consider sending this guy to the hospital and calling out the detectives.

"What for?" he says. "A superficial cut?"

I shrug. *It's his case; I'm just here for backup.* The brother-in-law is already gone and Zabinski doesn't seem too interested in looking for him. I help him with a few statements and then we're done.

Fortunately, the Indian loses the attitude and decides to go get checked out at the hospital on his own. Zabinski sticks around to see what the doctor says. Turns out they're admitting the guy for observation.

7:05 p.m.

I start toward the Espinoza house, but I'm preempted by another call. It's a burglary report on the main drag, all the way on the other side of my beat. The address is down a dark driveway that leads to a bunch of circa 1940's one-room cottages. They're tucked back off the street, and I never even knew they were here. There are about ten of them, all clustered around a flat area that was probably grass at one time. Now it's just a rutted flat of dirt and weeds.

I find unit number nine in the darkest corner of the property. A woman answers the door and invites me inside. There are no lights, just a couple of candles burning on the table. It's a seedy little place, but it's warm and she has it decorated the best she can. There's a stitched blanket type thing hanging across one wall, depicting a Mayan or Aztec scene. A bed takes up most of the room, and then a small counter with a hotplate on it is the extent of the kitchen. I'm not sure about a bathroom, and I don't ask.

The woman extends her hand to shake. "I'm Isabel Cota," she says. We shake hands. She's a Latino woman, small build, probably in her fifties, with wild gray strands woven starkly through mostly jet black hair. She's wearing pointy, librarian type, glasses. She's older and a little weathered, but she was probably a really attractive woman in her day. Something in her manner hints at a type of strength I'm unaccustomed to. I'd guess it has something to do with overcoming adversity.

Isabel shows me the backside of the door where the deadbolt hangs by a screw. "Someone kicked my door in earlier today when I was out."

I examine the splintered framing where the latch was once connected. "Anything missing?"

She shakes her head. "Nothing, really. Some cigarettes maybe, and some change off the dresser. I don't have all that much to take."

I take a property sheet from my clipboard and start jotting some notes. I want her to know that I'm taking her loss seriously. We talk a little while I'm writing, and she seems surprised that I haven't heard her name before. Apparently she's got a long record.

"You're probably too young to know about me," she says.

I ask what some of the old cops would tell me about her and she laughs. Her smile exposes a few missing teeth.

"I've been in and out of jail my whole life." She pushes her glasses up the bridge of her nose a bit. "I've been a dope fiend since I was sixteen."

She slides the sleeve of her sweater up her arm revealing a long row of deep scars. "These are *old* tracks," she says proudly. "I've been clean for three years."

"That's a great accomplishment." As if I have any idea what it's like to kick a heroin habit.

We talk some more. She puts a pan of water on the burner and asks me if I want tea. I decline, and she makes a cup for herself. She talks openly about her past—run-ins with other cops, mostly older guys, many of whom she mentions by name. She talks about occasions when she had to "work the streets." I take it to mean she was also a prostitute. I feel privileged, like I've been let under the barbed wire, behind the wall, into the underworld. Most people go to great lengths to hide that stuff from cops, but Isabel seems to take comfort in the openness with me. The small dimly lit quarters and the tenor of the conversation reminds me of a confessional.

I sit at her tiny table, writing my report under a candle's flickering light. For some reason, I tell her I hope to work undercover some day. A few moments of uncomfortable silence pass between us and I wonder if I've crossed some invisible line.

"I know a lot of drug people." Her words are barely audible.

I finish taking down her information and gather up my things. Isabel stares deep into her mug, quiet with her thoughts. We sit there for a minute without a word.

She looks up. "I never thought I would snitch, but it was probably one of the drug addicts around here who kicked in my door."

We talk some more, and both agree to let her think it over. I tell her that I work nights on the beat covering her area, and that I could stop by next week to talk more.

"Okay," she says. "But come late, and park out on the street so people won't know you're here."

8:22 p.m.

I'd like to check the Espinoza house again, and I'd also like to make an appearance at my dad's party. Then the radio calls my numbers, and it looks like I won't have time to do either.

They're sending me to cover Zabinski again. This time, it's to the lobby of an apartment building where a woman is reportedly "acting crazy."

Zabinski comes on the radio and asks for the cross streets of the address. I know he knows where it is, and I suspect he's just harassing the dispatchers. They give him the cross streets.

"The apartment manager states the woman is in the lobby now, slamming her head against the wall." The dispatcher's words are seasoned and raspy, like a lifetime smoker. She's a salty old gal we call Grace.

"And what's the manager's name?" Zabinski asks.

No response on the radio. I'm imagining Grace sitting there thinking, who cares? She finally answers, "Ed."

Zabinski keeps pressing her. "And can you give me a description of the suspect?"

Another long pause. Apparently Grace had as much of Zabinski as she could handle. "Well, if you get there and find more than one woman slamming her head against the wall, let me know. Then I'll help you narrow it down with a description."

That shuts him up.

We arrive at the same time. The apartment house is a square two-story building built around a courtyard. You have to walk through the lobby to get into the complex. The lobby has a large window, and through it I see a man standing near a Christmas tree, talking with someone out of my view. The wood paneled room is warmly decorated with colored lights, and fake snow sprayed around the large windows. The man opens the locked door to allow us in.

A blond woman in a bright red dress and high heals is seated on a couch. They are the only people in the lobby, and we quickly determine they are the parties involved. He accuses the woman of ramming her head into the wall, and she claims she didn't. Simple as that.

Zabinski deals with the woman and I move the manager to the opposite corner. He claims the woman does not live there and is not known to him. When I ask how she got into the locked lobby, he repeats my question.

"How did she get in?" He stares at the door for an answer. "I guess someone else let her in."

"That's a lie," she hollers from behind me.

I take down his information, and ask him to sit quietly for a moment. Just like separating two kids in a schoolyard.

I join Zabinski, and notice a red welt in the center of the woman's forehead. I scan the walls while they're talking. I find a round, greasy smudge on the wall above the couch, just to the left of where she's sitting. If she had been kneeling on the couch, her head would have been at about the right height. We keep them apart while Zabinski and I conference in a neutral corner of the room.

I tell him that the manager is playing dumb. Zabinski says the woman admits to being the manager's girl-on-the-side. Apparently they rendezvous in whichever unit happens to be vacant. Tonight they had an argument of some kind. He threatened to break it off and she threatened to go tell his wife. She still denies the head pounding scene.

Zabinski decides to send the woman on her way. She grabs her purse and storms toward the door, then stops and turns back toward the man. "I'm sure you'll have a happy holiday!" She walks out, slamming the door behind her.

I walk back to my car wondering if it was said to make the man feel guilty, or if it was a threat. If she's hell bent on ruining Ed's Christmas, she'll be back.

I check my watch. Still enough time to swing by my dad's party.

9:13 p.m.

I normally wouldn't go to a party while I'm working, but this is the first Christmas since my dad remarried, and they're excited to host something at their new house.

The house is teeming with people, some of whom I know and some of whom I pretend to know. There are the usual jokes, "Are we being too loud, officer?" or "Better give this guy a sobriety test." I have my plastered smile at the ready.

I see my brother, the college student, and make my way over to him. He gives me a rundown on the foods he's already sampled, what's good and what to stay away from. I pick up a couple of crunchy things wrapped in bacon, mounted on a toothpick.

"George-46," my radio squawks.

I balance my snacks on a napkin with one hand and pull my radio out of the case. "Go ahead," I say quickly, so dispatch doesn't hear the party in the background.

"Start to cover the downtown unit on a code-3 call," she says. "The fire department is responding to a fifteen year old . . . The caller says . . . Apparently her intestines fell out into the toilet."

I quickly turn down the volume knob, but it's too late. My brother turns ashen and sets his plate of food down. I give him an apologetic look and set mine down as well. I wave across the room to my dad, point to my radio, and shrug.

I'm outside and in my car, wondering what in the world this call is about. I've never heard of such a thing. Gory images flash in front of me like some macabre version of Rorschack inkblots. I'm driving through the city with my lights and siren on, passing cars, driving left of center, through crowded intersections, but I'm not seeing any of it. My mind is preparing itself for a new set of images. These will undoubtedly be more vivid, and more permanent.

It's another apartment complex, this one much bigger, with interior hallways on several floors. The fire rig and another police car are stopped dead in the street out front as traffic inches around them like spit on a window. The sound of black women screaming helps me find my way to the unit. The door is open and a fireman stands in the doorway, motioning me down the hall.

I step into complete chaos. Although there's screaming and crying and several large women in nightclothes, my eyes immediately focus on the floor next to a flocked Christmas tree. A firefighter and the other cop are hunched over a newborn infant, umbilical cord and placenta still attached, and white cheesy film covering it. The baby is blue and not moving.

Behind me, I hear the firefighter who was standing at the door. "These fucking people! What's wrong with them? They're fucking animals!"

I inspect the group of women for the one who appears most calm. She's a young heavy-set girl sitting silently on the couch. She's wearing a faded blue nightgown with blood all over it, and she's got a bloody towel wadded between her legs. I keep searching for someone else. I pick a woman who's trying to calm another one.

"Can I talk with you a minute?" I say motioning her toward a bedroom.

She follows me down a hallway littered with bloody towels and discarded feminine pads. I ask her if she's okay, and she nods yes. I ask her if she can tell me what happened tonight.

"We were just about to go to bed," she says. "Tinesha was in the bathroom."

"Is Tinesha the one on the couch?"

"Yeah. She's my niece. She's only fifteen." The woman wipes her eyes. "We didn't know she was pregnant. She's a big girl, and I guess she kinda hid it from everyone."

The woman tells me that while Tinesha was in the bathroom, she called out for someone to bring her some scissors. Her sister brought them to the door and Tinesha reached out, took them, and then closed the door. Later, Tinesha came out of the bathroom and went directly into the bedroom. Nobody thought much about it.

Sometime later, Tinesha's mother went into the bathroom and started screaming. There was blood all over, and what looked like a pile of intestines in the toilet. They thought they had come out of Tinesha while she was going to the bathroom. Someone called 9-1-1. When the firemen arrived, they pulled the baby out of the toilet and tried to revive it. The woman begins to sob.

I step into the bathroom. A purple handled scissors sits on a counter covered with bloody handprints. I stare into the toilet, trying to visualize what the mother saw. Unfortunately I can.

I jot down the aunt's information and what she is able to provide about Tinesha—age, school, etc. I would like to move Tinesha and her family to another room while they work on the baby, but the place is too small and I don't know if Tinesha's condition can handle being moved. Two ambulances arrive and they take Tinesha and the baby to St. Theresa's, through it's pretty apparent there is no hope of reviving the baby.

Things calm down a bit after they're taken out, and I take a few statements to help the cop who's assigned to the call. We're both numb. There's a pungent smell in the room like nothing I've ever been around. I'll be glad when I can leave. The sergeant stops by and gets the rundown from the other cop. I finish my statements and give them to him.

Before leaving, I stop at the door and take in the scene. The floor is littered with sterile wrappers and first aid paraphernalia. A tacky pool of blood, about the size of a football, has seeped into the carpet and has already started to clot. It changes color as the Christmas lights flash on and off behind it.

10:10 p.m.

I clear myself from the call and dispatch asks me if I want to take my lunch break. I switch to the utility channel and tell them I'll be taking it at my dad's house. I give them his phone number in case I can't hear them calling me on the radio.

I get back there and the party is still in full swing. I go directly into the bathroom and wash up. Even though I didn't touch anything at the call, I can't shake the grimy feeling. When I walk out I'm surrounded by my dad's buddies.

"What happened?" they all ask. "Did you have to go take care of a drunk or something?

"Yeah, something like that," I say with a forced laugh.

One of them nudges my dad, "Your kid had to go wrestle a drunk!" They all laugh heartily. I look across the room and see my brother watching me. He's not laughing.

After awhile, I say goodbye to my dad and step-mom and to their friends. My brother walks with me outside.

"You alright?" he asks.

"Yeah, how come?

He looks down at my radio and shakes his head ominously.

"Why?" I say. "Did you hear that call I got?"

"I heard enough of it."

I feel bad for spoiling his night. I wish he hadn't heard it. "Don't say anything to dad, okay?"

He shakes his head. "How can you even tell anyone about something like that?"

"I don't."

We hug each other, and I drive off.

11:15 p.m.

There is a lot of commotion on the radio—something about a possible sexual assault. The call must have come out as I was leaving my dad's. A woman was reportedly running naked down the street. I missed the initial call, but I'm listening to the bedlam it caused. Nearly every cop in the city is rolling, regardless of how far from their beat. The midnight shift just hit the street and a bunch of them are headed there as well.

The location of the call strikes a familiar note with me. I flip my radio to scan and pick up a car-to-car transmission that's been discretely moved to another, rarely used, channel. They're two sergeants talking about the call. When one of them mentions Tina, I recognize why the address is familiar. The call is at Tina's apartment, and she's the assault victim running naked. *Holy shit!*

I look around frantically for a car to stop. I want to make myself so busy that there's no way I'll be sent to help out there. A scandal like this, I don't need to be involved in. Other cops are starting to figure out who it is, and they're suddenly doing the same thing. A sudden rash of random car stops clogs the radio channel.

"George-46?"

I click my mic without saying anything.

"Forty-six, if you're clear, start for the area and assist with a search for the suspect."

"Damn it!" I write down the description and start toward the call. I visualize the suspect in my mind based on the description given, trying to match it with any of the cops, sergeants, or the lieutenant who've been rumored to have been with Tina. It's a generic description though, and could be almost any one of them.

I take my time getting there. I arrive just as an ambulance is driving off—presumably with Tina inside. The crime scene van is parked on the grass outside Tina's front door, illuminating the whole place with side-mounted halogen lights. Cops are going every which way, some arriving and some leaving, but none are sticking around. The watch commander's car pulls up and he and a sergeant get out. They go into the apartment and come out after only a couple of minutes. A couple of others do the same.

I wait until they all leave, and I walk from the parking lot over to the van. The evidence technician comes out with an embarrassed smile. He's a young guy they call Shorty. I think he really wants to be a cop.

"Is it a legit rape?" I ask.

He shakes his head. "I don't think so. Bet it's another attention getter."

Van Kirk joins us, and he's already laughing—obviously not one of the guys who has something to worry about.

"You guys see the parade coming in and out of here?" Shorty asks.

I nod. "What's that all about?"

"They're cleaning the entire place out," he says. "Tina had photographs of every one of the guys she's been with, all tacked up on her wall. Everybody's coming by to get rid of evidence. I've been ordered not to photograph the scene until all of it's gone."

Now I wish I hadn't been so nosey.

Shorty motions toward the inside of his van. "She says the guy raped her with a broomstick."

Me and Van Kirk glance at the broom lying in the back, labeled with an evidence tag.

Van Kirk lets out a roaring laugh. "Did you sniff it to see if she's telling the truth?"

The odd smile returns to Shorty's face. "What good evidence tech wouldn't?"

"Well?" Van Kirk asks.

"Oh yeah," Shorty says. "There's no doubt that broomstick has seen action tonight. Now, whether someone forced Tina or she did it to herself, who knows?" He grabs his camera out of the van and ducks back inside the apartment.

I head for my car and hear Van Kirk laughing all the way back to his. I drive away wondering whether or not Tina was really raped. She's obviously got some relationship issues, but does that make her a nut case? If she faked the rape, broom stick, naked sprint down the street and all, she's got real problems. But if it was a genuine rape, then the police department has real problems. I think back to her scorched cat in the middle of the night. Was that faked too?

12:05 a.m.

A call of a drive-by shooting goes out and I jump on the opportunity to clear from this call. A midnight unit is the primary officer on the shooting and I am one of three others sent as cover. The call is in the middle of a dilapidated neighborhood where the narrow streets are a maze of slum quality apartments. The streets are dark because many of the streetlights have been shot out, and every fence and street sign is covered with gang graffiti.

I'm flying down the street and see a fire engine lumbering along, code-3, ahead of me. They motion me to pass, probably to make sure the shooting is over before they roll into the scene.

I pass them and slide into a left turn that takes me into the pit of the neighborhood. Flashing lights direct me to the driveway where two cops have just pulled up. I stop behind them and the fire truck stops behind me. Other units are checking the area for a white Cadillac, described by a witness as the car the shots came from.

There's a black kid, about sixteen, lying on his side—a narrow red stream starting to work its way down the incline of the driveway. Another similar aged black kid is standing next to the victim, holding a spoon and soup bowl. The kid on the ground is barely conscious and won't say anything other than, "Nigga shot me." The firefighters start working on him, and it looks like he's got a small caliber entry wound just above his right hip.

An ambulance arrives and they begin loading the kid up. I move to the other kid who's busy eating whatever is in the bowl.

"Hey," I say. "Did you see what happened?"

"Yeah, my cousin got shot."

"Did you see who did it?"

He shovels another heaping spoonful into his mouth. "Naw, man."

"What are you eating, there?" I ask.

He peers into his bowl for a second. "Gumbo."

"You must be pretty upset, your cousin getting shot and all."

He plops another chunk into his mouth. "Yep."

Just then a plain tan sedan pulls up and two family counselors get out. They work out of the police department and, among other things, assist at traumatic incidents. They speak to one of the other cops who points them in my direction.

"I understand he witnessed his cousin getting shot?" one of the counselors says to me. "Do you think he needs grief counseling?"

The counselors follow my gaze over to the kid who's wolfing down the last of his gumbo.

"I think somehow he'll manage."

1:15 a.m.

I finally hit the wall. My eyes are beyond burning, and I feel like I could fall asleep at the next red light. I open the window and feel an arctic blast on my face. Things on the street are starting to quiet down a tad, and I'm thinking of asking the sarge if I could comp off a couple of hours. Before I do, I'll make a quick spin by the Espinoza house.

I turn onto the dead end street where they live. Colored lights twinkle from a few homes, but most are dark. The two women have hung a wreath in the window with the words, *Peace on Earth*. A message to Manuel perhaps, or possibly an expression of their unity and strength. Maybe it was the only decoration left in the store.

I search to the end of the block for the truck, but it's not there. All the cars are empty and covered in frost. I pass their house on the way out, and picture the makeshift alter in the corner of the room.

A pair of headlights swing in off the main cross street, heading slowly toward me. The outline of a truck comes into view and it slows to a near stop. He's seen me.

I get on the radio and tell them I have a possible suspect in a felony assault. Scenario options flash through my mind; he's drunk and going to take off, he's armed and going to shoot it out, he doesn't know there's a warrant out for him and he goes along with the program. I've already ruled out that he'll try to run on foot.

The truck starts moving again, and now I'm wondering if he's going to ram into me. I stay stopped in front of the house to discourage him from trying to run inside. He continues at a slow speed, passing within inches of my car. We make eye contact and I see that it's Manuel. I also see he looks drunk.

I make a hard turn into a driveway and flip around behind him. It's a dead end court and it'll be tough for him to turn the truck. I hit my lights as he comes to the end, and he stops. I switch from radio to loudspeaker and order Manuel to shut off the engine and drop the keys out the window. It takes him a few minutes of fumbling, but he complies. He slides out as I'm walking up, and I tell him to stay put. I give him a quick pat search and turn him toward the truck. My backup pulls onto the street as I'm handcuffing Manuel.

I ask the other cop if he would mind parking the truck for me while I transport Manuel to the station. Before I do, I make a quick stop at the house to let the women know he's on his way to jail. It's late, but I know it might help them sleep better.

Leticia answers the door and her mother is in the shadows behind her. They're visibly relieved, and very thankful.

3:00 a.m.

I finish booking Manuel and take a written statement from him. He admits throwing the ashtray at his daughter and uses his "drinking problem" and loss of a job as excuses. I finish the DUI report and end up getting off at my regular time. Manuel's arrest gave me a temporary burst of energy, but the exhaustion has caught up with me again. I turn in my paperwork, change out of my uniform and head home.

The bed is going to feel so good tonight.

4:13 a.m.

I wake up to Gale rubbing my shoulder.

"The police department is on the phone," she whispers.

"Hello?" I say, fumbling the phone from her hand to mine.

As the layers of confusion start to fade, I realize it's the desk officer calling. He's asking something about my car being broken into. I have no idea what he's talking about.

"My car wasn't broken into," I tell him.

"Are you sure? Because the jail recovered some of your property from a drunk who was brought in tonight."

I'm trying to figure out what Manuel Espinoza could have possibly gotten his hands on that belongs to me. "Was it Espinoza?"

"No," he says. "A downtown drunk by the name of Clem McMillen. He was wearing your jacket when he was arrested. The jailers found your name printed on the tag inside."

The guy in the bus stop. "Uh, yeah," I clear the night from my throat. "I know who you're talking about. Uh, there was no car burglary. I gave him my jacket."

Silence on the other end of the line. *I knew people wouldn't get it.* "Okay, whatever you say."

I'm lying in the dark after hanging up the phone. Gale has already fallen back asleep. A carrousel of images float past me; Clem, Lupe, Leticia, Manuel, Tinesha, her baby, the kid eating gumbo, his cousin, Tina, Shorty and his broomstick, Isabel Cota, the apartment manager and his girlfriend, the Indian guy with the knife wound.

I take a deep breath and let it out slowly, unsure if I'll be able to get back to sleep.

Chapter 17

4:45 p.m.
I check my mail slot on the way to the locker room and find a message from Lupe Espinoza asking me to phone her. I have a few minutes before lineup, so I give her a call. She and her daughter want to thank me for helping them. To show their gratitude they're inviting me to come by during my shift for an "authentic Mexican meal." We have a strict policy against receiving gratuities of any kind, but I accept the invitation nevertheless. I can tell it means a great deal to them. We shoot for around eight o'clock, barring any emergency calls.

4:59 p.m.
There is a goodly amount of speculation among the squad about Tina. One rumor is that she's been committed on a psychiatric hold. Another is that she had a fling with one of the lesbians in the department, which was the impetus to her downward spiral. Another story, and the one I find most intriguing, is that Tina's sexual conquests reached as high as the Chief of Police. Though a little far fetched, it would definitely explain why everybody is dancing on a tightrope around here.

The room falls silent as the sergeants and lieutenant come in. First order of business is the mall. We're reminded that with only two days until Christmas we need to keep the shoppers feeling safe. We're told to get out of our cars and walk through whenever we have some free time.

They briefly go over the vacation schedule, which gives me both Christmas Eve and Christmas day off. I had to trade another guy who wanted New Years Eve, which is no big deal to me. But it's the first time I've had enough seniority to actually be off on Christmas day.

5:35 p.m.

First call of the night. I'm sent to a possible injury accident on someone else's beat. Not real happy about it, and hope it isn't an indicator of the kind of night the dispatcher has in store for me.

I arrive at the intersection where the collision was reported, a major state route through the city. It leads west, toward a bridge that crosses the bay, and is heavily traveled by tractor-trailer rigs. There are no cars in the intersection, only broken glass and a horrendous set of thick black skid marks. A bus is stopped off to the side with its flashers on, and the driver is standing next to it waving me over.

"Craziest thing I ever seen," he blurts out before I can even stop my car.

I give the bus a quick look and see there's no damage. He follows my eyes and holds up his hands. "No, no. Wasn't me who got hit," he says. "Was a guy in a tiny Honda car. Poor son-of-a-bitch got plowed into by a big semi."

"Where are they?"

He points west, in the direction of the skids. "The guy in the semi just kept driving. I don't think he even knew he hit the Honda."

"Well, where's the Honda?"

"That's the thing of it! It's stuck to the front of the semi truck, and the driver's still inside. Me and some other people was blowing our horns to get the semi's attention, but he kept on driving along."

I thank him and pull onto the main highway, leaving a little rubber of my own. I'm trying to visualize the position of the car in relation to the semi, and how in the world this is possible. If what the bus driver says is accurate, I'd better stop the semi before it crushes the tiny car. I follow the skid marks, which look like a wide black set of train tracks running down the center of the third lane. I race through a couple of intersections where people are pulled over looking stunned. I go for nearly a mile before I catch up to flashing emergency lights on the back of a stopped big rig.

I drive past him and pull to the curb just ahead. I'll be dammed if there isn't a pale yellow Honda plastered sideways across the grill of the semi. Its tires, or what's left of them, are smoldering, and the driver is still inside. He's a white guy with a wild head of black hair and huge terrified eyes.

The semi driver jumps down from his cab, still a little confused about what happened. He helps me yank open the Honda's buckled passenger door. Out climbs the driver, one long lanky leg at a time, followed by a long narrow torso, and finally his bushy head. He stands so tall it's hard to believe he could have even fit into the miniature car.

I ask him if he's hurt.

"No, I don't think so," he says. "But I'm certainly glad to get off that wild ride. I didn't think he was ever going to stop."

The semi driver, a grandfatherly guy with a day old beard, is apologizing all over the place. He says his cab sits so high he never even saw the Honda pull out in front of him. He might have never known he was pushing the car sideways down the road if it weren't for all the people honking at him.

"I guess the toll taker would have told me about it when I got to the bridge," he says.

Zabinski pulls up to assist me. He surveys the truck, the position of the Honda, and the four-wheel skids stretching back up the roadway as far as the eye can see. He's speechless. After taking a statement for me, we get the Honda towed and the two guys are on their way. Zabinski sticks around to talk.

"You hear about the Indian with the hole in his stomach?"

"Sounds like a pathetic joke," I say.

"No, I'm serious." Zabinski hands me the statement he just took. "From the other day. You covered me on the stabbing."

"Yeah?"

"Well, I had to follow-up on the case, per the sergeant. The guy's in intensive care and may not make it. That's why I missed

lineup. I went to St. Theresa's and talked to him. They opened him
up and dumped all his intestines onto a tray."

"What the hell for?"

"I guess so they could wash 'em off. The knife punctured his
bowels and his shit got all over the place. Now he's laying there,
turban all askew and a tub full of guts on his lap. Pretty fucked up,
eh?"

"Yeah, pretty fucked up." Of course, in my mind I'm thinking
the fucked up part is that Zabinski nearly left that scene without
taking a report. Good lesson for me, too. A small stab wound
doesn't always equal small injury.

6:27 p.m.

Dispatch is calling me to see if I can clear.

"Affirmative," I say. "What do you have holding?"

"Attempt suicide," she says. She gives me the address and I
realize that it's another call off my beat. Now I'm starting to get
pissed off. I haven't even been on my own beat yet!

I get to the house and dispatch updates me that the victim,
Dave, shot himself with a rifle. *He shot himself with a rifle and it's only
an "attempt" suicide?*

The fire department and my cover unit pull up behind me, and
we end up all on the front porch together like a bunch of scouts
selling cookies. I'm thinking this guy might be on the other side of
the door with the gun, ready to shoot us. It's a small woodsy home
that looks as if it's had a custom remodel.

The door is unlocked, and we stand off to the side as I knock
loudly and then push it open. I call out Dave's name. A weak,
crying voice responds, "In here."

We make our way through the living room, into a wide
contemporary kitchen with an adobe looking tiled floor. We find the
victim, Dave, sitting on a kitchen chair holding his face. An
abundance of blood oozes between his fingers, and a rifle is lying at
his feet. I holster my weapon and use my foot to slide the rifle away
from him.

"What happened, Dave?" I ask.

He begins to sob. His head bobs spasmodically, flinging drops of blood in an arc on the tile beneath him. We all unconsciously take a step back.

"I can't go on," he cries. "I don't want to live anymore. Everything's gone wrong. Look, I even fucked this up."

He momentarily removes his hands from the left side of his face, revealing an irregular gaping hole that extends from the corner of his mustache to the top of his jawbone. The bottom half of his left ear appears to be missing, and a bloody chunk of flesh, roughly the shape of a cashew, dangles precariously in its place.

"Go ahead and keep pressure on that," says one of the firemen. Dave clamps his hands back over the wound.

My backup, Zabinski, examines the rifle. It's a long narrow 30-30, with a fancy western-style wooden stock. It looks like the kind of thing your grandpa would give as a gift if you lived in Montana.

"Couldn't reach all the way," he says. "The barrel was in my mouth and it slipped when I tried to pull the trigger."

Through the kitchen, I see a family room with a Christmas tree and stockings hanging from a mantel. As the firemen begin treating Dave, I walk over to check things out. There are four stockings with names stitched onto them; Leah, Coco, Susan, and Dave. A thought runs through my head: *What if Dave killed his family before he turned the gun on himself?*

I embark on my hunt to check the welfare of Leah, Coco, and Susan. Walking through someone's home definitely gives you an insight into their lives. You're privy to their most sacred belongings, their quirks, their habits, their cleanliness, and even their sexual practices. It's a lesser known perk of being a cop.

The remainder of the house is empty, and oddly enough only one of the rooms is set up as a bedroom. It has a king size bed and a wedding photo of Dave and a woman. They've also got a bountiful collection of pornographic videos in the stand beneath the TV.

I step into the backyard where two large but friendly dogs collide into me, leaving a wavelike arrangement of fur across the thigh of my uniform pants. I find a large shed in the corner of the yard, locked from the outside. The windows are covered and I can't see in. The ground outside doesn't have any signs of blood, drag marks, or shell casings, and I'm coming to the conclusion that Dave is the only one involved. I'm also assuming that Leah and Coco are the names of the two dogs.

Returning to the kitchen, I see that my partner and the firefighters have calmed Dave considerably. He has stopped bawling and is sitting quietly while they take his blood pressure readings. I ask Dave if there is a key to the shed in the backyard. He digs through his pocket and hands me a key ring. I go back out and try a couple of keys until I get one to open the padlock. Nothing inside but lawn furniture and tools.

I return his keys, but the thought of other victims still nags at me. Finally I see a lull in the activity.

"Where's Susan?" I ask.

Dave goes hysterical. He pulls away from the firefighters, heaves himself to the floor, and begins wailing like a sick cow.

"She left me!" He makes a halfhearted attempt to crawl toward the rifle and is quickly pounced on by Zabinski, me, and a fireman. "I don't know where she is! I want to die! Just let me die!"

The firemen look at me like I'm some kind of idiot.

"What did you do that for?" Says Zabinski. "We'd finally calmed him down."

I thought my question had been innocent enough, but in retrospect it was probably ill-timed. They must think I was taunting the poor guy. I consider trying to explain my logic, but when I look at their annoyed expressions I decide to let it go.

The ambulance comes and I follow it to St. Theresa's. Dave is admitted and taken into surgery. The nurses have instructions to call upon Dave's discharge, so we can bring him for a psychiatric evaluation.

I swing by the station to log the rifle into evidence, and then head back onto the street.

7: 20 p.m.

Bradford gets me on the air and wants to meet up at the mall for a walk through. He says it over the main channel to make sure the sergeants hear. We meet near the food court entrance, and because parking is a horrendous, we pull the cars right onto the sidewalk outside the doors.

I hold the door for a man and his young daughter who are laden with packages. The father manages to free one hand and raise it in the air.

"I didn't do it," he says, proud of himself for being so clever. I immediately have a fantasy that I let the door go, crushing him and all his gifts. Instead, I ignore him and wish his daughter a merry Christmas. Bradford doesn't react one way or the other. He's fiddling with something on his gun belt that's come undone. We stop for a second just inside the door.

I've never seen the mall so congested. Guess it'll be a good year for the city's revenues. Bradford finishes adjusting himself and we press on into the middle of the stampede. Above the white noise of the crowd, there's a sudden and perceptible clamor. We both scan the main mall ahead and see some kind of commotion. The mob splinters apart, and two people run past. We both take a quick step forward, reactively preparing to run after them. It takes only a second for the visual to be processed by my brain, and after taking only two steps we abruptly stop. The two people running are both naked, and they're both women. They had streaked past us on their way down the center of the mall, wearing nothing but tennis shoes and ski masks.

Bradford and I turn toward each other, amused and indecisive at the same time. We glance back at the two women, their white fleshy behinds undulating like tapioca pudding. Without saying a word, we turn and bolt out of the mall, laughing all the way to our cars.

The mental image of chasing two naked women through the throng of shoppers isn't even as bad as the image of us once we caught up with them. What the hell would we do? We jump in our respective cars and peel out, both clearing ourselves from the mall over the radio. We want to be as far away as we can when the *streaking* call comes in.

I quickly switch to an auxiliary channel and request an early lunch break. It's granted.

7:55 p.m.

I park in front of the Espinoza house and detect movement at the window drapes. Lupe and Leticia peek excitedly as I come up the walk. I'm greeted at the door by a mouth-watering aroma of home cooking. The two women are nicely dressed and the tiny house is immaculate. It's warm inside, and decorated for Christmas.

They guide me to the kitchen where the table is set for one. I ask if they're eating too.

"No, no," says Lupe. "We ate already. This is a meal just for you."

Leticia smiles. "We wanted to thank you somehow, for what you've done for us."

Lupe takes my jacket and Leticia pulls my chair back for me. I'm treated as if I were royalty. It's overwhelming and a little daunting, but I want to enjoy it with the same spirit in which they're offering it. I've never had people demonstrate such appreciation. The thought of me violating the department's policy against accepting gratuities edges into my mind, but I dismiss it as the first course is presented in front of me.

Lupe stands back admiringly as steam rises off chili rellenos smothered in shredded cheese. A plate of hot, handmade tortillas accompanies them. Leticia pours a Coke into a glass of ice and Lupe returns to the stove to scoop rice and refried beans onto a separate plate. I'm completely swept away with the delicious food, and even more so by their generous hospitality.

We talk lightly as I eat, and they're quick to refill and replenish whenever I pause. My portable radio murmurs quietly at my side the whole time, and I'm grateful that things have stayed quiet on my beat.

I thank them profusely, and they seem satisfied with the success of their gesture. I wedge myself back into my car, hoping I don't have to run after anyone tonight. They wave through the window as I drive out of the court.

9:00 p.m.

I get a cover call, another off my beat. It's some kind of noise complaint at a fairly nice condo complex overlooking a golf course on the west end of the city. I'm covering a guy who's also rolling from a good distance, which begs the question: where the hell is everyone else?

I arrive to find the neighbor standing out front. The condos are narrow three-story units, with a garage on bottom, kitchen and living room above, and bedroom with bathroom on top. This neighbor shares a common wall with our suspect, who's apparently been making a lot of strange noises. The neighbor describes it as a lot of moaning followed by glass breaking, and then more moaning.

The assigned officer hasn't arrived yet, so I listen at the door for a bit. Sure enough, there's moaning. I pound on the door and identify myself as a police officer. More moaning, but no other response. I ask dispatch how far out the other unit is and I'm told he's stuck in traffic, still a few minutes away.

I try the door and it's unlocked. I walk into a dark entryway with a door to the garage immediately to my left and a stairway directly in front of me. These are tight quarters and they don't offer a lot of options should I get into trouble. Up the stairs I go, to the empty living room. A nice TV and stereo system, some discarded clothes, and a few Hustler magazines. I take a quick peek into the small kitchen, which is also empty.

I call out again and begin climbing up the second set of stairs, my flashlight illuminating the way. I hear a little more moaning, but no lucid response. A mellow pink glow descends from the bedroom to light the third landing.

"Hey," I call out. "This is the police department. Is everything alright?"

I pause for an answer.

"Fritz."

Who in the hell is Fritz? There's a sloshing sound from behind the half-open door, and I see movement on what appears to be a waterbed.

"Are you okay?" I move to a protected spot behind the door frame.

"I want to fuck the cat."

I slide sideways with my hand on my gun. It's dark, but I can see his entire figure on a bed lit by the glow from a pink lava lamp. It's a man, and he's roiling up and down on a waterbed. The bed is stained in an inky liquid that glistens in the light. I ease the door open further and step into the room. I shine the flashlight directly on him. He's lying on his back, nude, and he's masturbating. Blood is everywhere. Lots and lots of blood.

The man doesn't react to the light. He's staring at a point high on the wall and stroking his penis, which is also covered in blood.

"I'm fucking Fritz the cat," he murmurs.

I follow his line of sight to a wall clock. It's a black and white cat with the time dial on its stomach. Its eyes flash right and left with each tick, and it's long, black, pendulum tail swings to keep time.

As the man sways back and forth, I also notice the sparkle of broken glass all over him and the bed. I radio for an ambulance, just as the other cop comes on scene. I hear him trudging up the stairs. As he gets to the room, I hear the obligatory, "What the fuck?"

We check the room while waiting for the ambulance. There's a small zip lock baggie on the nightstand, with a card inside printed with tiny Disney figures. Based on the guy's hallucinations, I'm certain they're LSD tabs. What's left of a lighted mirror hangs cockeyed on the wall above the waterbed. Blood is smeared on the wall next to it. I suspect that the guy tried to dive through the mirror, cutting the shit out of himself in the process. He probably fell back onto the bed, and then became distracted by the sexual magnetism of the wall clock. Fritz, as he called it.

The fire department arrives, followed by an ambulance. When they come into the room it's too congested to move. Their patient is still masturbating on the bed, completely mesmerized by the clock. We decide to wrap him like a mummy in the bed sheet, and then transport him to the hospital just like that. All at once we jump on the guy, spinning him over and folding the sheet tightly around him. The plan works. He's unable to move as we horse him down the stairs and into the ambulance.

When we're done, the other cop follows the ambulance to St. Theresa's and I clear the scene.

10:18 p.m.

I hear an evolving situation over the radio. It's the third call we've had about the same wild Christmas party. Three units and a sergeant are already there. From what I'm gathering, things are starting to get ugly. I hear it in the tone of the cops who are at the scene. Dispatch hears it too, and starts pulling units off other calls. I let them know I'm clear, and start toward the party as well.

It develops into an all out melee before I'm half way there. The sergeant comes on the air asking for expedited cover. He sounds out of breath and I hear yelling and screaming in the background. This is the kind of call that gets everybody rolling. I step it up and hear the midnight shift clearing their lineup to help. Suddenly the frigid night is filled with the sound of sirens.

I turn onto the street already filled with cop cars. Their rotating lights illuminate the situation in fits and starts. A lot of people, bottles crashing, fighting, and cops dragging people this way and that. It's the kind of scene where you don't have the luxury to ask questions. You're thrust into the middle of a battle about which you know nothing, but one that you better be physically and mentally prepared to deal with. That means you have to be at to full speed the moment you step out of your car.

I grab my nightstick and my car keys. I'm running past patrol cars with open doors and running engines, but there's nobody inside them. I smell smoking brakes, wet asphalt, and beer. The house, jammed with people, shudders to a thumping beat. A clot of bodies on the front lawn draws me in that direction. A couple of cops are wrestling a guy there, and they're surrounded by a dozen or so angry partygoers. The mob surges toward the cops and I position myself as a buffer. I have my nightstick extended, chest high, in both hands. I'm ready to make an example of the first guy who challenges my space, just to make sure the others pay attention. A bottle whizzes past my head, but the seething pack remains at bay for the time being.

A few more cops arrive. They splinter off, a couple heading into the house and a couple joining me in the face off with the crowd. It frees me up to help the two on the ground. They're still trying to gain control of their fighting prisoner. With three of us on him, we are able to twist his arms out from under his stomach and bend them behind his back. We're about to handcuff the guy when Bosworth comes driving across the lawn. He's coming toward us so fast that we momentarily pause for fear of being run over. He slides to a stop and jumps out, swinging his nightstick in the air.

"We got it!" I shriek. The other cops yell the same thing, but it's no use.

Bosworth dives over the top of us, walloping his stick onto the suspect's back and legs. Another whooping sound and Bosworth's nightstick comes crashing down on my arm. Excruciating pain radiates through my right elbow.

"Son-of-a-bitch!" I roll off the suspect, gripping my arm.

"Mother fucker!" Another cop yanks his hand back and shakes it in the air. "I think you broke my fingers, you dumbass!"

By the time we're through, Bosworth has managed to beat the shit out of us much worse than anybody at the party has. The guy on the ground is lumped up too, but at least he had it coming. My elbow is killing me, but it'll have to go unreported. I'd rather not have to tell anyone how it happened. The cop with the fractured fingers is in a worse spot. He gets splinted at St. Theresa's and just claims it happened during the fight with the suspect. Technically, that's true.

Why we keep protecting Bosworth I'll never know. The guy's a train wreck.

11:30 p.m.

By the time we clear the party and I get cleaned up at the station, I'm well over the hump of my shift. Though my elbow still smarts, the midnight shift has taken over the majority of calls and things are quieting down some. I hope to park somewhere quiet and write. I've just pulled up beside Kalani when dispatch calls me. It's the old dispatcher, Grace, who doesn't mind going head to head with the cops.

"Take a burglary that just occurred . . . off your beat."

I stare out the open widow at Kalani, who's laughing hysterically. Instead of answering Grace, I take my microphone and toss it out the window.

"I'm throwing her out of my car," I say to Kalani, which only makes him laugh harder. I drive off to the call, my mic dangling against the outside of my driver's door. All the way there I'm livid. With all the cops on the street, she keeps sending me to calls on someone else's beat. Not to mention, my elbow is still aching.

The call is at a place called Galaxy Manor. It's a mobile home park where the streets are all named after planets in the solar system. The trailers are old and the residents are even older. I pull up to a nifty blue and white singlewide at the corner of Mars Drive and Venus Court. An elderly gentleman meets me outside, holding up a handwritten list of the items taken in the theft.

He tells me that somebody broke in while he was at the recreation center playing bingo. He heard someone run out the back door as he was coming in the front. Suddenly a great idea comes into my head. Though it has little to do with this poor guy's burglary, it's perfect.

"Forty-six," I say into my radio. "I have an update."

"Go ahead," Grace says in her gruff smoker's voice.

"Suspect in my case is already gone—unknown description." I pause for a second. "However, a male figure was last seen running up Uranus," intentionally pronouncing it as *your anus*.

A long silence follows my transmission, and I'm certain Grace is checking the map to see if there is such a place. I'm smug in the knowledge that it's a legitimate street a few blocks over.

"Uh, check, Forty-six." Grace nearly spits the words out. *She knows I got her!*

Other cops momentarily key their microphones without saying anything. Suddenly the airwaves are filled with clicking sounds. It's their anonymous show of support for my zinger. It only lasts a few seconds and then it's over.

I examine the interior of the mobile home and write the report at the dining room table. When I'm done I give the victim a business card with the report number on it.

1:15 a.m.

The sergeant wants to meet me on the street to pick up my completed paper. He says he'd like to get out of here at a decent hour. Apparently he's taking Christmas Eve off too. I hand him my reports and he speeds off. A nippy gust of wind whistles through my car.

I'm sitting in the dark lot with the heater running at full force. I slink down in my seat and hope the next couple of hours are uneventful. There's a twinkling light on the other side of the lot, and I chalk it up to a holiday display in the thrift store window. I see the flash again and realize it's not in the storefront, but in the parking lot outside.

I put the car in gear and roll across the lot slowly and without lights. As I get closer, I make out the outline of a car. It's backed in next to a dumpster beside the store. The light is from a cigarette inside the car. I'm sure whoever it is in there has already spotted me, so I go ahead and light up the car. A white guy, mid-thirties, with short brown hair and glasses is sitting straight up on the passenger side of the front seat. I get out slowly, expecting a head to pop up from his lap any second. I stand next to my own car and radio in that I'll be checking a vehicle. The guy's expression doesn't change. He's just sitting there watching me while he smokes a cigarette.

I walk up with my light on him.

"How are you doing?" I ask through his closed window. I ease the light downward — there's nobody on his zipper.

"Okay," he says, rolling down his window. "Did I do something wrong?"

I tell him that he didn't, but that I saw the light from his cigarette and thought I'd check on it. He seems nice enough, cordial and respectful. Right away I like the guy. He tells me he was laid off recently and couldn't afford to stay in his apartment.

I aim the light into the backseat where a couple of boxes and some clothes are stacked. I take a step closer and illuminate the rear floorboard. There's a little boy asleep under an orange blanket.

"Who's the boy?"

He tells me it's his seven year old son, Brian. The man's head bobs lower as the obvious shame of his situation overcomes him. "Not good living conditions, I know. But I'm trying to get another job."

I take a deep breath in and let it out slowly. It helps me think. We talk about other options, friends, relatives, ex-wives. There's nobody who can take Brian. I ask what he'll do with Brian when he does get a job, and he doesn't have much of an answer. Turns out Brian hasn't been enrolled in school since before last summer. I can only imagine the kind of nutrition he's getting.

After a while the boy wakes up and climbs up front with his dad. He curls up under his dad's arm and it's obvious there's a great deal of love there. Living out of a car and going hungry has not impacted how Brian views his father. The guy is a hero in his eyes. Which makes my decision that much more difficult.

I take the father's identification and run a check on him. A hit would make it easier on my conscience. He's got no wants or warrants. I step away from the car where the boy still sits curled in his dad's lap. Going over the circumstances in my head, I realize that there's no crime against simply being poor. The boy is obviously being nurtured and loved. I wonder if worse emotional damage would be done by removing Brian from the only person he has in his life. The one person he loves. On the other hand it's pretty cold out here, and the boy's got little or nothing to eat. He's also been missing school.

It's a difficult call, but the idea of this little boy spending Christmas, freezing inside an Oldsmobile Omega tips the scale for me. Regardless of the admiration he has for his father, I'm feeling a heavy responsibility to ensure his physical health and safety. The potential emotional trauma notwithstanding, I can't turn away from this situation, even though there are probably much worse out here.

My sergeant stops back by with an annoyed look. He's probably thinking, another report I'm going to have to read. *I'm the one who has to write it!*

He listens from inside his car as I give him the rundown. I present it to him the way most of the sergeants prefer. I tell him what I plan to do, rather than ask what I should do. He agrees with my decision. He shudders in the cold, rolls up his window and takes off.

I explain everything to the boy's father, and though he's upset, he seems to know somewhere inside that it's the right thing. He holds Brian tightly in his arms whispering into his ear. They both tremble quietly and I know they're crying. I feel like shit.

He hands Brian over to me and I strap him into my front seat. I radio ahead and a family counselor meets me at the PD. She's a young Latino woman named Fabiana. I run the case by her as she sits comforting the boy. She agrees with my decision to take Brian into protective custody, which makes me feel a little less of a shit. I'm given a foster home address in the hills, and I head back out with the boy. The home is large, and in an upper class area—a small consolation. By the time we get there, the car heater has soothed Brian back to sleep. I carry him to the door where I'm met by a middle-aged woman and her husband. They look fatigued and half out of it. They take the boy from me and go back inside.

3:00 a.m.

I bring my completed report to the sergeant's office. Bosworth is ahead of me getting lectured about some mistake he's made. It doesn't sound like they're talking about beating me half to death, so I assume he's screwed up something else tonight. They finish and Bosworth leaves the room.

The sergeant doesn't look up when I set my paper in the basket.

"So you never found your suspect?"

I'm thinking back over the night, wondering which call he's talking about.

"The burglary?" I ask.

"Yeah." He swings his chair around to face me. "The guy who was running up Uranus?"

I try my best to keep a straight face and he does the same. Neither of us cracks.

"Never did find him, Sarge."

"That's too bad," He says turning back to his paperwork. "Have a good Christmas."

3:39 a.m.

The house is warm and quiet and the smell the Christmas tree gives me a good feeling. I'm tired and the bed will feel nice. I think of the things we'll do tomorrow; visiting family, hanging the girls' stockings, and me assembling their gifts late into the night. They're pleasant thoughts.

An image of the little boy, Brian, suddenly creeps into my head. I picture him in a strange place without his dad. I wonder what kind of Christmas he'll have. Will the foster parents even have a gift for him?

I tiptoe into the kitchen for a pen and a piece of paper. I write a short note to Gale and leave it on the table where she'll see it. I need to be woken up early—there's one more Christmas present I have to buy.

Chapter 18

4:42 p.m.

I'm in the locker room getting dressed and I hear the front office paging me. I drop my case in the lineup room before walking up to see what they want.

"Your sister called," the woman says. "She'd like you to phone her when you get a chance."

It's unusual that she would call me at work, especially on New Years Eve. I talk to my sister almost every day, and recently she's been too absorbed in the on-again, off-again relationship with her boyfriend to talk about much else. I don't particularly care for the guy, and given my perspective as an older brother, I don't think he's any good for her.

I give my sister a call and she tells me they've broken up. I want to let out a whoop and congratulate her but she's an emotional wreck right now. We talk for a few minutes, and I'm able to make her laugh a little. I assure her that I'm there for her, and give her my word that she'll survive the pain.

I hang up the phone and wonder how long before she goes back with the bum.

5:00 p.m.

Lineup starts with a threat: everyone on the squad is expected to arrest at least one drunk driver tonight.

"There are more drunks on the road on New Years Eve than any other night," the sergeant says.

Woodruff raises his hand, grammar school style. "Actually, Sarge, statistically there are more drunk driving fatalities on Thanksgiving than on New Years Eve."

The room grows uncomfortably quiet as the sergeant glowers at him from the dais. Why a guy would draw that kind of attention to himself is way beyond me. The sergeant continues without acknowledging Woodruff.

"At midnight I want everyone on the squad under an overpass or in a parking garage," he says. "Those aren't firecrackers going off, they're gunshots. And whatever goes up is going to come back down."

I know that traditionally cops always seek shelter as the clock ticks into the new year, but I always wondered if it was really necessary. Getting hit with a stray falling bullet seems about as likely as being struck by lightning. I've never actually heard of it happening. In any case, from the traffic over the radio it sounds like it's going to be a busy night.

I'm walking out to the parking lot with Woodruff and Zabinski. I realize that every time I look at Woodruff I think about how he accidentally shot that kid. I can't help it. He must feel the same way, always there, always in the back of his mind. He must go through each day under a dark cloud of grief and humiliation.

Woodruff wants to keep talking about drunk driving statistics, obviously something he read up on while preparing to test for the traffic bureau. Neither Zabinski nor I are interested. Zabinski has troubles of his own.

"My guy died," he says.

"The Indian?"

"Yeah. They couldn't stop the infection in his intestines. Who would have thought?"

Not that anything Zabinski did or didn't do could have changed the outcome, but the fact that he initially blew off the investigation doesn't bode well for him. His reputation with the investigators is totally trashed.

5:48 p.m.

The night is overcast and cold, but at least it's not raining. People are already out in droves. Lines at the convenience stores I pass are five and six deep. I see two men in their 20's balance a keg of beer on a skateboard as they push it slowly down the sidewalk. The bars are overflowing already, and traffic on the main streets is almost at a gridlock.

"George-46?" the dispatcher chirps. "Cover the fire department on a structure fire."

The address given is a low rent apartment house that backs up to a strip mall. The building is filled with government subsidized units and people of questionable citizenship. Depending how bad the fire is, evacuation of the complex may be required and I'm already going over the shift roster in my mind for a Spanish speaker. I drive there pretty quickly, flipping on the lights and sirens only to bust through congested intersections.

I arrive to find that the firefighters have already put out the fire. There is a single smoky apartment on the second floor with fat yellow hoses clogging the doorway. A couple of firefighters are tending to somebody in the parking lot below the apartment. Appears to be a Latino man in his 30's, and he's wallowing in agony on the pavement. Next to them is a gold Pontiac sedan up on jacks with its hood open.

I meet with the battalion chief who runs it down to me.

"Our victim here is some brainchild," he says. "Second and third degree burns all over his backside."

"How did he manage that?"

"He was working on his car earlier today," he says, pointing to the Pontiac. "Decided to dump some gasoline down the toilet in his apartment and then forgot all about it. Went in there later to take a shit, lit a cigarette, and boom! Nearly blew his ass off."

"Anyone else in there?"

"Nope, just him." The chief barks a couple of commands into his radio and then turns back to me. "The fire was contained to the one apartment. More of a flash fire, really. Quick ignition, sucked up all the oxygen in the room, and went out."

The ambulance arrives and they load him up. I follow them to St. Theresa's and try to take a quick statement from the guy. He's in a lot of pain, but I get enough to put together an informational report. It doesn't look like any crime occurred, but if there's a law suit or the guy dies, I don't want to be in the same boat as Zabinski.

The wannabe auto mechanic is stabilized and transferred to a burn unit across the bay. I pull a report number from dispatch and I'm done.

7:10 p.m.

I stop by Isabel Cota's place on the pretext of following up on her burglary two weeks ago. I park on the street and come down the driveway on foot, just like she requested. She peeks out the window and immediately peers past me toward the other cottages to see if anyone is watching. She opens the door and closes it quickly behind me.

I tell her about the burglary at the mobile home park. Although it's a good distance from her place and likely unconnected, I tell her it's probably the same guy. I'm making like her case is the only thing on my mind. After a while I work the conversation around to the drug angle.

"It's probably someone from the neighborhood looking for drug money," I tell her.

Isabel is quiet. I think she's weighing it out in her head. After a minute she looks at me with an expression that's hard to read. It's almost as if I didn't fool her and she knows exactly what I'm there for.

"The guy in the front house sells meth," she says. "But don't go bust him right now. Do it when I'm not around."

I smile at the crazy notion. I couldn't do anything without evidence anyway. "Don't worry," I say. "I'll make sure he can't connect you to it."

She doesn't know his name. Just a big white guy who rides a motorcycle and sells methamphetamine at night. It surprises me that she serves me up a meth dealer rather than someone who sells heroin. I figure she knows plenty more of them. Then it dawns on me. Isabel doesn't use meth, so why would she care? The guy in the front cottage is not her drug connection. I wonder if she's still closer to the heroin dealers than she wants to admit. In any case, she's my first real informant and I'm grateful for the information.

I pass the front cottage on my way out the long driveway. There's a motorcycle tucked up next to it and I have to strain to see the license plate. I repeat it to myself all the way back to the car, where I write it down on my clipboard. A radio check reveals the plate comes back to Reginald Cuthbertson at that address. I cross over the boulevard and back into a church parking lot where I have a clear view of the driveway. Anyone from one of the cottages would have to pass that spot. My plan is to follow the motorcycle when he comes out.

7:35 p.m.

No sooner do I get set up when they call me on the radio. I'm assigned to cover one of the downtown units on a problem at one of the liquor stores.

"Clerk reported a guy hanging around out front, possibly casing to pull a robbery," dispatch says.

The other unit, Woodruff, is working overtime on our shift tonight. He gets there before me and puts out over the air that the suspect is gone. "Description is a thin white male wearing a wool beanie and dark clothing."

I tell him I'll check around the area to see if I can locate the guy. There's no response on the radio and I assume Woodruff is busy at the scene talking to the clerk. I zigzag through the neighborhood streets a few blocks from the liquor store. They're narrow and dark, and covered in gang graffiti. Up ahead I see two dark figures standing on a corner. I get out, having positioned my car as a shield between us in case they start shooting. I rest my hand on my gun and eye them over the hood of my car before approaching. I pick up my mic with the other hand and put myself off, "out of the car on two subjects."

Curiously, I here my own radio transmission echoing with each word. "Woodruff?" I say, peering at the two on the corner. One of the figures turns and I see now that it's him, his badge glistening in my spotlight. His radio was the echo I heard. "Where is your car?"

"I thought I'd check the area on foot," he says with a cocky grin. "I left the car back at the liquor store."

I update dispatch that Woodruff and I are together, checking only one subject. The guy matches the description given by the clerk, and I recognize him as a crazy guy I dealt with a while back. Woodruff is patiently listening to the guy jabber on about a black hole in his pants pocket.

"Valentino," I say with a snap of my finger. "I talked to this guy a couple of months ago."

The guy frowns and wags his finger in my face. "Valentini!" he says. "Peter."

I tell Woodruff that the guy belongs in a group home downtown. Dispatch calls them again and we all wait on the corner. Woodruff's cavalier manner is starting to make me uncomfortable. He never radioed that he was looking for the guy, much less alone and out of his car. He was lucky it was only this harmless nut the clerk saw pacing around the front of the liquor store. It could easily have been a guy with a gun.

"Things can go to shit in a hurry out here," I tell Woodruff after Valentini's ride picks him up.

"That's why I wear these," Woodruff says. He shines the light on a pair of slick black low-cut tennis shoes he's wearing. "If things turn to shit, I can run like the wind."

I give him a lift, and he talks my ear off all the way back to his car. He wants me to go with him to check out the girls at a dance club on his beat, but I decline. I'd like to identify the dealer Isabel told me about.

8:41 p.m.

I'm driving back toward the little cottages and there's a new, black, full-sized truck in front of me. The guy is driving about 10 miles an hour below the speed limit, and keeps looking at me in his mirror. I'd like to find out what he's up to, and I certainly could use the DUI arrest tonight, but I decide to set up on Cuthbertson instead. I back into my previous spot in the church lot and maintain my surveillance.

I like Woodruff, but I can only take him in small doses. It seems like he's trying too hard, maybe to compensate for something. He's been a little reckless ever since he killed that kid.

Checking my watch, I start to wonder if the motorcycle left while I was off with Woodruff and Valentini. I'm thinking this whole thing could be a complete waste of time, when the same black truck passes by me going the opposite direction. The driver is looking the other way, toward the same driveway I'm watching, and doesn't even notice me. I see him go down to the next intersection and make a U-turn. He's coming by on his second pass, and now I'm sure he's up to something.

He slows, looks around, and turns down the driveway to the cottages. The taillights disappear into the dark and I can't tell whether he shut them off or drove further off the road. For all I know he could live there.

I think about driving in, but that might spook the guy. Besides, if Isabel saw me she'd probably never give me information again. Several minutes go by and I'm just waiting to get sent off on another call. My luck can't run much longer—especially on New Years Eve. A few more minutes pass and I see backup lights. The truck backs out of the driveway, onto the boulevard.

I stay put and watch as he starts southbound, then flips a U-turn at the intersection. As the truck passes by me, I see it's the same guy. There's only the driver—an old white guy, much older than the stereotype I had imagined. Maybe this guy isn't involved in drugs. He could have been visiting someone in another cottage, but then why did he back out? There's enough room to turn around at the end of the driveway near Isabel's place. Unless he stopped at the first cottage and didn't drive all the way in. I'm trying to convince myself that all this watching and waiting has been worth it.

I pull out and follow the truck at a comfortable distance. He's heading toward the downtown area where I know there'll be ample backup if I stop him. He makes a sudden turn before downtown and heads into the hills toward more upscale neighborhoods. It's another strike against my stereotype. I realize I had better do something, one way or the other, before we get too far into the highlands. I'm still going to need a valid reason if I decide to stop him. He takes a turn and I notice he doesn't use his signal. Technically a vehicle code violation, but I wouldn't normally bother stopping someone for that. I put out over the air that I'm making a car stop, and I request a backup unit. Things are starting to pick up around the city and I don't hear if anyone answered up for the cover. I've turned on my emergency lights and I'm focused on any movements the driver makes.

He stares into the rearview mirror as he pulls to the curb. We're stopped on a broad curve in the road, under a bunch of pine trees. He's driven so far off the main boulevard that there's barely any traffic here. I aim all my spotlights into his mirror, temporarily blinding him to my movements. He reaches up and aims the mirror away from his face. Even pointed downward, it still has the effect of illuminating inside his car.

I walk up to the driver's window and find the old guy fumbling with something dark. Startled by my tap, he tosses it onto the passenger seat. To say this guy is nervous would be a grave understatement. He gropes for the window switch and finally opens it. I'm trying to see what he discarded on the seat. It appears to be some kind of small leather case. I watch while he pulls his license out and hands it to me. The truck is so new that he doesn't have a registration yet. That also might explain why he couldn't open the window.

"Dino D'Annunzio," I read aloud from his license. All my stereotypes are going to hell. I'd like to ask him what he was doing at the cottages, but that would expose the fact that I'm watching the place. I know he didn't see me parked across the street, and probably never knew I was behind him until we were already in the hills.

D'Annunzio is stocky with thick hands and stubby fingers. He asks me why I stopped him and I tell him about the turning signal. He gives me a pleading look.

"I'm a tile setter," he says, showing me his hands. "I'm just coming home from work, planning to have a quiet New Years at home." I check his license and see he lives only a few blocks farther up the hill.

"Where were you working?"

"San Jose," he says.

"And you're on your way home?"

D'Annunzio nods. I'm seriously wondering if I've got a big nothing. I'm thinking maybe I should just let the old guy go on his way, but something's telling me not to.

"Stop anywhere along the way?"

He shakes his head. "Drove straight here."

I know that statement isn't true. I should go back to my car and run a check on him, but I don't want to let the leather case out of my sight. He notices me eyeing the case, but he won't glance at it himself. He's trying hard to appear calm and unconcerned. I ask him to step out of the truck. He slaps his hands against the steering wheel and lets out a long breath. He's not moving fast enough, and I'm feeling like he's using the time to think of a plan. I grab the handle and open the door.

"I asked you to get out," I say more sternly. I'm making a quick plan of my own, but it involves physically yanking him away from his little case. He glances down at the gear lever, but doesn't move. The engine is still running, and I'm sure he's going to try to take off at any moment.

"I'm not going to ask again!" I change the blade of my feet and slide my right hand near my holster.

To my surprise D'Annunzio turns off the truck. Slowly, he eases himself out onto the street. Then, as I start to step back to give him room, he leans back in across the seat. He's reaching for the case on the passenger seat. I scramble over the top of him and we end up stretched across the cab, me on top of D'Annunzio, both holding onto the case. He's not fighting for it like a madman, but more as if he's hoping I'll just let it go.

"Don't try it," I say right into his ear. "Leave the case on the seat!" I yank the case free and tuck it under my arm. D'Annunzio backs out, and then, on his own, leans forward with his head against the side of his new truck. Whatever is in the case has him convinced he's going to jail. He strains to bend his knotted arms behind him, and I put the handcuffs on him just as my backup arrives.

Once I get him secured in my backseat, I set the case on my hood and carefully unzip it. A loaded semi-automatic pistol sparkles under the spotlight.

The other cop, a guy, who's been on about a year and a half, looks at me the same way I used to look at seasoned cops—the guys who always came up with great arrests, presumably out of nowhere. I unzip an inner pocket and pull out two good size zip-lock baggies of meth. The younger cop stands there in awe. *If he only knew.*

9:13 p.m.

I log all my evidence, and then go into the jail to get a statement from D'Annunzio. He's worked himself into being pissed off now, and refuses to talk to me. Another cop is in there giving a breathalyzer test to a drunk driver. He completes the test and we both stand around while the jailers finish booking our prisoners. He's a guy named Tom Scheper—the one who has a thing for my sister. I start thinking that maybe he wouldn't be so bad for her. Even if they only go out once, at least it would keep her mind off of the bum.

They finish up with our prisoners and we walk them over to a cell. It's an eight-person, dormitory-style room with metal bunk beds along the walls, and it's already full.

I point to a stack of mattresses against the wall. "You'll have to use one of those to sleep on. We're probably going to be pretty crowded tonight."

"What about blankets?" Scheper's guy asks.

Scheper waits by the door while I go down the hall to the supply room. I return with a couple of blankets and Scheper holds the door open for me. I get as far as the first set of bunks when I hear the door slam shut behind me. Then the lights go out.

My heartbeat quickens. I drop the blankets and whirl around in the darkness. I slowly back my way to the far wall. It's completely dark, except for a narrow shaft of light coming through the small rectangle window in the center of the door. With my back pressed against the wall, my hands are extended rigidly in front of me, just waiting for an attack out of the darkness. I hear stirring on the beds, but no words. The light from the window is suddenly eclipsed by Scheper's gigantic laughing face. He turns the lights back on and opens the door. A couple of the guys who had been lying down are now sitting on their bunks with their feet on the floor. Though they may have been preparing to pounce on me, it's more likely they were simply wondering what the hell was going on.

I make a hasty exit and find Scheper outside doubled up against the wall laughing. I tell him he's psychotic, but that only makes him laugh harder.

"I was going to fix you up with my sister," I say. "But you just blew that."

"What do you mean?" He's no longer laughing.

"She finally broke up with that guy she's been dating. I *was* going to give you her number." I rub my chin like I'm thinking hard. "But now, with this childish attempt on my life, I'm not sure if I remember it."

He pleads with me, and now I'm laughing. I finally cave in and give Scheper her number. When I walk by the report writing room a few minutes later, he's just sitting there staring at the piece of paper.

"Is this some kind of payback?" He asks. "Did she really break up with her boyfriend? I don't want to look like some kind of idiot if I call her and she's still with him."

I lift my shoulders. "They were broken up as of a quarter to five this afternoon." Scheper's dialing the phone as I walk out of the room.

Dispatch has cleared me for my lunch break and there's a nice spread set up in the lunchroom. The police officers' association brings in food for the people who have to work Christmas Eve and New Years Eve. I fix myself a plateful of roast beef, mashed potatoes and gravy, and fruit salad. Then, just as I'm sitting down to eat it the jail alarm goes off.

There are actually three alarm locations in the building: one at the public counter in the front office, one upstairs at the detective's secretary station, and several on the walls throughout the jail. Since nothing ever happens at the other locations, the alarm sounding usually means some kind of emergency in the jail. Accordingly, everyone automatically rushes there.

This time is no different. I drop my fork and sprint down the hall toward the jail. A dispatcher comes over the building's speakers, "Assistance needed in the jail!"

A logjam rapidly develops in the hallway as eight of us try to funnel through the door. Inside, two of the jailers are fingerprinting a prisoner and another jailer is replacing an ink cartridge on the printer. They all look up in amusement as we come charging in.

"There's no problem back here," one of them says calmly.

By that time one of the front office clerks has called into dispatch to tell them that the problem is at the front counter.

"Assistance needed at the front counter!" The dispatcher's voice bellows over the building speakers.

Like a flock of birds, we all turn at once and head off in another direction. Squeezing back through the jail door, down the hallway, and past the report writing room where Scheper is still talking on the phone, oblivious to what's going on. We all race through the office, past the front counter, and out the door into the lobby. Nothing. A homeless woman is curled up on a chair sleeping, a man is filling out papers with a bail bondsman, and a teenaged kid is talking on the payphone.

Could it be upstairs in the detective section? Nobody's even there this time of night. One of the clerks catches my eye. She's in the front office, on the other side of the open bullet resistant window. She stands perfectly still, pointing downward toward her desk. By now all the cops are milling around, figuring it must have been some kind of alarm malfunction. A couple of us walk back inside and over to the clerk. She's still not saying anything, just pointing down.

I squat down and see a man curled up in a ball under her desk. *What the hell?*

"How did he get in here?" Me and another cop yank the guy to his feet.

"He came running in the front door and dove head first over the counter," she says.

The guy looks loaded and paranoid. "Don't let them get me," he cries. His eyes are wide and his pupils take up nearly his whole iris. "They're following me. They're going to kill me."

One of the midnight shift cops handcuffs the guy and walks him back to the jail. We slide the heavy window across the counter, locking it for the night. A couple of us are asking who the desk officer is supposed to be.

"It's me," a voice calls out from down the hall. Bosworth comes strolling out, tucking his shirt under his belt. "I had to go to the bathroom."

I return to the lunchroom and horse down my cold meal. The streets are jumping and I've been in here way too long already. When I get to the back lot I hear fireworks going off. Is it midnight already? I check my watch and see that it is.

Pam Halsey, one of the crime scene technicians comes driving in the lot as I'm walking to my car. She's about my age, but something about her reminds me of one of my aunts. Her ancient hair style, maybe. Pam's a big woman—really tall, with a narrow upper body and a wide butt. She pulls the van up next to me and stops.

"Happy New Year!" She throws open the door and lumbers out. I can see black fingerprint powder smudged all over her light blue uniform shirt, and some of it seems to be imbedded into the pours on her face. Her bright red lipstick is smeared and she looks kind of sweaty.

"Happy New Year, Pam."

She tosses an arm around the back of my head and pulls me into her, like a man would do with a woman. Suddenly I feel her face pressed against mine. I don't detect any tongue, but her mouth isn't closed either. It's a sloppy kiss that leaves me feeling like I've been socked in the mouth. The worst part of it is this: her breath reeks of alcohol. She's been out there, on duty, driving around in the tech van. Drunk!

"Are you all right?"

"Yeah," she smiles. "Why?"

"Are you in for the night?" I ask as casually as I can.

"Uh huh." Pam flings herself back into the van. "I'll be inside processing evidence until the end of my shift."

Thank God! There are a lot of things I just wish I didn't know about.

12:02 a.m.

The city sounds like a war zone. Aside from all the fireworks, there are definite gunshots. A burst of rapid gunfire stands out among the others and someone puts out over the air that there is machinegun fire several blocks south of the station. I should be under an overpass right now.

"George-46," dispatch calls over the air.

"Clearing the station now," I say. "Go ahead."

They send me to a gunfire call. I want to tell them that there's gunfire everywhere in the city, but I resist. I'm anticipating that it was called in by an elderly lady who was awakened and maybe frightened by all the noise. I find the house on a quiet block on a picturesque hillside below the university. It's actually quieter up here than the rest of the city.

I'm met at the door by a man and woman in their 30's. The woman is holding a little girl wrapped in a blanket. They tell me a bullet crashed through their roof and into their daughter's bedroom. She's okay, it didn't hit her. I'm shown a hole in the corner of the ceiling and chunks of sheetrock and dust that had fallen onto a toy box. I find an expended bullet from a rifle, pretty much in tact, lying on the carpet right next to the bed. It's about the size of a .223 round, which I recognize from our SWAT rifles.

They hadn't heard anything prior to the thump of the bullet, which they thought was their daughter falling out of bed. I look out the window to see if there are houses up the hill above them, but there's nothing but night sky. It could have come from blocks away, maybe even miles. Who knows how far a rifle round can travel?

There's a long beep on my radio followed by a request for "all units." I quickly take down the couple's names for my report and apologize for having to leave so abruptly. They seem to understand.

12:32 a.m.

I run out to my car and toss the clipboard across the seat. A party has grown out of control in a church hall downtown, and it's turned into something of a riot. There are already officers on scene, and one of them puts out over the air that there are shots fired inside. It's unclear if cops are involved.

With my lights on and siren wailing, I slide sideways off the side street onto the main boulevard. I slow for a huge intersection and two other patrol cars streak through. I fall in behind them and see several more in my rearview mirror. By the time we get there, one side of the six lane street is clogged with emergency vehicles. Hundreds of young, mostly black and Latino, teenagers pour out of the building. So many that the cops can't even see one another.

A lieutenant and three sergeants are there directing the action. Two cops are assigned just to keep watch over all the patrol cars. The K-9 units are posted near the front to help clear the crowd. Traffic units are setting up a single-direction route for departing partygoers, northbound toward the freeway.

I'm part of a group of four told to walk the block to prevent any other fights from breaking out. I hear a cop inside the hall ask for an ambulance. Apparently one kid was shot through the foot by an unknown suspect. It sounds as if none of our guys were involved in any of the shooting. I'm thinking we'll be lucky if a bullet in the foot is the worst that comes out of this call.

All I can think of is that they're going to call Pam out of the station to assist with the tech work. I keep listening for it, but thankfully they don't send her.

We run into groups of teens, most of them acting like they've been through this many times before. They size us up and give us challenging looks. Some mumble obscenities and some of them call us *white pigs*. For the most part we don't check them out, since our mission is to clear the streets as soon as possible. But I can't help but wonder how many of these kids are armed. It's an uncomfortable feeling to be so vulnerable, and to know that any one of these people can get at least the first shot at you anytime they want.

After circling the block on foot, we report back to the front of the hall. A station wagon screeches to a stop on the other side of the boulevard and a woman scurries toward us. She's a large black woman with her hair wrapped in some kind of cloth, and she's wearing a robe and bedroom slippers. She wants to know what happened to her son—the kid who was shot in the foot. One of the sergeants tells her what happened, and that he's been transported to the county hospital in Oakland.

"What happened to his shoe?" she asks.

"You mean his foot?"

"No," says the woman, "I mean his shoe. Where is it?"

The sergeant winces. "Maybe you didn't hear me right."

She heard him right. Instead of asking if her son was going to live, she wants to know what the police are going to do with his shoe. Apparently the kid was wearing an expensive pair of sneakers and she wants the missing one back—regardless of the hole through it or the sizable blood stain.

Angry that the shoe is going to be kept as evidence, she storms back across the boulevard to her car.

I check my watch. I still have to get a DUI tonight.

2:10 a.m.

After finally clearing the mess at the church hall, I make it back to my beat. I still have the bullet hole through the roof to write, and most of the D'Annunzio drug and concealed firearm arrest. I'd like to find a quiet spot to work on them, but I should also look for a drunk driver.

I hear one of the traffic units making a stop on the beat west of mine. I don't hear anyone covering him, so I turn the car around and head in his direction. At this pace I'll be here writing all night.

Like I suspected, the traffic unit stopped a drunk driver. He asks for a backup unit and I tell radio I'm almost there. I see his flashing lights and pull behind him with mine on. We're all the way over in the slow lane, and the traffic cop is talking to the driver who's still sitting in his car. When the cop sees me pull up, he gets the guy out and walks him over to the sidewalk.

The cop is taking his time and this sobriety test is going really slow. I look at my watch, hoping he'll get the clue and pick it up a little. My shift ends in 40 minutes and I'd like to get a drunk of my own. The guy stumbles while trying to walk the straight line and the traffic cop lets him start over. Now he wants to ask the guy all the questions off the DUI form out here instead of doing it at the jail.

A car driving slower than the rest of the traffic pulls to a stop behind my patrol car. I keep my eye on it in case it's a friend of the guy we're about to arrest. Finally the traffic cops signals me and we snap the cuffs on the drunk. He's cooperative and doesn't seem the least bit surprised. Like me, he's probably wondering what took so long.

I'm keeping an eye on the car stopped behind me as we load the prisoner into the back of the traffic car. I check my watch again and shake my head. This guy probably wants to report something.

I walk back to the car where a small balding white man sits patiently behind the wheel. I tap on the window and motion for him to roll it down. He does.

"Is everything alright?" I ask.

He stares at me for a second with glassy eyes. "Fine, officer."

"Do you need something?"

He points in front of him toward the rotating lights of my car. "No, sir. Just waiting for the red light to change."

Got my DUI.

2:49 a.m.

Instead of a breath or urine test, my drunk driver wants to have a blood test taken. What a pain in the ass. Now I have to drive out of the city to a county facility, not to mention all the paper I still have to write. I jump on the freeway and drive like I'm going to a hot call.

The hospital is as crazy as a psych ward, and I'm grateful the intake nurse has moved me to the head of the line. It still takes 35 minutes to get my guy in, get his blood taken, and get the paperwork back.

I get back on the freeway and speed back into the city. I take the off-ramp a little faster than I should. Suddenly, I'm blinded by a pair of headlights coming right at me. My car goes into a sideways slide as I mash down on the brakes, trying to avoid the car coming the wrong way. Doubtful I'll be able to prevent a head-on crash, I brace myself for the impact.

"Hold on!" I yell to my prisoner.

The roaring skid seems to last an eternity. We stop moving without feeling any collision. My car sits in a haze of burnt rubber, sideways across the off-ramp. I peek out my passenger window and see the pair of headlights, motionless, about two feet away. A man with a cigar in his mouth sits frozen behind the wheel. I turn on my emergency lights and get out of the car. After two words with the other driver I know he's shit-faced.

I radio for a CHP unit. Normally I would take it myself, but with the late hour and a prisoner already in my car, I'd like to hand this off. Besides, freeways, including the off-ramps, are technically their jurisdiction. A double unit arrives and they're actually happy to take the arrest—saying the DUI is easier than taking the accidents this guy would have caused headed the wrong way on the freeway.

4:55 a.m.

My sergeants are long gone, so I drop my reports on one of the midnight sergeants. He doesn't seem all that happy about reading them, and he gives me a nasty smirk in case I missed it in his tone. I'm thinking all this work was hardly worth it. I end up pissing off a midnight sergeant, and my own sergeant will have no idea what or who I arrested tonight. I walk down the empty hallway to the locker room taking solace in the possibility that I may have saved someone from starting their new year in the morgue.

5:17 a.m.

I slip into bed as quietly as I can.

Gale rolls over and whispers, "Happy New Year."

Chapter 19

4:17 p.m.
I feel like crap today and I'm hoping the night goes by without any problems. I must have caught another chest cold while standing on the perimeter of some crime scene in the middle of the night.

I stop by the uniform store on my way to work with the idea of replacing my hat. I've worn the same one since I was hired and it's gotten pretty tattered. An investment of $29 and I look like I belong in a marching band. I forgot how boxy and puffed-up they are when they're new. It also seems to highlight the shabby condition of the rest of my uniform.

5:00 p.m.
I walk into lineup carrying my new hat and sucking on a throat lozenge. My sergeant spots the hat and has to point it out to the rest of the squad.

"Take a lesson," he says to the group. "You want to be treated like a professional, you have to look professional."

The sounds of smacking lips immediately resonate around the room.

"He looks like a Mexican General," Enrique says. "All he needs is a pearl handled revolver." Enrique can get away with the ethnic jab because his family is from Argentina, anyone else might have been written up by the sergeant.

I pop another throat lozenge and take my seat. As one sergeant gives the lineup, the other, a slick salesman type named Evan Casey, walks around the room passing out messages, follow-ups, incomplete reports, and court subpoenas. He stops next to me and hands me a subpoena for tomorrow morning at eight o'clock. I had actually considered asking to get off early if it's slow tonight, but so much for that. What will that give me, a couple of hours sleep?

He also hands me a phone message from Isabel Cota. He wiggles his eyebrows at me and moves on to the next guy. I think back to what Isabel told me about her past, and wonder if the sergeant recognized her name. If not, he probably thinks I'm banging some woman on my beat. Either way it's not good. I consider stopping by his office to explain, but then dismiss the whole idea. He wouldn't believe me anyway.

5:39 p.m.

I'm loading my things into the patrol car when Scheper drives into the lot. I haven't talked to him since he called my sister. I knew they had plans to go out, because my sister told me so.

"Very funny," he says, "very, very funny."

I act like I don't know what he's talking about, but I'm already struggling to suppress the chuckle. I told my sister before their date that Scheper was deaf in one ear, and very self-conscious about it.

"I kept wondering why she was talking so loud," he says. "Then she kept moving around to the other side of me."

I'm laughing even harder as I imagine the scene.

"I asked her why she was yelling into my ear, but she didn't want to say. Finally she told me it's nothing to be embarrassed about. I didn't know what she was talking about, until the end of the date when I finally got it out of her."

"Well?" I say. "Are you going out again?"

"Oh no, I'm not giving you any more information." I can tell by his goofy smile that it went well. I'll get it out of my sister, no problem.

5:45 p.m.

I'm dispatched to a family disturbance. The location is a duplex on a decent street in an otherwise crummy neighborhood. It's the rear unit—a single-story brick building with a carport at either end. As I walk past the front unit, I recognize the resident. She's a sweet old lady, Mrs. Philpott, who belongs to the local neighborhood safety group. I stop to say hello and she gives me a hug. I tell her that I have a call next door.

Mrs. Philpott shakes her head sorrowfully. "Come by and see me after."

The front door is open and I tap on the screen. I hear yelling in a back room, but don't recognize the language. Some Slavic dialect, I think. A man appears from the hallway and storms toward the door. He doesn't have anything in his hands, but he's clearly upset and very serious. He's in his 40's, with short brown hair and a compact stature. He pushes the door open with a bang.

In a thick accent he yells, "This is my home and my family. I can do how I want!"

I step inside. It's a small room crowded with pieces of china and family photos. The walls are painted a dark grayish blue, which adds to the smothering feeling inside.

I urge the man to try to calm himself and tell me what's going on. He's joined by his son, about 22 or 23 years old. The son helps calm his father, and then acts as a translator.

"My father is very angry with my younger sister, Elena," he says. "She's been working at Taco Bell and she met a boy there. Someone she works with."

I can see the mother in the background. She's alternately listening to us, gesturing at me, and yelling in Romanian toward a closed door off the hallway.

"Does your father dislike the boy? Is that it?"

"We're from Romania," he says. "Stoica is our name. My father won't allow Elena to meet with any American boy. Where we come from, the parents pick a boy for the daughter."

The father says something, punctuated by pounding his fist into his hand.

"My father says Elena will be locked in her room. He says she cannot attend work at Taco Bell."

I nod to the father, acknowledging respectful deference to his position as head of the family. However, I'm not sure his methods are going to fly here in California. The boy seems pretty well socialized and I can only imagine the daughter is too.

"How old is your daughter?" I ask the man.

He looks at the son questioningly, as if that has no bearing on anything. "Eighteen years."

I see the mother in the background struggling to maintain her grip on a doorknob. I'm assuming it's the bedroom where the daughter has been confined.

"May I speak with your daughter?"

The son starts to translate and the father waves him off.

"One minute." The man storms off. As he does, I hear him mumble, "I am head of family."

The son is taller and more slender than his father. He glances back at his parents and then smiles sheepishly.

"I'm very sorry about this," he says. "They don't understand how things are here."

I ask how he's getting along and he tells me it's easier for a young man—not as many difficult customs. He says he's in school, studying to become a police officer and his parents are happy with that.

Elena emerges from the bedroom, a slight girl who appears young for her age. She's pale and has a sprinkling of freckles across the bridge of her nose. The girl is dressed in a brown restaurant uniform.

I ask Elena to step outside where she can speak freely. The parents' faces are pressed against the screen door, but we're far enough into the driveway that they can't hear us. Elena tells me that her father was reluctant to even let her get a job. He didn't want her outside the house. He relented after much debate, and she began working at the Taco Bell down the street. There she met her boyfriend, Brad, and now the two are in love. *How did I know that was coming?*

"You're eighteen," I say. "What do you want to do?"

"I want to go live with Brad. His parents support our decision and have invited me to come live with them. I want to go there."

I ask her to think about it very carefully, reminding her that the damage to the relationship with her parents may be permanent. That if it doesn't work out with Brad she may not be accepted back. She's made her decision.

I move my field case into the backseat and make room for Elena in the front of my car. She waits there while I go back inside to drop the bomb on her folks.

I start by explaining that California recognizes anyone eighteen or older as an adult. Legally, adults are free to make their own decisions, and it is not permissible to confine someone against their will. In fact, the law specifically prohibits false imprisonment. When I tell them that Elena has chosen to live with Brad, they go nuts.

The father is yelling in Romanian, repeatedly pounding his fist into his hand. The mother is worse. She is wailing at the top of her lungs. Initially she pleads with hands raised toward the sky, and then works herself into ramming her head against the wall. The son runs back and forth between the two, trying to calm them. I try to make a comment or two about the possibility of a positive outcome, but they're not even listening to me. At this point I'm the American devil to them.

They eventually calm slightly, and when I'm sure the woman isn't going to crush her own skull, I leave. The girl is sobbing quietly in the car when I get in. I'm sure she and the rest of the neighborhood heard the commotion. Mrs. Philpott is on her porch with the same sad look I left her with.

"The girl has been confiding in me," she says. "I told her it's best not to hide this. I urged her to talk to her parents. I hope that wasn't a mistake."

I tell her she did the right thing, and that sooner or later it was bound to come out. I ask Mrs. Philpott if she thinks the father will ever soften his position.

"Hard to say. They once told me he was with the Romanian Secret Police. Mr. Stoica is very strict."

I drive Elena to her boyfriend's house about a half mile away. It's a large, ranch-style home on a big lot. I'm introduced to Brad and his mother, and they're more than happy to receive Elena.

I drive off feeling happy for the young couple, and hopeful that it all works out for them. I'm also conflicted about Mr. and Mrs. Stoica. They're truly heartbroken. Through no fault of their own they've become wedged in a generational and ethnic fracture from which they're unable to escape. I imagine this situation would have been much simpler for them in Romania, though probably not so for Elena.

As I drive away, I think of my own daughters. How would I handle a similar set of circumstances? What kind of father will I be?

7:10 p.m.

I park on the street near Isabel's house. It's still early and there is nobody around. I walk in past the first cottage and notice that the motorcycle is not there. Isabel sees me from her window before I see her. She must have been waiting.

"Hurry up and come inside," she says, with her usual paranoid scan over my shoulder. "I found out something today."

She closes the door behind me. For some reason her place doesn't seem as cute as the first time I saw it. It's downright sweltering inside, and a greasy odor hangs heavy in the air—a confluence of fried foods, cigarettes, hairspray, and body odor. Even with the heat inside, Isabel's wearing a fleece jacket. Makes me wonder again about her drug use. *Could be wearing the long sleeves to cover fresh needle tracks on her arms.*

I pretend not to notice, and ask her about the new information.

"A guy's been coming around here with crystal," she says. I know *crystal* is a street term for PCP, the drug developed from an animal tranquilizer. Again, it's not the drug Isabel is supposed to be most familiar with, but whatever.

I ask her if she knows the guy's name.

"I only know his first name. Everybody just calls him Finn."

"Have you seen the PCP on him?"

She shakes her head. "Somebody around here bought it from him," she unconsciously motions toward the cottage next to hers. "I don't want to get her in trouble though."

"How much is he selling?"

She shrugs. "I don't know, a couple of joints."

I'm choking on the stale air and I can feel sweat dripping down the side of my face. A couple of joints are hardly worth staying any longer than I already have. I thank Isabel for the information and tell her I have an emergency call I have to leave for.

I think I have a fever.

7:44 p.m.

The wind is kicking up. I pick a few wet leaves off my window before getting in the car and letting dispatch know I'm available.

I know the guy Isabel was talking about. Finn McGrath is a punky 19 year old who I've arrested a couple of times for being under the influence of drugs. He's got a stout build—a little flabby but strong at the same time. We had to fight him once when he was high out of his mind. He lives with his parents and his sister a few blocks away, in a house that backs up to a little strip mall where he usually hangs out.

Dispatch is asking me to take a cover call off my beat. It's a possible burglary in progress. I'm backing up Lee, who works the downtown area. I hear him go off at the scene and I put my foot into it. Maneuvering through traffic and around clueless drivers is aggravating me to no end tonight. I'm cursing at a guy who didn't heed my lights and siren, and now decides to stop dead in the middle of the intersection. I manage to squeeze past him, hoping he can't read lips.

There's nowhere to park, so I leave my car with its lights flashing in the street. I run up the steps of the dilapidated Victorian and find Lee talking with an elderly man and woman. They tell him there's a strange noise coming from beneath the house, and they think someone is trying to break in. Lee looks at me and I know we have the same thought: Who breaks in through the floor?

The people are genuinely scared, and Lee assures them we'll check it out. I'm less comfortable about it. I have a rodent phobia and I hate basements. Most of the guys I work with know it and think it's hilarious. Once a couple of guys on my squad hung a dead mouse on my locker and I nearly had a heart attack.

Lee and I walk down from the porch and around to the side of the house. We stop at a cellar door that's flapping in the wind.

"You see?" I tell Lee. "The noise is nothing but the wind."

"They told me it sounded like moaning, and then they heard pounding. C'mon, we have to check down there."

Lee swings the door open and we both step inside, our flashlights held out tentatively in front of us. It's a dark, dusty space, deep enough to stand straight up in. We inch our way into the depths of the basement, side-by-side, hearing nothing but the wind. A clattering sound somewhere in the dark makes us both jump. There's a growling noise, and a flurry of light as we try to aim our flashlights toward it.

"There!" yells Lee.

I follow my beam to a compressed area way in the back, where the ground rises up to only a few feet below the floor. A cat, big and orange and covered with dirt, hunches and growls at something in the dark. I move my light a few inches over and I'm frozen in horror. A rat, nearly the size of the cat, stands on its hind legs bearing its teeth and pawing its tiny claws in the air. Nastiest thing I ever saw.

Next thing I know I'm running for my car. I fishtail around the corner and I'm gone. I still have to pull over and turn on the light to make sure nothing's crawling up my pants. Lee gets me on an auxiliary channel later and gives me a bad time for leaving him alone with the giant rat.

I tell him, "It's payback for giving my wife poison oak."

8:35 p.m.

I'm back on my own beat. It's beginning to sprinkle a little, so I put a plastic cover on my new hat. I set the hat back on top of my nightstick which sticks up from my field case, strapped with a bungee cord onto the headrest. I've always propped the hat there so it gives the illusion of a second officer sitting in the passenger seat. I don't know if it ever fooled anyone, but it's just an extra precaution I take.

I'm achy, my throat feels like it's on fire, and all I want to do is lie down. I check my watch and realize I'm not even half of the way through my shift. On top of that, I have court in the morning.

A car horn honks and I watch a cream colored Mustang swerve across two lanes to make a right turn. I can't get on the radio because they're dispatching a call to someone else. I pull in behind the Mustang, now traveling very slowly down a narrow side street. There's only one person in the car—a man, judging from the outline. I turn on my lights and the car speeds up momentarily, and then suddenly turns into the curb and stops. I try to get on the radio again, but now someone is running a license plate. The driver glances back at me and then dives out of the car, running hard for one of the houses.

In a flash, my mind races back to the Lopez house when I nearly got my clock cleaned by Johnny and his family. I grab my nightstick on the way out of the car, and see my new hat tumble out onto the street. The guy is heading for a house near where he bailed out of his car. However, in a stroke of luck for me, he overshot it when he stopped. Even with his head start, it'll be a race between us to see who gets to the door first. I want to block the entrance, so I'm running as fast as I can.

He's a big guy, young and fit, with a military-looking haircut. He's got that glazed look though, and I can tell by the way he's running he's drunk. *Why is it these guys always think if they can make it to their house, they're home free?*

He gets there a stride ahead of me. As he hits the second step to his porch, I grab his collar from behind and yank with all I have. He stumbles backwards down the steps and onto the lawn.

"You're under arrest," I yell. "Put your hands behind your back."

He wheels around to face me, sets his feet apart in a fighting stance, and rears back with a balled fist. This guy has me by several inches and he means business. I rush him before he's completely gotten his balance and give him a forearm across the chest. His foot catches on a tree root and he tumbles onto his ass. I advance again before he can get up, snatching my handcuffs out of their case.

"Stay down," I yell. "Hands behind your back." I'm thinking that nobody even knows I stopped a car. I wish I could get to my radio, but there's no time. I need both hands.

From a sitting position, he lunges forward and grabs onto the dangling end of my nightstick. I feel him tugging, furiously trying to get it out of the ring on my belt. I twist away from him, pull the night stick out of his grip, and now it's firmly in my hand. I swing it back across, cracking him as hard as I can on the meaty part of his upper arm. He rolls back with his legs bent in the air and I drive another arching blow into his knees. He hollers out in pain.

"Give up or I'll give you another one!" I raise it up again, hoping he has the intelligence to stop fighting. He struggles to his feet and I'm thinking this guy doesn't get it. This time, instead of trying to fight me, he takes off running. I finally manage to put my location out over the radio and ask for assistance. I follow the guy on foot around the side of the house where he pushes his way through a gate and continues into the back yard. There are no lights, and my feet are getting bogged down in tall wet grass. I'm tripping over things and trying to keep him in sight. I still don't know if he's got a weapon, or for that matter if he's trying to get to one. I'm calling out for him to give it up, and wondering the whole time if he owns a dog.

An approaching siren signals the arrival of someone to help me. I catch up to the guy in back of the house as he's trying to get a door open. I use my shoulder to drive him flat against the wall. He's out of breath and so am I.

"Just let me go," he pleads. "I didn't do anything."

I keep telling him to put his hands behind his back. He refuses, and continues struggling to get away.

My radio squawks, "I'm on scene, Forty-six's car is in the street but I don't see him."

It's my backup and I know they're looking for me. With both hands on the guy I still can't get to my radio. It doesn't matter through, because the cop quickly finds the open backyard gate. I hear footsteps behind me and then hear the cop shouting into his radio.

"I got him in the back yard." A crushing strike comes suddenly out of the darkness to the side of me, as my cover unit drives the end of his nightstick into the guy's ribcage. The guy gasps at the impact, with a sound that comes from deep pain. It actually hurts me just hearing it.

"Okay," he wheezes. "Okay! I give up."

I see that the other cop is a heavy guy who is working overtime on our shift tonight. He and I walk the drunk driver out to the front of the house where I hear another siren approaching. I get on the radio and advise that we have the suspect is in custody, and don't need any further assistance. A patrol car turns the corner and races down the street toward us, lights flashing. I repeat over the radio that we're okay, but he keeps coming.

I see my new hat lying in the roadway. It's like a slow motion train wreck that I can't do anything about. As I stand holding my prisoner by the arm, I'm watching the cop in the patrol car barreling toward us. He hits his brakes and slides right onto my hat, grinding it under the skidding wheels, chewing it to shreds, and spitting it out in his wake. My mouth opens but nothing comes out.

"Is that your new hat?" the big cop asks.

"It *was*."

11:50 p.m.

I'm clearing the station after booking my guy into the jail. Turns out he's a U.S. Marine on leave, staying at his sister's house. I consider myself lucky he was too drunk to get the better of me.

The fight didn't make me feel any better. I'm going to meet Van Kirk at a 7-11 for a cup of coffee. On the way, I hear him go off on a pedestrian stop at a small row of storefronts on his beat. Radio dispatches me to cover him, but I'm already headed there. I'm scanning the other channels and hear Van Kirk running a check on Finley McGrath, the guy Isabel told me about.

I get there and find Van Kirk's car in an alleyway behind the stores. It's a dark narrow area littered with garbage, and there's graffiti all along the wall. Van Kirk is out of his car talking to Finn when I join him. It doesn't look like the kid is high right now—he's talking calmly with Van Kirk and they appear to be joking around.

When there's a natural break in their chatter I pull Van Kirk off to the side and let him know what my informant told me. I try not to sound like I'm boasting, although that's exactly what I'm doing. Undercover narcs have informants, not street cops. Van Kirk looks at me with skepticism, and then goes back to Finn.

"You got any drugs on you?"

I can think of more subtle ways of getting around to searching the guy, but the question doesn't seem to rile the kid.

"Nope, go ahead and search me." He raises his hands and turns toward the fence.

Van Kirk conducts a quick pocket check, and then gives me a demeaning roll of his eyes. "Nothing on him."

I standby, watching while the two continue to talk casually. I'm wondering if Isabel's information was bad. I suppose Finn could have stashed the drugs in his house by now. For that matter he might have already sold whatever he had.

"You really like that PCP shit," Van Kirk says.

Finn laughs. "You should try getting dusted sometime."

The term *dusted* comes from another street name for PCP— Angel Dust. I've never actually talked to someone about what it's like. This would be good to know if I ever make it into the narcotics unit.

"What's it feel like?" I ask.

"It's like you're not even in your own body." He pauses as if he's recollecting fond memories. "Like you're seeing everything though a tunnel."

Van Kirk balls his hand into a ring and looks through it. I unwrap another lozenge and slip it in my mouth. I'd like to get out of this alley before a rat jumps out of one of these trash bins.

"I did my sister once when we were high," Finn says.

Van Kirk slowly drops his hand. "Say what?"

"Yeah, my parents were gone. Me and my sister both smoked crystal and got real horny." He's standing there grinning as if it's no more than mildly interesting—like telling us he's got a pet iguana, or he plays the banjo.

"No shit?" Van Kirk says. "You were high and you screwed your own sister?"

"Best fuck I ever had."

There's really nowhere to go with a conversation after a comment like that. Finn goes on his way and we walk to our cars. Van Kirk and I spend a few minutes discussing whether or not we believe him. The whole thing is just too weird for me.

1:00 a.m.

Van Kirk gets a call, so we decide to skip the coffee. He takes off to the call and I park with my heater turned up high. Now I'm cold and clammy. I work on a couple of reports while monitoring the radio. Van Kirk is heading to the bridge to cover the highway patrol. It sounds like they are investigating an accident that happened about mid-span, where the elevated section of the bridge drops down to about 15 feet off the water. From what I gather, the driver of one of the cars climbed into the bay and is trying to swim away. Must be drunk.

1:33 a.m.

My throat could sure use something to drink. I stop at the 7-11 and buy a cup of hot tea. The clerk is a woman with well-defined, tattooed arms, and hair shorter than mine. She's got a pretty smile and a warm voice, but I get the definite impression she holds her own against rowdy customers here at night. We talk for a few minutes, and I pull up my coat collar before I walk back out to my car.

I take a sip of the tea and then wedge the cup against my case. As I'm pulling out of the lot I see two figures, barely distinguishable, crowding together under the overhang of a repair shop. The shop is closed and it's dark. My lights hit them and I see they're two guys wearing black clothing. I immediately think they're breaking into the shop, or more likely, they're going to rob my friend at the 7-11.

I put myself off over the radio, and I pull in before the two guys have a chance to react. I barely get my door open when one of them, the one closest to me, makes a robotic half-turn and thrusts a hand into his jacket pocket. I reach for it at the same time, ending up holding his wrist with one hand and gripping the outside of his jacket with the other. I feel something squishy inside—not a gun, but probably a bag of drugs.

The second guy is frozen in place with his mouth partially open and a blank stare on his face. I realize they're both high on PCP.

The one I'm gripping drives an elbow into my chest, knocking me back against the side of my car. He starts to pull away, trying to run, but his feet aren't fully cooperating. His steps are short and rigid. He's still got one hand dug into his pocket, probably trying to discard the drugs.

I grab him from behind and spin him toward my car. He's fighting wildly now, whipping his arm backwards, hoping to land a lucky face shot. I'm ducking each swipe, trying to keep the other guy in sight as well. Still don't know if the partner is armed. So far, he seems too high to react.

I'd have to release the grip on my guy in order to get to my radio, but I decide against it. I'm suddenly aware that he's dropped one hand, which I now feel grabbing at my crotch. I swing my arm around his neck, trying now to turn the jewels away from his grasp. Bad move. The next thrust of his hand goes right for my holster. He's got a grip on my gun and I feel my gun belt jerk as he tugs. I maintain one arm around the front of his throat and try to clutch my holster with the other. No use.

The metallic clattering sound on the asphalt courses through me like ice water. My handgun has come loose and it's sliding across the pavement. All three of us see it at the same time. I'm pretty sure that I could die out here, in the dark, in front of this repair shop at any second. It all just depends on who gets to my gun first.

I yank the guy by the neck, and with all my might I slam his head against the door frame of my car. It hits with a nauseating thud and he drops straight to the asphalt. I stumble over him, dropping to the ground on my hands and knees. I dive for the gun but it isn't there. In the spot where it should be is a pair of feet. My heart drops as my eyes follow them up. I'm expecting to see the other guy pointing my own gun at me, but he's not. A sheriff's deputy stands there holding my gun in his hand.

"Lucky thing we passed by," he says with a grin. His partner is behind him handcuffing the other guy.

I thank them as I climb to my feet, trying to catch my breath.

"I was about to jump in and help," he says. "But then you dropped that guy pretty good."

I look at the withered mass on the ground. He's holding his forehead and his face is covered with blood. I handcuff the fighter and remove the contents of his pocket. It's a sandwich bag half full of something—either marijuana or parsley laced with crystallized PCP. I can't tell for sure in the dark.

I take down the deputies' names for my report and thank them again. My prisoner has to be cleared at the hospital, so I drop the first guy off at the jail and head to St. Theresa's. It takes a few sutures to close the gash on his head, but I doubt he feels anything yet. Another hour passes before the hospital clears him.

By the time I get back to the station my shift is over. The rest of my squad is leaving, and I still have these two arrests to write. I walk my guy into the jail and leave him in their custody.

"Hey, your other guy's already gone," one of the jailers calls to me from around the corner in the booking office.

I ask him which guy he's talking about.

"Your DUI from earlier, the guy who fought you."

"What do you mean, gone?"

"Sergeant Casey came in here about an hour ago and had us release him on a citation."

I stare at the jailer and feel the fever flashing in my face. "Did Casey say why?" I manage to ask the question without infusing it with the emotion I'm feeling.

"No, but he gave the guy a ride home."

A Goddamn ride home! I leave the jail and check around the station for Casey. I'd like to confront him, but he's already gone. Just as well. With the night I've had and the way I'm feeling, it's probably better to cool off before I talk to him.

I unload my car and find a cup of cold tea wedged against my field case. I warm it in the microwave oven and settle down in the report writing room for a long night of logging evidence, filling out forms, and writing.

5:00 a.m.

I drop my reports with the midnight sergeants. After putting my things away in my locker, I make my way back down the dark hallway to Family Services. Everybody's gone in that end of the building and it's warm and quiet. I use my key to get into one of the counselors' offices—a carpeted little space with a small couch. I have three hours to kill before I need to be in court. It's hardly worth changing out of my uniform, much less going home.

There's a stained old slip cover on the couch—one that I know has played host to thousands of nasty asses over the years. But tonight I'm too sick to care. I wad my jacket under my head and curl onto it. As tired as I am though, I can't fall asleep. I'm thinking about the two guys I fought tonight, and wondering if I used more force than I needed to. It's always in my mind afterward. On the other hand, I might have been killed had I not been as aggressive as I was. And yet, part of me wonders if it would have happened the same way if I hadn't already felt so lousy.

8:00 a.m.

I try to smooth my hair as I walk across the parking lot to the courthouse. The deputy district attorney tells me that the defendant's attorney called this morning to ask for a continuance. He apologizes for any inconvenience and tells me I'll be re-subpoenaed in a few weeks. I go back to the department and change out of my uniform.

8:29 a.m.

I walk into the house and find my two daughters on a blanket, watching Sesame Street. Gale told them I didn't feel well and they've made up a bed for me on the couch next to them. All of their stuffed animals are positioned around it. They've got a toy thermometer and stethoscope laid out on the end table next to a glass of orange juice. I kick off my shoes and stretch out on the couch. One of the girls gives me sips of the juice while the other puts a damp washcloth on my head. It's just what I needed.

Gale comes over and whispers, "Don't feel like you need to stay out here if you'd sleep better in the bedroom."

"Believe it or not," I say. "This is probably the only thing that will actually make me feel better."

Within minutes I fall asleep.

Chapter 20

4:10 p.m.

Tonight is going to be a good night, I say to myself as I'm driving to work. It's not only my Friday, but come three o'clock in the morning when I get off, I'll be on vacation for a week. I have plans to take Gale and the girls up to the snow, and I can't wait.

I pass Sergeant Casey in the locker room. He flashes a cheesy smile and I'm transported back to the night a couple of weeks ago when he released the guy who fought me. Casey's been away at a training class of some type, and I have yet to speak to him about it. I glance around the locker room, at the guys half-dressed and half-listening, and I realize it's not the time or place. I quickly get into my uniform and head straight for the sergeants' office.

"Sergeant Casey."

He looks up from the beat roster he's just printed out. "What's up?"

"I've been wanting to talk to you about the guy I arrested down on Longwood a few weeks ago. The guy who fought me and I had to chase."

Casey regards me with mild amusement. "What about him?"

"I was told you released him on a citation and then drove him home."

The sergeant stares at me with a stone face. Then, slowly, he walks to the door and closes it. I'm not sure if I overstepped and he's about to tear into me, or if he's going to apologize. He walks slowly back to the spot where he was standing.

"Let's just say, he's a friend of a friend."

I had gambled that it was something underhanded and he just confirmed it. If it was above board he wouldn't have closed the door, and he would have chewed my ass for questioning him. Now it's me with a stone face.

"I got a call from his sister," Casey says. "I know her . . . She's a friend, okay?"

And this guy had the stones to smirk at me when Isabel left me a message. Something about him I never trusted anyway, and I'll be glad when I can transfer off his shift.

"Sure, Sarge." I turn and walk to the door. "See ya in lineup."

5:00 p.m.

"They still haven't located the jockey," the Lieutenant reads from a bulletin. "He was last seen climbing over the side of the bridge after being involved in an accident. CHP suspects he was drunk."

I read about it in the newspaper. The guy was a jockey at Bay Meadows racetrack in San Mateo. I'm guessing if he hasn't turned up by now he's dead, but the lieutenant is reading it as if we might still spot him doing the backstroke somewhere out in the bay.

"His name is Tommy Jansen, and he's wanted for hit and run," he says.

Other than that and a few stolen cars, there isn't much in lineup tonight. The sergeant goes over the beat assignments, and for some reason I was moved to the downtown beat. It crosses my mind that Casey did it intentionally to bug me.

5:30 p.m.

I'm still loading my things into my car when dispatch calls me. She sounds frazzled. I toss my things in and answer the radio.

"Start for the City Center building," she says. "We've got a report that someone just jumped off."

I'm weaving through commute traffic with my lights and siren, and my mind is racing faster than my car. At twelve stories, the City Center is the tallest building downtown. I don't even want to imagine what a body looks like after falling that far. The walking beat unit shows up at the same time as me, and the fire rig sirens sound close.

We jog down a paved path onto a wide bricked pedestrian plaza at the foot of the building. From across the square I see her. She's lying on her side with the upper part of her body turned toward the sky. I walk toward her, slowly inhaling a deep bracing breath. I'm looking down at an angelic porcelain face, her blue eyes half open and still. Her tiny hands lay open on either side of her frail body. She's dressed in a pink tank top and denim pants. She appears no more than sixteen years old.

My heart feels like it's being yanked right out of my chest. Taking time to square myself away, I gaze straight up along the flush face of the building—each glass pane dark and unbroken. Around the courtyard, dozens of eyes watch in horror.

I take a breath before looking back down at the girl. A small trickle of blood has pooled in the grouted lines beneath her head. I kneel down to get a better look at her necklace. It's a colorful strand of beads with a small amulet resting just below her neckline. It reads: *Life's a Bitch.*

The fire engine rumbles across the plaza, stopping right next to us. They jump out and hook her up to a monitor—not a sound. They shake their heads.

I glance around the square where a few small groups have clustered. Some watch, some shield their eyes, and some turn away to be comforted by coworkers. I move between them asking if anyone actually saw it happen. Most of them only heard it, describing a loud crack when she hit. One woman thought it sounded like a sheet of plywood had been dropped from the top of the building. Another didn't know the girl had fallen, and thought she had simply collapsed while walking across the courtyard.

A man in a business suit tells me he saw the girl earlier. "I was sitting out here drinking a cup of coffee at about ten minutes to five," he says. "That girl walked right past me, and into the city building. I remember because she seemed like she was in a hurry. She was looking straight ahead, determined and serious, as she passed me."

I walk back as they carefully lift her onto a stretcher and into the ambulance. The crime scene tech pulls up and I ask her to take a Polaroid photo of the girl before they take her. She climbs into the ambulance and snaps a picture, then hands it to me. The girl has no purse and no identification, and at this point we haven't a clue about who she is.

I'm suddenly aware of someone nosing over my shoulder. As the Polaroid image begins to take shape on the gray background, I hear a voice.

"Is that the individual who fell?"

I turn to see a short Latino man. The first thing I notice is an oversized mustache that dwarfs his scrawny features. He's dressed in a blue sweater vest worn over a shirt and tie. It slowly sinks in that he holds a high rank in the city's administration. It occurs to me that this building also houses his office. Accordingly, I offer a polite correction to his assessment.

"We haven't determined exactly what happened yet, sir."

I begin walking around the building to visually check all the windows, hoping to rule out that the girl either fell or was pushed through of one of them. The guy from the city does a little two-step to keep pace with me.

"Of course she fell," he says. "She couldn't possibly have gotten onto the roof and jumped."

I stop walking. "Why is that not possible?"

"There is no public access. And even if she was able to get to it, there's a ten foot wall."

I take a breath and exhale slowly. "Okay, well, thanks for your help. I'll let you know what we find."

I start walking again and he's hot on my trail. "Do you know who I am?"

"Yes, sir."

"Then you'll do more than 'let me know' what you find. You'll take down what I say."

I pause again at the back of the building and I look right at him. "What, exactly, are you saying?"

"Clearly," he starts. "The individual was trying to climb up the side of the building and fell."

People annoy me when they start a sentence with *clearly*. If it were so *clear* they wouldn't be arguing their point. It also annoys me that the guy continues to refer to this young girl as *the individual*. It's as if depersonalizing her makes it somehow less tragic. I'm beginning to think this guy cares about one thing and one thing only—the city's liability.

"You think a tiny teenage girl scaled the face of a twelve story building?"

"I'm not suggesting she made it all the way to the top," he says. I note frustration in his voice which is now a few decibels louder. "The individual probably climbed up here." He points to a narrow fire escape housed in a column of vertical bars. The rest of the building is brick and glass. "Maybe one or two floors up," he says.

"How then, would she have landed on the opposite side of the building?"

His eyes narrow to little black peas. "Used her fingers to grip between the bricks." The words sputter like a sprinkler head. "Probably worked her way around to the other side and fell!"

Clearly, you are a total imbecile!

I check the remaining side of the building—no broken windows whatsoever. I finally shed the city hall guy and track down the building's security guard. I tell him what happened outside and ask if he's seen anything out of the ordinary. He hadn't noticed the girl and hasn't seen anything unusual all day. He's a husky black man with a soft voice and slightly graying hair at the temples.

I have him take me to the roof. We get off the elevator on the twelfth floor and walk up an internal flight of stairs to the roof. It's an expansive area dotted with pipes, machinery and radio antennas. A ten foot concrete wall marks the outer edges of the building. I glance around and there are no ladders or boxes, nothing that could be used to scale it.

"I notice you had to use a key to get into that last stairwell," I say to the guard.

"We keep it locked after five at night."

"And before five?"

"It's left unlocked during the day," he says. "A lot of the maintenance guys have to get up here. But the door is alarmed. It sends a signal to my desk downstairs if someone opens it."

"Did you happen to get any alarms from the door today?"

He tilts his head to think. "Matter of fact I did. Must have been right before five o'clock. I came up here to take a look around, but didn't see a thing. Went back down to my desk, and been there ever since."

"How long did it take you to get up here?"

"Gosh, I don't know. Ten minutes, maybe?"

Sounds about right to me. It's close to the end of the day and the door's alarm probably goes off all the time. He wasn't in any hurry to come all the way up here and check it out. I'll bet if he copped out to taking ten minutes, it was probably double that.

We walk to the northwest corner, directly above where the girl landed. A thick black antenna cable runs up and over the side of the wall. I grab it and hang on it with all my weight. It doesn't budge. I inspect the corner where the two walls join right next to the cable. Light brown crescent scuffs mark the wall about half way up. They are the kind of scuffs that would be made by someone using the cable to hoist themselves up.

It all fits. She got onto the roof before they locked the door. She set the alarm off, but by the time the security guard got up here, she had already scaled the wall and jumped. Now we need to find out who she is and why she did it.

I drive back to the station feeling hollow inside. What could make someone do a thing like that? How terrified she must have felt. What resolve it must have taken. Such a pretty little girl, with her whole life still to live. Gone, just like that.

7:38 p.m.

I'm in the station searching the missing person and runaway files. A couple of young women have a physical resemblance, but none close enough. I jot down the names for my report, just in case.

I pass Sergeant Casey in the office and he asks me about the call. I run down what I found and the probable sequence of events. I also mention the big wig from city hall, and the fact that he wanted me to report back with my findings. I barely get the words out of my mouth.

"I'll take care of calling him," Casey says. Then, realizing he sounded a little too eager to kiss some city hall ass, he continues in a more controlled voice. "I mean, no offense, but a call like that should probably come from a sergeant."

I'm being paged over the department intercom to come to dispatch. It's a great excuse to leave Casey to his phone call. I walk in and one of the women, a sweet girl named Judy, whose husband I went to school with, motions me over to her station. Her teary eyes are wide with panic. She motions to her headset.

"Okay, ma'am, I'm going to put you on hold for a second." She looks up at me and all the color drains from her face. "I think I've got the girl's mother on the phone. She's reporting that her sixteen year old daughter isn't home yet."

"Where does she live?"

"On McKeever, two blocks from city hall."

I tell Judy to take down the information as we normally would, and let the woman know we're sending an officer right out to take the report. Judy takes a moment to calm herself before repeating what I said into the phone. When the call ends, Judy turns in her chair and puts her hand on top of mine. Her eyes tear up and I can tell she feels the same way I do.

"Do you want me to clear someone to go with you?"

I think about it for a second. "It might be easier to do alone." I tell her that I'll most likely have my portable radio off. She nods.

8:20 p.m.

The address is a cute white cottage at the end of a short street that borders the business district. In fact, it's the last house on the block. I park at the corner and put myself off over the air, telling them again that I'll have my portable radio turned off. I turn down my car's radio as well.

A recently watered flower pot hangs over the porch, dripping in my path. I step around it and up to the door. I take a deep breath before knocking. A woman in her thirties answers with a warm smile and vibrant blue eyes.

"I'm so sorry to trouble you," she says. "I'm sure it's nothing. It's just that my daughter's pretty good about coming home before dark."

I step inside the tidy home, hoping and praying it isn't her daughter. I don't think I have what it takes to tell her.

"Can I get you something to drink? A cup of coffee?"

"No, thank you."

She tells me her daughter's name is Stacy Towner. I ask if there's anyone else at home, and she tells me she's alone. Her husband is in the military, serving at a base in Alabama, and Stacy has no brothers or sisters.

I ask if she has any idea what her daughter was wearing, but she's not sure. I follow her into the girl's bedroom where she picks through her things. While she uses the process of elimination to figure out what Stacy wore today, I gaze out the bedroom window at a clear, perfectly framed view of the city center building. It's illuminated now, towering proudly above the rest of the structures as if nothing had even happened. I quickly scan the tops of her dresser and nightstand for a note, but there's none.

As we walk back into the dining room, the woman takes a few guesses at what her daughter might have worn. She makes room for me at the dining table and sits down at an angle to my left.

"I'm sure it's nothing," she says.

I'm stalling. My heart is pounding so hard I'm afraid this lady is going to hear it. I don't want to scare her needlessly if it's not her daughter, but I have to find a way to tell her if it is. My voice cracks as I start to talk.

"The reason . . . The reason I'm asking all these questions about Stacy's clothes. Well, we had something happen today. Something very bad. And we don't know the girl's identity yet."

The woman studies me quietly. "You mean, like, a girl got into some kind of trouble?"

I take a gulp. "No, I'm afraid it's something worse than that. Can you describe her jewelry? Anything unique she was wearing?"

"I don't think she has any rings," she says. "But she does have a necklace."

The pause seems to hang in the air for several minutes. I don't want to hear it. *Please let it be something else.*

"It's a silly little thing." She smiles nervously and rolls her eyes, and I know what's coming next. "It says Life's a Bitch."

I can't feel my hands rubbing my face. I'm blinking the tears out of my eyes but they keep coming. I can't breathe. I'm shaking my head, trying to speak calmly.

"I'm afraid your daughter . . . There was a terrible accident."

The woman begins to cry too, shaking her head in disbelief."

"A girl died in a fall from a building this afternoon." I'm unable to tell the woman that her daughter hated her life so much she dove off a twelve story building. I just can't bring myself to say it.

"Was it her? Do you think it was Stacy? Another girl could have had the same necklace." The woman is still shaking her head.

I know she's going to have to identify the girl at some point. Seeing Stacy stretched out on a slab at the gruesome county morgue would be more devastating than what she's already going through. I've gone this far, I have to find the strength to just finish it.

"We took a photograph of the girl," I say.

"Show me."

"Are you able to look at it?"

She nods and steadies herself by gripping the table. I take the photo from my pocket and hold it in front of her. Slowly, her hands come up to meet her face and she sobs silently into them.

I want to put my hand on her shoulder. I want to hug her. I want to sit down and cry with her. But this grief belongs to her, it isn't about me. I'm unsure where the lines are. I don't know what's appropriate and what isn't. So I simply sit quietly with her. A long time passes.

"Stacy's had a difficult time adjusting. She'd been living with my ex-husband back in Illinois. Her boyfriend died in a motorcycle accident last year, and in September she moved out here to live with me and her stepfather."

"Had she seemed particularly depressed lately?"

"That's the strange thing. She's been really down since moving out here, but this morning she was different. I thought she's really turned the corner. She was happy and cheerful."

I'm wondering if that's because she'd made up her mind. She'd probably been looking out at that damn building for weeks, and finally decided to do it. That might also account for the witness's description of her, determined and in a hurry. I bet she went straight up to that roof, climbed that wall, and jumped without even hesitating.

After a long while I ask if there's anyone she'd like me to call for her. Although she's got no relatives in the area, she thinks it might help if I smooth the way with her husband's military commanders. After she calls and tells her husband about Stacy, she gives me the number for his command. I tell them what has occurred and offer them my name and badge number if they need to confirm anything.

Stacy's mother is more composed now, but her eyes are swollen and red. She's sits limp on her chair. I give her my card and the number to reach our counseling staff. I apologize to her again, and again. Finally, I back out the door and fall into my patrol car, shaky and emotionally spent. I sit there for a minute watching the house, empty and still against the backdrop of the towering city center.

I turn the key and the starter grinds loudly. I jerk my hand away, realizing I'd already started the car. I shouldn't be on the street tonight; my mind is not in the game. I carefully put the car in gear and start toward the station.

10:13 p.m.

There's a low static sound and I realize my radio volume is turned down. I crank it up and I'm bombarded with a flurry of activity. I've apparently tuned in at the middle of something, and it sounds heavy.

"The wife is on the phone now," the dispatcher's voice snaps. "She says the suspect is armed with a handgun and is holding her and their daughter hostage. We hear screaming over the phone in the background."

Police units are giving their identifying numbers in rapid fire succession as they arrive on scene. The sergeant comes on and asks for an update.

"Caller states that the suspect just went into the garage."

"Ask her if there's anything in the garage we should know about," he says.

A minute later the dispatcher comes back over the air. "Uh, she says he's got explosives and more weapons in there."

"How many units do we have at the scene?" The sergeant's siren nearly drowns him out.

"Five patrol and one traffic, so far," she says.

"Okay," the sergeant pauses, "We're going to have to make this a SWAT activation. Go ahead and make the callout."

I open my window to get some cool air on my face. I turn the car toward the west end neighborhood, apparently under siege. It's the worst possible time for me to be called to something like this. I'm a mess. Unfortunately, I don't have the luxury of going in and telling the watch commander that I'm an emotional wreck and would like to go home.

"Do we have any other SWAT personnel on duty tonight?"

The dispatcher pauses as she checks the log. "Forty-six," she says. "But he's still off on McKeever."

"I've just cleared," I say over the air. "I'm en route now."

I drive into what looks like a Viet Nam war evacuation zone. There are road flares everywhere, glowing eerily through the smoky discharge. Patrol cars litter the block, on curbs, halfway into driveways, and abandoned in the middle of the street. A police dog barks wildly from the backseat of one of them as I pull up.

We've apparently taken over the office of an elementary school around the corner, courtesy of a school security officer who happened to be monitoring our channels. It'll serve as a command post for the higher ranks and a staging area for the SWAT team when they arrive. I'm told by dispatch to respond there.

The address in question is dark, and I can see the outlines of uniformed cops hunkered down on every corner. They form an irregular perimeter around the house, preventing the suspect's escape. Meanwhile, it sounds like we have the entire 25 person SWAT team and the nine-person hostage negotiations unit responding. That number includes three of us on the team who already happen to be on duty.

"Pssst," someone calls from the dark. I walk toward the sound and find Chuckles, one of the motorcycle officers. "Hey," he says. "I think I got myself into trouble."

"How?" I'm wondering if this is important information I need right now.

"I'm supposed to be keeping traffic out of the area, but I had to take a dump really bad."

I'm pretty certain I don't need to know this. My face, I'm sure, twists into one big disgusted wrinkle.

"The people in that house right there let me use their bathroom, and I stunk it up really bad. Now I think they're going to call internal affairs on me."

"You could always plead insanity." I give him a pat him on the back. "And I'll even testify to it."

I continue around the corner to the school's office. The sergeant is assembling some of us and making assignments. As the other SWAT team members begin to arrive, the sergeant is relieved by tactical unit supervisors.

"The phone line's gone dead," dispatch says. "Sounds like he's pulled the phone out of the wall."

One of the cops on the inner perimeter suddenly comes on the air. "The front door is opening. I've got someone in sight. It's the wife. She's running from the house."

They put the grab on the woman and escort her to the command post. Two of the hostage negotiators whisk her into a side office to question her. I'm hoping after learning the status of the little girl they find out more information concerning the explosives and weapons.

I listen at the door. The woman's telling them she saw a chance to escape and took it. Now she's crying because she left her four-year-old daughter, Kelly, in the house alone with him. She wants to go back in. There's a scuffle and the cops have to physically restrain her.

"What set him off tonight?" one of the negotiators asks.

"Me and Kelly came back from the store and Keith was laying on the couch," she says. "He was drinking and watching porno videos, and I could tell he was high."

Seems like it would have been logical time to take the girl and leave, but obviously she didn't. I continue listening.

"Keith was real cross. He threw a beer can at Kelly when she walked in front of the TV set, and was yelling and cussing at us."

Yet another red flag ignored. She stays there and exposes the girl to a violent father watching pornography.

"When Keith hit me, I decided it was time to take Kelly and leave. That's when he pulled out his gun and wouldn't let us go."

The negotiators finally get to the subject of weapons. Turns out he has a couple of sticks of dynamite in the garage, along with several handguns and rifles. According to the woman, "He's got more ammunition than the army."

I pass on the information I overheard. The explosives and access to rifles changes our strategy a little. Those weapons give the suspect greater range, and subsequently cause the evacuation of several more houses nearby. Although I'm not designated as a sniper, I'm given a scoped rifle and tasked with finding an elevated position where I can cover the backyard.

I climb onto the roof next door and inch my way up the protected side to the crest. I brace myself against a brick chimney and rest my elbows over the peak. The position allows me to look straight into the fenced back yard. The door from the kitchen into the yard faces me, and at times I can see shadows of movement inside.

With no immediate way to communicate with Keith, it's a waiting game. I can see beyond the suspect's house into those of his neighbors; lights flashing in the dark, hurried movements, and panicked expressions as they're escorted to their cars by police in black jumpsuits. I see a mother and her teenage daughter run across the street carrying clothes still on a hanger. I think of Stacy Towner. I imagine her mother in her house tonight, alone with her anguish. A clot of emotion begins to grip my throat and I clear it away.

I'm staring through the rifle scope, lost in my own thoughts. Why does this affect me so much? I didn't know the girl. Am I feeling her mother's grief or am I feeling my own? I picture my two little girls, laughing, playing, and watching cartoons. Perhaps I'm feeling the grief of a parent, replacing Stacy with one of my own daughters.

My portable radio crackles and I blink to clear my eyes. I've been shivering in the dark up her with no concept of passing time. I pull my face way from the rifle and stretch my neck. I glance around. There's nothing moving in the quiet darkness. I slowly settle back into my position, and back into my thoughts.

"There's movement through the front window!" A voice suddenly calls out over the air. "I can see him going into the garage. Standby . . . there's more movement . . . standby on the perimeter!"

I clench the rifle tight in my arms, driving the butt hard against my shoulder. I feel blood coursing through me, pumping furiously inside my veins. My ears ring and my field of view narrows. I'm pressed against the scope, moving the lens from the door to the window and back again. A shadow moves behind the curtain.

"Something's happening," a unit on the inner-perimeter reports. "Standby . . ."

A creak suddenly emits from the kitchen door. I tighten my grip and slide my finger down, slowly releasing the safety. Stay focused, I tell myself. I watch intently through the scope as the door inches open. It's dark and it'll be hard to differentiate a weapon from the shadows when he comes out. I take a measured breath and hold it.

I see his dark outline—he's outside now. I strain to focus my eyes. It's a small figure, too small for a man. Slowly I make out the round face, the one-piece, zip-up, yellow pajama, and the tiny hand gripping the teddy bear. I pull my eye away from the scope and gasp in some air. I aim my flashlight into the yard and see her innocent face, her red cheeks, and her blue eyes.

"It's the little girl," I say into the radio. "Need a ground unit on the north side, now!"

A rustle comes from the bushes beyond the fence. "Come toward my light," an officer calls to her. She wanders sleepily toward them, and is quickly lifted to the other side of the fence. I watch the whole thing take place, and it's over in a few seconds. I'm covering the door and windows in case Keith appears, but I feel like the life's been sucked out of me. I honestly feel as if I've reached beyond my emotional limit tonight.

A figure appears at the door, nothing more than a solid black frame against a dark gray background. This one is big—it's Keith. I advise the units over the air and everyone holds tight their positions. He steps into the yard, looking back and forth. I can't tell if he's looking for cops or for his daughter.

"No weapon visible," I whisper into the mic.

Keith steps silently across the yard, still glancing around. When he nears the fence, a blinding flash lights the entire yard brighter than day. Almost simultaneously a flash-bang grenade is detonated by the perimeter team, causing a thunderous boom. It stuns Keith, dropping him to his knees. There's a popping sound as two darts from a stun gun fly into him. The wires arc and Keith writhes and flops like an eel. Three cops suddenly appear over the fence. They handcuff him and drag him out of the yard.

The entry team moves in to clear the house, normally part of my job on the team. I climb down as the sheriff's bomb unit comes around the corner from where they've been staged, and they go in behind the entry team. I check-in at the school and turn in the rifle. I'm officially released from the scene, so I jump in my car with the heater on full, trying to thaw my frozen fingers. I don't remember driving back to the station.

Since I'm leaving on vacation, I need to finish the Stacy Towner report before I go home. I spend the next thirty-five minutes alone in the report writing room.

4:17 a.m.

I change in the locker room and then check-in with the watch commander before I leave. He tells me the coroner's office called about my "jumper." The lieutenant hands me a message slip with their number.

I speak to one of the pathologists who asks a couple of questions about the scene. Since they don't have a copy of the report yet, I fill him in. No suicide note, no actual suicide threats, but recent depression over the death of a boyfriend. I mention that the decedent's mother identified her via a photograph taken at the scene. He thanks me for taking care of that for them.

4:55 a.m.

I park my car and come up the walk to my front door. There's a pink plastic hand shovel and bucket on the porch, and two tiny pairs of muddy shoes. I tiptoe into the house and hang my jacket in the closet. It's warm and quiet, except for the tapping sound our wall heater makes.

I walk down the hall to my daughters' room where they both lie quietly sleeping. I lower myself to the floor, reclining in the narrow space between their beds. I need to be here tonight. I tilt my head back and listen to them, dreaming and breathing softly in the dark. There's not a more comforting sound for me than this.

Chapter 21

Wednesday, 12:00 noon

I'm packing the car in the shadow of last night's unhappiness. It's no surprise that I didn't sleep well, but I'm trying hard to shake it off. The girls are excited and Gale's been looking forward to getting out of the house.

It's been awhile since we've been up to The Cabin—a rustic place in the Sierras shared by my mom, her sister, and the two respective families. Although we're only planning to stay five nights, I've reserved a whole week just in case. It's the first time my daughters have seen snow and there should be plenty of it. We sit with the girls while they fidget through their lunches, and then we embark on our three hour drive.

3:50 p.m.

After a couple of bathroom breaks and a stop in town for groceries, we finally arrive. My first clue that something is amiss are the tire tracks pressed into the snow covering the driveway. There's no car, but the bounteous footprints around the cabin look as if a troop of Boy Scouts has just passed through. I cautiously put my key in and push the door open. Dirty dishes fill the sink, beneath which is a cooler overflowing with beer bottles. The smoky remnants of a fire lingers in the fireplace and there are sleeping bags rolled out here and there. Gale and I exchange looks, and I can hear the girls asking her what's wrong. I feel my teeth grinding as I step inside and examine the nametag on a suitcase propped against the wall. I don't recognize the name, but the address helps me fill in the blanks. An unscrupulous cousin is making a little money on the side by renting the place out to friends.

I come back out and the girls are playing in the snow, oblivious to the whole thing. Gale and I talk about what to do. I can hear the disappointment in her voice, but it's trumped by her worry about what I'm going to do to my cousin. We make some phone calls, and out of sheer luck, we're able to line up another place nearby. By the time we load everything in the other cabin, it's starting to get late. Gale works on dinner while the girls and I go outside to work on our snow angels.

8:55 p.m.

With our daughters finally tucked into bed, I start a fire in the fireplace and Gale opens a bottle of Cabernet. All the lights are out and she's illuminated only by the crackling fire. I take a sip of wine, my first one, and the telephone rings.

I look at Gale in disbelief. "Who even knows we're here?"

"You're sister is the only one," she says. "I gave her the number in case of an emergency."

I answer the phone and immediately recognize the intermittent *beep* of the police department's taped lines.

"Guy's dead."

"Who is this?" I say

There's a sniffling sound, like the person's crying. "It's Clarence Scheper."

"Tom?" I'm totally confused. It sounds like Tom Scheper.

"Yes, it's Tom Scheper. Guy Woodruff was just killed."

I'm not saying anything. Woodruff's image fills my head—a guy I see smiling at me, pointing at the new black shoes he wears on patrol. A guy who once accidentally shot and killed a kid, and had worked so hard to come back.

"Dead? How?" The words finally eke out.

"We were working the desk together tonight," he says. Scheper's voice is high and squeaky, like he's about one syllable away from completely loosing it. "There was a call a few blocks from the department. He wanted to go. I told him to forget it, stay inside where it's warm." Then Scheper starts to weep.

My insides feel empty and my stomach burns and churns. I'm bogged down with a glut of disjointed thoughts and feelings. The most coherent is the unanswered question of how this happened. When Scheper steadies himself, I ask again.

"The killer stabbed Guy in the neck," he answers.

I finish the call and walk unsteadily back to my spot by the fire. Gale's eyes are teary, having overheard enough to get the gist of the call. I tell her who was killed and how Scheper said it happened.

"They were friends, Tom Scheper and Guy." Gale says it softly, as if she's thinking aloud. "How's Tom handling it?"

"He doesn't sound good." I think about the way he told me. "Weird thing, when I first answered the phone he said he was Clarence."

Gale reminds me that Tom had a brother named Clarence who died when they were kids. We figure that Woodruff's death had somehow jolted those twenty-year-old memories back into Tom's mind. I doubt he even realized it.

We sit quietly, thinking, until the fire finally dies out. I know the police department will be a mess. The cops that were there, they won't be able to function. "We'll all need each other," I say. "I need to be there."

3:30 a.m.

It's a tough night. As tired as I should be, I lie awake staring at the knotholes on the bedroom walls. I'm shaky and scared, though I don't know exactly what I'm scared of. I've left the light on next to the bed like a little kid afraid of the dark. I can only guess that my fear is about the hazards of this job, and of my own mortality. The reality of which I've successfully managed to avoid . . . until now. I picture Woodruff heading off to work, like any other night, never knowing that this night would be his last. I realize the same could happen to me any time I put on my uniform.

Thursday, 2:45 p.m.

The police department parking lot if full. There are dozens of cops in the building, eyes swollen and red, just milling around the station. The entire investigative bureau is in, working on various aspects of the homicide. I can't even put myself in their place — investigating the murder of one of our own.

I track down a couple of friends and we walk out to the back lot. It's not as if we anticipate our conversation will be all that private, but it may be. I think we all want to talk about what really happened, how it happened, and whether it could have been avoided. It will also be useful to be outside, away from others, should one of us suddenly be overcome with emotion. As it turns out, we all hold together.

Enrique, who's been there a couple of hours already, has gathered the facts from a variety of sources, which also include the local newspaper. He shows us the front page photo of the scene, with a smaller inset of Woodruff's departmental photograph.

He tells me and Kalani that the original call went to Bert Usher, a guy who's been in and out recently with a work-related back injury. Usher apparently got a call of a motorhome parked in a residential neighborhood a block from the police department. It was a nothing call, and nobody thought anything about it.

"When Usher gets there he's got some nutcase inside the motorhome," says Enrique. "The guy refuses to talk to Usher. Keeps telling him to go away. Then, the guy takes a match and holds it to a can of hairspray like a flame thrower."

Kalani and I are absorbed in the details. I can picture each step as if I had been there to see it all firsthand.

"Usher comes on the air asking for cover," Enrique says, "and Woodruff rolls from the station."

"Damn it!" I smack my fist onto the hood of a patrol car. "Usher's always making things into something bigger than they need to be." My two friends look at me with no expression. It dons on me that I'm just searching for something tangible to blame, as illogical as blaming Usher is. Fortunately, Enrique and Kalani understand where it came from.

"Anyway," Enrique continues, "Woodruff shows up and decides he's going to go in by himself to arrest the guy. So he runs inside and ends up in a wrestling match in the back of the motorhome. By the time Usher gets in to help him, the dude's on top of Woodruff. He had picked up a filet knife and jammed it into Woodruff's neck."

I'm standing there breathing like I was in the fight myself. I'm resisting the urge to tear up, and instead I find myself replacing the emotion with anger. I can't stand hearing it, but I can't stop myself form listening.

"The knife broke off in his neck," Enrique says. "They think it severed Woodruff's jugular, because he bled out within a couple of minutes."

"Did Usher know Woodruff had been stabbed?" I unconsciously lean against the car for support.

"Not right away," Enrique says. "The sergeant and a couple of other guys showed up by then, and they handcuff the suspect and drag him outside. Then someone asks, 'Hey, where's Guy?' They go back inside he's laying on his back with his eyes open, not moving. They do CPR on him until ambulance and fire get there, but it's too late."

"Did Woodruff ever say anything?" asks Kalani.

"When Usher got in there to handcuff the guy, Woodruff said, 'Get this guy off of me.' That was all he said."

Several minutes go by. The three of us stand around the car in silence. Finally someone says something.

"Are you going to work the street tonight?"

"I doubt his squad will be here," I say.

They nod. "Let's go ask the watch commander if they need us."

5:00 p.m.

A collection of big wigs are crammed into the lineup room, already taking initial steps to plan Guy Woodruff's funeral. I listen at the door and hear them discussing teletype notifications, honor guards, family liaison, and the massive task of traffic and parking. It seems unreal to me.

We're told to forgo lineup and hit the street. The shift is a hodgepodge of officers from a variety of squads and assignments, all volunteering to work on their normal day off. Everyone looks as if they're sleepwalking. There are none of the usual vigorous debates, shouts across the parking lot, or cackling laughs. Instead, small groups of two or three talk quietly among themselves. Remarkably, there are demonstrations of physical affection and emotional support—relatively rare in this testosterone-driven environment.

5:40 p.m.

I drive out the gate and down the street to where it happened. The investigators have finished interviewing witnesses, the crime scene techs are gone, and the motorhome has been towed to an evidence yard. All that remain are a few measurement markings on the pavement and the white chalky residue left by dozens of burnt road flares. A guy on the corner is mowing his lawn, and two teenage boys toss a football in the street. It's as if it never happened.

I sit in my car staring at the spot, wondering. How many times have I passed by this corner? How many calls have I gone on, just like the one Woodruff was sent to?

Why the hell did he go charging in there?

6:17 p.m.

I drive through my beat seeing all its inhabitants through a different set of eyes. Now they're dangerous, angry people, armed with filet knives. Every call carries the threat of sudden death, and the next one could be mine. I don't want to answer my radio, I don't feel like stopping any cars, and I don't want to arrest anybody.

I pull into an apartment parking lot where a bunch of kids are playing. I stop and watch them for a while, and then I get out and sit on the hood of my car. Some of them glance at me for a moment and then go on playing. They're young and innocent, and for the most part they haven't been exposed to the cynical world yet. They're free from all that consumes me. What I'm watching isn't complicated, it's simple. Just kids playing.

I watch them for a long time.

7:10 p.m.

Dispatch calls me and I answer. They're sending me to a possible drug overdose in an apartment building I'm all too familiar with. It's a large complex with subsidized housing—generally equating to low income, high crime, and every ethnicity and language under the sun. I notice they're also sending two cover units and the fire department. It could mean the guy's extremely violent, or simply an overreaction by dispatchers as a result of Woodruff's death. In either case, I don't mind the extra backup.

I walk into the interior hallway on the first floor and I'm met with the strong smell of Indian spices. A TV news program plays loudly in one apartment and the sound of a baby crying comes from another. Two firefighters tromp in behind me and their voices echo off the scuffed, yellow, high-gloss walls.

"Hey, sorry for the loss of your officer," one of them says.

I thank them, and we continue to apartment 115 where we find an open door.

"Police department!" I call out as I rap my palm against the wall. I listen, but there's no noise inside. I slide my gun out of the holster—my own overreaction to Woodruff's death. A cigarette butt smolders in an ashtray on the counter and there's a half drunk bottle of beer next to it. Whoever was here certainly left in a hurry.

I make my way through the apartment to the bathroom. The overhead light inside is muted by the dark purple paint on the bathroom walls. I edge my head around the corner and see a reflection in the mirror of a body in the bathtub. A white man in his late twenties lies naked, covered in ice cubes.

"In here," I call out to the firemen. "Heroin overdose."

The guy is unconscious and barely breathing. I suspect heroin because I've heard of the ice routine before. A legend of drug mythology is that submersion in cold will shock an overdose victim back to consciousness. This guy is proof that it doesn't work.

The firemen pull something called *Narcan* out of their tackle box, and inject it into the nearly dead bather. Almost immediately he comes around, sits up, and tells us to "Get the fuck out." I liked him better when he was comatose.

I advise dispatch to cancel my cover, but the two cops come anyway. When the ambulance shows up, the guy is loaded onto a stretcher and taken to St. Theresa's. It's a policy thing with overdoses—a precautionary medical clearance before our jail will accept custody of them. I'll check his arms for injection sites, and arrest him at the hospital. Meanwhile, everyone leaves and I take a few minutes to look around the apartment. No syringes, no drugs, just an average apartment with a dark purple bathroom and a bathtub full of ice.

I meet up with the manager before leaving. She gives me the name and description of the guy who rents the place. It doesn't match with the man in the tub. I make the assumption that the renter is the one who called it in, and then gathered up the drugs and took off. A tidbit of information I can forward up to the narcotics unit.

On my way to my car, I pass a Latino man hefting several trash bags into a bin. He looks at me as if he's wrestling with a decision, then speaks to me in broken English.

"Did you know the officer who died?"

I nod. "He was a good friend of mine."

"I'm very sorry for his death," he says. He makes the sign of the cross and walks on. I watch him walk back into the building, and a sick feeling sweeps over me. Guy Woodruff wasn't *really* a good friend of mine.

I get into my car and rub my forehead with my palms. I remember the time the whole SWAT team went away for a two-day training together. The lieutenant had paired me in a room with Woodruff. I traded roommates with Tom Scheper so I wouldn't have to room with him. I ended up rooming with someone else, and now I'm wondering if Woodruff knew. I wonder if I had hurt his feelings. It wasn't that I didn't like him, I did. He was just a little too loud, too animated sometimes. Now those things don't seem like such a big deal. I should have been a better person to Woodruff. I should have made more of an effort.

8: 35 p.m.

My prisoner is cleared at the hospital and I finish booking him at the jail. The place is nearly empty. I guess none of the other cops are doing much on the street tonight. The jailers mope around listlessly, and a couple look as if they want to talk. I sit with them for a while listening to their memories of Guy, the emotions they felt when they had to book his killer, and their questions about what might or might not have happened. It's a reminder to me of how something like this affects everyone.

9:13 p.m.

I cruise up and down the streets of my beat, watching everything but not seeing anything. I find myself at the duplex driveway where the Romanian family lives—the Stoicas. Mrs. Philpott's light is on and I see her sitting at her kitchen table drinking from a mug.

I tap lightly on the door and she flicks on the porch light. I apologize for the late intrusion but she doesn't seem to mind. She hugs me and tells me how sorry she is about Guy. I'm suddenly worried that she thinks I stopped buy just to be comforted. *Why did I stop by anyway?*

"So, anything new next door?" I ask, trying to casually change the direction of the conversation.

"You haven't heard? Elena and Bradley got married."

"Wow. How did the parents handle it?"

Mrs. Philpott smiles and shrugs. "You know how Mr. Stoica is. He says he's disowned Elena, but I hear that the mother secretly meets with her."

I picture my two young daughters, and then I think about Woodruff.

"Life's too short," I tell her. "I sure hope he comes around."

We talk at her table for a little while longer and then she gives me another hug before I leave. As I walk to the car I realize that *is* why I stopped by. Mrs. Philpott knew it all along.

10:30 p.m.

I'm advised over the radio that I'm cleared for my lunch break. I drive back to the station and call Gale. She sounds like she's been sleeping but she tells me she's hasn't. She asks how I'm doing and how everyone else in the department is doing. I only want to know how the girls are doing. She tells me they're both asleep.

"There's a Romanian family," I say. "The father disowned his little girl." I hurry through the rest of the story, rambling over parts, skipping details, and then backing up to try to fill in the blanks. I know Gale thinks I've lost my mind, yet she listens patiently.

When my story finally sputters to an end, Gale reassures me; about my daughters, about myself, about our life together. She ends by telling me that we'll get through Guy's death.

12:14 a.m.

Dispatch sends me to the movie theaters on the west end of the city, for a man found sleeping inside. I'm wondering why the ushers don't just wake the guy up.

I arrive as the last of the moviegoers head out of the building to their cars. A pimple faced boy in a bow tie and gold blazer meets me at the door. He tells me his manager instructed him to call; otherwise he would have kicked the guy out himself. The kid walks me into one of six theaters where a small Filipino man in a brown jacket is slumped in a seat. I hear him snoring peacefully as I approach.

Kalani's silhouette appears at the theater doors. I surmise that either dispatch sent him or he decided to cover me on his own. Again, I'm fine with it either way. I give the old guy a little shake and step back in case he wakes up swinging. Instead, he yawns and stretches like a cat. I recognize him as a goofy little guy who doesn't seem to be all there. I see him around the city from time to time, wearing a silly grin and waving to passing cars.

I ask him if we can call anyone to come get him, but he says there's nobody. I end up giving him a ride to his home outside the city. Apparently it's a converted garage he rents from someone. I find the place a few blocks into the county's jurisdiction. As I let the man out of my car, a sheriff's unit rolls by.

"Everything alright?" the deputy asks out his window.

I give him a wave. "Just giving this guy a lift home."

The old man flashes a toothless smile and waves at the deputy like they're old friends. The deputy laughs and waves back.

"My condolences for the officer you guys lost last night," the deputy says to me.

I thank him and drive off.

1:46 a.m.

Kalani gets me on the auxiliary channel and wants to meet for coffee. We back our cars into stalls in front of the 7-11 then stand with our backs to the brick retaining wall while we drink. Mine is my usual half coffee and half hot chocolate—it's easier on the stomach.

We usually talk, laugh, tell stories and compare calls, but not tonight. We sip our drinks in silence, both lost in our thoughts, both trying to come to terms with Woodruff's death in our own way.

"Did you hear about the guy who did it?" Kalani says after a long while.

I shake my head as I take another sip from my Styrofoam cup.

"He's on parole out of Southern California."

"Figures. What's he on parole for?"

"He murdered his landlords."

I look at him in disbelief. "You're shit'n me!"

Kalani shakes his head in disgust. "Killed two people, paroled out of jail, came up here in his motorhome and stabbed Guy in the neck."

It's almost too incredible to believe. Neither of us says anything after that. We just finish our drinks in front of the 7-11. I'm not sure if I feel better or worse. Something about the fact that the guy wasn't from here seems to give me a strange satisfaction. And then there's his criminal record—convicted of a double homicide. Not too many of them walking around free. Then again, it makes the whole thing that much more senseless.

I want to blame someone, but whom? The judge who sentenced him? The parole agent who wasn't tracking him? The Supreme Court who limited his prison terms? The society that allows it all?

I shake my head, like I'm trying to get something out. It's too much to process, or maybe too much to just file away. There are no categories in my mind that this kind of information will fit into. It's absolutely absurd.

3:00 a.m.

I turn in my one arrest report and go to the locker room to change. Woodruff's lock has already been cut and all his personal belongings have been taken out of his locker. Presumably, his things will be inventoried and turned over to his family. The nametag has been pried off the locker door, which now stands open and bare. I wonder how long before they reissue the space to a new officer.

Chapter 22

4:45 p.m.

I got in early and dressed before the rest of my squad. Three new patrol cars were delivered from the city garage this morning, and I'm determined to grab one of them. Can't even imagine what it'll be like to drive a unit that isn't cluttered with coffee cups, doesn't reek of cigarettes, the seat springs haven't been squashed down to the floor, and my hands don't stick to the steering wheel. When I've just about convinced myself that everyone else is to blame for the disgusting condition of the cars, I remember back to the time I was racing to a call while trying to eat a kraut dog. I took a sharp turn and lost a blob of sauerkraut between the seats. A few days later one of the women on my squad complained that the car was infested with worms. When the garage mechanics found that it was only dried sauerkraut, everyone on the squad knew I was to blame.

At the key board I find myself quickly joined by Kalani and Enrique. We're all looking for the three new units, but two have already been taken by the overlap shift and won't be turned in until ten o'clock. The other one is out on the dayshift. That car will be brought back in at five—the beginning of our shift. The three of us jostle for position as we struggle to find our nametag and hang it on the hook first. Enrique somehow gets his hung before us, leaving Kalani and me to drive a couple of old turds with over 100,000 miles on them.

Our new sergeant, Danny Jenner, was recently promoted out of the narcotics unit. Something about him makes me feel relaxed, like he's seen it all and won't get too worked up about anything. During lineup he reads a bulletin requesting the C-Charles unit to extra patrol the Arborwood area. Evidently there have been a couple of residential burglaries on the street in the past week.

"And I live a half block away," says Van Kirk. "So somebody better catch that son-of-a-bitch before he hits my house."

I'm just as concerned as Van Kirk, because Gale's parents live on Arborwood Avenue. We all look at Bosworth, who works that beat, and shake our heads in unison. Doubtful Van Kirk's burglar will be caught anytime soon.

The sergeant picks up a stale lookout bulletin that's more than a couple of months old: "Be on the lookout for the horse jockey, Tommy Jansen." Everybody starts laughing.

"I think I saw him riding a Sturgeon under the Golden Gate Bridge," Enrique yells.

"A great white had him for breakfast," another says.

"Did you hear they found his shampoo out in the salt flats?" says Van Kirk. "Yeah, it was Tommy Jansen's Head and Shoulders."

Even Jenner laughs. He shakes his head as he surveys his motley band of cops. This guy really seems to enjoy the squad. He's so much better than Sergeant Casey was.

"Get out of here, and be careful."

5:35 p.m.

After lineup, I walk through the second-floor maze of inspector cubicles, to the door at the far corner of the building. It's always closed and locked, and often there'll be music or laughter on the other side. This time, the rumble of low voices is all I hear behind the door. I tap just below the sign which reads, *Narcotics Unit*.

Talking ceases, replaced by drawers closing and other assorted sounds of furtive movement. I suddenly feel like Dean Wormer at the door of Animal House. It's finally opened by a scraggly guy named Skip, who's wearing a Corona t-shirt and worn Levis. Their talking resumes when the other three narcs see it's only me.

I hand Skip a large envelope containing the booking photo, rap sheet, and vehicle license printouts of a guy who's supposedly dealing grams of cocaine on my beat. As he looks over the contents, the other guys are congratulating each other on their big case.

"Look at this," says a guy they call Moose. "It's a kilo of pure Persian heroin." He folds back the ends of a pillowcase to show me a neat, plastic wrapped bundle about the size of a meatloaf.

"It's the biggest heroin seizure we've ever had." Moose gingerly wraps it back into the pillowcase. "Almost 100 percent pure."

Suddenly my little gram dealer doesn't sound so important. They don't seem to mind, though. While they talk and Skip looks over my information, I scan around the room. I'm taking in as much as I can, hoping to glimpse some secret piece of intelligence I can use on the street. My eyes stop on a handwritten bulletin posted on a corkboard behind Skip. It says, *Beauty Queen of the Month*, and on it is a Polaroid photograph of a naked woman with the biggest boobs I've ever seen.

The guys thank me for bringing the info to them, and I take it as my cue to go. I walk back out to my car thinking how much of an anomaly the narc unit is in this otherwise tightly structured environment. Something about that kind of undercover work really intrigues me.

6:00 p.m.

I make a quick phone call to Gale and let her know about the burglaries around her parents' neighborhood. "Remind them to be careful," I tell her.

When I get back to my car, I hear the gate opening up. It's Enrique in the brand new patrol car, already coming back in. His serious face is devoid of its usual comic expression. Something's obviously wrong. I step up on the curb as he passes, and see the driver's door is buckled and dangling, clamped against the frame by Enrique's left arm holding tightly to it.

He backs into a stall with the door facing away from the building—like nobody's going to know.

"What the hell did you do?" I call out as I cross the lot toward him.

He holds up a finger to shush me. "Keep it down!" He waits until I get all the way to him before he tells me. "I pulled over a car and when I opened the door, some asshole sideswiped me. The traffic unit say's there's no way they can clean it up for me; it'll go against my record."

"No safe driving pin for you."

"Now I've got to tell the sergeant and lieutenant. It's one of the new cars, too."

I'm just glad it wasn't me. I remember an old veteran cop once told me that it's better to take out the older cars. Nobody notices new dents and dings, and if you mash one up, everyone is glad to be rid of it. More than the sergeant, all the guys will be pissed at Enrique. A brand new car.

6:18 p.m.

I'm sent to a burglary at a townhouse in the hills above downtown. It's a nice, woodsy-looking complex that backs up to a canyon, thick with oak trees. I meet the man and woman who live there—a professional couple in their 30's, who got home from work and found their place ransacked.

They show me around, pointing out the dresser where money and credit cards were taken, and a cabinet that's missing a bottle of Schnapps. There's mud all over their white carpet, and the owners tell me it was left by the burglars. I find an unlatched window in a room that looks like a home office, where the muddy footprints seem to originate.

I walk around to the rear of the building and work my way up a slick hillside. From there I can examine the outside of the window. Something had been used as a wedge between the latch and the frame, splintering them apart. Small pry marks resembling the blade of a pocket knife pepper the area around it. A flat muddy spot just below the window has impressions of shoes facing both into and out of the window. There are two different sizes, one set is very small and the other extremely large. Shorty shows up and I have him photograph the footprints for me.

I'm inside recording the owners' information when Shorty finishes up.

"We're looking for at least a size twelve," he says. "The other one is either a female or a kid." He leaves and I go back to filling out the report.

7:39 p.m.

We're interrupted by a phone call and the man excuses himself to answer it. I note the alarm in his voice and I stop writing. He motions to me excitedly, "It's the credit company. Someone's trying to use my card."

The guy hands me the phone and I identify myself to the caller. He tells me the card is being used to purchase something at Tanager Liquors, a store two miles away. I get on my portable radio as I'm jogging to my car, and I ask dispatch to send a couple of units there right away.

"I don't have a name on the suspects, but we're looking for a large male and either a female or smaller built male. They should have credit cards belonging to my victims, and one of the suspects is probably carrying a knife."

I hit the main boulevard just as a downtown unit advises dispatch of his arrival. My sergeant goes off with him a few seconds later. Lights are changing in my favor and I get there a little more than a minute after them. They've stopped a tall, burley, biker-looking guy in big boots and a leather jacket, and a skinny woman with a pockmarked face. They're standing with their backs to the liquor store window, which is plastered with handwritten discount ads and lottery logos.

The girl looks worried. I watch the biker's eyes and detect a coolness that tells me he's unconcerned. *He's already dumped the evidence.*

"Nothing on him but this buck knife," the cop says, handing it to me.

The guy tosses his long hair over his jacket collar and grins at me. "Can we go now?"

I ignore the question. Sergeant Jenner is watching me, but says nothing. I glance down at the suspect's boots when he's not looking. There's mud caked on the sides of the heel, but I can't see the tread. I step into the liquor store, and approach the clerk. His East Indian accent is rough to decipher, but I'm getting that he doesn't want to be involved. He's saying something about the biker possibly coming back to hurt him.

"Can you just tell me about the credit card he tried to use?"

"Don't remember." He shoos me away with his hands like I'm a fly. "Don't remember."

By the time I get back outside, the other cop has dumped the contents of the girl's purse onto the hood of his car. Nothing of interest.

Now she's looking more confident. "Can we go?"

The guy grins again, "Yeah, we're done here."

"Sure," I say. "But I'll need to take your shoes as evidence."

The girl protests that her feet will get cold. I note a flash of worry cross the biker's face. I'm guessing it's got nothing to do with his girlfriend's cold feet.

"Don't worry," I give him the same grin he gave me. "I'll give you a receipt for them, and you can pick them up once the lab analyzes the mud." That last part was a bluff. We haven't got the resources to make chemical comparisons of mud, but he doesn't know that. However, we might be able to match the tread to the impressions photographed by Shorty.

He bends slowly down and begins unlacing one of his massive boots. His stringy hair dangles over his face and I can't see his eyes. Something tells me he's moving slowly because he's trying to think of a plan. The sergeant and the other cop step back, thinking he's getting ready to bolt. I lean in close, thinking he's going to do something with the boot. He gets it unlaced and starts to slowly pull it off his foot. In one sudden movement, he spins around and smacks the sole against the window ledge. Partially dried chunks of mud fly every which way. My instinct is to dive for the boot, which I do. But at the same time I find my other hand driving his head back. I'm peripherally aware of a wet, mushy sensation against my palm as his head bounces against the window. Thankfully it doesn't break. The boot drops to the pavement and the biker comes up holding his nose.

"You broke my fucking nose," he says in a nasally voice. I aim my light as he takes his hand away. It's a little red and there's a small trickle of blood, but I doubt it's broken. I hadn't pushed him that hard.

My sergeant tries to suppress a laugh as the guy gives up the other boot without any problem. I look them over; mud packed between the groves of the tread, and they're size 13. I handcuff both suspect, hoping I find more evidence. Right now I've got mud to support a circumstantial burglary case, and a weak misdemeanor charge of attempting to destroy evidence.

"Where were they when you pulled up?" The sergeant says to the other cop.

He raises his chin in the direction of a trash dumpster on the other side of the small lot. "Over there."

I feel like asking the cop why he didn't mention that before. Sarge rolls his eyes and I know he's thinking the same thing. As they all stand there watching, I walk over and shine my light into the bin. Turning a couple of cardboard boxes, I find the two missing credit cards lying among the refuse. I use a handkerchief to pull them out and slip them into my jacket pocket.

9:30 p.m.

The girl gives me a statement admitting that they both broke into the townhouse and then fraudulently used the victim's credit cards. The guy refuses to talk, complaining to the jailers that he needs an icepack for his nose. I see from his rap sheet that this isn't his first offense, and that he's already spent time in prison. It amazes me how this big, tough, ex-con is such a puss.

I finally get back out on the street and immediately get a call. Dispatch sends me to cover Enrique on some type of overdose up in the hills. It's on a rural section of road high on a ridge bordering the county's jurisdiction. It takes me a while to get up there, and when I do I find Enrique leaning against his second car of the night, shaking his head.

"What?" I get out and start toward him.

"I can't believe it. I just ran into the fucking fire hydrant."

A long jagged crease runs the entire length of the right rear quarter panel just above the wheel. I'm trying not to laugh, but I can't hold it in. Enrique starts laughing too.

"The sergeant's going to kick my ass."

"How the hell did you do it? It looks like you took a can opener to it."

He shrugs and we start walking up the drive. "I was trying to spotlight the address and didn't see the hydrant."

A howling noise comes from inside, and the discussion about Enrique's car quickly ends. We take positions on either side of the door and Enrique pounds on it with his nightstick. A woman's voice screams out something unintelligible.

Enrique tries the door and it's locked. He raps again. There's a thumping sound like someone running across hardwood, and the door swings open. A woman stands there, out of breath and with a panicked look on her face. The first thing I notice is her hippy look—long unkempt hair, no makeup, a faded halter top and a long paisley skirt.

"What's going on?" Enrique asks.

"My boyfriend," she gasps. "He's on some kind of bad trip." The woman raises her arm to point toward the back of the house and a manly tuft of armpit hair springs free like a jack-in-the-box.

"Does he have any weapons?" Enrique says.

"No, of course not."

Enrique looks like he wants to slap her. *"Of course not"—as if it's common knowledge that someone on a bad drug trip would never have a weapon.*

She follows us as we slowly make our way down the hall. We try to step quietly, but the creaking wood floor telegraphs our otherwise stealth approach. The hall ends at an expansive recreation room with high beamed ceilings and large windows. In the middle of the room stands a naked man covered in blood. He's got dark curly hair and a full beard, and he's standing with his arms and legs apart like da Vinci's Vitruvian Man.

One of the plate glass windows is shattered and huge irregular shards of glass litter the floor. A lagoon of dark, clotting blood collects below him, nearly submerging his toes. His face is placid and his eyes have no expression.

"Okay then," I hear Enrique say in his usual jovial tone. "Did someone decide to take a swan dive through the window tonight?"

The guy doesn't answer. I notice a particularly large gash on his thigh, filleted down to the bone, and a tinny smell permeates the room. It's a distinctive odor that only comes from a whole lot of blood. It's so deep on the wood floor that it appears black and chunky in spots. Yet, he's standing there like he hasn't a care in the world.

Enrique's eyes meet mine and I lean toward his whisper. "All the gloves and disinfectant in the world won't protect us if this guy decides to fight."

I nod. There's a knock at the door—the fire department and probably an ambulance crew. I ask the woman to let them in. Meanwhile, Enrique and I keep it light and friendly with the guy.

Three firefighters step in. "Hey," one of them says. "It looks like someone used the Jaws of Life on one of your patrol cars out front."

"Thanks for noticing." Enrique nods toward their massive first aid kit. "You think you got a band aid in there for this guy?"

With a little coaxing from all of us, we manage to get the guy willingly into the ambulance before he bleeds to death. Enrique, in his second dented patrol car, follows them to St. Theresa's. I stay at the house with Janice Joplin to see what she'll tell me about the acid her boyfriend took. Unfortunately, she's developed sudden-onset memory loss, and won't admit anything. She insists she's never used it, and it's her boyfriend's first time. *Right!*

10:15 p.m.

I'm backed into the driveway of an RV dealership, writing reports. There's good light and I'm tucked back out of sight. After a while, I find myself re-reading the same line as my head droops lower and lower. I rest my eyes for a minute and they open with a start.

"George-46?" Dispatch is calling me. I answer quickly, not knowing if this is the first or one of several attempts to raise me. She tells me that I'm clear to take my lunch break. Just in time—any longer and I'd have fallen asleep.

Enrique is in the lunchroom eating when I come in. He seems a little quiet at first, probably from the ass-chewing he got from the lieutenant, but bounces back once we start talking.

"What do you think this is?" He parts his sandwich bread to expose a mottled slab of meat.

"I don't know." I shrug. "Looks like either spam or rotten baloney. Who made it for you?"

"Nobody," he says. "I forgot to bring a lunch, so I just took this one out of the refrigerator."

I shake my head. "Some poor midnighter is going to come in here and find his headcheese sandwich gone."

Enrique finally gets around to telling me about his talk with the lieutenant. He wasn't real happy about the second crash. We discuss whether or not it's a record—two in one night. Neither of us has heard of it happening before. We finish eating and walk out together. I try not to laugh when I see the considerable dent as he drives past me.

I get in my car and follow Enrique through the back lot to the security gate. It opens and Enrique pulls forward, then he stops halfway out to adjust his mirror. I cringe as the gate automatically starts to draw closed. In his mirror I see his eyes widen with dread as he watches it happen . . . a third time. From my vantage point, it unfolds in slow motion. Enrique panics, steps hard on the gas, and his car lurches forward. It's as though he's going to try to outrun the rapidly closing gate. The gate catches on the handle of his back door, warps forward with a perverted sound of stressed metal, then launches off its track, slamming against the side of his car. He stops with a sudden jerk, and everything falls silent. Enrique steps from his car with a horrified look, first at the dangling gate, then at the new damage to his car, and then back at me.

I get out, afraid to say anything. What little of the gate that is still coupled in place finally gives way. With an abrupt release, the entire gate plunges to the ground, sheering the side mirror with it.

Another patrol car drives up on the other side of the driveway, and I can hear Kalani's raucous laugh before it even comes to a stop. His prisoner is in the backseat, watching the show with amusement.

"What's this, number three?" Kalani can barely speak between howls. I'm laughing too, but poor Enrique is just standing there, pale and silent.

Kalani's horse laugh suddenly stops and he speeds past us to the jail sally port. I look over my shoulder and see the sergeant standing there with his hands planted on his hips. I quickly snuffle out any remaining semblance of laughter. I clear my throat and step back to my car without a sound.

12:20 a.m.

Traffic is light and the radio is quiet. I haven't heard Enrique come back on the air and I have a feeling I won't. Three pulsating beeps straighten me up in the seat, and the dispatcher follows with my identifier.

"Armed robbery in progress at Pang's Market," she says. "Clerk states suspect's leaving now—white male, large build, with a full beard.

I'm pretty close and I see headlights coming toward me. "Any vehicle?"

"None seen."

This is the part that I always get wrong. I was always trained that the most important thing is getting to the scene to ensure the safety of the victim, secure physical evidence, and get a more detailed description of the suspect. But my gut is telling me that the guy who did it is in one of these passing cars. Some of the best cops I know would stop one of them, the right one, and make a great arrest. I'd undoubtedly stop the wrong one, the guy who did it would get away, and nobody would be there to handle the scene. Can't do it.

I put out the description and direction of the cars as they pass me, hoping one of the other units will be in position to make a stop, and I continue to the market. I speak to the young Asian woman behind the counter and then update the suspect's description over the air. His hair and beard are sandy or reddish, and he's wearing a green army jacket. Meanwhile, nobody is in position, the guy gets away, and I'm pissed off at myself.

Judging from the young lady's account, the robbery doesn't appear well thought out. She says the guy came in asking to buy cigarettes, and when she opened the register, he demanded that she give him all the money inside. She tried to close the drawer and he pulled out a knife and pointed it at her. She reopened the register and the guy grabbed all the bills out himself, and stuffed them into his jacket pocket.

I have a tech dust for prints while I take the victim's statement. For some reason, the whole thing strikes me as the desperate work of a heroin addict. Although I must admit, most addicts I've seen are dark, greasy, and emaciated looking. Never heard of a husky, white, hairy, redhead.

On the way out, the tech tells me that the bosses sent Enrique home. Evidently they felt that he was a hazard, and three crashes was their limit for one night.

1:35 a.m.

I return to my cozy spot at the RV dealership. I'm just about done with my robbery report when I feel my head bobbing again. Afraid I'm going to fall asleep here where someone might spot me, I start the car and drive toward the station. Unless I'm parked with another cop, I feel awfully vulnerable nodding off alone out on the street somewhere. I pass the broken gate which someone has already cordoned off with street barricades and crime scene tape. I drive slowly through the lot, making sure nobody is back there, and then tuck myself in against the back fence. With the transport bus on one side of me and the SWAT van on the other, I'm all but invisible. I kick my heater up a notch and sink into my seat to wait out the remaining 75 minutes of my shift.

The silent radio and the idling engine join forces to lull me into a place somewhere between meditation and true sleep. I'm pretty sure I'd still hear my call sign, but I also find myself submitting to fleeting fragmented dreams.

2:18 a.m.

My eyes spring open to the sound of my numbers over the radio. I sit up, sweaty now because of the heater and the insulating effect of my jacket. My heart pumps hard to bring conscious thought back to my brain.

"Go ahead," I say into the mic, with a little croak I hope no one else can detect.

"Cover the midnight Charles unit on a robbery alarm at Denny's Restaurant on Jackson Street."

I pull out of the lot hoping I caught the radio on their first attempt to raise me, and that nobody saw me leaving. I hit the emergency lights and check my watch—almost made it to the end of the shift without another call. A piece of something fluttering against the windshield catches my eye as I race along nearly empty streets. Some paper or something trapped under my wiper blade.

I get to the restaurant and see that two cops have already arrived. It must have been a false alarm, because they're both talking casually as I drive up. They turn toward me and their expressions go from perplexed, to amazed, and then to hilarious laughter. I get out apprehensively, and see that my entire car is plastered with red tow stickers.

People walking from the restaurant to their cars slow to get a better look. The two cops can't stop laughing, and all I can do is shake my head. Someone on my squad did me good while I was asleep in the back lot. Although, as many pranks as I've pulled I probably had it coming. The list of suspects seeking to pay me back is pretty long. The only one I can rule out for sure is Enrique, and that's just because he was sent packing.

I drive back to the station as quickly as possible, and spend the rest of my shift peeling all the stickers off. I know there's a whole squad in the report writing room laughing their asses off.

2:53 a.m.

I'm unloading my car when Sergeant Jenner appears at the back door motioning to me. I leave my case on the seat and follow him into the watch commander's office. The lieutenant sits silently behind the desk studying me as the sergeant and I walk in. It's a power game I've seen before—keep him guessing if he's in trouble, and then maybe he'll admit to something we don't even know about. Not a chance. It could be anything from falling asleep to wanting me to give a statement about Enrique's driving.

I take a seat under the message board and wait for one of them to say something. They glance at each other, like, *which one of us should tell him?*

"We need an FTO on this shift," the lieutenant finally says. Sergeant Jenner smiles at me as if my silence had pleasured him.

He nods, "I've been watching the squad and you've got what we're looking for."

Now my silence feels like a liability. I'm too surprised by their offer to know how to respond. The Field Training Officer positions usually always go to the most senior and trusted officers.

"Sure," I finally say. "Whatever you need."

"Bernardo Perenti is going to be assigned to us in a few weeks. He's going to need a lot of work."

I shift my gaze back and forth between them. *Are they blowing smoke up my ass just to get me to do a job nobody else wants?*

"Perenti's too timid," says the lieutenant.

Jenner looks me directly in the eye. "He needs to be more assertive on the street, or the crooks will eat him alive. You know how to talk to people. You know when to go easy, and you know when it's time to kick some ass."

The whole pitch catches me off guard. For one thing, I've never heard someone of rank talk about kicking ass. Usually it's like they're only about keeping citizens from making complaints to internal affairs. The second thing is; they seem to really like me. I know I work hard to do a good job, but I never thought anyone paid attention.

I'm thrilled to be viewed in such a positive light, and feel privileged to be let in on their little secret: *It's not always a bad thing to use physical force.*

I stand and shake both their hands, thanking them. I stop myself before I go too far and give them cause to doubt their decision. Don't want to appear too stunned.

3:00 a.m.

I stop by the report writing room, not because I need to, but just to let them get their jollies. The whole squad starts snoring when I come in, and then the room erupts into laughter. I tell them I was exhausted after watching Enrique crash his car so many times, and we all laugh even harder.

A few of us walk to the locker room together, still joking and retelling stories from the night's calls. We pass Guy Woodruff's still-empty locker, and the laughing trails off. It's been over a month. Some of us have moved on easily while others still struggle. None of us says anything.

Sometimes it's just easier to stow it away than to talk about it.

Chapter 23

4:53 p.m.

I greet the usual cast of characters as I enter the lineup room: Kalani, Van Kirk, Zabinski, Pigeon, Bosworth, Lee, Enrique, and The Village Idiot. Two people are on vacation, and Shorty, the evidence tech is sitting in the back. That rounds out our swing shift. I grab my usual seat and join in with the joking already in progress. The room grows quiet and I look up at the door to see the new guy, Bernardo Perenti. I suddenly flash back to my first shift, and my field case being tossed here and there by all the veteran cops. We must look like that to Perenti.

He stands there like a kid in Sears who lost his mom. I would swear he's about to wet his pants. I nod to him and motion to the seat next to me. There's a low murmur from my partners as he tentatively sets his things down and takes the seat. When the talking resumes, I ask Perenti how he's doing.

"Okay, I guess." His head is down and his voice is barely audible. "They have me inside doing an orientation this week, and I guess I'm assigned to you starting next week."

"Do you feel like you're ready?" I try to infuse the words with enthusiasm.

Perenti's shoulders hunch in a pathetic shrug. "Sure. I guess."

I give him a slap on the back. *This boy is going to take a lot of work!*

Sergeant Jenner walks in and lineup gets underway.

5:33 p.m.

I pass several older people in the hallway as I'm heading out to the parking lot. I realize they're holding a neighborhood group meeting upstairs, and I escort a few latecomers up to the assembly room. I pop my head in and wave to a couple of people I recognize from my beat. Mrs. Philpott rushes over and gives me a hug.

"Did you hear the latest about our Romanian family?" she says with eyes that smile with excitement. "Elena and the boy are going to have a baby. She's due in a couple of months."

I ask how the parents are dealing with it and she waffles her hand back and forth. "Mrs. Stoica is happy, but she tries to hide it from the mister. Between you and me, I think even he's getting used to the situation."

I consider the idea of dropping by just to say hello. If things have smoothed over so well, they may not still blame me for what happened.

5:49 p.m.

I hear a burglary call go out to an overlap shift unit, two blocks from my in-laws' house. Van Kirk hears it too, and we both take off out the gate. A woman came home from work and heard the back door slam closed as she walked in the front. No suspects were seen, but they couldn't have gotten far.

We crisscross up and down a four block area of the neighborhood, while another cop contacts the lady. I'm driving slowly, eyeing cars and people, looking for anything that appears out of place. Nothing stands out, only a nagging sensation that whoever is doing these break-ins is right under our nose. I pull up to the side of Van Kirk's car and ask if he's sure the suspect isn't one of his sons. We're still cackling back and forth in the street when Bosworth drives up.

"It's his beat and he's the last one to arrive." Van Kirk gives him a disgusted look and drives off.

6:15 p.m.

Dispatch asks me if I can clear.

"Go ahead with the next call," I say.

"Start to cover the downtown unit on a . . . some kind of . . ." Her voice trails off and I'm already shaking my head. This is going to be a good one. Finally she comes back on the radio. "Fire and ambulance are also responding to this. It sounds like someone was injured during some kind of sexual act."

I roll into the court, and park in front of a pale green house with a nicely landscaped walk. The house is set against a hill, and a steep stairway leads to the porch. A handful of kids are playing tag in the street, and the neighbor on the right is washing his car. Pigeon is already there, and is at the top of the stairs waiting for me.

He knocks and we are let in by a 30-ish white man with a neatly trimmed beard. He's wearing a golf sweater, slacks, and an embarrassed expression.

"Hello officers. One of my roommates was injured and needs an ambulance." We follow him toward the kitchen while he's talking. Pigeon tells him that it's on the way.

I turn the corner into the kitchen, and see a door leading outside with the glass window broken out of it. In front of the door, in the middle of the kitchen floor, are two men standing stark naked. One of them is holding a towel against his upper arm, trying to stop it from bleeding. From the pint or more smeared all over the tile floor, it doesn't look like he's having much luck. I also notice that his penis is erect, and appears as if it's being strangled by a brass ring around its base. Much of the blood has dripped and smudged on his body, although it doesn't appear there are any other wounds.

"It's called a cock ring." He says with an intellectual air, as if explaining a sacred custom to the uninformed foreigner. "They're used as a sexual aid."

No shit? Silly me, all this time I thought you misplaced your wedding ring.

The other man's deep set eyes are darting back and forth like a scared cat. His naked body is hunched and taut, adding to the animalistic look. Then I recognize him.

"Peter Valentino!" I say, like I ran into an old friend.

"Valentini," he corrects me.

"Don't you belong back at the board and care home? What are you doing here?"

"He couldn't achieve an erection," Valentini says, motioning to the other guy. "So he tied me up. I agreed to it, but then I changed my mind."

"The guy just suddenly freaked out," says the guy with the ring.

Pigeon asks the golfer where he was during all of this. He says he had just come home and found the two of them struggling in the kitchen.

"We were just trying to quiet him down," he says.

The guy with the ring motions toward the broken window. "I stumbled into it during the struggle to calm this guy. Accidentally stuck my arm through it."

Pigeon continues to question them, and I leave the room to let the fire department in. They pick up on my look, but it seems that dispatch has already given them a heads up. Their gloves are on, and they're donning their masks, and goggles. Into the kitchen they go, while I take a snoop around the house.

The front bedroom seems to be where the struggle began. It's got a huge pulley bolted into the ceiling, directly above the bed. The rope over the pulley separates into four leather straps, each with a belt-like buckle at the end. Gay pornography is playing on a television set in the corner. The bed us unmade and stained with an odd looking, yellowish, greasy substance. On the headboard I locate a gallon container of animal lard. Judging by the deep gouges already scooped out, it appears to match the substance on the bed.

I join the group just about the time the ambulance crew carts the roommate out on a stretcher. He bolts upright before they reach the door.

"I'm a nurse," he says. "This won't affect my job, will it?" Pigeon and I both shrug.

One of the firefighters asks us to find out the name of the hospital where he works. "Just so I know where *not* to go," he says.

Valentini starts down the hallway to get his clothes—yellow chunks of lard still caked on his ass. For the third time, we call the board and care home to have the goofball picked up.

Pigeon eyes him as he emerges fully dressed. "I hope you tell your group home counselors what a naughty boy you've been."

"I will."

7:49 p.m.

As soon as I clear, dispatch advises they have another call waiting for me. I'm sent, along with two other units, to cover Tom Scheper on a traffic stop. Either the car he stopped is stolen, or something's gone haywire. Whatever it is, he and my sister are almost living together, and if for no other reason I figure I'd better get there in a hurry.

The intersection is already clogged with police cars when I show up. Scheper is standing waist high to the most gargantuan man I've ever seen. The other cops have deployed in a sort of semi-circle around him. I hear Scheper's voice over my radio checking the guy for warrants. The name he's running is one I recognize—a notorious Oakland Raider football player with a reputation for knockdown-drag-out fights with the cops. The bad news, or good news, depending on your point of view, is that he does have an arrest warrant. I join them, filling an open spot in the ring around the giant. I notice we all have our nightsticks, and a couple of the guys already have them in hand.

Drivers slow as they pass, either recognizing the famous player or because of all the cops. Maybe it's just sheer size of this guy. He's got a bushy head of hair that descends into a wild beard, and then down his open collared shirt to his chest. His eyes are thin slits of anger as he looks from one cop to the next, sizing us up. I'm certain we'll end up taking him into custody, but it won't go down easy. At least a few of us will end up making a trip to St. Theresa's.

Dispatch confirms that the warrant is good, and Scheper tells the guy he's under arrest. His giant hands roll into fists as each of his breaths comes faster and more exaggerated. Tense seconds pass and nobody moves.

"Look at you guys," the NFL star finally says. "I see the way you're looking at me. Like you want to kick the shit out of me. You want to hit me with your sticks, don't you?"

"Just go with the program and nobody hits anyone." Scheper takes his handcuffs out.

The big guy slowly turns away, dropping his head as if the coach had just pulled him out of the game. Even though he's put his hands as close to the small of his back as possible, Scheper can barely get one wrist cuffed. Someone reaches up with another cuff and he snaps it on the guy's other wrist. With both sets of handcuffs still dangling several inches apart, a third set is needed to connect them in the middle. It takes all of us to load him into the back of the car, sideways across the seat, with cops tugging his shoulders from one side and pushing his massive legs from the other. It ends up being a cooperative effort that garners a couple of childlike giggles from the big guy.

9:30 p.m.

I clear the scene, happy to be in one piece. I'm thinking of phoning my sister and taking credit for saving Scheper's life. Although I did next to nothing, it would annoy him that I twisted the story to make myself the hero. I'm near the station, and about to stop and make the call when dispatch raises me on the air. It's a *cold burglary*, meaning whoever broke into the house was long gone when the victim called it in.

I forgo the call to my sister and drive to the burglary instead. It's a single-story, ranch- style home in a nice neighborhood. The house is at the end of a court and backs up to park district property, so it's fairly private. Another set of headlights follows me into the court and I see it's one of the evidence techs—Maureen Repasky from the overlap squad. She comes out with her fingerprinting kit and we start up the walk together.

"I've been to this house before." Maureen slows to view the front of the house.

"A prior burglary?"

"No," she shakes her head. "I did the tech work on a death investigation. It was about a year ago, I think. The woman who lives here found her husband dead. Turned out to be a heart attack. Nice older lady."

I knock on the door thinking how sad it is; she looses her husband and then some bum breaks into her house.

The door is answered by a tall, thin woman around 60 years old. Her perfect posture and short, but stylish, silver hair gives her a distinguished look. She greets us with a nice smile and introduces herself as Patricia Nance. She shows us through the living room, to her bedroom.

"This is where the things were taken," she says, motioning toward a large dresser. "Money, a camera, and a coin collection my husband kept."

The rest of the house appears in perfect order. I ask if anything else was disturbed and she tells me there was nothing touched except the dresser. Seems pretty sure of it. I ask if she could tell where the burglar entered, and she brings me into a wood paneled family room.

"The sliding door was partially opened when I got home."

I look beyond the door to a kidney shaped in-ground swimming pool surrounded by manicured trees and flowering plants. It's protected from view and there's nothing but parkland on the other side of the fence.

Maureen dusts the dresser for prints and then the sliding door. "Nothing but smudges," she says on her way out.

I give her a wave, and then sit down on the family room couch to take down a detailed list of property from Mrs. Nance. Something in her certainty that troubles me. Most women, especially those who live alone, are usually much less composed. They're typically too frazzled to know what is missing and what's not, and often ask me to double check the house to make sure the burglar isn't hiding somewhere.

I start fishing. "Anything like this ever happen to you in the past?"

"Never."

"Notice anyone in the neighborhood watching you leave?"
She shakes her head.

"How about the things that were taken, anyone know they were kept in the dresser?"

A momentary pause. "Not that I . . . not that I'm aware of."

I look her in the eye, knowing by her last answer there's more than she's telling me. "Mrs. Nance. You do want me to help get your things back."

"You won't get them back," she says, again with certainty. "Those things have already been sold. I mainly need the report for my insurance."

"Is there someone you're not telling me about? Someone you think did this?"

Mrs. Nance takes in a deep breath and cradles a cushion in her arms. "I have a son who doesn't live here. But he comes by every now and then for money."

"And?"

"And, he's got a drug problem. Heroin," she says. Now things are fitting a little more neatly. That explains why nothing else was touched; why she wasn't fearful, and why she was so certain her things were gone for good. It also tells me why Mrs. Nance didn't want me to dig too hard—he's her son and she still loves him.

I talk with her awhile about what she's been through with her son's addiction. I'm understanding, even sympathetic. When she cautions me that the burglar might be someone other than him, I agree ardently. We finally get around to *his* information.

Stephen Nance, a 33 year old with a minor criminal record— theft and drug possession. Mrs. Nance assures me that Stephen is neither violent nor dangerous. I ask for his description.

"He's a big boy," she says. "About six foot-two, with a thick red beard."

My mind immediately goes back to the Pang's robbery a couple of weeks ago. I had a hunch it was the work of a dope fiend. I ask if she has any idea where he lives, but she has none. No car, no job, and no friends that she knows of. I'm lost in thought about where this guy might be staying. Without wheels, it's got to be somewhere out here on the south end of the city. A couple of fleabag hotels quickly come to mind.

Mrs. Nance suddenly sniffles, and I'm aware my thoughts have drifted away from my burglary victim.

"I'm really afraid for him," she says, her eyes moist with tears. "He's either going to overdose or get killed by some drug dealer."

"Whether he did this or not, I'd like to get him the help he needs." I say, not really specifying exactly what *help* that might be. In any case Mrs. Nance seems thankful. She reaches over and squeezes my hand.

I finish up and blow out of there as soon as I can. I want to get back to the station and do a little follow-up on Stephen Nance.

10:53 p.m.

I request my lunch break and it's granted. I return to the station and find Enrique sitting in the front office. He tells me that he's been temporarily put on desk officer duty, pending a disciplinary decision about his three accidents. He's eating a piece of barbecued chicken, and his grin tells me that it doesn't belong to him. I don't even want to know — as long as it's not mine.

Between bites of my own sandwich, I print out Nance's rap sheet and pull up his mug photograph. I also need similar looking pictures for a photo lineup. The stack of prints for *male, red hair, beard*, is small, but I manage to locate the five others I need.

12:09 a.m.

I'm heading to Pang's Market in the hopes that the same clerk is working tonight. I'm almost there when a three-beep call goes out over the air.

"Any unit to respond — we've got a fully involved house fire with people trapped inside."

It's on the beat next to mine, and I'm all the way on the other end. I start in that direction with my lights and siren on. I'm racing to get there, but have to slow considerably as I near Sneakers Nightclub, where several silhouetted figures dart back and forth across the roadway. Cars are parked all up and down the street, and I make a mental note to walk through the lot before I get off duty.

I slide around a corner onto the street where the fire is. I see the lights of a police unit about a block ahead of me. It's Lee. I hear his numbers as he hits off at the scene. The blaze is out of control, heat radiating up and down the street, bathing the whole block in daylight. I skid to a stop behind Lee's car, and we both run past pajama-clad neighbors, toward the house. The fire spits violently, heat and smoky embers in a whirlwind of its own making. A single figure claws feebly from behind the window.

"There's a guy inside," yells Lee, his voice barely audible over the combustion.

We get to the window, face-to-face with the man. He's old, and appears disoriented. Though the front door is only feet from him, he's frozen there against the glass. I try the door and it's locked. The fire rages behind the man, and it's clear we don't have time to concoct a decent plan.

"Stand back," I shout to the old man. "We're going to break the window!" He doesn't move. By now he's covered with soot and the smoke is so thick that it's difficult to see the fire behind him. He's fading, barely able to stand.

Lee and I use our nightsticks to smash through the window. As soon as we do, the fire thunders with new oxygen, belching glass and more embers in our faces. I clear as much of the glass as I can with a couple of quick sweeping motions, coughing and choking, and trying to shield my face with my free arm. Smoke now pours off the old man, and we can't tell whether or not he's on fire. He collapses just as we reach for him. As he starts to drop into the flames, both Lee and I lean through the broken glass and grasp for him. With only the slightest handhold, but our adrenaline working double time, we drag the poor old guy through the shards and out the window. His steaming body flops onto the ground like a sack of sand.

I reach back through the window and grab hold of a thick window curtain, yanking it as hard as I can. The rod falls into the flames, but I maintain my grip on the curtain.

"Grab the other end!" I don't know if Lee hears me, but he gets the idea. He reaches in and takes hold of the opposite side of the fabric. Both of us pull and it comes slithering out, singed and smoldering. We throw it on top of the old man, patting it against his body, and then quickly roll him up in it. Lee takes one end and I take the other, and we use it as a litter to haul him to the other side of the street.

An explosion of flames shoots through the window, blowing fragments of glass and burning wood behind us. The first of several fire rigs pulls up and they begin to unroll their heavy hoses. I run back to ask the neighbors if they know of anyone else inside the house. They tell me the old man lives alone, and they believe he was the only one inside.

When I get back to the victim, a paramedic is slipping an oxygen mask on him. He's barely conscious but alive, and miraculously, only slightly burned.

Lee gives me a high-five as the realization of what just happened starts to sink in. We're both coughing and spitting soot as we stand there watching the house go up in a conflagration of flames. The guy is put into an ambulance and taken to St. Theresa's. Lee follows and I stay at the scene to help with traffic direction.

Later, when they're mopping up what's left of the house, the battalion chief tells me they think the fire originated on a recliner chair. Apparently they found evidence that the old guy was smoking cigarettes, and they suspect he fell asleep.

1:40 a.m.

I'm in the Sneakers Nightclub parking lot watching over the mostly calm crowd. Their security people eye me almost more than they do the patrons. Regardless, as long as they all know I'm out here, it's less likely there'll be any problems. I'm about to get on the auxiliary channel and ask Kalani if he wants to meet me here for a walkthrough when I get a call.

"Forty-six, can you clear the nightclub?"

"Go ahead," I say, pulling out my pen to start writing the address.

"We have a hysterical female caller reporting that she thinks her father just hung himself."

I'm wondering why someone would *think* that their father hung himself, and I'm debating whether or not to ask. Thankfully, before I can, the sergeant comes on the air.

"Did the caller say *why* they think that?"

The dispatcher answers in a matter of fact tone. "She sees him out the window, hanging from a rope."

I guess that's a good enough reason. Though if it were my dad I think I would try to cut him down, but that's just me. Who knows what the story is?

It's a two-story apartment complex, large and with a confusing numbering system. I've parked at the wrong end and have to jog through the maze of buildings to find it. The complex is dark and quiet. A strong wind has kicked up, clearing the air and magnifying the brightly shining moon. I slow to check the numbers with my flashlight and suddenly hear something to my left. I swing my light around and see a shriveled old man in a white hospital gown, hanging from a rope. He's in the dark stairwell between apartments. His gown billows like a sail as his frail body rocks back and forth in the breeze.

It looks more like a Halloween decoration than a man. I move closer until I'm almost directly under him. With the suddenness of broken fishing line, the rope snaps and the hanging man falls to the pavement. Unfortunately, my natural instinct was to jump back instead of dive forward to catch him. At the same time, I'm aware of another man on the dark stairs above him. I hit him with the light and see he's holding a shiny buck knife and wearing only boxer shorts.

"I cut him down," his quivery voice says. "He's dead."

I kneel down and feel for a pulse. There's no pulse, no breathing, and the man's skin is as cold as a stone. In yet another heart stopping surprise, the door to the downstairs apartment flies open and a middle-aged woman in a bathrobe runs toward me screaming. I hear more footsteps running up behind me, and I wheel around. A man in black clothes is rushing toward me.

"Get out of the way! I know CPR," he shouts. I hold him off with one hand while trying to calm the woman. I'm straddling the dead man, and still have no idea what the guy with the knife on the stairwell above me is doing. I'd really rather nobody touch the body, since this is a crime scene and a death investigation.

After barking a few commands to grab their attention, I finally get the two guys seated on the steps where I can see them. The woman in the bathrobe doesn't appear to know the two men, but she does seem to know more about what's going on. So, I try to get the story out of her first. My cover officer arrives and I have him keep an eye on the guys. Instead of watching them though, he's just staring at the wizened corpse on the ground.

I pull the woman aside and ask her to start from the beginning.

"That's my father," she says, pointing to the dead guy. "He's been in very poor health with emphysema. In fact he's been on a breathing machine."

"Does he live here?" I motion toward the apartment.

"Yes. He and my mother. I've been staying here to help out."

She lets out a sob and I urge her to continue when she can.

"He often has so much trouble breathing, even with the oxygen, that he has to come outside for fresh air. I thought that's where he was tonight. But he was gone for over an hour." She starts crying again.

I figure the rest of it out for myself. She must have looked out the window and spotted him blowing in the breeze.

"Does your mother know what's happened?"

"No," she says. "She's sound asleep. She's hard of hearing."

"What's your story?" I say, turning to the CPR guy in black.

"I live here," he says, motioning to the apartment directly above the dead guy's. "I was at work when I heard the call go out." He shows me a half-baked security guard badge. "I listen to the police scanner while I'm on duty."

My cover officer rolls his eyes.

"I recognized the address as the apartment below mine, so I called him." He elbows the guy sitting next to him in boxer shorts. "He's my cousin. He's visiting from out of town."

"Welcome to our fair city," I say with a friendly wave.

"So anyway," the guard continues. "I called him and told him to go outside and check for a guy hanging."

We all look at the cousin for his part of the story.

"Well, I came out once and took a look around, but I didn't see anything. So I went back inside and called him back. I told him I checked outside on the landing but there wasn't anyone hanging."

"I told him to go out and check again," says the guard. "I said to look down this time."

I raise my hands in submission. "I get it. So you finally saw the guy hanging and cut him down about the time I show up."

He nods vigorously. I'm finally starting to feel like I have a handle on this thing when the downstairs door comes open again. Out comes an old lady wearing a nightgown and holding a metal walker.

"Where's Papa?" she asks in a loud screechy voice.

"I'm sorry, mama, he . . . passed away." The daughter moves to block the lady's view of her dead husband.

"What?" The old woman squawks, cupping a hand to her ear.

"Papa passed away."

"What? Papa's across the bay?"

"No! Papa died!"

"What?"

"PAPA'S DEAD!"

About this time, the old woman notices her husband crumpled on the ground and starts screaming bloody murder. I deputize the guard and tell him to keep the woman inside while we wait for the body to be removed. His visiting cousin goes back to bed.

I explain the situation to dispatch and ask if they can expedite the coroner's office. It's a slow night in the county and they arrive within the hour. Meanwhile, I have Shorty take a few photos of the scene.

2:55 a.m.

By the time I get by Pang's Market, the place is closed. It's my Friday, the last day of my workweek, and I'd rather not leave this robbery investigation for someone else to do. I return to the station and run it down to Sergeant Jenner. He has me put everything I've got into my folder in case an investigator needs to locate it, but assures me I can finish it up myself next week.

3:00 a.m.

I change out of my smoky uniform and bundle everything up for the dry cleaners. I visualize the night's calls as I'm driving home, almost like a score card. The guy with the cut arm will live, and we all survived an almost fight with the football player. We saved one guy from a fire, but another guy hung himself. Sad as it is, it wasn't a bad night, all-in-all.

Chapter 24

4:45 p.m.

I'm in the locker room changing with Kalani and Van Kirk. They want to know how I'm ever going to get Perenti out of the patrol car.

"He's scared of his own shadow," Van Kirk says. "He needs to grow a pair."

I peek around the corner of the lockers to make sure Perenti's not around. "He'll be alright," I tell them. "Just leave it to me."

They both laugh and go back to changing. I'm left wondering how, exactly, I'm going to do that. I don't think the kind of *Drill Sergeant* pressure some trainers put on their recruits would work on Perenti. It would drive him back into his hole, and it isn't my style anyway. I'm thinking that I've got to find a way to show him how fun the job can be. Get his self-confidence up.

"Hey," yells Kalani. "At least you'll get free dinners out of it." It's then I remember that Perenti's mom and dad own an Italian restaurant on the west end of the city. It's not on our beat, but Kalani's right, we'll probably be stuffing ourselves with his dad's stromboli before the night is over!

5:00 p.m.

Perenti is already in the room when I come in. He's all spit and polished, looking like he just left the uniform store. The lieutenant starts lineup, going over a list of new department policies. Sergeant Jenner moves around the room passing out unfinished work and court subpoenas. He takes my file from the squad folder and tosses in on the table in front of me.

"Doesn't look like any of the detectives have moved on your armed robbery," he says, knowing I'm happy about that. "You gonna finish it up tonight?"

I tell him what I have left to do: show the photo lineup to the victim, and hopefully get Nance identified. I don't mention that I'm also going to do everything I can to track Nance down and arrest him. Although, by the way he's grinning at me, the sarge knows exactly what I'm planning.

5:46 p.m.

It takes awhile to check out the car, mainly because I'm showing Perenti how it's supposed to be done. He listens carefully, but the whole time he has a look on his face like he'd rather spend the rest of the shift in the station doing nothing. When we're finished, I tell him what we *are* going to spend the rest of the night doing.

"We're going to have some kick-ass fun tonight!"

Perenti's eyes, already magnified by his round glasses, now seem to take up his whole face. "Yeah?"

"Yeah!" I give him a slap on the back. "We're going to go get some gas in the car and then we're going on a hunt. Before tonight is over we're going to get us an armed robber!"

"Yeah?"

"Yeah!"

We pull up to the city garage and the gate is already opened. Two other police cars are filling up, so we take our place in line. Bradford, from overlap shift, and Tom Scheper, from Traffic, are at the pumps. Enrique follows me in and waits behind me. The first to leave is Scheper. When he gets just past the gate, he stops, closes it, locks the padlock on the outside, and drives off laughing. Everyone is yelling and cussing at him, but he keeps driving. Sometimes I seriously wonder why I ever introduced that nut to my sister.

Dispatch is calling Bradford on the radio. He doesn't want to come on the air and say that he's locked in at the pumps, so he tells them he's still filling up. Meanwhile we have to get on an auxiliary channel and ask someone else to stop by and unlock the gate. By the time we're freed, Bradford is a mess. He jets away from the pumps, forgetting to take the nozzle out of his car. It stretches like something in a Roadrunner cartoon, and then finally snaps. Bradford skids to a stop, the nozzle and hose still dangling from his car. He looks at us with his mouth hanging open.

Enrique shakes his head. "Oh shit, am I glad that wasn't me."

Perenti's eyes bulge again, as he watches in astonishment. The rest of us get our gas from the lone functioning pump, and clear out before the sergeant gets there.

6:28 p.m.

We hit Pang's Market first. I have my photo lineup all ready to show the victim, but she's not there. An older man working behind the counter tells me that she's expected in for work at eight o'clock.

I buy a pack of Swisher Sweet cigars before leaving. Although I rarely smoke cigars, this is part of my plan to toughen up Perenti. I stick one in his mouth and take one for myself. He stands there looking at me as if in shock. *Again with the eyes?*

"Are we going to smoke these?"

"Damn right!" I say. "C'mon. We're going to light 'em up, and then we're going to find us some action."

I see a shy smile creep across his face. We light our cigars and jump back in the car.

"First stop?" I say. "There's a burglar stalking my in-laws' neighborhood. We're going to cruise around and look for him."

We pull out of the parking lot, onto the main boulevard. We're stopped at a huge intersection crowded with commuters. The light changes and the car in front of us inches forward, then stops. There's only one person in the car—a man, judging from the outline. People pull out of the lane to go around him, and all the while he just sits there.

"C'mon, Perenti. We're going to see if this guy needs a push." I turn on my overhead lights and go off on a traffic hazard over the air. With our cigars hanging from our lips, we both get out and approach the car.

"What happened to the car?" I say, as I reach the open window. The guy inside turns and looks at me with a familiar blank stare.

"Put your hands on the wheel," I say. The lights have changed again, and now we're halfway into the intersection dodging cross-traffic. He's got one hand on the steering wheel and I can't see the other. I open the door and the guy lunges out at me.

"Knife!" I holler, as I see the glint of the blade in my periphery. It's down the front of his pants and he's struggling to get at it. My cigar goes flying as I focus all my energy on isolating the hand reaching for the knife. Perenti dashes to my side of the car and joins me in tackling the guy to the pavement. I'm vaguely aware of honking horns and flashing headlights as we roll on top of one another, wrestling for the knife.

I suddenly smell something burning, and at the same time feel a stinging sensation on my forearm.

"Perenti! I think I'm on top of my cigar. See if you can get it."

Perenti sweeps the cigar from beneath my arm as I manage to knock the knife away from my drugged out suspect. A couple of cars have stopped and their occupants tentatively approach to help. Sirens whine in the background, but by now we've gotten the guy in handcuffs and secured the knife. I check my arm and there's an inch-long welt where the cigar burned me.

We advise dispatch of our situation, and request a tow truck. Perenti and I lean back against our car, catching our breath.

"Lesson number one," I say. "Don't roll on top of a lit cigar."

Perenti laughs and shows me his—still lit. I tell him he did a good job.

9:05 p.m.

"Ready to go at it again?" I ask Perenti as we clear the jail. "The night is still young."

Perenti grins like a kid. "Want another cigar?"

"Not yet," I tell him. "Let's see if we can get my robbery guy identified, and then we'll have something to celebrate." The truth is, I'm beginning to wonder if this cigar thing is such a good idea. So far, all I've got to show for it is a burnt arm. At least Perenti seems to be pumped up.

We get back out to Pang's and Doris, the slightly built clerk, is there waiting. I tell Perenti to man the counter while I show Doris the lineup. He takes a spot behind the register and stands there like an old pro.

In the storeroom, I remind Doris that the photo lineup may or may not contain a picture of the suspect. She only takes a second to pick him out.

"That's him, number two," she says. "I'm sure it's him." I take a quick written statement and we're done.

I run it down to Perenti as we're pulling out of the lot. "We've got one more stop to make, but you'll have to wait in the car."

He looks like his feelings are hurt, yet he doesn't question me.

"It's an informant," I tell him. "She's really nervous about giving information."

Now that he knows it's nothing personal, he's much happier. We stop at the mouth of the driveway leading back to Isabel Cota's place. I leave Perenti in the car and quietly make my way to her little bungalow in the back. Isabel peeks out the curtain before I even knock. *What does she do, sit at the window watching all night?*

She lets me in, and then does her furtive glance around the environs before closing the door. I set the photo lineup on her tiny table.

"I need your help with a case," I say, pointing to Stephen Nance's photograph. "You know this guy?"

Isabel studies it for a minute. "He's called Big Stevie." Then she points to photo number four, "I know him, too."

I tell her I'm not worried about any of the other guys, just Big Stevie. "Do you know where he hangs out?"

Isabel looks at the photos while she's thinking. She always takes her time answering, almost like she's weighing how much of the truth she wants to tell me. That's probably as much as I can hope for out of a street informant. Still, I'm grateful for whatever help she can give me.

She slowly shakes her head. "Just around. No place in particular that I know of."

"How about a motel?"

"Might be." She studies the photos. "That's where a lot of people score their dope."

For some reason the photo lineup seems to make it more real for Isabel. Maybe she's afraid she'll have to testify or something. I slide the lineup back into my folder.

"Hey," I say, sitting down at her table. "I'm not going to burn you on this. I'd just like to know where the guy stays. I'll take it as an anonymous tip."

"What did he do?" She stands across from me, her eyeglasses catching the light. I wish I could see her eyes.

Now I pause, weighing how much of the truth I should tell her. "Robbed a store."

Isabel nods slowly. "I heard." Another long, uncomfortable silence. She knew all along.

For whatever reason, she's balking tonight. Maybe he's a friend, or maybe they get their drugs from the same connection. Who knows? No use pushing her though. I'll just have to find Nance on my own. I take a deep breath and get up.

"Okay, well, thanks for taking a look at these." I've got my hand on the doorknob when I hear Isabel speak in an even voice.

"I'd check out the Red Carpet Motel on Mission if I were you."

9:58 p.m.

"C'mon my boy," I yell, giving Perenti a high five. "Let's go get us an armed robber." Perenti is already lighting up his cigar and all I can do is laugh. He's loving it!

We're about a block away when dispatch calls my identifier. "Cover the Charles unit on a domestic dispute."

Damn it! I twist, hoping to loosen the knot in my neck, and then pick up the mic. "Ten-four."

We arrive at the address given, and it's a nail salon. The small cluster of storefronts are all dark and appear deserted, but the door to the salon is open. Pigeon, the primary unit, is already there. We join him at the door, flashlights in hand. It's quiet now, but Pigeon says he heard yelling when he first pulled up.

A squat Asian woman emerges from the back. As she stomps toward us, an Asian man appears out of the darkness behind her. They're both around 40 years old.

The woman points back at the man, and begins yelling in a thick, and I mean *thick*, accent. "Dat mudda fawka, cheata on me."

"Is that your husband?" asks Pigeon.

"He maya husband. He cheata on me."

The man walks up tentatively, carefully stepping around the woman. He's wearing a white collared shirt and slacks. I note the scent of a strong aftershave as he approaches. We keep them separated. I step over to my car with the man and Pigeon stays just inside the doorway with the woman.

The man speaks without a discernible accent. He identifies himself as Yong Kim, and tells me that he and his wife own the nail salon together. She actually runs the place, and though he's unclear about what he does with his time, I have a pretty good guess. The only thing he'll tell me about their current situation is that they are separated and having marital problems. I'm getting more by eavesdropping on Pigeon's conversation with the woman. I take down the man's name and information, and have him wait by the car with Perenti.

When I join Pigeon, I notice he's trying to conceal a grin.

"Maya husband. He fawka Tina Wrinch."

Pigeon leans over and whispers in my ear. "She's saying, 'Tina Lynch,' the chick who used to work in our front office."

"I know who she is," I say. "But how does this guy know her?"

Pigeon shrugs. "Guess Tina knows a lot of guys." Pigeon and I both look back at her husband and shake our heads.

The woman's been watching us whisper back and forth, and apparently she's now convinced there's some kind of conspiracy.

"Yeah, you go head and laugha. You fawka Tina Wrinch, too!"

Pigeon tries to explain that we were talking about something else, but she's not listening.

"You fawka Tina Wrinch! Maya husband fawka Tina Wrinch! Evwybody fawka Tina Wrinch!" Exasperated, the woman throws her hands in the air and storms back inside the salon.

I'm rubbing my face to cover my mouth, and Pigeon has to turn away. The husband looks guilty as hell, and poor Perenti hasn't a clue what we're talking about.

We leave the woman there to calm down, and Pigeon drives the man to stay with a relative. Perenti and I are itching to get back to our hunt.

10:30 p.m.

As soon as we leave the call, dispatch advises that we're clear to take our lunch. For once I'm too worked up to eat, but Perenti really wants to show off his uniform to the folks. He says they'll be hurt if we don't stop by their restaurant for dinner. The more I think about it, we might have better odds of catching Nance later in the night.

We light up our cigars again and start for the restaurant. As we crest a section of road elevated over the freeway, I see someone ahead, streaking across the traffic lanes. Something about the way he's running—he's holding something in his hand. He makes it to the other side of the street, and I'm watching him out my driver's side window as we pass. Suddenly the sound of gunshots ring out. I look to my right, near where the guy ran from, and there's another guy crouched near a fence, firing a pistol. The bullets fly in rapid succession, followed by blinding flames and sharp cracking sounds. By this time, the man who had run across the street has taken up a shooting position on the far curb. He's firing back toward the man by the fence, and we're right between the two of them. Bullets fly over the top of our car, and I hear the tinny sting as a couple of them ricochet off our hood and roof.

"Forty-six, we've got shots fired!" I'm giving our location to dispatch, and the description of both men. In a split second decision, I crank the steering wheel and slide into a left turn skid. Cutting off oncoming cars, I drive right at the first guy we saw. He turns to run and I jump the curb, following him across an unpaved construction area. The car slides wildly as it bucks and jumps over deeply gouged dirt. I catch a glimpse of Perenti in my side vision. He's gripping the door with one hand and the radio mount with the other. His glasses appear sucked onto his corneas, and he's all but swallowed his cigar.

"Wooo-hooo!" I let out a cowboy-like hoot, hoping Perenti will see the fun in this. Actually, I'm running on pure fear and instinct, but the last thing I want is for Perenti to crumble now. To my surprise, he lets out a pathetic hoot of his own.

The guy is still running with the gun in his hand, heading for a fence behind a row of homes. He's yet to turn on us at this point.

"Okay, get ready!" I yell to Perenti. "When he hits the fence he's either going to turn and shoot it out, or dump the gun. Just stay behind cover if he fires on us."

The suspect gets to the fence just as we skid to a dusty stop. I see the guy's hand go up, but I can't tell if he's still got the gun. He throws an arm across the fence and swings himself over it in one quick movement. As I run up to the fence, I play out the scenarios: he could be waiting on the other side with the gun aimed right at me, or he could have hit the ground running on the other side. I hear a clattering sound beyond the fence and realize he's still trying to get away. I dive onto the fence, hooking my left arm over the top and giving myself a stable shooting platform with my right hand. With my gun resting atop the fence, I scan the yard before jumping over. The drop is farther than I anticipated and I feel my knee pop as I hit the ground. Perenti follows me over.

"Watch the drop on this side," I warn. We move slowly and quietly through the yard to a large doghouse. I listen for a second and can feel his presence. Whether it's his heart beating, his breathing, his perspiration dripping, or all of the above, I know he's in there. Perenti orders him out, and sure enough he crawls out with his hands in the air.

We handcuff the guy and dispatch other units to deploy on the house across the street. Rather than hoist our prisoner back over the fence, we walk him through the yard, to the street, and around the block. Once we secure him in the car, we return to look for the gun.

Shorty is already in the yard with his camera. "I found the gun," he says. "Suspect must have tossed it. Look where it landed."

The gun had landed facing straight down, partially piercing the fabric of a folding lawn chair. It hung there, suspended oddly in the center of the chair.

By now my knee is throbbing. I casually reach down and feel that it's about twice its normal size. I limp back to the car and we drive across the street to the house where the incident appeared to have started. It's a known gang hangout, and several of the cops who responded already have a bunch of young guys detained. A couple of guns have been recovered, and the other guy we saw shooting is there as well.

The sergeant shows up and assigns out the work. We take the arrests and the original assault with a deadly weapon report. Zabinski and Kalani handle the supplement reports covering the search of the house and the suspects detained there. Shorty collects the guns and all the evidence.

11:12 p.m.

We drive toward the station with one of our two prisoners in the backseat. Perenti tells me he's having a great time. We pull up to the gate and I stop the car next to the trash cans.

"I'm starting to think these things are bad luck," I say, dumping the cigars out the window into the can. Perenti hands me his and I chuck that one too.

While I stay in the jail during the processing of my prisoners, Perenti goes out to call his dad and tell him what happened. Turns out the whole family was waiting for us at the restaurant a block away from the shooting scene. They heard all the sirens and wondered if it was us.

I question the two guys in custody, but only the guy arrested at the house talks. He claims he never shot at anyone. Other than that, he says nothing. When I check his record I can see why. He's got prior arrests for assault with a deadly weapon, and possession of firearms.

1:39 a.m.

I run into Bosworth in the report writing room and he tells me about another burglary in the Arborwood area. This one was around the corner from my in-laws, on the same street where Van Kirk lives. It's beginning to really piss me off.

I track down Perenti in the lunchroom. Unfortunately, I've been writing all night and never got a chance to eat. My stomach feels like a mop bucket and there's only one thing I can think of that will make me feel better: Stephen Nance.

We hit the street with just over an hour left on our shift. Perenti's rubbing his hands together like it's Christmas morning. I think he's liking this. I call for an additional unit and we wait for him a block away. Together, we pull up in front of the Red Carpet Motel office, essentially a glass enclosed cage. The night clerk looks up with a malaise that comes only from working nights in a drug infested, rat hole motel, and probably using some of the drugs himself. The guy looks like a bulimia patient—emaciated, sunken eyes, and a graying goatee that only partially covers his pitted face.

I walk in and nod to the guy like we're playing on the same team. "How's it going tonight?"

"It's going." The guy looks into a stack of room registration cards as if I caught him in the middle of an important filing project.

I stand there staring at his bald spot until he becomes uncomfortable enough that he finally glances up.

"Help ya?"

"Yeah, as a matter of fact." I step up to window and set my photo lineup on the counter. "This guy look familiar?" I point to photo number five—a guy I have no interest in.

"Nope." He says it before he even looks at the photo.

"Take another look." I say it in a flat tone, thinking that this isn't going as well as I'd hoped.

The night clerk lets out a short huff. "No."

"How about this guy?" I say, pointing to number six—another nobody.

He studies the photo a bit longer this time before telling me he doesn't know him.

Now I let out an irritated huff. "Do any of these guys look familiar to you, or are you going to tell me you've never seen any of them?"

The clerk rolls his eyes and leans over the lineup again. "I don't know, maybe this guy." He waves a pale hand over Nance's photo.

"Yeah, I know that guy too. He's a local guy, but he's not the one I'm looking for."

The clerk slides back in his chair. "Whatever. Anything else you officers need tonight?"

"What the hell," I say. "Maybe this dude knows the guy I'm after." I glance at Perenti and shrug. "As long as we're here."

The clerk gnaws at a piece of his fingernail and spits it out. "Room 185," he says without expression.

I whisper to my cover unit, "Stay here and make sure he doesn't call the room to warn him." Then I motion to Perenti to follow me. We use the interior hallway until we get to the building room #185 is in. I tell Perenti to stand at the front and watch the door while I take the outside route along the pool, to the back of the room.

I hear low voices as I make the corner. It sounds like a few people talking and laughing outside. I turn my radio down as far as it will go and I cover my badge with my hand. I'm pretty much a shadow coming down the path. Ahead of me are several people sitting in an open back patio of the room I'm aiming for. I keep my head down, peeking through my hair to size up the group. There are three men and two women—the man sitting on the railing next to the building is Nance.

When I get up to them I hit my flashlight on the group. It looks like a herd of deer staring directly into the beam. One quick look around the group and I can tell they're all addicts. Birds of a feather and all that, which happens to be particularly true with the tightly-knit heroin community. The good thing is they're usually pretty docile, except when they need a fix.

"How's everybody doing tonight?" I ask casually, as if I just happen to be taking a friendly stroll through the complex.

They murmur responses that are mostly unintelligible. It's not like I really wanted to know. My eyes are mainly on Nance, who's just looking back at me. He hasn't uttered a word.

"Nance, right?" I say, fixing my light on him. "Steve?"

He nods and slides a leg off the railing. He stands erect and for the first time I have an appreciation for how big he is. He looks like a red haired Grizzly Adams.

"Can I talk with you privately for a minute?"

He nods again and steps down from the patio. The guy's towering over me as we take a few hesitant steps up the path together. He seems calm though, and I don't get the feeling he's going to make a run for it.

"Steve," I say in a low voice only he can hear. "I'll be honest with you. I've got you ID'd in the robbery at the store a few weeks ago. We're here to take you in."

He takes in a breath and lets it out slowly. "Yeah. I guess I knew you'd catch up with me. Probably for the best."

I'm amazed, but try to act like I'm taking it in stride. "I'd rather not put the handcuffs on you in front of your friends. You're not going to be a problem for me, are you?"

"No, sir."

I call Perenti on the radio and have him meet me at the car. The other cop is waiting there, too, when I show up with Nance. It's then that I put him in handcuffs and wedge him into the backseat.

2:39 a.m.

I interview Nance in a holding cell inside the jail. He admits to everything, explaining that he had no intention of robbing the store clerk until she opened the till and he saw how much money was in there. He would have just grabbed the cash and run, but panicked when the girl slammed the drawer closed.

"I guess I kind of blew it when I pulled the knife." He throws a palm against his forehead.

"Well, at least you didn't hurt anyone."

"I knew you'd find me." Nance looks at me with surprisingly soft eyes. "Thought you'd catch me that night."

"Why?"

"I saw you pass me when I was driving away from the store."

"You were in one of those cars? I wondered about that."

He nods. "It was only a matter of time. How did you know it was me?"

"Your mom was ripped off." I say it without any sound of accusation. I just look at Nance.

He drops his head. "Yeah, that was me, too."

"What happened to the money, and the camera, and the coin collection?"

He gives me a funny look. "I sold the coins and used the cash to buy dope, but I never took a camera."

I raise my eyebrows and give him a grin.

"Can't blame Mom for trying to pad the insurance claim."

He signs the statement and we shake hands. "Good luck," I tell him. "I hope you get some help kicking your habit."

He thanks me, and I walk him back to the booking counter. As I'm heading down the hallway, Nance calls to me.

"I appreciate the way you did it."

I look back at him, not sure what he's saying.

"Walking me away from my friends before you arrested me. I appreciate the respect."

3:00 a.m.

I'm looking for Sergeant Jenner. I finally find him in the watch commander's office talking with the lieutenant. They quiet down as I come in, and I can't help wondering if they're talking about me.

I hand the sarge my reports and he thumbs through them, stopping on the robbery arrest. He pulls that one out and lays it on top of the pile. A big grin comes over his face as he looks at the lieutenant.

"What did I tell you?"

The lieutenant leans up in his seat to look at it, and then gives me a nod.

I'm still not sure what it's all about. It would be nice to know the whole context, but at least it doesn't seem to be a bad thing.

I walk to the locker room where I find Pigeon telling a group of cops about the old Korean gal who had accused the entire police force of bedding Tina Lynch. Thurmond Morris, the blabbermouth of the department, comes in on the tail end.

"Hey, you know why Tina's not working here any more?" he asks.

Pigeon laughs. "Because she's crazy?"

"That may be part of the reason," says Morris. "But here's the other part. One night when I was working the industrial area, I rolled up on a car with a couple doing it inside. I hit them with my spotlight and as soon as I did, I recognized the car. It was the police chief's car, and he was with Tina."

A murmur of disbelief rustles around the audience. "Bullshit," a couple of guys bark.

Morris raises his hands. "Hey, believe what you want. But I'm telling you it was the chief's car, and Tina was going down on him."

Another guy shakes his head. "If that was true, *you* wouldn't be here to talk about it."

"Headquarters-One never knew it was me. I kept the spotlight on him as I backed all the way down the street, so he couldn't see. And I never went off on the radio."

A few of us walk away shaking our heads. *Not impossible, but doubtful.*

I catch Perenti trying to listen in from the back of the group and I grab him by the sleeve. Ushering him out of the locker room I say, "You don't need to hear that crap." I let him know that the sergeant and lieutenant seem to be pleased with our work tonight. I also remind him we're going to take a rain-check on his dad's strombolis.

As we walk down the hallway toward the parking lot together, I detect a notable difference in his bearing and a smile on his face.

Chapter 25

11:10 a.m.

After sitting in the district attorney's waiting room since eight o'clock this morning, I'm finally called to testify. It's a preliminary hearing for the burglar I arrested several weeks ago in front of Tanager Liquors.

The Deputy DA meets me in the hallway outside the courtroom. "The defense is pushing hard to get the burglary dumped to a misdemeanor," he says. "He's trying to keep his client out of prison."

I follow him into the courtroom. The judge peers down at me over the top of his reading glasses as the bailiff motions me up to the witness chair. I see the big biker sitting at a table next to his attorney, and there's a court reporter and clerk in front near the judge. I tighten the knot of my necktie and walk past all of them.

"Do you solemnly swear to tell the truth, the whole truth, and nothing but the truth, so help you God?" The bailiff says it fast and serious.

"I do."

I take a seat and begin by answering a series of introductory questions—my full name, how long I've been with the department, when I attended the police academy, and things like that. Meanwhile, I keep glancing at the biker and the way his attorney has him made up for court. For starters, his long stringy hair has been neatly cut away from his face, resembling something between a Dutch explorer and Andy Gibb. Instead of his black leather jacket, he's wearing a business suit and humongous black dress shoes. To top it off, he's got on a pair of thick black-framed glasses. The whole getup looks more like something Ward Cleaver would wear.

The DA asks me a bunch of questions about the case, and I answer them, one by one. The whole time, the biker sits staring at me. I try to address the judge while I'm talking, and occasionally spread my attention around to the DA, the other attorney, and the court reporter. Throughout my entire testimony I'm aware of the biker's burning glare. I see that he's shed the phony glasses. His eyes narrow as he holds his gaze fixed to mine. Slowly, so that nobody else can see, he makes his hand into the form of a gun, pointing at me. Barely perceptible, he nods his head and drops his thumb like a hammer.

I answer the next question with a smile, checking first the judge, and then the attorneys, to make sure they're not paying attention. Everybody else is in their own little world, unaware of this silent battle of body language and intimidation. I fix my eyes on the biker and stare back at him. Then I slowly slide my hand up to my face and begin rubbing my nose—a subtle reminder of how I broke his. I smile at him as I continue rubbing it. The biker eyes widen and then he quickly looks away.

The DA asks another question and I answer it. When I look back, the biker is no longer staring at me. He's leaning back in his seat with his arms folded, staring at the blank wall. I finish testifying, employing all the pleasantries of a used car salesman.

When they dismiss me, I walk past the table where the biker sits. He keeps his head down, never looking back at me.

1:10 p.m.

I walk across the courthouse parking lot to the police department where I parked my car. As I pull out the back gate onto the street, I see a pickup truck driving up behind me. We stop for a red light and I notice it's a man and a woman, but I'm unable to make out any facial details.

I continue on my route home, noticing they're behind me at each turn. I've driven about three miles, making several direction changes in the process, yet the truck is still right on my tail. I know they saw me leave the police lot, and possibly the courthouse before that. It crosses my mind that it could be the biker and his girlfriend. I wish I could see past the glare on their windshield.

A mile or so from home I make a turn, heading in another direction. I watch as the truck takes the same turn. I go down a few different streets, finally pulling into a driveway of a house I don't know. The truck passes slowly as I get out of the car, and for the first time I can see them. The man is not the biker, but a mangy, tattooed, parolee-looking guy nevertheless. I start up the walkway and the truck disappears down the street. He had followed too closely for me to catch the license plate number.

I jump back in my car and head down the street in the opposite direction, starting back for home. The truck suddenly comes around the corner toward me, apparently having only driven around the block. As we pass each other I see the driver laughing uproariously and pointing at me. At this point it's clear he knows I tried to throw him off my track. I'm a little embarrassed at being caught, but more concerned about being followed. They take off and I don't see them again. I drive the rest of my route home checking my mirrors, wondering if someone is really after me or it was a chance thing. I convince myself of the latter, reasoning that they wouldn't have been so obvious had they really wanted to know where I live.

2:45 p.m.

It's the first really warm day we've had in a while, so I blow up the little inflatable pool and fill it with water. Gale and I sit on the backyard lawn watching the girls splash and play together. The stereo is on just inside the house, tuned to a light jazz station. Gale calls it elevator music, but it has a way of relaxing me.

As we sit there together in the yard, I realize how much my family means to me. Twice today I've felt threatened in subtle ways, first by the biker in court, and then by the guy who tried to follow me home. I worry about what would happen if someone I arrested actually came after me. Worse yet, what if they found my house when Gale and the girls were here alone? I would never want to be in a job that would put them in danger.

I shake off the angst and check my watch. I have to get ready to go back pretty soon.

Gale notices my tranquil expression shift to edgy. "Time for work?"

"Yeah, I should probably start getting ready."

"I'll pack you a lunch."

I tell her not to worry about it. Since it's my Friday, I'll plan on picking up something on the street.

"Besides," I add. "Nothing's safe in that lunchroom when Enrique is around."

I give Gale and the girls a kiss and then head out the door. All three of them wave at me through the window as I drive off. It's a little ritual they have done every single day since the girls were old enough to wave. Gale once told me she has them do it just in case it's the last time they see me. Besides being a nice image to leave with, it also serves as my strongest motivator to make it home safely.

5:00 p.m.

Bosworth called in sick. His beat, the one that has been hit with all the burglaries, is now empty. The sergeant asks for two volunteers: one to stay inside and work the front desk, and the other to move over and cover Bosworth's beat. Before I can think, I realize the sergeant is pointing at me and my raised hand. What had I just volunteered for?

"You'll be on the C-Charles beat tonight," he says. The rest of the squad puckers their lips as if I did it to look good. Most of them don't realize that some burglar has been running rampant in my wife's parents' neighborhood, not to mention it's the same neighborhood where Van Kirk lives. He's the only one who gives me an encouraging nod.

We break lineup, and I walk toward the parking lot thinking that it's going to be a good night. I remind myself though, that I've been wrong before.

5:42 p.m.

I make a stop at the gas pumps before going on the air. Two of the motorcycle officers are there filling up; Chuckles, and Tom Scheper. I wait behind Chuckles, thinking about the problem spots on tonight's beat, when Scheper motions me over to the corner of the facilities yard.

"What?" I ask. "You gonna lock me in here with Chuckles?"

He shakes his head in irritation. "Just come here."

I leave my car and walk across the yard with Scheper. He digs his hand into his inside jacket pocket and comes out with a tiny black box. I see it and my eyes widen. *This, I'm not sure I can handle.*

"I'm going to ask your sister for her hand in marriage."

Scheper has been watching too many old movies. *Her hand in marriage! Who are you, Jimmy Stewart?* Of course, I shake his hand and wish him luck.

Tom Scheper, my brother-in-law. Holy shit!

6:08 p.m.

I start for Mrs. Nance's house as soon as I clear the gas pumps. I want to fill her in about her burglary report, but more importantly, I want to let her know that Stephan is in custody and getting the help he needs. I'm sure she'll rest much easier at night.

I'm about halfway there when I'm diverted to a call. It's an injury accident involving a child. I'm on the opposite end of my beat, and I let dispatch know I'm rolling from a distance. Tom Scheper comes on the air, and since he's a traffic unit, they cancel me and send him. I'm headed there anyway, to help Tom out, but dispatch comes over the air calling me again.

"Charles-46, start for the frontage road along the salt flats, south of highway 92."

Frontage road along the salt flats? I don't think I've ever been out there. I pick up my mic, but she continues before I respond.

"Possible dead body."

I drive quickly, but without any lights or siren. Why risk it? The *dead body* isn't likely to go anywhere. I pull up behind a city pickup truck. I'm assuming he's with the sewage treatment department. Must have found the body during his rounds. I get out of my car and see that the guy is green. Not the dead guy, but the city worker. He's leaning over his bumper, gagging. I have him take a seat, and then I walk down a slight embankment to the salt-caked water's edge.

The remains of a small man lies curled against the shore. The first thing that comes into my mind is the jockey, Tommy Jansen. Other than the bone stubs jutting from his gnarled feet, the body is fairly well preserved—probably from the salt and wind. He looks almost as if he's been freeze-dried, or dehydrated like a piece of beef jerky.

I lean down with my flashlight to check for anything that might help positively identify him. A lot of people who jump from the Golden Gate Bridge are washed south by the bay's currents. This body could actually be anybody.

I feel along the back of his pants for a wallet, but there's none. The waistline of his pants slips down and inch or two, and I see his white underpants beneath them. Monogrammed right on the elastic around the top are his initials: TJ. I shake my head in amazement. Who the hell monograms their underpants? For a second, I imagine all the jockeys in the Bay Meadows locker room swiping one another's' clothes. *Maybe they all put their initials on their underwear.*

Well, here's one long-running mystery solved.

7:46 p.m.

After the coroner's office takes the jockey, I drive toward the home of Mrs. Nance. This time, I go over the air and get permission to do a follow-up off my beat.

I tap lightly on the door and it's opened by Mrs. Nance. She's wearing a red, floor-length bathrobe. I apologize for the intrusion, and I tell her I came by to give her an update on her burglary case. She asks me to sit with her at the dining room table, and offers me something to drink. I thank her and decline.

"I wanted to let you know that your son, Stephen, has been arrested."

Mrs. Nance is quiet, looking at me through watery eyes. "Did you arrest him?"

"Yes, I did." I glance toward my clipboard, electing not to show her the photo lineup. Not sure why I even considered it. "It turns out that Stephen had also committed a robbery."

She looks puzzled. "Robbery, burglary, aren't they the same?"

"No, they're not." I had forgotten that most people aren't sure of the difference. "He forced a clerk to give him money from a cash register."

She shakes her head in disbelief. "Stephen isn't violent." Tears fill her eyes.

"I know," I say sympathetically. "I talked with him for a while. We wrote out a statement that will show the judge he was cooperative. I think it will help him. He seems to care about you a lot."

She gives me a courteous smile. I can't tell if what I said makes her happy, or if she thinks I'm being insincere.

"At any rate, he seemed remorseful, and at least he'll get the help he needs to start fighting his heroin habit."

That part seems to genuinely please her. I start to tell Mrs. Nance that her son also admitted to burglarizing her house. But when I look up toward where she's been sitting, the chair is empty. She's standing now, and walking around the table toward me.

I clear my throat. "So I've included his admission in your report." She's standing to the side of me now. "That should help persuade the judge . . ."

I'm suddenly aware of this woman's hand cupping the back of my head. She pulls me gradually toward her until my face is flush against the midsection of her robe. She stands there, motionless and stoic over me, as I sit like a chump with my face buried in Mrs. Nance's bosom. *What the hell is she doing?*

I don't want to be rude. After all, the poor widow has been through enough. Maybe she's just showing me her gratitude. I guess that's okay, although I hope she doesn't show me anything else. Maybe I'm making too much of this.

I hear her inhale deeply. "You're a handsome officer." She pauses and I imagine my eyes bulging like Perenti's. "A sweet, young . . ."

I pull back, disengaging my head from her robe. "Was that my call sign? Yes, I think that's me they're calling." I gather my things and inch myself out of the chair. Mrs. Nance is standing in the same spot, crowding me as I straighten up and edge past her.

She motions toward the backyard. "My pool doesn't get much use anymore."

I'm almost running by the time I hit the front door. For some reason all I can think of is the fact that her son, Stephen, is older than me. What would he think? More importantly, what would my wife think? I don't even want to think about that.

8:56 p.m.

I haven't had much to eat today, and by the time I clear the Nance house I'm starved. Since I'm already off my beat, I decide it's a good time to quickly slide downtown and grab a dog.

Kalani eyes me suspiciously from the lane next to me as we pull up to a red light. He rolls down his window. "Hey Bosworth, what are you doing off your beat?"

I wave him off. "I'm dying for a hotdog. Let's get together later—I've got to tell you about the follow-up I was just on."

He turns left and I continue straight, through downtown, to der Wienerschnitzel. I park in front and run in, hopefully before my sergeant comes by and spots me.

"I didn't do it," a guy in line says, raising his hands. His girlfriend pulls at his arm, obviously embarrassed.

I point my forefinger at him, giving him a wink and a click of my tongue. "Good one."

It takes a few minutes to get my order. Apparently the funnyman in line ahead of me took the last corndog and they have to make some more. I come out with two fresh ones, hot and ready to eat. I'd like to get back to my beat first, but I'm too hungry. I use my teeth to tear the pack of mustard, and then I squeeze an abundance of it onto the dog.

9:16 p.m.

I flip a U-turn in front of der Wienerschnitzel as I lift the steaming corndog gently to my lips.

Beep-Beep-Beep! "Charles-46, with a unit to cover, residential burglary just occurred on Arborwood."

"Son-of-a-bitch, that's him!" I say aloud. I set the corndog on the bag next to me and pick up the microphone. "Four-six, I'm rolling." I take off like a bat out of hell toward my in-laws' neighborhood.

I'm weaving in and out of traffic, zipping down side streets, and avoiding congested intersections by means of every shortcut I know. With my lights and siren manhandling traffic out of the way, I accelerate around the back side of the mall, and into the neighborhood. I shut down my siren—amazed at how fast I got here.

I turn onto the street, heading for the address, when a set of headlights hits me coming the other way. My mind flashes back a few weeks to the Pang's robbery. Not knowing it at the time, I passed right by Stephen Nance as he fled the scene.

I slow to nearly a crawl and inch my car toward the middle of the street, so much so that the other car can barely squeeze by me. As it does, I aim my spotlight right into the window, blinding the occupants in the process. I see two panicked faces. Both are young, white, teenagers, about 16 years old. They're both dressed in nice sweaters, as if heading to a school dance. Neither of them matches my mental image of a couple of burglars. Should I continue to the scene and contact the victim, or stop this car?

As they inch past me, a third head pops up from the backseat. I get only a glimpse, but it's the face of a man about ten years older than the other two. I flip the car around as quickly as you can on a narrow street, and start after them. As I put it out over the radio, they're already making the turn. A few seconds later, I come around the corner and I'm right behind them. Something's changed. I only see two heads. The older guy is either ducking down in the back or he jumped out in the seconds before I caught up with them.

I hit my lights and siren and the car pulls to a stop. I take the shotgun out of its mount and jump from the car with it. Crouching in the wedge of my open door, I level the gun at the car. I slip one hand down to adjust the spotlight directly into the back window. Still only two heads.

My cover unit comes tearing around the corner and then another. It's Enrique, followed by Kalani. I yell to them that a third suspect may have jumped out a half-block back. Enrique stays with me and Kalani continues down the street to check. I'm calling out for the two boys to step out of the car with their hands up. When they do, I move away from my car to get a view into their back window.

"What the hell is all over your pants?" Enrique says to me.

"What?"

"Your pants. What happened, you get so excited you took a dump?"

"What the hell?" While holding the shotgun on two suspects, I stretch my neck to look down the backside of my uniform pants. A long jagged column of bright yellow mustard extends from my gun belt all the way to my knee.

"Damn corndog." I see one of the suspects peek over his shoulder. "It's mustard," I tell Enrique, loud enough for the two boys to hear. "Mustard!"

We handcuff the two kids, but the older guy isn't in the car. Kalani can't locate him, but we do find all the stuff taken in the burglary in the backseat. I have Kalani transport them to the station for me while I meet with the victim to take the report. They identify their stolen property, and there are other items we recovered that don't belong to them. I'm certain those things will connect these suspects to several of the other burglaries in the area.

10:52 p.m.

I return to the station and interview the two boys separately. Both admit to all the break-ins, and also give up their uncle as the mastermind. They provide me with his name, address, and description. It turns out that the two boys live a block from one another, smack in the middle of the neighborhood that's been getting hit. The uncle, who was recently let out of jail on probation, lives nearby on the other side of the freeway.

The boys also confirm my suspicion that their uncle jumped out of the car as they were making the corner. They say the car was still moving at the time. According to the boys, he told them to keep going and don't look back.

Just to be on the up and up, I have Kalani put together a photo lineup that includes their uncle. I take a look at it, just as a witness would, and identify the guy I saw in the backseat. I might not have needed to do it since both boys named the guy, but what if they changed their testimony? At least this way we'll have an airtight case against him.

11: 39 p.m.

Dispatch is paging me over the building's intercom. I phone in and they tell me that Zabinski and Lee have stopped my guy. Apparently he was making his way home on foot and they spotted him on a pedestrian footbridge over the freeway. Trapped at mid-span, he had nowhere to run. He gave up without a fight.

When I approach the uncle in the jail, he refuses to say anything.

12:00 Midnight

Kalani gives me a hand logging evidence in the report writing room. Two other cops are in there, a female officer from the midnight shift and a motorcycle traffic cop who's also logging evidence. He had apparently rolled out to the scene of the earlier injury accident with Scheper.

"How's the kid?" I ask. Kalani and the female officer turn to hear his answer.

He smiles lightly. "He's going to make it. Broken leg, but that'll heal."

"That's good." I turn back to my paperwork.

"Funny guy, Scheper," the motor cop continues. "This kid was really banged up and scared when we got there. He had gotten hit on his bicycle a few blocks from where he lives, so nobody from his family was even there."

We all turn in our seats again, to listen.

"So there's the kid, lying in the middle of the street, shaking and pale, and looking like he's about to go into shock. Scheper starts talking to him, trying to keep him calm while we're waiting for the ambulance. Then Scheper takes off his helmet and I'll be damned if he doesn't lie right down in the middle of the street next to the kid."

"You're kidding," Kalani says. We look at one another.

"Serious as a heart attack. Scheper just lies there in the grease and grime, uniform and all, keeping the kid company until the ambulance gets there."

12:18 a.m.

I ask Kalani if he wants some coffee, then I head off to buy a couple of cups out of the machine. The lights are out when I get to the lunchroom. I stop in the doorway, wondering what's going on. A dark figure scurries into the kitchen area, just out of my sight. *What in the hell?*

I flick on the lights and walk hesitantly across the room to the kitchen. I turn the corner, fully expecting to find a couple against the refrigerator in some sort of lascivious repose. To my shock, it's my old academy roommate, Timmy. He's alone, which has me even more concerned.

"Timmy?" I give an exaggerated look back and forth, letting him know how freek'n weird it looks that he's alone, at night, hiding in the dark police kitchen. And he's a detective, too. They don't even work this time of night.

"I know this seems strange," he says, glancing cautiously around the empty room.

"Ya think?"

He motions me to lower my voice. "I'm on an undercover assignment. I've been ordered to investigate a series of thefts from the lunchroom. Apparently several lunches have turned up missing."

"You're kidding."

"Nope. Sandwiches, cookies, fruit . . ."

"No. I mean you're kidding that you've actually been assigned to investigate this."

Timmy smiles sheepishly. "I'm the newest detective, I guess. Besides, it wouldn't have been that big a deal, but the watch commander has lost two lunches in the past month."

"So, undercover," I chuckle. "Shouldn't you be hiding over there in the trash can, or behind the coffee machine?"

Timmy growls and shakes his head. "You know what I meant. I just don't want anyone knowing I'm doing this. I've placed several bait lunches in the refrigerator and sprinkled them with an invisible tracking dust. It only shows up under a UV light source. That's what I was checking when you came in."

I look down and notice a small zippered case on the floor next to him. I'm laughing and shaking my head. "Let me get out of your way then. Kalani and I will hit the 7-11 for our coffee. Good luck with the investigation, Timmy."

I'm thinking that this place is hilarious. If he shines that thing on Enrique, his whole face will light up like the moon!

12:40 a.m.

I follow Kalani out to the 7-11 on his beat, content for the first time in a while that my in-laws' neighborhood won't get hit. We park in the empty lot and get our coffees—mine is cut with the usual half hot chocolate. The night is cool, and although I should be tired, I'm not. We both lean back against the retaining wall out front and stare up at the crystalline stars.

A motorcycle drives into the lot and a solid looking kid of about 18 years gets off. He gives us a look as he toes the kickstand down then sets his helmet on the seat. The kid turns to look back at us again before going into the store.

While he's in the store I notice him still checking us out. He's a big, good looking kid who's obviously spent a lot of time in the gym. He comes out drinking from a quart bottle of orange juice. When he starts over toward us, Kalani pauses his story.

The kid stops directly in front of me and extends his hand. I grasp it hesitantly, studying his face for recognition. Suddenly something in his expression seeps through.

"No way!" I say, stepping back to take in the whole sight. "McDonough?"

He pumps my hand wildly. "Yep! It's me, and now I have a license for the motorcycle." We both laugh heartily.

"I can't believe you're the same guy. What have you been doing?"

"I'm a senior in high school now. I've played football all four years, and I'm boxing Golden Gloves."

We talk for a while, laughing about all the times I chased him. He graduates soon and plans on going on to college. I give him a slap on the back as he turns to go. It's solid as a rock. I can only stare at him as he drives off, amazed, and even a little proud.

Kalani and I sip our drinks quietly for a while, taking in the flavors of the night. How many shifts have we stood out here swapping stories of the calls we had gone on? Stories that nobody would even believe. I lean back against the retaining wall and remember back to my first nights on the street. Like Perenti, I was unsure and indecisive. I hadn't figured out who I was as a cop. How could I have known? I had just turned twenty-one. I was only a kid.

We check our watches and finish the last of our coffees. I drive back to the station through nearly vacant streets, the cool wind on my face. It's nights like these when I am in love with my work and invigorated by the people I meet. Some of them have been lost in a jumble of partial memories and unremarkable calls. Others I will never forget. I find myself thinking about the ones whose lives have touched me in ways they will never know.

2:30 a.m.

I'm in the report writing room with my squad, finishing up the last of my burglary investigation. The laughter and joking is as comfortable to me as family. It's easy banter that no one seems to take seriously. I realize that beneath all the jokes and the nicknames there truly is a passionate loyalty to one another that our lives depend on.

Sergeant Jenner appears at the door and gives me a nod to follow him. A couple of the guys lock eyes with me and I can only shrug.

I walk behind him down the hall and into the watch commander's office. The lieutenant is sitting behind his desk watching me. I notice his lunchbox on the floor next to the desk and remember he's closely guarding his sandwiches these days. There's a moment of silence, again, before the sergeant speaks.

"We really like the way you do business. You write well, conduct solid investigations, and you know how to deal with people."

"Thanks," I say softly, wondering who they want me to train this time.

"You've come a long way," the lieutenant says. "And the main thing about you is you're dependable. All of the sergeants you've worked for say the same thing—they never have to watch you, and they can count on you to do your job."

I swallow. Though I feel a little hot and dizzy, I remain standing in front of his desk. "Thank you, sir."

"An undercover position has just opened up in the narcotics unit." The lieutenant leaves the comment hanging long enough to look to the sergeant, who nods, and then back at me. "I understand you submitted a request to transfer into the unit."

I'm thinking back. "Yes, I did. That was almost a year ago."

"Do you still want it?" the sergeant asks with a laugh.

My head spins with a million thoughts. The Narcotics Unit has been a goal of mine ever since I got off probation. "Of course," I say hoarsely. "Who would I have to interview with?"

The two of them look at one another, then back at me. "Nobody," the lieutenant says. "It's already been discussed upstairs by the command staff. The position is yours."

A wave of apprehension washes over me like a heat lamp, and then it's gone. I have more questions than I can even separate in my mind. I clear my throat, and then try to come up with my foremost concern.

"When do I start the assignment?"

"Next week," the lieutenant says. "Tonight is your last night in uniform."

Made in the USA
Las Vegas, NV
28 June 2022

50822589R00226